# CULTURE AND IDENTITY

*Sponsored by the Joint Committee on Japanese Studies of the American Council of Learned Societies and the Social Science Research Council.*

# CULTURE AND IDENTITY

JAPANESE INTELLECTUALS DURING THE
INTERWAR YEARS

*Edited by J. Thomas Rimer*

PRINCETON UNIVERSITY PRESS   PRINCETON, NEW JERSEY

Copyright © 1990 by Princeton University Press
Published by Princeton University Press, 41 William Street,
Princeton, New Jersey 08540
In the United Kingdom: Princeton University Press, Oxford
All Rights Reserved

*Library of Congress Cataloging-in-Publication Data*

Culture and identity : Japanese intellectuals during the
interwar years / edited by J. Thomas Rimer.
"Sponsored by the Joint Committee on Japanese Studies
of the American Council of Learned Societies and
the Social Science Research Council"—
Includes bibliographical references.
ISBN 0-691-05570-X (alk. paper)
1. Japan—Intellectual life—20th century. I. Rimer, J. Thomas.
II. Joint Committee on Japanese Studies.
DS822.4.C85   1990   306′.0952—dc20   90-8099   CIP

This book has been composed in Linotron Sabon

Princeton University Press books are printed
on acid-free paper and meet the guidelines
for permanence and durability of the Committee
on Production Guidelines for Book Longevity
of the Council on Library Resources

Printed in the United States of America by
Princeton University Press, Princeton, New Jersey

10   9   8   7   6   5   4   3   2   1

# Contents

*Preface*                                                                   vii

**PART I:** THE MOVE INWARD                                                   1

**1.** Abe Jirō and *The Diary of Santarō*
    Stephen W. Kohl                                                           7

**2.** Kurata Hyakuzō and *The Origins of Love and Understanding*
    J. Thomas Rimer                                                          22

**3.** Taishō Culture and the Problem of Gender Ambivalence
    Donald Roden                                                            37

**PART II:** CULTURE AND SOCIETY                                             57

**4.** Sociology and Socialism in the Interwar Period
    Nozomu Kawamura                                                         61

**5.** Tsuchida Kyōson and the Sociology of the Masses
    Eugene Soviak                                                           83

**6.** Disciplinizing Native Knowledge and Producing Place:
Yanagita Kunio, Origuchi Shinobu, Takata Yasuma
    H. D. Harootunian                                                       99

**PART III:** MARXISM AND CULTURAL CRITICISM                                129

**7.** Marxism Addresses the Modern: Nakano Shigeharu's
Reproduction of Taishō Culture
    Miriam Silverberg                                                      133

**8.** "Credo Quia Absurdum": *Tenkō* and the Prisonhouse of
Language
    Brett de Bary                                                          154

**9.** *Ikkoku Shakai-shugi*: Sano Manabu and the Limits of
Marxism as Cultural Criticism
    Germaine A. Hoston                                                     168

**PART IV: JAPAN IN ASIA** 187

**10.** Nitobe Inazō: From World Order to Regional Order
*Thomas W. Burkman* 191

**11.** A Vast and Grave Task: Interwar Buddhist Studies as an Expression of Japan's Envisioned Global Role
*Jackie Stone* 217

**12.** A Turning in Taishō: Asia and Europe in the Early Writings of Watsuji Tetsurō
*William R. LaFleur* 234

**PART V: ART AND THE CONCEPT OF CULTURE** 257

**13.** Kuki Shūzō and *The Structure of Iki*
*Hajimu Nakano* 261

**14.** Natsume Sōseki and the Development of Modern Japanese Art
*Shuji Takashina* 273

**15.** Yūgen and Erhabene: Ōnishi Yoshinori's Attempt to Synthesize Japanese and Western Aesthetics
*Makoto Ueda* 282

*Contributors* 301

*Index* 303

# *Preface*

In RECENT decades, studies of Japan undertaken by Western scholars have brought a great deal of knowledge, and a certain amount of wisdom, to the West concerning the development of the Japanese view of themselves and the world in this century. Movements in politics, history, and literature have been articulated, often with considerable skill, so that the flow of events and ideas in those areas have begun to reveal both the working interrelationships between thought and action and a certain line of historical coherence in their development, or at least as much coherence as one might expect to find in this turbulent century. One area, however, that has yet to receive the attention it deserves—not only because of its importance to the development of ideas in modern Japan, but for its own intrinsic interest—is what might be loosely defined as the intellectual history of modern Japan as revealed in the cultural field. The essays here concentrate on the important interwar years, from the Taishō period (1912–26) through the early Shōwa era (1926–40). Collectively, they represent our attempt to prepare a rough sketch of this terrain, which yet awaits a systematic charting.

Why should this area of ideas have received so little attention outside Japan? During the conferences that stimulated the composition of the essays included here, a number of hypotheses emerged. First of all, the development of modern Japanese intellectual life, at least until the beginning of World War II, was inspired by an attraction felt by the Japanese for European models of cultural criticism, and the configurations among the intellectual, philosophical, and artistic worlds of Japan drew closer to similar circles in Europe rather than to the prevalent Anglo-American models, which generally pursued a more pragmatic approach to cultural and philosophical speculations and methodologies. American scholars, because of their national disposition and traditions, often take the value of such pragmatism for granted, but such assumptions have not, on the whole, been prevalent in Europe, or in Japan.

To take the simplest example, a British or American reader is altogether prepared to regard a poem, a novel, or even the written text of a drama as literature. Yet a philosophical essay may seem to that same reader to be removed, almost by definition, from that category and so will be relegated to what is often regarded as a text of secondary status, that of speculative criticism. In the United States, certainly, the current generation of readers seems to regard philosophical texts as specialized material. In our tradition, we doubtless must go back as far as Henry Adams, William James, and Ralph Waldo Emerson to find texts that the general reader can accept in terms of both ideas and literary style. In Germany, on the other hand, Heidegger has been as powerful a force as Thomas Mann in shaping modern cultural attitudes. In France, a thinker such as Jean-Paul Sartre was able to move from one genre to another; his readers followed him from formal philosophical texts to the novel, the theater, even to the autobiographical confession. Many of the Japanese writers discussed in these essays occupy a similar pride of place in terms of wider definitions of literature held in modern Japan. To encompass them, Anglo-American suppositions concerning the nature of the literary impulse must be expanded to grasp fully the continental, and Japanese, assumptions.

By the same token, an examination of Japanese intellectual life during the first four decades of this century requires some knowledge of, and sympathy for, the high European intellectual traditions of the same period. It was to Germany and France that the majority of Japanese turned for their heroes, who ranged from Kant and Hegel to Nietzsche, Marx, Durkheim, and Bergson. Japanese intellectuals studied such thinkers in order to grasp, then sometimes adapt, their methodologies. The American scholar working in this area is thus asked to take on new sets of complex loyalties in order to comprehend with any precision the means by which the foundations of modern thought were laid down in Japan, and the means by which important Japanese assumptions about the workings of the life of the mind developed.

In this regard, Americans have, at several stages in their history, made the European connections as well. As did the Japanese, American intellectuals travelled to study with European masters, and they were, as often as not, impressed by what they experienced. William James, for example, meeting Wilhelm Dilthey in 1867, found him to possess a prodigious mind, "overflowing with information with regard to everything knowable and unknowable. He is the first man I have ever met of a class, which must be common here, of men to whom learning has become as natural as breathing."[1] In 1867, Japan was just opening its doors to the West, but a decade before Dilthey's death in 1911, his work was already being read and absorbed by eager students in Japan, among them such eminent philosophical writers as Nishida Kitarō and Abe Jirō.

Given these continuing Japanese proclivities, the usual methodologies commonly in use in the United States—history, literature, and sociology, for example—can only provide imperfect mirrors in which to capture or recreate the motion of ideas and enthusiasms flowing through Japan during those years. The attitudes they chronicle are often elusive, and the

---

[1] William James, *The Letters of William James* (Boston: Little, Brown, 1926), p. 110.

effect of the Japanese intellectual world on its larger society is difficult to quantify to the American taste. Certainly the traditional prestige of learning as an endeavor in Japan, as well as a widespread admiration for the accomplishments of the European intellectual world now being assimilated there, put a number of Japanese intellectuals in positions of prominence. Still, little careful research has yet been done, either in Japan or in the West, concerning the sociology of the structures of modern Japanese high culture. It is not yet clear, for example, what constituted the precise nature of the relationship between the universities and the world of publishing, nor has much data been compiled so far concerning the nature and extent of the connections between the ideas of the urban intellectuals who wrote for the leading Tokyo newspapers and their meaningful reception by a larger public. In many ways, the larger effect of the efforts of Japanese intellectuals during those years can only be grasped intuitively, at least at this point in the study of the period. Still, there is no question but that, for many Japanese, such thinkers as Watsuji, Abe, Miki, and Yanagita were thought to have captured, and at the deepest level, the truth of their civilization, and Japanese intellectuals today continue to accord such thinkers of the interwar years high status. Such men seem heroic in Japan in the same way that Germans find Hegel and Simmel, or the French Durkheim and Sartre, to be so. Read, even unread, such writers stand within the context of their civilizations as symbols of high achievement.

The present volume contains essays devoted to five areas of inquiry, all related to the general area of cultural criticism. The insights presented, both in the individual papers and in the larger ordering of the volume, represent a collective hope on the part of all those who participated that such new areas of inquiry might be sustained and developed by others. Eventually, a synthetic examination of the ideas of the interwar period, which produced concepts and assumptions still so important in Japan today, should become possible. To those conversant with modern European intellectual history, the composition of the kind of general synthetic treatment provided by H. Stuart Hughes in his *Consciousness and Society* (Vintage, 1961) may seem unproblematic, yet given the present state of research in the West on modern Japanese intellectual history, any equivalent study, the participants in our project agreed, is still beyond our reach. The essays included in this book, however, are intended to point in the direction of such a possibility.

In choosing a means to locate an area within which to examine the outlines of the development of Japan's intellectual traditions in this century, the participants agreed to focus on the problems encountered by Japanese intellectuals in defining the concept of culture, both on an individual basis and on the basis of national perceptions. The development of

a knowledge of European cultural achievements brought to Japanese intellectuals a crucial self-consciousness, first concerning their personal
selves, then, almost simultaneously, of the special characteristics of the
society in which they lived. This self-consciousness and concomitant desire for self-definition provides, from our contemporary vantage point, a
useful link that can connect the various constellations of ideas that developed during the period.

The Japanese thinkers whose work is described in this volume conceptualized culture in different ways, as the various essays will make clear.
Some defined the concept in terms of personal self-understanding, others
in terms of the problematic nature of the relationship between a personal
sense of culture and its social contexts. During the period, culture as a
metaphor for qualities felt to be innate in human society helped create a
common rhetoric that could be shared by intellectuals representing
widely varying disciplines, ranging from sociology to aesthetics. Indeed,
the act of addressing the matter of culture helped to guide the development of various academic disciplines that came to be established in Japanese universities; concepts of culture aided in the accommodation of foreign methodologies to the felt nature of the Japanese experience. In one
sense, these continuing discussions during the interwar years as to the
nature of culture in general, and of Japanese culture in particular, helped
advance the development of what might be termed a "common problem-
consciousness" in Japan, one that cut across academic disciplines, narrowly defined, to allow for a wider, and often an international, dialogue.

During this process, some European conceptions of culture were accepted; others were tried, then abandoned. Perhaps such a dialectic of
attraction and rejection was not so surprising. Concerning Western definitions of culture, Raymond Williams has remarked in his *Keywords*
(Oxford, 1971) that "culture is one of the two or three most complicated
words in the English language," since the concept deals with "several distinct and incompatible systems of thought." As Japanese intellectuals, re-
acting to European culture, found themselves forced by a new self-consciousness to define culture for themselves in order to examine their
traditions, as well as the place of those traditions in the context of a larger
and different world, they fell prey to the confusions of defining a concept
that held within its potential of meaning so many contradictions. Some
Japanese definitions of culture involved the notion of progress; others denied its possibility. Some saw culture as operating inside history; some
located its essence in layers deeper than any chain of historical cause and
effect. For others, modernity was the touchstone in any definition of the
term. The perceived need among Japanese thinkers to determine what
elements or qualities might be defined as truly Japanese in the context of
the development of their general concept of culture, itself inspired by un-

derlying categories familiar to Western thought but new to them, remained a matter of central concern. The term "culture" could be and was employed by Japanese intellectuals to create a number of strategies by which to examine the realities of personality and society, some psychological, some artistic, some political. In this examination of culture, the relationship between objective fact and subjective value also came to be sensed, then articulated, often with the aid of imported ideologies and methodologies. The difficulties of the quest were infinite.

In that regard, the reader of this volume will note that the various contributors whose work is included here have also employed a wide variety of methodologies to explicate their chosen subject matter, ranging from biographical description to Marxist techniques of literary and historical analysis. It is our hope that these varieties of approach will be stimulating to the reader. The wide spectrum of analytical techniques employed both indicates the multitude of viewpoints available today and suggests the diversities that can be found among scholars in Japanese studies, in Japan and in the United States. On the whole, these differing intellectual methodologies support and complement each other. Each contributor has approached the subject of inquiry undertaken as he or she sees fit. The congruence between the material treated and the means chosen to do so remains agreeably close.

Each section is introduced by a brief statement of the larger and more general themes addressed by the individual essays. These introductions are intended merely to provide a simple framework for those who may be approaching the subject matter for the first time. It is hoped that those interested in the development of modern European intellectual history will find the Japanese experience relevant. These introductions may serve as a brief guide to them as well.

A note on usage is in order here. Japanese names mentioned in the body of the text are written in the Japanese fashion, the family name first, followed by the personal name. Japanese contributors to this volume, however, have been listed in the customary Western way, with the personal name preceding the family name.

This book is the result of the enthusiasm and labor of a great many people. The Social Science Research Council, which organized the series of workshops that gave rise to the present collection, is particularly to be thanked. Ronald Aqua, Sophie Sa, Stefan Tanaka, Blair Ruble, and, in particular, Theodore Bestor all helped shepherd the enterprise along at various crucial stages. The Japan–U.S. Friendship Commission, which generously provided funding for the meetings, was of signal help, and both Francis Tenny and Richard Erikson took an active interest in the development of the project.

A number of participants whose energies and insights made the sessions particulary stimulating were not able themselves to contribute papers. Among them, special thanks should go to Carol Gluck of Columbia University, who provided invaluable insights on modern Japanese history, and Gerald Izenberg, of Washington University, whose background in European intellectual history gave crucial perspectives, as well as to Yamazaki Masakazu of Osaka University, who brought a wealth of scholarly understanding to the discussions. It is especially to be regretted that several essays presented at the conference could not be included in this volume, among them thoughtful contributions on the work of the philosopher Nishida Kitarō by William Haver and Naoki Sakai, a valuable study on the art of the modern woodblock artists Onchi Kōshirō by Elizabeth Swinton, an essay on the critic Takayama Chogyū by Randy Petralia, and an examination of certain cultural concepts in the work of Yanagi Sōetsu by Brian Moeran.

Many of the ideas presented in this preface and in the introductions to the five sections of the book were developed in discussions held during our series of five meetings, and the rapporteurs who prepared useful transcripts made a signal contribution. They include Randy Petralia, Susan Griswold, Joan Ericson, and Clifford K. Uejio. Special appreciation goes to Darlene King for her conscientious preparation of the manuscript.

In particular, thanks to our indefatigable editors at the Press, Anita O'Brien and Beth Gianfagna, who have done so much to make the final book both readable and attractive.

Finally, it should be said that all who participated continue to hope that sustained and more systematic work can be done in the area of modern Japanese thought. Japanese intellectual history in this century is of great potential interest outside Japan, perhaps in particular to Americans, who have turned to many of the same European sources, and often during the same historical periods, for a means to develop their own intellectual traditions and their own sense of selfhood.

*J. Thomas Rimer*
*March 1989*

# Part I

## THE MOVE INWARD

THE GENERATION that came to maturity in Japan between the turn of the century and World War I was faced with new and difficult challenges. In one sense, young intellectuals believed they required some kind of basic understanding of the functions of society; on the other hand, they found themselves encouraged to respond to a growing sense of a need to search out the authenticity of their own interior selves. If any synthesis was to be created between the sometimes congruent, sometimes conflicting demands of civilization, self, and society, each element would have to be examined and defined before any genuine relationship among them might be posited. Many during the period decided to begin with an examination of the self, that realm of the personality that heretofore had been relegated, indeed conceptualized, as an adjunct to the primacy of social relationships and obligations. The search for that self was often to prove a painful one.

It was not surprising that the urgency of these questions was most strongly felt by the young, university-educated youth of the period, exposed as they were to an increasingly sophisticated level of European learning, particularly in the romantic German classics, where interiority, from Goethe's time onward, was deemed a central virtue. In addition they found themselves inspired by the high accomplishments of several important Japanese writers and intellectuals of the preceding generation, who had brought to their own lives and writings a new level of self-conscious discourse concerning the nature of culture and the way in which the growth of the individual spirit might be fostered by an understanding of the subtle relationships between self and society. For those in that earlier group as well, the growth of a sense of individuality had proved extremely painful. The suicide in 1894 at age twenty-six of the poet and essayist Kitamura Tōkoku, a romantic with a singular interest in Christianity, marked the end of the career of a man who had done much to develop in his readers an expansive idea of the nature and role of the self; the doubts and dangers that his own quest revealed were to cast long shadows over the next generation. The novelist Shimazaki Tōson was to write his 1902 novel *Haru* (Spring) as a partial attempt to come to terms with, if not to exorcise, the specter of his spiritual mentor. Writers like Mori Ōgai and Natsume Sōseki had returned to Japan after undergoing powerful personal confrontations with European culture. They made clear in subsequent novels, essays, and articles the need for the Japanese to discover who they were, as well as what their individual identities would and could be in relation to the rapidly changing culture in which they found themselves.

The younger generation, troubled and moved by the power of the writings of their precursors, now felt a need to seek out a sense of interiority, which seemed a mandatory first step toward an understanding of the relationship between the individual and the surrounding culture. The early phases of cultural criticism, then, were often most concerned with a search for an authentic sense of self. Implicit in that search was the need to discover where within that self might lie some realm of personal freedom.

These currents of thought were to some degree inevitable. The kind of statism that produced Japanese victories in the Russo-Japanese War in 1904–5 also produced the suppression of civil liberties and socialist thought in the 1911 Kōtoku Shūsui affair. Those who questioned the policies of an increasingly autocratic government were forced in turn to examine themselves, in order to think through the implications of their own divergent responses to what was perceived as an increasingly autocratic attitude on the part of government authorities. The suppression of individual rights, as it were, brought to many a stronger awareness of the need to define the necessities of their own spiritual existence. A generation found itself asking where the uniqueness of an individual might lie. Further, did that uniqueness constitute his or her freedom, and if so, how could it be manifested, particularly in relation to a society that, officially at least, seemed increasingly suspicious of individual choice? Such was the range of questions that forced themselves to the surface in various guises.

A number of intellectual paradigms had by now been made available to the elite students who pursued their studies at the great Japanese universities. Particularly at Tokyo University, but elsewhere as well, the study of Western philosophy was by the turn of the century considered a central part of the curriculum, and the introduction into Japanese intellectual life of Kant, Hegel, Schopenhauer, Nietzsche, and other important figures in the German tradition did much to help define the terms in which the self and its relationship both to society and to history were to be defined. Given the strong centralization of Japanese higher education during this period, an impressive number of those who would later assume leading roles in the foreign service, journalism, law, and the arts took up the study of this idealistic tradition of German philosophy, which provided both a new set of modes in which the questions they asked themselves were to be framed, and new methodologies by which they might be explored.

In this regard, the importance of a teacher such as Raphael Von Koeber (1848–1923) cannot be overestimated. Koeber, at the suggestion of the German philosopher and aesthetician Eduard Von Hartmann (1842–

1906), whose writings on art were later to so influence the thinking of Mori Ōgai, was sent from Germany to Tokyo University in 1893, where he continued to teach philosophy until his retirement in 1914. Staying in Japan until his death almost a decade later, he remained an important force in the thinking of many of his former students. His dedication provoked in his students a fierce loyalty to him and his ideas; from the later testimony of such important figures as Natsume Sōseki, Abe Jirō, and Watsuji Tetsurō, among many others, Koeber served in one way or another as a major influence on the development of their thinking. Koeber, and others like him, helped set the level and the intensity of discourse concerning the individual. For many of Koeber's best students, philosophy thus became not an academic subject to be studied objectively from the outside but a new and powerful means to search for a new faith in the self.

Those who learned to seek out a greater personal understanding of themselves through their contact with the study of European philosophy soon helped spread these ideas, and a sense of their importance, to the educated levels of society all over Japan. In this regard, both the spread of journalism and large-scale publishing were crucial. By 1915, for example, a series of translations of the texts of modern European philosophy, predominantly of the German Neo-Kantian school, had been made available, and at reasonable prices, thanks in large part to the enterprising work of Iwanami Shigeo (1881–1946), whose efforts through the Iwanami Publishing Company did so much to bring the written products of Western culture to a wide audience in Japan. The work of such popularizers of ideas as Hasegawa Nyozekan (1875–1969) was crucial as well. Hasegawa, an important intellectual and writer who in 1908 joined the staff of the *Osaka Asai shimbun*, perhaps the leading intellectual paper at the time, helped encourage high standards that were both politically liberal and philosophically individualistic. In such publications, the goal of an examined interior life could find a public forum for discussion.

One of the first literary and philosophical products of this inward search is represented in the early work of the writer and critic Abe Jirō (1883–1959) entitled *Santarō no nikki* (The diary of Santarō), first published in 1914 and frequently amended and enlarged in later editions. The author's continuing attempts to grasp and fix his shifting sense of self, as chronicled in Stephen Kohl's essay, found a wide and enthusiastic readership among his young contemporaries, whose sense of sympathy with Abe's search kept the book in print for many decades. Other young intellectuals, emboldened by Abe's example, composed books of a similar confessional nature. Perhaps the best-known of these remains *Ai to ninshiki to no shuppatsu* (The origins of love and understanding), written in 1917 by Kurata Hyakuzō (1891–1943), whose later writings, often overtly religious in tonality, were to gain him recognition abroad as well. Kurata, as J. Thomas Rimer's essay explains, found himself caught between a series of tensions and countertensions that, he eventually came to believe, could only be resolved or transcended through faith in some set of higher spiritual principles.

The search for self was not an easy one, and the gulf between public image and private vision often revealed an ambiguous gap between expressed ideals and personal desire, seldom more than half-acknowledged. For many in the interwar years, the roots of self-understanding proved shallow. Many who searched for a unique individuality ended during the war years in supporting the very nationalism that would have been anathema to them two decades before. This kind of ambiguity marked social, interpersonal, and sexual relationships and attitudes, as illustrated in striking detail in Donald Roden's essay.

Ideals and reality, self-knowledge and self-ignorance, exaltation and denegration—all formed part of the search for the self during the interwar years.

# 1

## Abe Jirō and *The Diary of Santarō*

STEPHEN W. KOHL

THE PASSING of the Meiji emperor marked not only the end of an age; it was a watershed in the development of Japanese thoughts and attitudes about the world in which they lived. The Meiji period had begun with great determination and enthusiasm as Japan undertook to modernize and Westernize. Forty-five years later when the period ended, Japan had achieved many of its goals. The entire political structure of the nation had been reorganized, a new educational system was in place and functioning, a modern judicial system had been installed, and a modern military had been established. In its relations with other countries, Japan had achieved equal treaty status with the world's leading nations and had successfully triumphed in war against Imperial Russia.

And yet, as the Meiji period drew to a close there was a sense of uncertainty about what the recent past had meant and what the future held. Some of the leading intellectual figures, such as Natsume Sōseki and Mori Ōgai, were beginning to express misgivings about the ultimate success of the great Meiji experiment. The execution of Kōtoku Shūsui and other socialists in 1911 because of an alleged plot to assassinate the emperor raised questions about some of the new ideas that were being introduced from abroad. At the same time, the Ashio Mine Incident raised disturbing questions of social responsibility while the labor movement, the feminist movement, and the rice riots made it clear that whatever the success of modernization, social equality had not been achieved.

In this context Abe Jirō (1883–1959), a bright and promising schoolmaster's son from remote Akita Prefecture, came to Tokyo to attend the First Higher School and then Tokyo Imperial University, to get a new and thoroughly modern education and to become one of the intellectual elite of the new Japan. Yet despite the eagerness and assurance with which Abe and his classmates absorbed the great intellectual traditions of East and West, they could not help but be acutely conscious of how fragile their intellectual foundations were.

On the one hand, they were following in the giant footsteps of the pioneers of the Meiji period and often felt intimidated at the need to accomplish so much. On the other hand, they also knew that the earlier generation had lived in a much simpler world, one in which almost anything

Western could be introduced into Japan with revolutionary implications. Abe and his generation could no longer merely introduce Western thoughts and concepts. They had to break new ground, and, at the same time, they had to seek some suitable synthesis between Eastern and Western ways of thinking. Natsume Sōseki had already pointed out that it was no longer adequate merely to imitate the West; Japan had to find its own identity.

The history of philosophy in Japan in the Meiji period is largely one of a political or social philosophy. Fukuzawa Yukichi's utilitarianism had given way to a more complex concept of political and social equality, but essentially these systems of the period dealt with the outward rather than the inward aspects of human life.

By the end of the Meiji period the issue of the self in relation to society had been clearly defined if not resolved. The novelists Futabatei Shimei and Natsume Sōseki had presented their readers with highly self-conscious heroes who found themselves in conflict with society. The new society had brought about a fresh self-awareness on the part of the individual, but the question remained of how to reconcile the needs of the individual with the demands of society. By 1907 the writers of the Naturalist movement had fallen back on the traditional concept of sincerity combined with the modern concept of confession, arguing that no matter how beastly one's behavior, redemption could be gained through a sincere recounting of one's motives and feelings. Beastly behavior, however, no matter how redeemable it may have been, was not sought or practiced by everyone. What was clearly needed was a new definition of the individual self and a road map showing how that self could find its way to a satisfactory relationship with society.

In April 1914, at the age of thirty-two, Abe Jirō published the first part of *Santarō no nikki* (The diary of Santarō), a collection of philosophical essays dealing with the discovery of the self. The work provided the needed philosophical guidebook. Where earlier philosophers had been more concerned with establishing systems that defined the self in terms of new systems of social rights and obligations, Abe opened up the whole world of the introspective self as a ground for philosophical inquiry. The hero of Abe's inquiry is not the modern man of will and ambition who organizes society according to his own ideas, but rather a Werthersque figure who must first come to terms with the self before attempting to reconcile himself with society. In outlining his larger purposes in composing these philosophical essays, Abe expressed the need for an alternative to the Naturalist thinkers whom he opposed, saying, "They write about a self they do not know."[1] He also rejected as trivial Nagai Kafū's so-

---

[1] Abe Jirō, *Santarō no nikki*, in Kitazumi Toshio, ed., *Abe Jirō, Watsuji Tetsurō shū*, vol. 35 of *Nihon kindai bungaku taikei* (Tokyo: Kōdansha shoten, 1974), p. 12.

called hedonism. He reviewed Sōseki's novel *Sorekara* (And then) and pointed out that while it was critical of Japan's modern culture, the hero, Daisuke, lacked the will to do anything to improve the situation. Abe also criticized Futabatei Shimei, saying that although that celebrated novelist may have written in a realistic mode, "his realism is nothing more than the product of a philosophy of the sort we see in many idealists who agonize over the ideal of the individual self."[2] Consequently, in reviewing the current intellectual situation in Japan, Abe found himself philosophically very close to the position held by the well-known idealistic writers associated with the *Shirakaba* (White birch) magazine. The chief point that separates Abe Jirō from the best of those writers, men like Mushanokōji Saneatsu and Arishima Takeo, is the fact that Abe lacked what might be called a social consciousness. When Mushanokōji spoke of asserting the self, he was calling for the improvement of both the self and society at large. Abe's concern for the self is so inward-looking that his vision rarely goes beyond the identification and edification of the individual self.

Through the Taishō and prewar years of the Shōwa periods, *The Diary of Santarō* proved to be an immensely popular work read avidly by young intellectuals, providing them with a new realm for philosophical speculation. Tayama Katai's literary journal *Bunshō sekai* praised Abe's work, saying, "*Santarō no nikki* is like a spring dawn bringing a unified melody to our impoverished philosophical world. The fact is that our conventional rhetoric has always merely trifled with abstractions, but Abe, as a serious philosopher, in considering the nature of the self for the first time, has discerned some shadows of what it really is."[3] Similarly, *Araragi*, a leading poetry journal, hailed the work for its power of expression and its emphasis on the inner life which "provides the basis of true philosophy."[4] What these early readers admired was not only the power of Abe's writing, but also the sincerity of his approach. Again, an article on Abe's philosophy in *Bunshō sekai* exclaimed, "in our present philosophical world where triviality is carried to extremes, Abe's philosophy shows a remarkable sincerity and steadiness. With his unfailingly solemn attitude he looks unflinchingly upon cosmic life, and he throws his own life into the spotlight, revealing its essential significance."[5] Finally, a measure of the popularity of Abe's work can be gauged by the fact that between 1914 and 1943, when extensive publication was interrupted by the war, the

[2] Ibid., p. 13.
[3] *Bunshō sekai* 10, no. 3 (March 1915), as quoted in Inoue Masaji, "Kaisetsu," *Gappon Santarō no nikki* (Tokyo: Kadokawa shoten, 1981), p. 479.
[4] *Araragi*, June 5, 1914, quoted in Inoue, *Gappon*, p. 479.
[5] *Bunshō sekai* 9, no. 11 (October 1914), quoted in Inoue, *Gappon*, p. 479.

Iwanami Publishing Company brought out thirty editions of *The Diary of Santarō*.[6]

In later years Abe added a second and a third part, and he also made deletions and revisions in the original. Subsequent editors have taken it upon themselves to publish the work in many different forms. Even today, twenty-five years after Abe's death, this collection of essays continues to exist as a work in progress, as editors reissue it in a variety of formats. The first twenty essays represent the heart of the collection, which comprises the original *Santarō* as published in 1914.

This work is constructed in an unusual manner, consisting of a series of essays, some several pages in length, others no more than a few lines long, ranging over a wide variety of topics. There are selections from a philosophical journal, imaginary dialogues, fictional vignettes, and translations from European works, in addition to more conventional philosophical writing. The use of such a varied and loosely constructed form is intentional. In a series of companion essays entitled *Jinsei to bungei* (Life and art), appended to some versions of the diary, Abe explains his choice of format. "To be suitable for depicting one's inner life, drama, poetry, fiction, and essay must all be more internalized. They must be more honest, more simple, more direct, and more blunt."[7] Apparently one of Abe's intentions in this work was to find or create a new form of writing that would be a more suitable vehicle for describing his inner life.

Abe arranged his essays in the form of a philosophical journal following the spiritual odyssey of the persona he created, Aota Sangoro, as he attempts to come to terms with his own life. Like the form he chose, the author's narrative stance is also atypical. While the work is written in the first person, as one would expect of a diary, it is not always clear who that first person is. In his introduction to an edition published in 1918, Abe explicitly states that the work is to be regarded as Santarō's diary, not as Abe Jirō's diary, yet most of the episodes make no specific reference to Santarō. Since most of them were originally published in newspapers as short, independent essays under Abe's name, they can be considered his own reflections. To cloud the issue still further, Santarō mentions in chapter 12 that his original name was Segawa Kikunojō. Thus, Santarō, who is really Kikunojō, speaks for Abe, while in chapters 12 and 13 Santarō introduces Aota Santarō, who speaks for Santarō, who is speaking in turn for Abe. Yet despite the narrative distance, in his original introduction, Abe says that this work represents "the most direct account of my own inner life." He also admits that some of the episodes are composed of pages taken directly from his own diary.[8]

[6] Inoue, *Gappon*, p. 484.
[7] Abe, *Jinsei to bungei*, in Kitazumi, ed., *Nihon kindai*, 35:198.
[8] Ibid., p. 48.

The first conclusion that can be reached regarding both form and content is that the work is constructed in the loose, episodic manner used by Nietzsche in many of his works, especially in his *Genealogy of Morals*, and that in terms of content, although the collection surely represents Abe's own philosophical odyssey, he is able, by attributing the thoughts to a fictional Santarō, to maintain maximum flexibility in shaping and modulating his thought. This format allows Abe to examine his inner life and to create a new philosophical self, but to keep that new creation at arm's length. There is some uncertainty here; it is as though the author wants to create a new self but also wants to be able to disclaim it at any moment if this method should lead to the consciousness of a self he does not wish to accept. The reader has the feeling that Abe wants to explore the inner life of the self as completely as possible in a fictional sense. He wishes to be certain of where all this self-examination is going to lead before he commits himself to the new identity he has created.

In the introduction to *The Diary of Santarō* Abe writes, "This work represents my meditations concerning my own conflicts and weaknesses. . . . Yet at the same time it is a cry from one who lives in darkness and who is seeking light. It is also a record of how I moved gradually from darkness toward the light."[9] In the same introduction he also writes, "This is an account of the opening of my small soul from the time when I had lost my naive faith in both human life and I myself and was in confusion, up to the present time when I have, to some small degree, regained my faith."[10]

By arranging these various essays, written over a period of six years, into a single work attributed to Aota Santarō, Abe is able to present a guidebook for the young intellectuals of his age, to show them how they might successfully come to terms with the philosophical problems that concerned them. Abe's conclusions, as with most significant philosophical conclusions, are rather banal when stripped to their bare essence. He says, for example, that to create the true inner life of the soul, we must be humble, sincere, and deeply introspective. But in *The Diary of Santarō* he stresses that the conclusions are not so important; for him it is the process that counts, the journey of the spirit as it deals with the many problems it encounters.

As a voracious reader of Western philosophy Abe was first stimulated, then finally overwhelmed, by the many ideas to which he was exposed. In a sense *The Diary of Santarō* represents his way of sifting through all that he had read, then digesting it, in a way that may finally be very Japanese. It has already been suggested that Abe's literary format resembles that of

[9] Ibid., pp. 50–51.
[10] Ibid., p. 51.

Nietzsche. Certainly much of Abe's later reputation was based on his translations and interpretations of Nietzsche's writing, but at this early stage of his career he was reading Hegel. Abe's style of presentation probably reflects the influence of Hegel in the sense that he tries to advance his argument by setting up two opposing ideas in order to resolve or synthesize them.

In the introduction to *Santarō*, a piece called "Dampen" (Fragments), Abe outlines his problem by saying that for him it is not merely a question of knowing the new or modern approaches to philosophy; rather, he is assaulted by so many possible modes of thought and behavior that his inner world has become fragmented and chaotic. Consequently, he has made up his mind to find out first of all what he is, and then what he could be or should be. In establishing this basis for introspection he uses Hegel's terms *an sich* (being-in-itself) and *für sich* (being-for-itself) to distinguish between what he is and to what he aspires. The conflict between these two states of being causes him great sorrow and anguish. He is weary of being a man and an adult and wishes to be a woman, a child, anything but himself as he now is. In a style appropriate to this intellectual confusion, his introduction is filled with images from Greek mythology and quotations from the New Testament, and the text is littered with English and German words. Surely much of the appeal of Abe's work to several generations of young intellectual readers lies in this eclectic scattering of terms, references, and allusions with which they would have been proudly familiar.

In the first several chapters Santarō is so alienated from himself that he creates a fictional character, Hermanov, to speak for him. Hermanov establishes an epistemological dialectic that identifies two sorts of knowledge—a pure, inner knowledge of the soul, and a more calculating, worldly knowledge. He also locates one source of anguish in the fact that an individual can say and think things he can never hope to accomplish. In the outer mode of being, this impossible dream is mere ambition, while in the inner world it represents aspiration. In Abe's case, the aspiration is for a life of truth. Santarō chooses to devote himself to the pursuit of this inner sort of knowledge, and to become an aspirant for the life of truth.

At this point everything is happening inside Santarō's head. There is no trace of communication with other people, nor any suggestion of the environment in which he is living. The imagery is all of twilight and shadows, with much use of the word *tasogare* (dusk). He notes that he prefers obscurity not only because it helps him hide his defects, but because it gives his imagination sufficient latitude to create its own environment. This environment is important for Santarō, since everything in his present life is false, and he must turn to abstraction and imagination to define his new life. He also maintains that abstraction reveals the essence of things.

He uses here the Japanese term for essence, *honshitsu*, as well as the German word *Wessen*.

Abe develops his idea of abstractions by observing that some abstractions deny reality, while others enhance it. He realizes that there are those who would ridicule the notion of an inner, spiritual world of the sort he is trying to establish, but he insists that such is indeed the highest form of reality. His argument goes like this: Experience consists of our impressions of things. Therefore the significance, value, and essence of things come from within us. Thus, feelings are more important than events or actions. This line of reasoning will become important later when it comes to defining morality. It might be noted, incidently, that Shiga Naoya echoed the same notion some years later when he wrote about the characters in one of his novels, saying, "My concern was not so much with what they did, but with how they felt about it when they did it."[11] Abe hopes to use his notion of abstractions to define for himself a world of possibility or aspiration which he can use to subjugate his current self and to create a new, better self.

Having spent the first few chapters laying the foundations for his philosophical explorations, Santarō pauses in chapter 5 to introduce some new elements. He reaffirms the notion that everything must come from within himself, but at the same time, and for the first time, he introduces the idea of romantic love, and thereby the idea that there might exist anyone other than himself. Typically he sets up a dialectic opposition between men and women in which men are depicted as a pretty poor lot. He wants a woman to love him, but first he must established himself as a man and as an individual, otherwise he will not be able to respond adequately to a woman's love.

Chapter 5 shows as well the first step, albeit a negative one, on his journey toward truth. He observes that although he suffers anguish while others feel complacent about their lives, he believes he is better off than they, for at least he realizes how worthless and superficial he is. It is also here that he has his first encounter with others and with nature. He describes leaving a temple and walking down the mountain. On the way he encounters a leper with whom he shares his food. He finds joy in helping the leper, and he finds joy in nature. But his is only a fleeting experience. Reaching out to other people will have to wait until after he has come to terms with nature.

Dreams represent one form of available abstraction. Santarō finds that dreams provide solace for lonely pilgrims like himself, for in dreams he can escape the world as it really is and immerse himself in the finer world of his aspirations. In dreams he can create his environment. Another way

---

[11] *Shiga Naoya zenshū* (Tokyo: Iwanami shoten, 1955), 10:180.

to create his own environment is to build his own castle. Japanese philosophers have always found a close correlation between the individual and his residence. We see examples of this throughout Japanese literary history. Prince Genji, tired of life as it is, tries to recreate life as it could be by building a palace and bringing together all the women who love him. Although Genji's attempt fails, his search prefigures Abe's in many respects. Similarly, Kamo no Chōmei's *Hōjōki* (A record of my hut) also defines the self in terms of dwellings and seeks to put aside life as it is in favor of life as it can be. Finally, in a broader sense, the Japanese word *uchi* can refer to one's dwelling and can also be used as a first-person pronoun. Given this context, then, it is not surprising that Abe, who had earlier written on the subject of architecture, should now make the Japanese home the central image of his philosophical inquiry into the nature of the self. He says that architecture should reflect the ideals of a people, and that for the Japanese this means bringing nature into the house. This inner world of the home contrasted to the outer world of nature not only reflects his earlier inner-outer world dichotomy of the self, but also puts the heretofore isolated self in touch with nature. The author observes, however, that although men ought to be immersed in nature and its rhythms, modern houses are designed to keep nature out and to shield humans from its force.

In making the house a metaphor for the self, Abe says the ideal home is a Western one and should be made of stone to keep sound out—society's sound, not nature's. The house, like the self, should create its own inner world and not depend on nature, especially in terms of the lighting employed. Just as the house is independent of the outside world, so too, within the house, each room should be independent of all others. Traditional Japanese homes with their sliding partitions are not like this, but Santarō feels that one should have absolute privacy in which to read, think, and make love, for only in true isolation can the soul look inward. He says the rooms should be carefully decorated in accordance with one's moods, but in his text he describes only a study and a bedroom. The ideal house has balconies, awnings, and crimson velvet sofas. The garden, on the other hand, should be equipped with a traditional tea house where one can go to escape the modern world. The ideal house does not reject nature but controls it. Such a house, with the isolation it provides, should keep the real world as removed as a distant dream.

Chapters 7 through 9 were written while Abe was on a hiking trip on Mt. Akagi in Gumma Prefecture. They depict the narrator emerging from his isolated self far enough to encounter nature. This experience gives him another perspective on the self. When he encounters a storm on the mountain he is terrified and impressed by the awesome power of nature. This brings him to the realization of just how small and trivial a single human life can be in the face of such an indifferent force. He realizes how meager his own spiritual resources are and feels that a person who knows the full sublimity of nature will be able to embrace it fully and will thus entrust his very life to nature. He also understands how far he has yet to go on his journey to understanding the self.

Not only has Santarō here moved out of his introspective self far enough to encounter nature, but he takes another step forward when he indicates, "My life cannot be complete unless I can achieve a harmony of nature, society, and self."[12] In the beginning he had rejected society and was concerned only with his own inner self; now, immersed in nature, he realizes the importance of society. But he is not yet ready to fling himself into society, or even commit himself to a personal relationship such as love. He believes that loving another person leads the self into compromise and falsehood, while nature is always uncompromising and true to itself. Thus he declares, "I can openly, egotistically reveal my heart to nature. . . . In the face of nature I am not alone."[13] This is the first time he is able to state that he is not alone.

Recognition of how frail the individual is in the embrace of nature leads Santarō to thoughts of his own mortality. He decides that the best preparation for death is to live the best possible life. Although he feels that he is not now living a good life, he nevertheless has the "will to live"—a term he borrowed from Schopenhauer. He sees this "will" as a blind, instinctive fear of death which is the driving force of life. He decides he will make no preparations for death, but merely struggle to go on living as long as he has the strength to do so. This conclusion is similar to that of Shiga Naoya's anonymous hero in *Kinosaki nite* (At Kinosaki), who, in order to come to grips with the idea of his own mortality, withdraws into isolation and introspection and finally dissolves almost completely into nature.

Having confronted nature, Santarō turns once more to the matter of the inner life. On the one hand, he is conscious of the meagerness of his inner life, but, on the other hand, he is determined to create for himself the sort of true life to which he aspires. However difficult his situation may be, he is certain that he is well ahead of all others who do not possess the capacity to think deeply. He says that like Dante he suffers the sins of pride and envy, but he is without Dante's strength. Here Abe speaks of the importance of creativity and rejects all forms of imitation. He notes that it is a delicate matter to distinguish between simple imitation and the act of understanding something and making it one's own. What reason, he asks, does he have for living if his life and thought are not different

---

[12] Abe, *Jinsei to bungei*, in Kitazumi, ed., *Nihon kindai*, 35:90.
[13] Ibid., p. 92.

from that of others? This mountaintop experience has thus enabled him to reach a reconciliation with nature, to resolve his uncertainties about confronting death, and it has clarified as well the problem of living creatively. In all, the experience has been the longest step yet in Santarō's journey. In much the same fashion, Shiga's hero in *An'ya kōro* (A dark night's passing), Tokito Kensaku, climbed Mt. Daisen to achieve his enlightenment, Kurata Hyakuzō climbed Mt. Tsukuba, and Moses climbed Mt. Sinai. Santarō does not receive the law of God in this experience, but he does come as close as he will ever come to an encounter with God. There on the mountain he says, "I feel as though I am embraced by a strange power. Shall I call thee God? Shall I call thee Satan? Shall I call thee providence or fate or nature or history? I do not know. What I do know is that you are the absolute strength that buoys up all that is my life—my joys, sorrows, loves, and wrongdoings. I have no choice but to call on thee to have mercy on me who is weak."[14] Not surprisingly, this view of God seems to be quite close to the one held by Goethe, that of a deity who comprises all nature, but not one that will provide individual salvation.

Chapter 10, entitled "Kaya" (Mosquito net), marks a radical shift in both style and content. Instead of cold, abstract thinking about concepts and principles, the author now becomes warmly specific in his descriptions. In contrast to the earlier chapter in which he identified the ideal house as being made of stone with separate rooms to insure isolation, now he speaks of the joy of living in intimate contact with others—in the same house, in the same room, within the same mosquito net. He evokes the intimacy of mother and child and recalls memories of his own happy childhood. Having made some progress in coming to terms with himself and with nature, he is now prepared to take on relationships with other people.

The first and perhaps most important matter Santarō takes up when he turns his attention to human relationships is the condition of parting and separation. He was impressed with Nietzsche's emphasis on the inevitability of separation in human life, although he might have been equally inspired if he had read *The Tale of Genji*. Santarō feels that in order to progress toward truth and the new self there is much that has to be left behind. Consequently, there is much sadness in the life of the pilgrim. If this is true for individuals, it is also true for cultures. He observes that Japan has broken with its past and is moving into an unknown future. He worries, however, that too much of the past lingers in the present, and that Japan has not been strong enough to make a clean break with the past.

14 Ibid., p. 98.

The problem of human relationships gives Abe the opportunity to discuss the suicide of General Nogi. Abe views the relationship between Nogi and the Meiji emperor not as one of master and servant, which would require this act of loyalty, but as the ideal personal relationship between two people. He admires one who could give his life for another and is ashamed that he has never been selfless enough to experience such a thing. Nogi's death suggests Tolstoi's concept of a life of service to others. Abe feels that there is a difference in emphasis in Nogi's case in that his life represented service to the state rather than to mankind in general. Nevertheless, the extent of Nogi's devotion to service is an ideal that makes other public servants nervous, so they ridicule the idealism it represents—a response Zarathustra would have predicted.

Through these middle chapters Abe as pilgrim has made good progress. He has broken out of his obsessive, introspective isolation and has been able to confront both nature and society. In chapters 12 and 13 he appears to backslide once more into a confusion of identity. First Santarō confesses that his real and original name was Segawa Kikunojō. Kikunojō is a stage name used by *onnagata* (female impersonators) in the Kabuki, although it was not in use during the Taishō period. The fact that the narrator's original name is that used by onnagata may suggest a confusion of sexual identity. As if this were not enough, Santarō again introduces another character, Aota Sangorō, to speak for him.

This backsliding of identity, however, is not as serious as it first appears, and indeed in one sense the situation marks the progress Santarō has made. Originally he changed his name to Santarō, a name often used for apprentices or novices and here suggesting the hero's new philosophical beginnings. Santarō adopted this name because, although he seemed outwardly to be a perfectly good person, he felt that his life lacked content. Kikunojō was clever with logic and good at thinking, so everyone was impressed with how smart he was, but inwardly he knew that his ideas were no more than mere cleverness and without any real depth or substance. When he changed his name, people misunderstood and supposed it meant he was becoming more sophisticated and decadent. In reality, however, it signaled his determination to find a new life for himself. As we already know, the attempt failed. Although he could do things Kikunojō was unable to do, his life was still false.

Nonetheless, Santarō was able to conceive of a better life in his imagination. Thus he now creates the character Sangorō, who is free of the physical, social, and philosophical limitations that burden Santarō. He hopes that Sangorō can do, experience, and express all that Santarō cannot.

At this point the author introduces the topic of Plato's *Symposium* and the views on the nature of love as expressed by Aristophanes and Socrates. Aristophanes identifies three sorts of people—man, woman, and man-woman. According to Plato, he explains we were originally a combined man-woman; now, as individuals, we have been separated from our other half and are searching to regain it. Often the union of the man and the woman is profane, but somewhere in the world there exists the perfect match for each one of us. Through this ideal union we are able to transcend the scientific and the natural, and reach the level of the sacred and the sublime. In considering this ideal of love, man and woman made one, it is hard to know how much emphasis to read into the suggestion that Kikunojō as onnagata may represent that ideal in himself. In any case, Santarō had originally rejected love because he did not have a well enough defined sense of self to be able to respond adequately to the love of another person. Later he rejected love again because it led the self into falsehood and compromise. Now he has found the theoretical ideal of love in which the self and other can become uncompromisingly one.

Santarō is now prepared to deal with other individuals, but he is still uncertain about how to come to terms with society as a whole. The relationship of the individual to society is a matter of morality, and here the inherent conflict between the self and society must be resolved. This conflict is inevitable because what is evident to the self may not be evident to society. If an individual follows his individual morality he will come into conflict with the moral values of society, and yet this is exactly what each person must do. Just as Abe had earlier contrasted an inner and an outer self, and an inner and an outer knowledge, now he posits an inner and an outer morality.

Inner morality, of course, is far superior to outer morality because it derives from the imperative of the true self. If morality is taught, that is, imposed from the outside, moral values will diminish correspondingly because true morality comes from within. In all matters, including chastity, adultery, faith, and friendship, outward moral standards can never match the subtle shading of light and dark found in the moral judgments of the self. The most important factor in making moral decisions is the individual's spiritual attitude, which ideally will entail a purity and nobility of spirit. Actions are less important than the attitude and condition of a person's spirit while performing the action.

Many moral philosophers may find this subjective standard of morality to be highly questionable, but at least it is consistent with every other part of Abe's philosophy. One may be reminded here of Shiga Naoya's story *Han no hanzai* (Han's crime) and Akutagawa's *Rashōmon* (The Rashō gate), both of which surely reflect the influence of Nietzsche's superman in defining his own morality. One can also recall Shiga's rather blunt judgment in *A Dark Night's Passing* when he writes, "if I like a person, I assume he's good, and if I dislike him, I assume he's bad,"[15] where matters of good and bad are determined entirely by one's individual and subjective judgments. In Abe's case he uses this concept of morality as a justification for adultery, saying that if the sin is confessed sincerely and with remorse, it can enable one to achieve a new and better spiritual foundation. He hastens to assure his readers that he is not promoting adultery, but merely saying that by applying his concept of inner morality, good can come even from that. Abe's main point is that external morality is insincere and therefore causes the soul to wither. It is only something for lawyers to quarrel over.

In chapter 15, Santarō examines another facet of the relationship between the self and society. He points out the conflict between the need to work for a living and the urge to devote oneself single-mindedly to the pursuit of truth. Here Abe wants to answer the question raised by Sōseki in *And Then* in a more comprehensive way than Sōseki did. In a fashion by now familiar to the reader, Abe posits two conflicting modes of being. Abe distinguishes between absorption, that which one takes in from the outer world, and creation, which comes from the inner self. Life is composed of a blending of these two into a synthesis that can place our lives somewhere on a continuum between heaven and hell. The key is to find a sort of work in the outer world with which the soul has a certain resonance, so that the anguish will not be so great as the soul flickers back and forth between the two states.

Santarō is always the purist and the romantic. He tells us that he has dedicated himself to the search for tranquility of the soul, and as he feels a new world beginning to open up for him, he decides he cannot work and be creative at the same time. Thus, he is living on borrowed money and eats poorly; he fails to buy adequate medicine for his ill and aged mother, and to provide adequate school expenses for his younger brother. In short, he has shirked all conventional social responsibilities, but he feels that his thoughts about the true life are beginning to coalesce.

From chapter 17 onward, the young philosopher is much more comfortable with himself and with the world around him. Now, far from disparaging himself as being weak and trivial, he launches into a discussion of the question of individual genius. Though he has not yet attained the true life he seeks, he nevertheless reaffirms the possibility of living such a life. He declares his belief in genius or the natural talents of the self, and he says that through developing the self, the individual can attain a true life.

[15] The quotation is taken from the Edwin McClellan's translation of the Shiga Naoya novel *A Dark Night's Passing* (Tokyo and New York: Kodansha International, 1976), p. 340.

Santarō first asserts that through meditation or introspection even a weak person's self-consciousness can become significant. He says such a positive development involves the mastery of hostility, and he speaks of the importance of true humility, saying that while humility often appears to be self-denial, it is, in fact, self-affirming. Putting this last thought into practice, Santarō says that although he is speaking of genius, he himself is the most ordinary of men. Finally, as in the introduction, he reminds us of Tolstoy's teaching that for the seeker of the true life, aspiration is more important than ambition.

In the final chapter, the growth and enrichment of the self become a conscious act. Santarō now sees himself as an evangelist of truth. He also fancies himself a critic of society and culture. Santarō never supposes that he has achieved his goal of the true life, but he does come to the conclusion that whether one's talents are great or small, whether one is a genius or an ordinary person, has nothing to do with one's value as a human being. The important thing is to recognize one's own self and to maintain a high sincerity of purpose. One must have the same respect for the ordinary man of sincerity that one has for the genius. If individuals create their own value with the talents they have been given, this creativity can imbue them with significance as human beings.

In this manner Santarō has progressed from anguish and uncertainty to a position where he has hope, aspiration, and strength. The true life he has sought is not a condition one finds and then maintains, but rather a process of a continual striving for self-improvement. To be consistent with this argument, Abe cannot present his conclusions as universal rules, but can only indicate the path he followed, inviting his readers each to search out and follow their own path.

During the course of this philosophical inquiry, which took six years to write, Abe alludes to the work of many prominent European thinkers. He says that the greatest influences on him came from Goethe, Dante, and Nietzsche, but the most consistent references in this work in terms of the arguments and the terminology used appear to be a combination that includes Shopenhauer, Hegel, and Nietzsche. Abe liked to call himself a follower of Nietzsche, but his views as expressed in *The Diary of Santarō* can hardly be called Nietzschean.

The source of this work's great and continuing appeal lies first of all in the fact that the author speaks to the universal groping of youth for answers to the large, philosophical dimensions of life. Second, he does not demand of his readers any rigid principles of thought. Everything can be as the individual wants it to be, as long as he can justify that goal with an expressed purity of intention and nobility of aspiration. These lofty ideals are stated in terms of references and allusions to the great thinkers of the

European tradition with which Abe's readers would have been familiar. Finally, it might be argued that *The Diary of Santarō* touched a responsive chord in the youth of Taishō Japan because the book, while creating a synthesis based on a broad spectrum of Western thought, is by no means rigidly sectarian.

# 2

## Kurata Hyakuzō and *The Origins of Love and Understanding*

J. THOMAS RIMER

IN MORI ŌGAI'S 1910 novel *Seinen* (Youth), Jun'ichi, the protagonist, writes moodily in his diary, ". . . what to do? That is the problem. For what purpose has the self been liberated? That is the problem."[1]

Ōgai was attempting to record the feelings of the young would-be intellectuals of his time, and certainly in this novel, at least, he did so with remarkable precision, if the writings of the much younger Kurata Hyakuzō (1891–1943) can be taken as a sample. Kurata's essays, begun when he was a student in the First Higher School in 1912, were first collected in the 1917 volume *Ai to ninshiki to no shuppatsu* (The origins of love and understanding), then reissued in 1921 with several additional items added. As a number of critics have pointed out, Kurata's book became a kind of Bible for young people, who found in it remarkable resonances of their own concerns. Indeed, Kurata's work helped them articulate to themselves their own sense of being and gave them, presumably, a method for coming to terms with their own adolescent feelings.

These essays were written early in Kurata's own career and mirror a phase in his own personal development. His later turn to religion (already clear in the final essays of *Origins*), and then to patriotism before and during the Second World War, is of interest for other reasons, but his contribution to the development and indeed validation of a new sense of self among young educated Japanese represents his major contribution as a writer for the younger generation at the time of World War I.

Kurata's main concepts, and his own emotional responses to the ideas he expounds, are set out chiefly in the long essays written during 1912 and 1913, when he was still a student and before his various illnesses caused him to drop out of the First Higher School. By the end of this period, humanistic and often specifically Christian concerns begin to loom larger, questions posed earlier now begin to be answered, another

All citations from *The Origins of Love and Understanding* are taken from *Abe Jirō, Kurata Hyakuzō*, vol. 74 of *Gendai Nihon bungaku zenshū* (Tokyo: Chikuma shobō, 1956).
[1] Mori Ōgai, *Seinen*, in *Mori Ōgai zenshū* (Tokyo: Chikuma shobō, 1971), 2:35.

rhetoric emerges, and the book loses some of the force of its opening thrust. The example of Kurata's finding a religious solution to his metaphysical and youthful anguish was doubtless a powerful one to a certain number of his readers, but his particular resolution was no more than one way through the thickets of doubt. Few others were to embrace it specifically.

In the first essay in the collection, "Longing" (1912), Kurata, who writes in the form of a letter to a friend, reminds his correspondent how necessary it is to examine life with the utmost seriousness. He contends, in turn, that such seriousness must bring with it a real sense of loneliness. Unlike Ōgai, however (whom he occasionally quotes), Kurata does not wish to remain a bystander; he does not wish to give up on life but rather wants to find something on which to fix the yearning, the human longing he feels within him. For Kurata, life must have a significance, and it must be led with the highest regard for the demands of the inner life.

It is clear after reading even the opening pages of this first essay, written when Kurata was twenty-one, that he exhibits a real vocation for the sacred, at that point still unarticulated within himself. It was one that he came to discover, or at least to describe, some three years later. In the opening essays, however, his vocabulary is couched in that of romantic philosophy, with a heavy emphasis on terms borrowed from German idealism and neo-Kantianism. By this time, such men as Raphael von Koeber (1848–1923) had been teaching German philosophy at Tokyo University for twenty years, and translations into Japanese of a wide variety of nineteenth-century German materials were available. As Donald Roden has pointed out, this kind of material had already reached the level of the higher schools, and Kurata was thus writing for an audience that was relatively familiar with the vocabulary of Western philosophy.

Kurata's sense of vocation produced as well a set of attitudes that give his existential anguish a special sense of urgency. It is clear from his first essay that his purpose is not merely to raise the "great questions of life" ("What is youth?" "What is truth?" "What is friendship?" "What is love?" "What is desire?" "What is faith?") but to develop a plan of action and a point of reference so that he might set out to solve those questions in terms of the conduct of his own personal struggle. At this juncture, Kurata chooses philosophy as the highest and most appropriate means by which he hopes to come to grips with his inner life.

In choosing European philosophy, Kurata does not seek to comprehend it in an academic mode. He examines philosophy not for its possible contribution to the history of ideas but as a living force that may hold the secrets for which he searches, if he can adopt the appropriate emotional attitudes. Kurata's desire for an emotional commitment to a set of intellectual ideas may now appear naive, but there remains something appeal-

ing, and courageous as well, in his ardent search for the truth. He insists
that philosophy is the highest form of study. The discipline provides him
with the only sufficiently powerful point of reference available to him;
after all, he says, the purpose of philosophy is to raise just the kind of
questions that are so important to Kurata himself. Kurata cites a number
of philosophers and writers in the book (indeed, one can index to some
extent his changing ideas with the works of Western writers whom he
selects to quote or paraphrase), but at this point in his thinking he is
drawn to Schopenhauer's *The World as Will and Idea*. He had either read
this work in its entirety or learned of it through a summary in Wilhelm
Windelband's *A History of Philosophy*, a well-used text for philosophy
in Japan. Kurata's attraction to William James is also fairly clear, but this
may have come about through his contact with the eminent Japanese philosopher Nishida Kitarō (1870–1945), described below. In James, in any
case, Kurata found justification for his conviction, again perhaps
strengthened by his contact with Nishida, that human experience rather
than abstract thought must produce in the individual a state of wisdom
and enlightenment. He was also much affected by his reading of the
works of the Japanese novelist Kunikida Doppo (1871–1908), himself a
Christian at one point in his career, whose elegiac and anguished stories
of Meiji youth must have served as both a stimulus and an objective correlative to Kurata's growing and painful sense of his own self. Like
Doppo, Kurata insisted on the primacy of "metaphysical desires" over
"mere pleasure," and Kurata's expressed sense of wonder and shock at
the magnitude of the universe surely echoes the crucial remark of Doppo's
protagonist in that remarkable short story "Meat and Potatoes," written
in 1901, some ten years earlier.

> Faith by itself can never suffice. I wish for the mystery of man and the uni-
> verse to plague me to the point, in fact, where without faith I could never know
> a moment's peace. . . . if only I could shake off this frost and free myself from
> the pressure of wornout custom. I wish that I could stand on my own two feet
> and preserve my capacity to be surprised.[2]

"I cling to ideas like mountains," Kurata writes, and he goes on to ex-
tend the natural simile by indicating that the first barrier that he and perhaps his readers must overcome is that of nature, which seems altogether
indifferent to human concerns. For Kurata, nature acknowledges man's
being but laughs at his will. Again, the importance of Schopenhauer as a
source of inspiration and consolidation for Kurata is clear when he goes
on to stress his belief that in order to connect ourselves with the temporal

[2] Kunikida Doppo, "Meat and Potatoes," in Maurice Schneps and Alvin I. Coox, eds.,
*The Japanese Image*, trans. Leon Zolbrod (Tokyo and Philadelphia: Orient/West, 1966),
pp. 187–88.

world, we must use our will to pull ourselves up and away from our acceptance of mere passive experience. Here, Kurata's intellectual understanding of his sources and his own instincts reinforce each other.

What quality is necessary to bring about the activation of the individual will? Understanding, or cognition, is the crucial state of mind, a mental quality that, along with love (which is added in a later essay), becomes for Kurata the basis for all spiritual growth in the soul. Once we have reached a state of cognition and self-awareness, Kurata writes, we are then prepared to take the crucial step of relating our own inner world to the outer temporal world in which we live. It then becomes possible to open up to life and to nature.

How does one reach the level of cognition? Perhaps, says Kurata, by means of loneliness, which can put us on a painful, slow path that forces us toward self-understanding. Yet, he concludes, there are further barriers, even should a level of self-awareness or cognition be reached. For cognition may itself lead to egotism, a state of soul that itself forms a well-constructed barrier to thwart any efforts expended in order to know oneself and the world, the kind of knowledge that is meant to herald the arrival at a state of goodness and altruism.

"Longing" sets out the urgent need for a plan and lays down some of the groundwork necessary to search out a requisite process to achieve self-understanding. The second essay, "The Cognitive Effort of Life," written later the same year, deepens the concept of the power and importance of cognition and chronicles in a much more complete form than the preceding essay Kurata's spiritual debt to Nishida.

> We are alive. And when we look into ourselves, we can observe for ourselves things of such import that an outpouring of tears could well result. The shadows of all the myriad things of this universe weave themselves into our senses. All the impulses that lie hidden in our inner life are thus set moving, creating in us consciousness, emotions, volition. And so it is that life itself, the substance of which lies concealed within us, begins to differentiate and develop, and our own interior experiences grow more complicated day by day. This complex inner life tries of its own accord to make itself complete. This force moves inside, going beyond the ordinary means of expression, to stir us up from within. Needless to say, two means to express this interior life are represented by art and philosophy. Art attempts, in a realistic and partial manner, to reveal interior experience, while philosophy, in the form of general conceptions, tries to express this experience as a whole. What comes as a result of this is a projection of the inner life, a reflection of the self, and the aim which has been accomplished is the creation of the self-consciousness of one's own existence. (p. 306)

Still it would be a mistake, Kurata continues, to say that life is only made up of sentiment; in fact, it is a mixture of knowledge and sentiment, and the two cannot be separated. The world of sentiment and feeling may be pursued through art, but the seeker must pursue as well the more difficult course of searching out the important role of the intelligence for true inner life. All of this must be undertaken so as to escape from the fragmentary nature of everyday life; all efforts must be made to achieve a whole being than can transcend our normally broken state of being. Art and philosophy alike are required.

It was at this point in his thinking that Kurata, in despair, happened upon Nishida's *Zen no kenkyū* (A study of good), published in 1911.

> I was truly suffering. I no longer knew why I should find it a worthwhile thing to live. I merely went on existing in the vague, like some idiot frog. Because of these disturbances within me, it was no longer possible for me to go to school. I wandered vaguely about outside. I let my feet guide me as I walked around silently, then returned home. Such was the easiest way for me to go on living. It was altogether impossible for me to study or to do anything.
>
> One day, as I was loitering about with no object in view, I stopped into a bookstore on my way home, where I bought a book, bound in pale, dark colors. The author's name was quite unknown to me, but the title of the book somehow possessed some power to console me.
>
> The book was *A Study of Good*. I began to read the preface in a desultory sort of fashion. After a bit, my eyes were transfixed by the words I found on the page.
>
> > Experience does not exist because of the individual; the individual exists because of experience. On the basis of the idea of that experience, and not on individual human difference, it is possible to escape from the theories of the ego.
>
> How sharp and vivid those words that were written there! A way of escaping from the self had been found! The words seemed to make a powerful print on my retina.
>
> I wondered if the palpitations of my heart would stop. I felt myself filled with the kind of quiet seriousness that constitutes neither joy nor sadness, and I could find no means to continue on with my reading. I closed the book and sat quietly before my desk. A tear trailed down my cheek. (p. 321)

In Nishida, Kurata insists, he found a description of a real wholeness of which he could at that point only catch a glimpse by means of his own tortured and unsystematic reflections. Nishida therefore provided Kurata not only with a point of reference, but with a possible plan of how to proceed as well.

The essay continues with a reading of Nishida through the eyes of Kurata, who wrestles both with the difficult text and with his own convictions. The results often tell as much or more about Kurata's mental state as they do about his rather selective view of Nishida's concerns, but these pages make particularly intense reading as Kurata, half explicating, half confessing, searches for a means to understand himself through his confrontation with the thought of a powerful philosopher.

For Kurata, the basic value of Nishida's work lay in the emphasis the philosopher places on the value of pure experience as a means to work toward both understanding and moral goodness. Nishida assumes a genuine moral grandeur based on the importance he places on experience as opposed to mere conceptualization. Although Nishida appreciates the value of cognition, which can become a crucial tool to help the mind in its attempt to synthesize experience, he does not abandon his belief in the power of intuition, which itself grows out of "pure experience." On the other hand, writes Kurata, Nishida is no "mere pragmatist," for he understands the power and truth of the classical Japanese virtue of *mono no aware*, that deep sense of the sadness and mutability of life. For Kurata, therefore, Nishida's writing might best be defined as an "aesthetics of cognition."

But, Kurata continues, there is still more to Nishida than that. Man "burns with a desire to be good," and thus Nishida's work might also be read as a study of ethics, since man's powers of cognition and self-understanding can give him freedom from the ultimate bonds of the external world. Such a consciousness represents the highest level to which mankind can aspire, since we can use this consciousness to escape the "tyranny of the instant." In Kurata's view, religion and a sense of awe before the divine represent the true end of Nishida's thinking. Thus, as one reads his philosophy, one can feel the greatness of his soul.

Kurata's third essay, "Finding Oneself in the Opposite Sex," continues along with many of the themes first explicated in the opening two essays but adds to them the second element required as equipment for life, that of love. In this essay, written a year later, in 1913, Kurata begins for the first time to reflect back on his own experience, suggesting that he has now reached a higher state of self-understanding. His ability to engage in such reflection, he indicates, confirms his conviction that the individual's interior life must be at the base of all human wisdom and endeavor. By the same token, he insists, concern with the self must eventually be replaced by and transmuted into concern for others. One can come to know one's own existence, he writes, but how can one truly imagine the existence of others? This essay might be best described as an attempt to sketch out an escape route from the kind of egotism that Kurata felt represented such a danger; for him, intellectual life alone cannot bring progress unless it is combined with and informed by human experience. In this regard, he concludes, a "psychological truth" can hold as much truth as an "intellectual truth."

His close reading of Nishida, Kurata says, permits him to discover the idea of love, particularly in terms of its power to go beyond the range of any individual human consciousness. At the end of chapter 2 of *A Study of Good*, Nishida wrote that "pure experience can transcend the individual." Kurata quotes Nishida's text:

> Thus, although it may sound extremely strange, we can say that because experience knows time, space, and the individual, it is above time, space, and the individual; it is not that since there is the individual there is experience, but rather that since there is experience there is the individual. Individual experience is nothing more than one particular small area delimited from within experience.[3]

This kind of thinking seems to confirm for Kurata the existence of a kind of transcendental ground with which human destiny seeks an intimate relationship. Both love and conscious understanding therefore represent the means by which the individual can go through the various stages in a process. Love, in particular, provides the means to come to terms with the human beings who live around us, so that we can experience life and learn from it.

Still, Kurata reflects, self-knowledge is hard won and can only come through the pain of personal experience. Kurata describes how, even as he experienced these thoughts, he made a pilgrimage to Mount Tsukuba, north of Tokyo, where, in his despair, he brooded over the difficulties of finding a means by which he might entrust himself to nature and pondered over his doubts as to whether or not he might ever find a means to come to terms with another human being, particularly with a woman. After the trip, he found himself slipping back into his old ways; he had still to find a way to avoid the purely intellectual. What could give him the necessary inner strength? God? Friendship? Woman? All these concepts now seemed tangled up in his mind. At this point, the concept of God seemed the most difficult for Kurata to come to terms with. "In fact," he writes, "it was harder to believe in God's love than in God himself." The problem of learning to understand women was difficult for him as well. He found himself suspicious of them, and yet he knew that his view was colored by his own egotism. More than anything else, Kurata confesses that he found himself worried about the relentless conventionality of women, the fact that they doubtless could not share the grandeur of his own feelings. "I did not want tradition, but a blending of souls," he writes, quite sure at the same time that he would be laughed at for his ridiculously high ideals.

[3] Nishida Kitarō, *A Study of Good*, trans. V. H. Vigilielmo (Tokyo: Japanese National Commission for UNESCO, 1960), p. 19.

Kurata, chronicling his own feelings, finds that, as a means to solve his spiritual crisis, he seemed to find himself ready to make an idol of life, perhaps ready to fall "into superstition and live a myth as a means to sustain himself." Love, then, came to seem to him not a pleasure, but a burning demand, and in the midst of such love, a religious yearning, the need for a "bitter pilgrimage," emerged. Now he realized that what he sought was a person for whom he was ready to die. Yet how was he to find a partner with the same degree of commitment? Reflecting on the suicide of General Nogi the year before, Kurata analyzes the event less as a traditional act in terms of Japanese society than as a natural religious act growing out of love; the general "could not bear to live." These thoughts in turn lead him to reflections of the state of loneliness that is man's lot.

> The word "loneliness" is one that has become familiar to our ears. Yet I think there lies concealed within this word a profound meaning. Thus I do not appreciate the fact that we tend to use that word lightly. Before we put the word "loneliness" on our lips we must reflect on the extent to which we can truly love another. In what way have we truly been able to touch the soul of another, in what way have we been able to unstop the mouth of our own soul, with the idea of accepting another's? It is on such things that we must reflect. To tell the truth, at this time, I am not lonely. I have no desire to flee from the souls of others. How I have wanted to thrust into myself, to the depth, and to tremble with this mystery. I want to adore my beloved to such a degree that the sweat will pour from me, so much that I could die. I want to know the shame of loving someone so much that I might fear death itself. (p. 326)

So it was that Kurata came to feel an ambition to realize a true love that could permit "a great strength to well up" in him. "Truly, love is *life*. And I want to expand every effort for that life. I will pursue such love for the rest of my life. But the heights of love, not the easy kind."

Although the essay is written in a confessional form, Kurata makes relatively few references to the external details of his personal life at the time. Still, it is clear that the kind of psychological fever chart his essays represent was indeed mirrored in his own experience; in that regard, Kurata had reason to maintain that thought and cognition did grow out of human experience and so must represent the most valuable and authentic access to genuine abstract thought. During his days at the First Higher School, when these essays were written, Kurata had suffered a series of serious illnesses, fallen in love, and been rejected by the young woman he had chosen to idolize. He had also managed to call on Nishida Kitarō in Kyoto. Shortly after the young woman who did not respond to his advances returned home and married, Kurata contracted a severe case of tuberculosis and was forced to retire from school in 1913. The combina-

tion of the two events caused him to plunge into a period of quiet reflection and study, during which he lived a somewhat hermit-like existence
in the countryside near Hiroshima. Although he was able to visit a protestant Bible study group on a fairly regular basis during those months,
by the end of 1914 his condition had so degenerated that he had to be
hospitalized.

By the time Kurata was twenty-four, he had set down in the five opening essays of the book his general principles for a plan of life. For him,
the search would now devolve on the area of religion. As early as the 1913
essay "The Road of One Who Has Lost Love," Kurata asked himself the
question, "How am I to sustain my belief in my path: By love? By work?
By faith?" He had come to the conclusion that no purely private suffering
was possible for him, and that, as "love is the highest function of consciousness, and will its clearest expression," he must dedicate himself to
a search for God. The twelve short essays that conclude the collection,
written from 1915 to 1920, range over a wide variety of subjects, and
show the results of Kurata's reading, in particular his emphasis on the
religious humanism of Strindberg, Tolstoi, and Dostoevski, as well as a
deepening interest in the writings of Nietzsche. Once the decision to embrace God is taken, Kurata's rhetoric changes, the scope of his question-
ing narrows, and the tonality of his prose begins to suggest a combination
of the evangelical and the condescending.

These essays, even within the humanist Christian framework developed
by Kurata, do nevertheless go on to refine and reexamine the premises
and intuitions that give the earlier seminal essays their force. Kurata attempts to separate the concept of selfless love from the egotism of the
lover; he sees that the disinterested love of neighbor, exemplified by the
sacrifice of Christ, rather than the egotistical love of husband for wife or
parent for child, must become one's goal. As Nishida himself understood,
Kurata insists, one must go beyond the individual in oneself to locate the
universal. The reading of literature, he adds, might provide a way to lead
one to a greater understanding of this vital principle. For Kurata, the nat-
uralists were wrong in their failure to understand the need to put goodness before mere beauty; by simply accepting that everything that exists
can be put into art, they lost the power of the moral distance that can be
found in great writers like Blake and Nietzsche, who, although they do
not deny what has been created, can use their genuine humanity to pass
judgment on what is evil. His reading of the New Testament too, on the
evidence of a few sentences in the essays, seems to have led him to see
certain parallels between the Christian experience and that of Shinran
(1173–1262), the priest who founded the Amidist sect of Buddhism.
Shinran, Kurata writes, "is a man who knows how to cry out to God."
This interest in the famous saint eventually led Kurata to compose his

drama *Shukke to sono deshi* (The priest and his disciples) (1917), written only to be read but later staged in 1919. This play, doubtless Kurata's most popular work after *The Origins of Love and Understanding*, brought him fame not only in Japan but abroad as well, when the play was translated into English by Glen W. Shaw and published in 1922.

By 1921, when the second and more complete edition of *Origins* was published, Kurata, then thirty-one, could look back on the development of his thought and life as reflected in his essays, written over a ten-year period, in order to place them in perspective. There remains in his new preface something of a pedantic tonality, but he is remarkably successful in explicating the way in which his essays had already been understood by his younger contemporaries.

> This book is a collection of virtually all my thoughts and my essays set down until this point. For me, the appearance of this book has two meanings. The first is that it serves as a memorial to my own youth; the second is that it serves as a gift to the hearts of those young people who will come after me. For me, it seems that the end of my youth has arrived. Thus I have decided to bury the "youth" of my young years, and, without reference to my actual age, live from now on in a spirit of "eternal youthfulness." On the occasion when one decides to bid farewell to one's youth, one must find oneself completely absorbed in boundless and deep emotions. One feels a powerful reluctance to part with one's youth. And it is very difficult as well to repress a sensation of thankfulness. Truly, one's youth was a time of great earnestness, of purity, and, furthermore, of bravery. A time filled with suffering and severe trials. And yet, as one reflects back, it seems that in the midst of those sufferings and those trials, one has been able to open up a road that will permit a proper life; progress has been made in finding a way that can lead the human soul forward. (p. 293)

This brief summary of Kurata's book may help to suggest the kind of concerns that he, and others like him, felt in the early Taishō period. Kurata's chronicling of his own plunge inward toward a spiritual journey provided in published form some general route markers for many in the generations that followed him. Indeed, by indicating that the need to follow such a path was the highest duty that a man could undertake, Kurata validated the feelings of others who also found themselves troubled and unsure of their own purposes in an increasingly complex society.

The question might be raised as to whether any objective conditions, beyond the nature of Kurata's own temperament, caused him to spend so much effort on plumbing what he took to be the depths of his own soul. He certainly did possess within himself in great measure the spiritual raw materials, as it were, to do so. But without the heritage of German philosophy and of earlier Meiji writings by such important writers as Kunikida Doppo and Kitamura Tōkoku, it is unlikely that Kurata would have been able to find either the requisite forms of thought or the appropriate vocabulary in which to couch his speculations. Even a cursory look at *A Study of Good* by his mentor Nishida Kitarō reveals an enormous and genuine assimilation of both concepts and examples of Western art, philosophy, and literature by this first, and perhaps greatest, master of modern Japanese philosophy. Through the example of Nishida, Kurata was able to assimilate this kind of vocabulary and, indeed, to express himself in a more natural fashion. By the second decade of the twentieth century, the efforts of Koeber and others had resulted in the creation of a core of highly educated students, many turned intellectuals and writers, whose absorption with continental European thought had naturalized those terms of reference in Japan. By 1915, for example, a group of respected writers and thinkers, among them Natsume Sōseki, the Kantian expert Kuwaki Gen'yoku, Nishida Kitarō, Abe Jirō, and Tanabe Hajime, edited a twelve-volume set of essays and translations of philosophy published by Iwanami that easily found a wide readership. The contents were mostly made up of Kantian and neo-Kantian material, and the fact that these modes of thought were widely enough accepted to permit a large readership suggests to what extent these terms of reference had become familiar to those with a university education. Some of the editors of the series were older men of distinction, such as Sōseki, but the importance of younger writers is clear as well. Abe was thirty-two; Tanabe was only thirty; and Abe Yoshishige, who later wrote important works on the history of Western philosophy, was also thirty-two. A majority of these men had studied philosophy at Tokyo University, and their mutual enthusiasm and further study helped to make these texts available to a larger public. Kurata himself, born in 1891, was only twenty-four when the series appeared, yet his use of European literary and philosophic terminology seems fully as assured as that of any of those who contributed to the series.

Still, there was one crucial difference between the essays in the monumental collection described above and the kind of writing that can be found in Kurata's work. The Iwanami collection might be described as an academic one, albeit of the most significant sort. The writers and editors set out to explain contemporary and near-contemporary currents of European thought, but they themselves did not necessarily become personally or emotionally involved with the texts. Kurata, on the other hand, plunged inside his European texts with the same kind of intensity that Bashō urged his *haiku* poet friends to plunge into nature; Kurata had the idea that he must "lose himself" in order to find a deep level of truth beyond his individual concerns. In the end, the most striking literary fact about *The Origins of Love and Understanding* doubtless remains not its contents but the confessional style in which it is written.

The major essays in the collection use two modes, the letter and the first person confession. A number of the early sections are couched in the style of letters sent to friends. Later research by Japanese scholars has indicated that indeed some of these essays did begin as personal letters that Kurata later expanded into literary documents. Such comparisons shed light on the processes of Kurata's compositional technique and are thus of some interest in terms of his biography. More germane to matters here, however, is the fact that he seems to have couched his arguments in that form because, as so many other Japanese writers in the period had discovered, the epistolary form brought with it the possibility of producing a powerful confessionary thrust less easily managed in the more regular third-person narrative style. One of the greatest of the epistolary works of the period, of course, is Natsume Sōseki's 1912 novel *Kokoro*, where, in the long letter that makes up the bulk of the novel, the protagonist finds himself able to explain his feelings through the means of a letter. Given the strictures of ordinary Japanese conversation, Sōseki doubtless would have found it difficult to use a third-person narrative mode to do the same. But there are also earlier letters in Sōseki novels, notably *The Wayfarer*, and there are celebrated uses of the form as well by other important contemporary writers, as in Chikamatsu Shūkō's novel, *A Lesson to My Divorced Wife*, written in 1910, or in *Friendship*, written in 1919 by Mushakōji Saneatsu. Again, this confessional style is related to the larger problems of the "I" novel and the whole relationship between literal truth and emotional authenticity that the form of the "I" novel raises.[4] A discussion of those problems would take us too far from the matters at hand, but it can be pointed out in any case that the first essays in Kurata's collection read very much as though they are passages from a confessional novel. He doubtless chose the form unconsciously as the surest way to validate his documentation of the flow of his emotions. One certainly can read the early essays as though they were fiction; or, conversely, they might be seen as fiction so successfully composed that they seem to represent fact. Kurata always provides an emotional environment that can allow him to demonstrate the inevitability of the reciprocal development of his intellectual ideas and his emotional attitudes. A few passages at random will indicate his general implicit methodology.

I am a pitiful, woeful insect. Like a stray dog, I loiter about, with no fixed and peaceful place of abode. Tangled as I am in desolation, grief, agony, and desire, all contained within me, I sometimes sigh and think that I am unique and alone in the whole universe. Now I feel sprouting in my heart a ghastly disgust with the world. Those feelings have taken the form of a bleakness, a

[4] See, for example, an extended treatment of these issues in Edward Fowler's study, *The Rhetoric of Confession: Shitshōsetsu in Early Twentieth-Century Fiction* (Berkeley: University of California Press, 1988).

desolation that appears in the midst of my consciousness, menacing me, ridiculing me. (p. 307)

Just as, for example, a pure white flower might suddenly open itself in a vast field at dawn, so, when we first realize that we have escaped from convention and tradition into a genuine life of our own, it is as though a glittering bright light surrounds us. One's eyes are stretched at the miracles in all things. Light has dawned on the long night of life. From now on, one must truly strive to live. So thinking, we set our hearts to dancing, step out with our shoulders held high. So it is that we set out to follow along this great road of life, with bravery, seeking a sense of completion. There has never been a time when one has had such a powerful sense of consciousness of oneself. (p. 317)

I have no wish to cry out over the pain I feel, nor to seek any sympathy. That is not how I should respond at this time. That is because, at this moment, I stand in a particularly unworthy position in relation to life itself. Now is the time when I must be resolute. Wretched, my spiritual life crushed, and my anxiety over the collapse of the body which must support it—my life from inside and outside as well presses on to the point of danger.

Indeed, is this not the time when I must try to save myself: Yet what is it that I should achieve? "In serving life, remain absolutely faithful!" So I close my eyes to the depths of the chill, the urgency in the complexities of all things in my life, and I cry out. And when I cry out, I find that what rules the innermost depths of my heart is a deep moral consciousness. This is a feeling of the sort of duty that transcends any promise, one that faces the reality of life itself. This is not the kind of duty that arises in response to the will toward any particular purpose. Rather, this is a feeling of duty that contains an imperative within itself. From the first time I felt that I had come to find myself in agreement with Kant and his moral imperative, and I am struck with his profound understanding. At this time when my being is threatened by danger, and I hear the sounds of crumbling and destruction within me, what gives me a sense of perseverance and strength of support is nothing other than this feeling of a duty toward life itself. (p. 334)

In many pages of the book confession transcends its function as mode and comes to represent virtually the purpose of the passages involved. In this regard, Kurata, like many of his contemporaries, followed the dictum of the writer and actor Shimamura Hōgetsu (1871–1918), who said that literature must bear witness to the age: "Eschew falsehood, forget ostentation, and behold acutely the realities of your own situation. Having beheld, then confess them earnestly."[5]

And yet, for Kurata there was one crucial difference. He bore witness to his own interior life, yet he made almost no references whatsoever to

[5] Quoted in Nakamura Mitsuo, *Modern Japanese Fiction 1868–1926* (Tokyo: Japan Cultural Society, 1968), p. 2.

the political and social situation in which he found himself. Thus if one characteristic of this early phase of the Taishō discovery of the self lies in confession, another seems to be a blocking out of social concern, at least in any analytic sense. True, in Kurata's case, he makes constant reference, especially in his later Christian-humanist essays, to the need to love one's neighbor. Yet even here, his motives lie in his apparent conviction that such attitudes represent a kind of therapeutic technique to repair the ravages of egotism to the soul, rather than a means to redress civil inequalities. Commenting on a later edition of *The Origins of Love and Understanding*, published in 1936, Kurata added a few paragraphs to his original preface, pointing out that some of his critics had found him "deficient in social character" and without any understanding of the materialist basis of society. He replied that before a human can grasp the nature of society, he must know himself, and this knowledge, he maintained, came from the twin poles of love and consciousness. Out of such a metaphysics of life, connections with others could develop. The process, however, could not be reversed. Indeed, he concluded, did not the development of his own thought bear this out? There is no question that the ultimate impact of the book on his contemporaries lay not in Kurata's eventual humanist and religious solutions but in the example he provided of the need for an authentic self-examination, which he created so forcefully in the opening sections of the book.

Another quality of Kurata's thinking and one that seems symptomatic of Taishō culture is its cosmopolitan character. Kurata's own reading, insofar as it is revealed in his citations, was more in Western sources than in Japanese ones, and there is little to indicate on the basis of internal citations that Kurata's book is by a Japanese. The very word "Japan" seldom appears, and almost never in a political context. The one political reference he makes to Japan in fact is quite critical: Kurata views the bellicose attitude of Japan toward China as a kind of national neurosis of desire paralleling the egotism of the individual.

> The feelings of a cat who plays with a mouse before eating it resemble closely the feelings of a man with a woman whom he seeks to violate. And this consciousness of subjugation serves as a stimulant for sexual desire. When I see a snake eating a frog, my desire is aroused. To give an extreme example, reading an article in the newspaper concerning the fact that Japan menaces China brings on desire. There is an inevitable connection between these things. (p. 375)

This emphasis on the centrality of the interior life of the individual suggests another assumption on the part of Kurata that, although never explicitly explicated, seems apparent from a close reading of the text. Kurata posits his ideas on the basis of an assumption that all men are at least potentially equal and have access to the same possibility of finding the significance of their own inner lives. One can say, of course, that the book, however widely read and admired, found its way only into the hands of the intelligentsia and does not represent any particularly democratic statement. Such may indeed be the history of its text and its readership; nevertheless, Kurata felt that his own responses to the human situation were universal, and the abstractions he takes from European philosophy provide him with the support for this assumption. The question for him always remains as follows: Once any individual becomes conscious of his own existential state, what plan of action must he undertake? Here, in Kurata's thinking, one's highest duty to oneself will inevitably lead to contemplation, a reading of philosophy, and eventually, just as he was convinced he saw in Nishida, the development of a religious understanding. In this regard, Kurata takes the emotions and responses of his youthful readers as significant and serious. Some of Kurata's attitudes may have been refined and developed through his reading of such humanist Christian writers as Tolstoi, but in the early essays they seem to spring naturally, from his own deepest convictions. For Kurata, therefore, the experience of literature is secondary to the experience of life.

A related assumption that a reading of the text reveals is Kurata's conviction that human knowledge is by nature experiential. Philosophic or religious doctrine is not merely something to be accepted or mastered intellectually, but a challenge to be judged, examined, and perhaps embraced on the basis of the development, and the suffering, found in one's own individual interior life. Intellectual "truth," then, must always be tested against the real truth of one's own personal experience. Life therefore informs art (and ethics), and not the other way around. Religion, literature, and philosophy become crucial means to instruct the soul in its own development and are without any separate, ultimate value as abstract ends in themselves. There is a genuine sense of vocation in Kurata's formulations, and an emotional force that remains compelling. In the earlier Meiji period, older ideas of Confucian duty were turned toward the strengthening of society and the nation. Now the same high-mindedness was to turn inward, and onto the individual.

Kurata's sense of commitment, and his shifts in consciousness undertaken in his attempt to describe his inner state of being, show qualities that would surely have appealed to the French philosopher Henri Bergson, who is often praised in laudatory terms throughout the essays. Had Bergson, with his own emphasis on the movements of time and intuition, known Kurata's work, he might well have appreciated the way in which his Japanese admirer found the courage to cut himself loose from the traditional verities of Japanese ethical and moral belief, in order to allow himself to float, at whatever psychological cost, toward the open sea of the twentieth century.

# 3

## Taishō Culture and the Problem of Gender Ambivalence

DONALD RODEN

CENTRAL to the iconoclastic spirit of the 1920s was the fascination for gender ambivalence in both the high and middlebrow cultures of the industrial world. What some called the "sexual madness" of the postwar decade was all the more striking because, as Stefan Sweig observed, the promoters of the new decadence were those very "bourgeois circles" that formerly had been "unshakable in their probity."[1] Sweig had Berlin in mind when he made this statement in 1926. With its cabarets, "wrestling salons," all-girl revues (the Tiller Girls, the Admiral Girls, the Paris Mannequins), and transvestite balls, Berlin clearly stood out as the "Babylon" of the Western world, a reputation enhanced by the conspicuous presence of Magnus Hirschfeld's Institute for Sexual Science. But while the flamboyance and daring of Berlin's nightlife may have exceeded that of other cities in Europe or the United States, the underlying fascination for sexual inversion and the intentional smashing of gender distinctions was by no means a geographically isolated phenomenon. Paris, London, New York, and, as will be seen, Tokyo were never far behind Berlin in the marketing of sexual ambivalence.

Nor was the naughty spirit of the age restricted to the cabaret stage or the "vulgar arts." A persistent theme within the European avant-garde before and after World War I was a disdain for conventional bipolar views of manhood and womanhood. In Buñuel and Dali's surrealist classic, *Un Chien andalou* (1928), the hero first appears on bicycle, wearing a nun's headdress with white wings and a skirt over his pants. His passion is later ignited by sight of a wistful androgyne, who stands immobile on the street poking at a severed hand, until she/he is struck by a passing car. The fascination for androgyny is further revealed in Carl Theodor Dreyer's *La Passion de Jeanne D'arc* (1928) and the films of the German ex-

---

[1] Quoted in Otto Friedrich, *Before the Deluge: A Portrait of Berlin in the 1920's* (New York: Harper and Row, 1972), p. 129. In writing this paragraph, I have also used Wolf Von Eckardt and Sander Gilman, *Bertolt Brecht's Berlin* (New York: Anchor Books, 1975), esp. pp. 22–43.

pressionists. From *The Cabinet of Dr. Caligari* (1919), recall the character Cesare, with long eyelashes, a mouth smeared with lipstick, cheeks caked with rouge. Kracauer reminds us that for Fritz Lang, prescriptive models, sexual or otherwise, were confined to the madhouse.[2] Lang's Cesare finds his musical counterpart in Arnold Schoenberg's decadent clown from the song cycle *Pierrot Lunaire* (1912). To enhance Pierrot's variant image the composer insisted that his part be spoken (Sprechstimme) by a female narrator who could exploit the dissident nuances of his atonal music.[3]

The intentional subversion of gendered polarities in music and film extended to literature. In the words of Virginia Woolf, perhaps the most outspoken champion of the androgenous vision, the "fusion" of masculine and feminine sensibilities "fertilized" the mind and made complete use of its capacity for psychological insight. "A mind that is purely masculine cannot create, anymore than a mind that is purely feminine."[4] Among German writers, Rilke and Hesse stand out for, in effect, putting Woolf's bisexual principle into practice. Rilke, who, at the behest of his neurotic mother, spent five years of his childhood dressing like a girl, continually mixed masculine and feminine imagery in his poems. In the fifth of the *Duino Elegies*, for example, the robust image of the acrobat— "tightly packed with muscles and dumbness"—gradually dissolves before the person of a young girl spectator, who is none other than the poet himself. The little girl, the doll, the angel—not the Nietzschean superman—were the "objective correlatives" for Rilke's aesthetic self-conception.[5] Similarly, self-awakening in Hesse's novels often hinges upon discovery of, and eventual union with, the feminine side of the masculine self. Emil Sinclair, the hero of *Demian*, discovers his real self through his dreamlike encounters with Frau Eva, the Jungian projection of *anima* or the feminine archetype of the soul. The feminine impulses of Frau Eva converge with the masculine impulses of Demian (the Jungian *animus*) to reconstitute Sinclair's sense of who he is. The atmosphere is decidedly hermaphroditic as even Frau Eva emerges in Sinclair's mind as "masculine" or a "half-male, half-female dream image."[6] The *anima-animus* di-

[2] Siegfried Kracauer, *From Caligari to Hitler: A Psychological History of the German Film* (Princeton: Princeton University Press, 1947), pp. 65–70, 81–84, 220–22.

[3] Erwin Stein, ed., *Arnold Schoenberg: Letters* (New York: St. Martin's Press, 1964), p. 149. For further information on Schoenberg and *Pierrot Lunaire*, I am grateful to my wife, Chie.

[4] Virginia Woolf, *A Room of One's Own* (New York: Harcourt, Brace, 1929), pp. 170–71.

[5] Rainer Maria Rilke, *Duino Elegies* (Berkeley: University of California Press, 1963), pp. 28–43; J. B. Leishman, *Rainer Maria Rilke: New Poems* (New York: New Directions, 1964), p. 25.

[6] Hermann Hesse, *Demian* (New York: Bantam, 1968), esp. pp. 103 and 111; Joseph

alectic that is introduced in *Demian* is greatly elaborated in *Narcissus and Goldmund*.

The elevation of sexual ambiguity as a problem, especially among German writers, film makers, and composers, says something about the broader nature of culture in the 1920s. For *Demian, Pierrot Lunaire, The Cabinet of Dr. Caligari*, the Tiller Girls Revue, and the Institute of Sexual Science are all constituents of what we now call Weimar Culture. And what might they signify? Above all, and here I employ and expand upon a brilliant formulation by the late Warren Susman,[7] the products of Weimar Culture suggest a pervasive interest in personality, as opposed to character, and an accompanying disinterest in the technical, bureaucratic, and political instruments of civilization. Let us look briefly at both sides of this question.

Like Victorian England and postbellum America, Wilhelmian Germany was a civilization of character, a civilization dedicated to the accomplishment of deeds, the fulfillment of duty, and the exemplification of bourgeois honor and respectability. As referred to here, character is synonymous with manliness or the values of masculine domination: asceticism, achievement, public service. In his orientation toward external goals, the man of character is no *Naturkind*, he is rather the product of development or "building" from without, the recipient of rigorous training in institutions like the Gymnasium, which restrained all natural impulses, sexual or creative, and rendered absolute the do's and don'ts of manhood and middle-class status. The simple optimism that informs the character ethic (the belief that institutions can indeed mold the ideal man of honor and respectability) was challenged in the early 1900s by an array of European writers who emphasized feeling over accomplishment, traits over morals, and being over doing—a vision that, in effect, gave primacy to "feminine" sensibility over "masculine" action. "Personality," wrote Henri Laurent in 1915, "is the quality of being somebody."[8] And who one happened to be was, for Laurent, no longer a question of moral training or pedagogy. Rather, man and woman emerged in early twentieth-century literature against a backdrop of moral as well as scientific relativ-

---

Mileck, *Hermann Hesse: Life and Work* (Berkeley: University of California Press, 1978), p. 94.

[7] Warren Susman, "Personality and the Making of Twentieth-Century Culture," in John Higham and Paul Conkin, eds., *New Directions in American Intellectual History* (Baltimore: Johns Hopkins University Press, 1979), pp. 212–26. Susman focused on the transition in American thought from a nineteenth-century "culture of character" to an early twentieth-century "culture of personality." For the purposes of the analysis of Meiji and Taishō Japan, I prefer to distinguish a *civilization* of character from a *culture* of personality, as the transition from civilization (*bunmei*) to culture (*bunka*) parallels the transition from character to personality.

[8] Quoted in Susman, "Personality," p. 218.

ity, of "dissolving certainties" about the beautiful, the righteous, and the evil, and of a fundamental tension between man's instinctive nature and his existence in a "civilized" social order.[9] Although Freud accepted many of the premises of bourgeois morality, he viewed the human being as an essentially neurotic personality, trapped between his or her own unconscious instincts and society's regulations. As a man or woman of character, the individual had full reign over his or her deepest impulses; as a man or woman of personality, such self-control was open to the most agonizing doubt and skepticism.[10]

The ambiguities and uncertainties of the Freudian view of personality undoubtedly inspired many Weimar artists in their explorations of the unconscious mind—the murky realm of the aberrant, the grotesque, the mystic, the unusual, the androgenous. The complete severance of personality from character, however, would not take place without a coincidental removal of culture (a basically spiritual realm that embraced literature and the arts) from civilization (a basically material realm that embraced the institutions of state and the technology of the machine age). In the 1920s, writes Wolf Von Eckardt, "technology and culture, once thought to make up what was called civilization, [had] become things apart."[11] Of course the separation of culture from technology and politics predated the 1920s. "All great ages of culture are ages of political decline," wrote Nietzsche at the turn of the century. "What is great culturally has always been unpolitical, even anti-political." This view was subsequently elaborated by, among others, Kurt Hiller, who, as spokesman for the expressionist literary circle Der Neue Club, claimed that "culture can only be grasped subjectively through feeling and not through logic," and then by Meinecke in his much belabored distinctions between *Kultur*, a supperrational entity, and *Macht*, the power of the state.[12] Moreover, unlike civilization, defined by Spengler as "the most external, artificial state of which humanity is capable," culture springs from the inner spirit of every person; it is "intrinsic and spontaneous" and thus indistinguishable from personality or the qualities of being over doing, feeling over accomplishment, and madness over reason.[13] In differing ways, the literary andro-

[9] George Mosse, *The Culture of Western Europe* (New York: Rand McNally, 1965), pp. 227–78.

[10] Susman, "Personality," p. 213.

[11] Von Eckardt and Gilman, *Bertolt Brecht's Berlin*, p. 43.

[12] Nietzsche quoted in Harold Poor, *Kurt Tucholsky and the Ordeal of Germany* (New York: Scribners, 1968), p. 85; Roy Allen, *Literary Life in German Expressionism and the Berlin Circles* (Goppingen: Verlag Alfred Kummerle, 1974), p. 194; Robert Pois, *Friedrich Meinecke and German Politics in the Twentieth Century* (Berkeley: University of California Press, 1972), pp. 49–50.

[13] Spengler is quoted in Mosse, *The Culture of Western Europe*, p. 1; also Pois, *Friedrich Meinecke*, p. 50.

gynes of Hesse and Rilke, together with Berlin's flaming transvestites, signify this shift from reasoned intellect to neurotic feeling, from a civilization of character to what Susman calls a culture of personality.

The transition from civilization to culture and from character to personality is as important to the social history of Japan as it is to Germany or the United States. No less than the Gymnasium, the Meiji secondary schools for men and women were character-molding institutions that, as Dewey phrased it, relied upon "a literal building into the mind from without." What concerned educators in the 1880s and 1890s had little to do with the innate sensibilities of young people. Instead, attention focused upon the content of the curriculum and the external environment of the school. The selection of textbooks, the balance between mental and physical activity, the design of uniforms, the planting of trees around school buildings, the location of lavatories—on such questions nothing was left to chance.[14] In a similar vein, Meiji educators drew elaborate distinctions between the character-building missions of young men and women, especially in the secondary schools. "Liberals" and "conservatives" agreed that the "duties of womanhood" (onna no honbun) destined the "weaker sex" to devote themselves to the home, as "good wives and wise mothers" (ryōsai kenbo), while the "duties of manhood" (otoko no honbun) demanded that young stalwarts seek their fortunes in the outside world of politics and commerce. Accordingly, just as the spokesmen for women's secondary education stressed the virtues of chastity, modesty, submissiveness, and good taste, the headmasters of the all-male middle and higher schools trumpeted the countervailing values of performance, unyielding determination, and fortitude. To be sure, Iwamoto Zenji and other "liberals" justified such sexual distinctions as a separation of spheres, each with a dignity of its own, whereas "conservatives," like Miwata Masako, argued that the juxtaposition of publicly aggressive men with domestically submissive women served the interests of the nation; that the sexual hierarchy within the family became, borrowing Sharon Nolte's words, the "organic component" of the orderly state.[15] Their differences notwithstanding, both Iwamoto and Miwada contributed to a polarization of manliness and femininity and a privileging of social character over individual personality. And social character, in the form of feminine do-

[14] For more on this, see my Schooldays in Imperial Japan (Berkeley: University of California Press, 1980), esp. chap. 2.

[15] Sharon H. Nolte, Liberalism in Modern Japan (Berkeley: University of California Press, 1987), p. 67; Roden, Schooldays, chap. 2; Fukaya Masashi, Ryōsai kenboshugi no kyōiku (Nagoya: Reimei Shobō, 1981), pp. 138–65; Hirota Masaki, "Bunmeikaika to josei kaihōron," in Joseishi Sōgō Kenkyūkai, ed., Nihon joseishi (Tokyo: Tōkyō daigaku shuppankai, 1982), 4:1–40.

mesticity and masculine performance, supported the material and technological needs of Meiji civilization.

Similar to Germany, a new obsession for culture and personality arose
in the 1920s in conscious reaction to the earlier dominance of character,
civilization, and the politics of public nationalism. As Harry Harootunian
puts it, "Meiji civilization summoned purpose and goal—self-sacrifice
and nationalism—whereas Taishō culture . . . evoked new associations
related to the nuances of consumers' life, to individualism, culturalism,
and cosmopolitanism." Moreover, "the ethics of the Taishō intellectual
were . . . largely an ethics of being, rather than a morality of doing," of
personality more than performance.[16] Indeed, already by the end of the
Meiji period, the existential concern for being over doing struck a responsive chord among a broad cross section of young intellectuals and students. Even the most civic-minded educator, Nitobe Inazō, pronounced
his support for this ideal, provided that self-revelation remained on a high
philosophic plane and did not interfere with public duties.[17] To a large
extent, of course, the problem of the self in Taishō Japan remained within
the stratosphere of phenomenology, where most philosphers wanted it
and where there is abundant discourse of considerable import. But after
World War I, the fascination for the inner psyche spread to the readers of
popular fiction and the patrons of movie houses. And what especially
drew the attention of the literate populace were those qualities of hysteria, temperamentality, and nervousness that departed from the insipid
character norms of an earlier era. In an age that was recognized by many
as neurotic, *shinkeibyō jidai* to use Hirotsu Kazuo's phrase, the mysteries
and ambiguities of personality superseded the hollow and straightforward formulas of character. Accordingly, the sex roles that had been so
carefully delineated in Meiji civilization grew ever more blurred and confused in Taishō culture.

Japan's post–World War I fascination for sexual ambivalence sprang
in part from a preindustrial cultural tradition in which distinctions between male and female were not nearly as clear-cut as was the case in,
say, medieval Europe. Even after 1600, when straitlaced codes of official
Confucianism dictated a strict adherence to gender role, sexual confusion
abounded in the urban entertainment quarters, where impersonation developed into an art form on the Kabuki stage. After the Restoration, and
in deference to an emphatically Victorian conception of respectability, the

---

[16] H. D. Harootunian, "Introduction: A Sense of an Ending and the Problem of Taishō,"
in Bernard Silberman and H. D. Harootunian, eds., *Japan in Crisis* (Princeton: Princeton
University Press, 1974), pp. 15–18. Earl Kinmonth also affirms the late Meiji and Taishō
transition from character or "performance" to personality. See *The Self-Made Man in Meiji
Japanese Thought* (Berkeley: University of California Press, 1981), esp. pp. 272–76.

[17] Roden, *Schooldays*, pp. 200–10.

Meiji leadership did its best to squelch the ribaldries of the old pleasure quarters and succeeded to a remarkable extent with proclamations and laws that transformed Yoshiwara into a sordid zone for legal prostitution; that forbade the casual mixing of the sexes in bathhouses and other public places; that curbed the publication of "lewd and debauched" prose; and that greatly reinforced the patriarchal authority of the family, extending from the emperor (a "deified patriarch" according to Carol Gluck) to the lowliest peasant head-of-house.[18] To be sure, beneath the sanitized and boring normality of "civilization and enlightenment," there existed an underground culture of peep shows, street carnivals, and masquerades that appeared to make light of the reformulated codes of masculine and feminine etiquette. For the educated elite, however, these back-street entertainments remained peripheral to the central thrust of Meiji civilization: the strict delineation of gender and the building of character.

On the other hand, after the turn of the century and especially during the 1920s, the expression and representation of gender ambivalence captured the imagination of a cross section of the literate urban populace in a manner that was simply unthinkable in the heyday of "civilization and enlightenment." Perhaps the first suggestion of this more flexible attitude toward gender identity among intellectuals surfaced in the writings of late Meiji romantics like Kitamura Tōkoku, whose explorations of love and the tormented inner self underscored the fragility of male feelings. The "anguished youth" in the early 1900s, and the naturalist writers who served as their literary voice, further embellished a new image of manhood fraught with anxiety, indecision, nervousness, and a susceptibility to falling in love, all of which challenged the ideology of the male as household head and stalwart provider. Conversely, Yosano Akiko's celebration of the power of feminine sensuality contributed to the conceptualization of a "new woman" (*atarashiki onna*) that emerged from the early issues of the literary feminist magazine *Seitō*. If the "new man" of late Meiji was sensitized to the point of emotional dependence, the "new woman" exuded what Itō Noe called in 1913 "a firm self-confidence" (*kakko taru jishin*) and an emotional independence from the patriarchal family.[19] It was the "new woman," more than her masculine counterpart, who triggered most of the late Meiji and early Taishō debate over sex role. Special symposia devoted to the "women's problem" (*fujin mondai*)

---

[18] Carol Gluck, *Japan's Modern Myths* (Princeton: Princeton University Press, 1985), p. 37; Jay Rubin, *Injurious to Public Morals* (Seattle: University of Washington Press, 1984), p. 20; Ishikawa Hiroyoshi and Noguchi Takenori, *Sei* (Tokyo: Kōbundō, 1974), pp. 89–98; Edward Seidensticker, *Low City, High City* (New York: Knopf, 1983), pp. 167–75.

[19] Itō Noe, "Atarashiki onna no michi," *Seitō* 3, 1 (January 1913): 21; Sharon Sievers, *Flowers in Salt; The Beginnings of Feminist Consciousness in Modern Japan* (Stanford: Stanford University Press, 1983), pp. 169–76.

became a standard feature, appearing in such monthly magazines as *Chūō kōron, Taiyō, Kaizō*, and *Fujin kōron*. In terms of a structural transformation of the family or political system, the debate, which focused on the dignity of separate spheres and distinguishing resources of nurture and maternal love, had nominal effect. But in drawing attention to a feminine self that broke down the psychological barriers of delicacy and submission (symbolized in Hiratsuka Raichō's overnight visit in 1912 to the males-only brothels of Yoshiwara), the spokesmen for the "new woman" forced the reading public to reconsider the Meiji legacy of sexual hierarchy and discrimination.

For some, of course, talk of feminine self-assertion sparked fears of dire social consequences. In a 1920 essay entitled "Contemporary Society and the Convergence of the Sexes," Nogami Toshio criticized the Taishō feminists for blurring distinctions between males and females that were ordained by nature. (Ideology of all stripes, but most certainly gender ideology, always rallies behind that which is deemed "natural."[20]) "Because of the deviant conditions that have recently arisen in our society, especially since World War I," Nogami averred, "women who perform men's work have significantly increased in number." Some had responded to this phenomenon by arguing that "the former spiritual and physical differences between the sexes no longer existed, and that men and women should proceed henceforth as one and the same entity." Such views, Nogami countered, hastened the "degeneration" of both sexes.[21] Could it be, a more sympathetic critic wondered, that by "parading through Yoshiwara, drinking at bars, and wrapping themselves in woolen capes," the new women had merely appropriated "the masculine model for living?"[22] Of greater concern to some male critics was the suspicion that once the new woman had internalized the masculine ethos, she might prefer single life to marriage, and, perhaps, the company of other women to men. Hiratsuka Raichō's attacks on the customary institution of marriage and her special friendship with Odake Kazue undoubtedly confirmed the opinion of some male alarmists that the new woman harbored lesbian sensibilities.[23] The new woman was not alone as an object of scorn, however. Since the turn of the century, moralists like Ōmachi Keigetsu and Inoue Tetsujirō had subjected the anguished young men of late Meiji to a

[20] Harry Harootunian, "Ideology as Conflict," in Tetsuo Najita and J. Victor Koschmann, eds., *Conflict in Modern Japanese History* (Princeton: Princeton University Press, 1982), p. 28.

[21] Nogami Toshio, "Gendai seikatsu to danjo ryōsei no sekkin," *Kaizō* 2, 4 (April 1920): 185–204.

[22] Kataoka Teppei, "Modan gāru no kenkyū," in Minami Hiroshi, ed., *Kindai shomin seikatsushi* (Tokyo: San'ichi shobō, 1985), 1:161.

[23] Sievers, *Flowers in Salt*, p. 225.

barrage of criticism that centered mainly on their alleged lack of masculine resolve. Tokutomi Sohō continued the attack in 1916 with his famous declaration that the young men of the new Taishō era had no unifying sense of character, settling instead for divergent shades of materialism, anguish, debauchery, and colorless nonchalance.[24]

Before World War I the censure of young men and women who did not abide by prescriptive models for manliness and femininity was largely the preserve of educators. But the dawning of Taishō saw the rise of a new group of critics distinguished by their expertise in the recently introduced fields of psychology and sexology. What Michel Foucault calls the science of sexuality, a taxonomical discourse centering on variant erotic behavior that emerged in the late-nineteenth-century writings of Richard Krafft-Ebing and continued in the early twentieth century through the contributions of psychologists like Havelock Ellis and Magnus Hirschfeld, quickly captured the imagination of Japan's earliest students of psychology.[25] Several of the pioneer psychologist-critics were amateurs, who studied on their own the works of Freud, Krafft-Ebing, and Ellis; others were medical professionals, who, dissatisfied with the purely experimental orientation of academic psychology in Japan, turned to the more exciting, and lucrative, task of writing guidebooks on intimate relations. Many of these were simple marriage manuals that went about telling, in rather unromantic detail, when, where, and how to do it; but there were also a surprising number of tracts on variant sexuality that attested to the depth of concern over gender ambivalence in Taishō culture. Perhaps the classic representation of this latter genre, first published in 1915 and reprinted eighteen times over the next decade, was *Hentai seiyokuron* (The theory of deviant sexual desire), coauthored by "Dr." Habuto Eiji and his "amateur" colleague, Sawada Junjirō. The format of the book bears a close resemblance to Krafft-Ebing's *Psychopathia Sexualis* (1886), to which the authors refer explicitly throughout the text. And like their Viennese predecessor, Habuto and Sawada seemed obsessed by the destructive threat that "unnatural desires" (*fushizen seiyoku*) posed for the Japanese social order. At the most obvious level, aberrant sexual feelings underlay criminal acts of brutality, but of more concern to the authors was the less dramatic but more widespread pattern of antisocial behavior that arose from the confusion of the sexes. Before the Restoration, according to Habuto and Sawada, inversion assumed the character of a paid "profession" for certain actors, monks, or vassals, who served the diver-

---

[24] Tokutomi Iichirō [Sohō], *Taishō no seinen to teikoku no zento* (Tokyo: Min'yūsha, 1916), pp. 1–35.

[25] Michel Foucault, *The History of Sexuality* (New York: Vintage, 1980), 1:53–73; Carroll Smith-Rosenberg, *Disorderly Conduct* (New York: Oxford University Press, 1985), pp. 268–72.

sionary sexual needs of samurai and townsmen. But in recent years, "Homosexuality has almost become a fashion, spreading throughout society, even among the ranks of amateurs [everyday people]." The authors refer specifically to the military regiment, the office, the school dormitory and the prison as distinctive modern institutions that are particularly vulnerable to the spread of this "unnatural disease." In addition, they leave no doubt that the more general phenomenon of "masculine women" (*danseiteki joshi*) and "feminine men" (*joseiteki danshi*), expressed in clothing, language, and etiquette, led inexorably to sexual inversion.[26]

With an introduction by a Tokyo police chief, the Habuto-Sawada volume addressed itself specifically to law enforcement officials, educators, and youth-group supervisors: those defenders of normality for whom early detection of the tell-tale symptoms of variant sexuality assumed, as the authors explained, a special urgency. But the readers of *Hentai seiyokuron* were by no means limited to the custodians of the civilization of character. Quite the contrary, the more Habuto, Sawada, and others exposed the dangers of aberrant relations, the more bored, urban middle-class readers turned to their books as a recreational escape from the very "civilized" norms the "doctors" said they were upholding. Herein lies one of the great ironies in the history of Taishō guides to proper sexual behavior. What started out as prescriptive literature quickly lost the blessings of educators and police and thus descended into the underground culture, where sexology thrived for most of the interwar period. *Hentai seiyoku* (Deviant sexual desire) and *Hentai shinri* (Deviant psychology) were among the half-dozen underground magazines that lavished attention on variant sexuality in the late 1920s; and these were accompanied by scores, perhaps hundreds, of independent books and articles. Indeed, an entire generation of sexologists, led by Habuto and Sawada, evinced great skill in gracing their tracts with just enough pseudo-scientific information and prescriptive advice to limit government censorship without dampening the curiosity of their middle-class audience. Less inhibited were certain underground writers of popular fiction, who, like the author of *Futanari monogatari* (Tales of a hermaphrodite), celebrated sexual ambiguity as the wave of the future.[27]

The problem of disorderly sexuality in post–World War I Japan could be overlooked if it had only attracted the likes of Habuto Eiji and Sawada Junjirō or been confined to the underground culture. But, as in Weimar Germany, the androgenous spirit pervaded a host of cultural endeavors from the frivolities of the vaudeville revues in Asakusa to the nobler ru-

---

[26] Habuto Eiji and Sawada Junjirō, *Hentai seiyokuron*, 18th edition (Tokyo; Sun'yōdō, 1925), pp. 103–14, 185, 266–75.

[27] Itō Matsuo, *Futanari monogatari* (Tokyo: Banrikaku shobō, 1930).

minations of esteemed critics. One did not have to explore the back alleys of Tokyo or patronize the most sleazy of bars to discover a woman dressed in an oversized business suit or a man with rouge-caked cheeks. Such oddities were among the identifying affectations of the "modern girl" and "modern boy," who not only promenaded down the Ginza but appeared prominently in movies, popular magazines, and novels. As Inage Sofū detected as early as 1918, Taishō was the era of "the feminization of masculine beauty" and "the masculinization of feminine beauty."[28] To allow a fuller appreciation of the accuracy of Inage's characterization, I would like to examine briefly two of the most striking symbolic representations of androgyny in Taishō mass culture: the *dan'yaku* actress in Takarazuka Theatre and the *nimaime* actor in the burgeoning cinema.

Founded in 1913 by Kobayashi Ichizō, the great private railway magnate of the Kansai, the Takarazuka Theatre typified the ambivalent spirit of the age.[29] True, the owner embossed his theatre with platitudes about a "garden of purity" for the "innocent, correct, and beautiful" development of character; and as a single-sex community of women, the theatre, with its affiliated school, appeared to mirror the Meiji pedagogical ideal of keeping adolescent males and females in isolation. But for all of the owner's pontifications, Takarazuka was a money-making enterprise, and as such, the presence of men on the stage—if not real men then women dressed up to act like men—was an economic necessity. Hence the raison d'etre for the dan'yaku, the male impersonators whose presence electrified the Takarazuka stage and assured full houses for decades to come.

From the opening of the first Takarazuka stage production on April 1, 1914, the dan'yaku star occupied the limelight of public attention. The inaugural production, *Donburako*, was based upon the story of the legendary boy-wonder, Momotarō, and featured the fourteen-year-old actress Takamine Taeko in the lead role. Meiji textbooks and childrens' literature had so inculcated the public mind with the manliness of Momotarō that the decision to launch Takarazuka with a feminized version of this quintessentially male tale was something of a risk. But so convincing was Takamine in her portrayal, as she strutted back and forth on stage with her arms akimbo, that fans called her "Momotarō" even when they spotted her sitting quietly on a commuter train. The enormous success of Takamine as Momotarō inspired the troupe to reenact the life histories of other masculine heroes from Yamato Takeru to Christopher Columbus.

In 1924, with the completion of a huge theatre, Takarazuka launched

---

[28] Inage Sofū, "Seibi no junka," *Nihon hyōron* 2, 1 (January 1917): 136.

[29] The following details on the Takarazuka Theatre, unless otherwise stated, are taken from Ichihashi Naoji, ed., *Takarazuka kageki gojūnenshi* (Takarazuka: Takarazuka kagekidan, 1964), pp. 88–159.

a new era of stage productions that featured multi-piece orchestras, elaborate sets, star-spangled costumes, and librettos based upon "modern" love stories rather than the legendary heroes of the past. The dan'yaku stars adapted enthusiastically to the new stage productions that bore a close resemblance to the revues in Paris and Berlin. For now, they could perform the role of the romantic suitor and thus objectify the deepest sexual fantasies or yearnings of their largely feminine audience. In such early box office hits as *Mon Paris* and *Revue Parisette*, the rotating dan'yaku stars brought tears to the eyes of their patrons through extraordinary displays of tenderness, courtesy, chivalry, sensitivity, and ardent pursuit. Recall that exquisite moment in the thirteenth scene of *Revue Parisette* when the ever gallant Kanbara proposes to the fair "Rorotto" in song:

> Wilt thou laugh or cry
>   Upon hearing my confession?
> My heart trembles to see thee
>   For years I struggled in confusion
> But now, at last, I must tell thee
>   The secret of my heart . . .
> Thou art beautiful
>   Loving thee my heart is aflame . . .
> Only lend me thy hand.[30]

The dan'yaku stars brought down the house with this ditty and captured the hearts of high school girls around the nation, for few male actors were as convincing in their entreaties. Thus by the early 1930s, Takarazuka's Nara Miyako, Kadota Ashiko, and Ashiwara Kuniko had established themselves as the Clark Gables and Gary Coopers of Japan.

The delightful confusions of the Takarazuka stage were compounded in the cinema by the growing popularity of the masculine counterpart to the dan'yaku: the effeminate male star, referred to in the vocabulary of Kabuki as the second or *nimaime*. According to Satō Tadao, the rise to prominence of the weak male second in the 1920s corresponded to the discontinuation of the *onnagata* tradition and the appearance, instead, of real actresses on the screen.[31] Particularly in the modern, domestic dramas, this first generation of film actresses quickly established a domineering presence that required the weakling, indecisive, and love-smitten male as a foil. The nimaime performed that role and, together with his feminine antagonist, perfected an entire genre of films that featured sturdy women and flimsy men, beginning with Urabe Kumeko's powerful rendering of the passionate Okane in *Seisaku's Wife* (1924) and continuing through

---

[30] *Parisetto*, in *Takarazuka Shōjokageki kyakuhon* 139 (July 1932): 40.

[31] Satō Tadao, *Nimaime no kenkyū* (Tokyo: Chikuma shobō, 1984), pp. 20–21.

Tanaka Kinuyo's performance as the indomitable nurse in *Aizen Katsura* (1938).

Of the male seconds who quivered and wept before the likes of Tanaka Kinuyo, none achieved greater popularity, nor expressed more plaintively the sexual ambivalence of the age, than the late Hasegawa Kazuo (1908–1984). One of the secrets to Hasegawa's ascent as a matinee idol was his late-adolescent training for female roles on the Kabuki stage. In his autobiography, Hasegawa concedes that he entered show business "with the intention of performing as an *onnagata* from childhood to old age."[32] But the lure of the motion-picture industry changed all of that, and Hasegawa, with coaxing from the head of Matsutake Studios and new-wave director Kinugasa Teinosuke, abandoned the Kabuki stage. At the age of nineteen, he launched a career as a new type of nimaime, who performed in both historical dramas and contemporary romances. As it turned out, the affectations of the onnagata that he cultivated in his early years served Hasegawa very well in perfecting the uniquely androgenous film image of a robust swordsman, on the one hand, but a swordsman who also emitted lovelorn sighs and self-conscious giggles. Indeed, still shots from his earliest films highlight Hasegawa's distinctively feminine manner of pressing his knees tightly together when sitting; of standing on tiptoes; and of tilting his head slightly when staring wistfully askance of the camera. Androgyny had no finer emblem than when Hasegawa, as Tsurujiro in 1938, shuffled down the street with a little purse dangling from his arm, or when, in the 1935 movie *Yukinojō henge*, he crisscrossed gender lines while performing the twin roles of a sword-swinging thief and the most beautifully seductive courtesan.

As in Weimar Germany, the "vulgar" expressions of sexual ambivalence—on stage, screen, or among those "modern boys and girls" who decked themselves in unisex attire—were accompanied by a nobler vision of androgyny in the "high culture" of Taishō Japan. Hints of this vision can be discerned in the early works of Abe Jirō and Kurata Hyakuzō, whose *Santarō no nikki* and *Ai to ninshiki to no shuppatsu* have already been discussed by Stephen Kohl and Thomas Rimer. As Kohl suggests, Abe's narrator in *Santarō no nikki* has real difficulty accepting his male sexuality. At one point he calls himself Segawa Kikunojō, a name formerly reserved for onnagata, and expresses great sympathy for Aristophanes' bisexual notion of love as man's recovery of his feminine self (his *anima*) and woman's recovery of her masculine self (her *animus*).[33] Such confusions also abound in *Ai to ninshiki to no shuppatsu*, wherein Ku-

---

[32] Hasegawa Kazuo, *Butai ginmaku rokujūnen* (Tokyo: Nihon keizai shinbunsha, 1964), p. 36. Other details about Hasegawa are taken from this autobiography and my own viewing of several of his prewar films.

[33] Abe Jirō, *Gōhon Santarō no nikki* (Tokyo: Kadokawa shoten, 1964), pp. 66–70.

rata's personal quest for self-meaning commences with a homophilic
yearning for a friend, continues with the discovery of who he is within
the soul of an ideal woman, and concludes with self-identity springing
from an asexual conception of Christian love of neighbor.[34]

Literary artists also participated in the shaping of the androgenous
ideal in the interwar period. The inversion of conventional sex roles fig-
ured prominently, for example, in the early writings of Tanizaki
Jun'ichirō, particularly in his explorations of masochism among men and
his dual quest for motherhood and the "eternal feminine." The pursuit of
the latter, as Minami Hiroshi and others have suggested, required a psychological transformation of the author into a woman.[35] Inspired by
Rilke's dream world of little girls and angels, the poet and novelist Hori
Tatsuo (1904-53) further embellished the androgenous vision by his outright adoption of a feminine voice in such works as *Kagerō nikki* (1937),
while Kawabata Yasunari, as Maeda Ai has argued, raised the androgyne
to new aesthetic heights in his surrealistic characterization of Yumiko in
the novella *Asakusa kurenaidan* (1929–30).[36] Alternating between the
guises of a "masculine" young woman and a "feminine" young man, en-
tailing changes of clothes, language, gestures, and even name, Yumiko
epitomizes the gender ambivalence of the new age. When her sister's former lover tauntingly suggests that she might be afraid of men, Yumiko
responds contentiously: "I'm sure not afraid of you. Besides, since spending half my life pretending to be a man, I find that men really mean nothing to me." Later, she adds: "If you look closely at me you will understand. I am not a woman. Since observing my sister's torment as a child,
I have decided never to be a woman . . . and no man can make me into a
woman." While proclaiming her defiance of conventional "femininity,"
Yumiko and her suitor sit in the audience for the Casino Follies, the
bawdy revue that had taken Asakusa by storm in 1929. The gender flu-
idity that Yumiko embodies manifests itself simultaneously on stage as
actresses impersonate young males in routines like the "Ginza Jazz
Dance."[37] Such explorations of gender also appealed to several contemporary women writers, notably Miyamoto Yuriko (1899–1951), who, in
the wake of her 1923 divorce from Araki Shigeru, temporarily experienced and later wrote about a world of women acting like men—as
breadwinners and as lovers.[38]

[34] Roden, *Schooldays*, pp. 214–15.

[35] Minami Hiroshi, "Bosei kara no tōsō," in Ara Masahito, ed., *Tanizaki Jun'ichirō
kenkyū* (Tokyo: Yagi shoten), p. 594.

[36] Maeda Ai, *Toshi kūkan no naka no bungaku* (Tokyo: Chikuma shobō, 1982), pp. 409–
16. I am indebted to Miriam Silverberg for calling my attention to *Asakusa kurenaidan*.

[37] Kawabata Yasunari, *Kawabata Yasunari zenshū* (Tokyo: Shinchōsha, 1970), 2:31–33.

[38] Noriko Lippit, "Literature, Ideology, and Women's Happiness: The Autobiographical
Novels of Miyamoto Yuriko," *Bulletin of Concerned Asian Scholars* 10 (1978): 4 and 9.

Perhaps the most telling expression of the androgenous vision in interwar Japan came from the most unlikely of sources—the venerated teacher of ethics and philosophy. In their commitment to living as isolated bachelors, ensconced in a world of neo-Kantian verities, the so-called teachers of life in the late Meiji and Taishō higher schools and universities presented themselves as ascetics who disdained the vulgarities of male or female sexuality. The asexual image may have approached reality in the cases of Ichikō's Iwamoto Tei or Nikō's Awano Kenjirō, but arguably the most illustrious "teacher of life," former Ichikō headmaster and Kyōdai professor, Kanō Kōkichi, took the principle of *dokushinshugi* (bachelorism) in quite a different direction, from celibacy to self-indulgence, with the ultimate consequence of further disrupting the lines between the sexes. In public, Kanō adhered steadfastly to E. H. Norman's flattering characterization of a dedicated scholar, "erudite in many fields" and "endowed with a critical and skeptical mind."[39] But in private, the energies of the dispassionate scholar and civic moralist turned to the collection of pornography and other, less learned matters. Entries in a personal diary for the late Taishō years detail a solitary world of autoeroticism, complete with calendars, charts, and descriptions of various accessories (including a microscope to ascertain the vitality of the emissions).[40] Before each event, Kanō would assemble his own sketches of nude women. But of most interest for this essay is Kanō's infatuation with a neighborhood girl named Chiyoko. So involved was the professor with the entirety of her life that Kanō kept a running log of her menstrual cycles in his diaries and took special pleasure, apparently, in predicting the onslaught of each period, along with its probable duration, as if he were experiencing the cycles himself. All of this would be of little account if it were not that for a generation of late-Meiji youth, Kanō Kōkichi symbolized the elevation of moral character over the urges and idiosyncrasies of personality. The case reveals that no one, not even the scholarly recluse, was immune to the lures of interwar eroticism and nonsense (*ero-guro-nansensu*).

Although an extreme example, Kanō stood not alone among educators or moralists in expressing the deep ambivalence of the age. Nitobe Inazō, the eminent educator and diplomat (whose public career is discussed by Thomas Burkman in this volume), confessed to the readers of a women's magazine in 1915 that he was governed by a fundamentally feminine disposition.[41] Several of his former students agreed, having referred earlier to Nitobe as the Ichikō headmaster with a "woman's temperament"—

[39] E. Herbert Norman, *Andō Shōeki and the Anatomy of Japanese Feudalism* (Washington, D.C.: University Publications of America Reprint, 1979), p. 11.

[40] Aoe Shunjirō, *Kanō Kōkichi no shōgai* (Tokyo: Meiji shoin, 1974), pp. 544–72.

[41] The information on Nitobe comes from my paper, "Nitobe Inazō and the Masculine-Feminine Convergence in Modern Japan," from the Nitobe-Ohira Memorial Conference at the University of British Columbia, May 24–26, 1984.

soft-spoken to the point of inaudibility, sensitive to the most minute details of grooming and decorum, lachrymose, and fearful of interpersonal confrontations. Nitobe's obsessive fascination for Joan of Arc, about whom he hoped to write a definitive biography and whose footsteps he literally retraced in 1900 and again in 1921, further enhanced his androgynous image.

The expression of gender ambivalence in both the popular and high arts of interwar Japan produced a variety of interpretive responses, most of which were decidedly negative. Writing in 1922, General Ugaki Kazushige said the following: "The feminization of men and the masculinization of women and the neutered gender that results is a modernistic tendency that makes it impossible for the individual, the society, or the nation to achieve great progress. Accordingly, since the manliness of man and the femininity of woman must forever be preserved, it is imperative that we not allow the rise of neutered people who defy nature's grace."[42] For Ugaki, Victorian codes of respectability, which had been firmly anchored in the social institutions of the Meiji state, required fortification against the subversive lures of Taishō culture. He was not alone. Spokesmen from the ministries of Education and Internal Affairs, from the conferences of normal-school principals, from the National Organization of Young Men, and from women's high schools and colleges waged a vociferous campaign—in the name of bourgeois gentility, natural order, and civilized morality—against the perceived distortions and excesses of Taishō culture. These included feminism, homosexuality, recreational sex, and the blurring, whether intended or not, of the sacred and inviolate lines between the masculine and feminine. The defenders of respectability spared no effort in championing the immiscibility of the sexes with long-winded explanations of male aggression and female passivity, of male rationality and female hysteria, of man's destiny to work outside and woman's to stay at home, and of the necessity to prevent the "masculinization" of feminine language.[43] Behind such assertions were the supposedly irrefutable physical and, based on the latest medical science, endocrinological distinctions that rendered any transversal of sexual boundaries a perversion of nature. As Yanagisawa Sanji argued, hormones, not culture, dictated the polarization of sex roles.[44] Even the Joan of Arc story raised consternation among the most alarmed educators, who took great pains, in a 1924 edition of a reader for high school girls, to explain that the Maiden from Orleans was not a "transformed male" (*hensei dansei*),

[42] Ugaki Kazushige, *Ugaki nikki* (Tokyo: Misuzu shobō, 1969–1971), 1:363.

[43] *Tōkyō asahi shinbun*, Aug. 8, 1938; Nogami Toshio, "Gendai seikatsu to danjo no sekkin," pp. 191–96. An earlier sounding of these alarms can also be found in Umagami Kotarō, *Shōjo no kyōiku* (Tokyo: Meguro shoten, 1914), esp. pp. 20–48.

[44] Yanagisawa Sanji, "Naibunpi gakushi yori mitaru dansei to josei," *Bungei shunjū* 8, 7 (July 1, 1930): 106–10.

but a young woman with uniquely feminine resources of energy.[45] To belabor the point at all suggests the depth of insecurity over such issues.

The campaign to sanitize Taishō culture took many forms: Naimushō censors banned the publication of thousands of sex-related books and blotched out kissing scenes from movies; normal-school principals combatted masturbation with declaration of a link between the "odious habit" and tuberculosis; insecure schoolboys, perhaps coaxed by their equally insecure teachers, reviled the likes of Hasegawa Kazuo and other nimaime "pansies"; conservative journalists in Osaka called upon Kobayashi Ichizō to recruit "real men" to replace the dan'yaku on the Takarazuka stage; and sword-wielding, rightist thugs, on at least one occasion in 1924, intruded upon the floor of a Tokyo ballroom, parading their manliness in front of the disdained moderns.[46] But censorship and intimidation would not put an end to what interwar critics called the public fascination for "the erotic, the grotesque, and the nonsensical" (ero-guro-nansensu), a fascination that inevitably confounded the male-female assumptions of the classroom. For ero-guro-nansensu was much more than an isolated novel about hermaphrodites, a dan'yaku star who posed as Momotarō, or a popular song in 1936 about the housewife with a mustache. As more thoughtful observers understood, these were merely symbolic manifestations of a deeper phenomenon that was rooted in history.

At least three interwar critics spoke directly to this point. In his 1930 collection of essays, Modansō to modansō (Modern class and modern phenomena), Ōya Sōichi equated the eccentricities of the age with "a society in the late stage of capitalism" (shihonshugi makki no shakai), a society in which industrial productivity and expansion had surrendered to consumption and stagnation. Ōya maintained that the Japanese economy had exhausted its potential for growth; that the entrepreneurial ethic of Meiji civilization was a thing of the past; and that a distinctively bourgeois culture known as "modernism" had taken its place. Whereas the early capitalist spokesmen for "civilization" had praised hard work and active engagement, the late-bourgeois advocates of modernism accepted their role as passive consumers and indolent connoisseurs of what Ōya called a "culture of feeling" (kankaku bunka). When the quest for sensual stimulation guided human behavior, as occurred in a "culture of feeling," then decadence and perversity would prevail. Ōya explained: "Those who unceasingly seek for new and more exciting stimuli inevitably become dissatisfied with ordinary sensations; instead they would find great

[45] Fujii Itsuo and Kasuga Masaharu, eds., Shihen joshi kokubun (Tokyo: Tokyo shubunkan, 1924), 8:89–91.

[46] Hisa Gentarō, ed., Hakkinbon kankei shiryō shūsei (Tokyo: Kohokusha, 1977), 4:214–15; Yamamoto Senji, Yamamoto Senji zenshū (Kyoto: Sekibunsha, 1979), 2:37; Satō Tadao, Nimaime no kenkyū, p. 72; Minami Hiroshi, Taishō bunka (Tokyo: Keiso shobō, 1977), p. 369.

happiness in artificially transposing gender traits. Namely, one grouping of women will become consciously masculinized while one grouping of men will become consciously feminized," through conversions of speech and apparel. And the "modern boys" and "modern girls," who shared each others' clothes and cosmetics, represented for Ōya the "vanguard" (*sentan*) of the late-capitalist age. Criticism of their brash defiance of early bourgeois respectability required, therefore, a tempering realization that their very presence bore an important historical message.[47]

Ōya was not alone in assigning an historical meaning to the sexual confusions of Taishō culture. Eight years earlier, in his perceptive essay "The Feminization of Men and the Masculinization of Women," the neo-Kantian philospher Kuwaki Gen'yoku stated that "the development of culture is prone to a reduction of the previously existent distinctions between male and female culture. Herewith arises the so-called feminization of civilization (*bunmei no joseika*)." Like Ōya, Kuwaki recognized an evolutionary pattern from a wholly masculine civilization of the late nineteenth century to a more androgenous culture of the twentieth century, a culture wherein men and women could freely "experience each other's emotions." It was culture, not nature, that constructed barriers between the sexes; and hence a reoriented culture, which granted a certain level of sexual flexibility, would pull those barriers down.[48]

Kuwaki's views were echoed by the psychologist Yasuda Tokutarō in his 1935 essay on homosexuality in interwar society. Although more narrowly focused than Kuwaki on questions of inversion among young women, Yasuda arrived at a similar conclusion that freer sexuality would propel Japan to a higher level of cultural development. "For future historians, reviewing the history of homosexuality in Japan, there will be considerable historical interest in the fact that homosexual love among consenting women, something that could not be expressed in the literature of the Tokugawa period, increased steadily from Taishō to Shōwa." Of particular importance was the "splendid masculinization of women" (*joshi no subarashii danseika*) that, in Yasuda's opinion, accompanied the inversion of sexual love. Yasuda welcomed the phenomenon of women speaking and acting like men, for such behavior heralded a "third stage" in Japan's cultural development that began with matriarchy, evolved into patriarchy, and now stood at the threshold of an epoch of fused sex roles, where neither women nor men could be reduced to servile status.[49] Although they employed somewhat different terminology, the combined insights of Ōya, Kuwaki, and Yasuda affirm, in my opinion, this article's opening proposition that the sexual ambiguities in Taishō Japan reflect

[47] Ōya Sōichi, *Ōya Sōichi zenshū* (Tokyo: Sōyōsha, 1981), 2:3–5, 16, 94–96, 110–15.

[48] Kuwaki Gen'yoku, "Danshi no joseika to josei no danseika," *Fujinkai* 6, 4 (April 1922): 3–5.

[49] Yasuda Tokutarō, "Doseiai no rekishikan," *Chūō kōron* 50, 3 (March 1935): 152.

the transition from a civilization of character to a culture of personality. Ōya and Kuwaki, among others, are quite explicit in their distinction between Meiji as civilization and Taishō as culture. And, by implication at least, all three writers call attention to the replacement of character with personality when they emphasize consumption over production, feeling over doing, the idiosyncratic over the normative, and self-expression over self-restraint. Just as character connoted a self-sacrificing, "external morality" (to use Abe Jirō's terms), personality sprang from "internal morality" and the self-actualizing needs of the individual. And this brings one to an important point of distinction between the Taishō conception of self and the Meiji vision of character. For in the culture of personality, the self-actualizing needs of the individual derive from sexual urges as well as philosophic quests. The Taishō personality combines Abe Jirō's personal self (*jinkaku*) with a Freudian concession to eros. This combination resulted in what Sawada Junjirō called the sexual personality (*seiteki jinkaku*)[50]; and quite apart from anything that Freud said about bisexuality within the Viennese middle class, the "sexual personality" of interwar Japan stood halfway between the masculine and the feminine, a blurred space where character simply could not exist.

Sensing the collapse of their ideology of character and civilization, the custodians of respectability sounded the alarm, warning of dire social consequences should nothing be done to curtail the "unnatural" excesses of Taishō culture. But where Tokutomi Sohō and Inoue Tetsujirō saw degeneration and backsliding, Ōya, Kuwaki, and Yasuda saw vitality and progress, not measured in industrial growth or working hours, but in the more flexible expression of sexual identity. In effect, the entire notion of historical development was turned upside down in the interwar period; for when Yasuda Tokutarō spoke of Japan as a "first-class nation" (*ittō koku*) in 1935, he was not invoking the Meiji shibboleth for industrial or military power. Rather, he spoke, as a translator of Freud and avid reader of Magnus Hirschfeld, of a nation that boasted within its population young women who dared to wear business suits, neck ties, and spectacles à la Harold Lloyd.[51] The breakdown of sexual barriers, the assimilation of manliness with femininity, the freedom to adopt the mannerisms of either sex: Whether Taishō Japan or Weimar Germany, these were the marks of a "first-class nation." Such a view could only emanate from a culture of personality.

[50] Habuto Eiji and Sawada Junjirō, *Hentai seiyokuron*, p. 93.
[51] Yasuda Tokutarō, "Dōseiai no rekishikan," pp. 146–47.

# Part II

CULTURE AND SOCIETY

THE SEARCH by intellectuals for models of society constitutes a second phase of Japanese intellectual history in the early decades of the century. In one sense, this search provided a new stage for those who had begun by probing the nature of the self. This second stage amounted to an attempt to locate that self in a larger social context. Such a psychological thrust, first inward, then outward, can be seen in the work of even such a self-absorbed writer as Abe Jirō. Kurata Hyakuzō, too, tried to place the individual back in a social context through the commonality of religious experience.

In some ways, the search for social and cultural models that might prove applicable in creating an understanding of the Japanese social situation can also be viewed as a development parallel with the importation of European methodologies to define and understand the self, described in part I. Just as the use of certain concepts in Western philosophy helped legitimize the acknowledgment of a new interiority, so the introduction of Western canons of social thought brought new ideas as to how the state, society, and community might be conceptualized with respect to Japan. Some of these European models tended to reinforce certain earlier nativist concepts of culture and society, while others forced a reexamination of prior assumptions.

As Nozomu Kawamura makes clear, there came to exist, in the attitudes of the early generation of Japanese interested in European social thought, a certain blurring in distinctions between academic theory and committed activism. For many, social science and sociology were understood less as analytical methodologies than as tools by which society might be reshaped. This was particulary true with respect to the issue of socialism itself, which attracted so much interest among Japanese writers and intellectuals at the beginning of the century, while causing such powerful negative reactions from the Japanese government. Nevertheless, as Eugene Soviak indicates in his essay, some intellectuals, such as Tsuchida Kyōson (1891–1934), continued to combine a strong interest in the disciplines of Western social science with a firm commitment to maintaining an activist stand in society.

Many of the imported models (Simmel, Durkheim, and others) important in the creation of the Japanese disciplines of social science provided intellectuals with a means to study the structure of their society in ways that were not directly related to concepts promulgated by the state apparatus. Such methodologies were therefore looked on with increasing suspicion by the more conservative elements in government circles. In this regard, culture as a focus of inquiry took on an especially charged significance. For example, anthropological models made it possible for scholars to examine Japan through the study of the common people in rural villages. Such research helped in turn to provide new conceptualizations of Japanese culture at some remove both from the movements of political history, since folk patterns were of long duration, and from the effects of powerful individuals, since the focus of understanding emphasized the communal. For many intellectuals, as H. D. Harootunian points out, the work of such scholars as Yanagita Kunio (1875–1962) and Origuchi Shinobu (1887–1953) seemed to point to new methods to bring about a reintegration of values to unite both urban and rural culture. Their respective studies of those deeper layers of culture that, they were convinced, lay beyond the superficial events of political history allowed them to bring together under one common set of assumptions diverse elements in Japanese society, which, by the end of the nineteenth century, risked becoming virtually estranged from each other.

Earlier thinkers, such as Motoori Norinaga (1730–1801), examined Japanese culture in an attempt to identify its particular features against a consciousness of China. Before the turn of the century, China as a model or foil had largely been replaced by an image of the centrality of the Western nations, which now came to represent a more diverse and dynamic cosmopolitanism. The availability of Western categories of social analysis permitted some thinkers to posit the possibility of defining Japanese culture as one specific example that could be located within larger and consistent world patterns. Others, however, took from their experience in learning these Western categories an opportunity to arrive at quite a different set of conclusions. They were to find the Japanese experience unique, one which could not be reduced to Western categories of analysis. Such views became particularly prominent during the war period.

The encounter of those witnessing the development of a Westernizing Japan with new cosmopolitan methodologies for understanding the mechanisms of society thus elicited a considerable variety of sometimes contradictory intellectual responses as the struggle to evaluate the efficacy of theory and practice continued.

# 4

## Sociology and Socialism in the Interwar Period

NOZOMU KAWAMURA

THE INTERWAR period in Japan witnessed a sustained attempt by intellectuals in many fields to make use of imported methodologies to understand and analyze the often dislocating processes through which their culture was moving. The discontinuities with traditional thought were great in every field of endeavor, and nowhere more so than in the field of sociology, where traditional concepts of social order, and of its purposes, were based on assumptions considerably different from those on which the great nineteenth- and twentieth-century European social thinkers, so much admired by the Japanese, based their own theories. In this regard, an examination of the development of social theory in Japan during this period, and of the relationships deemed useful between theory and practice, can serve as a model for the study of similar challenges in all aspects of modern Japanese thought.

During the late Tokugawa era, Japanese scholars of the West began to introduce European philosophy and social thought to Japan. At that time, such scholars had difficulty grasping the idea of modern civil society. When sociology was first introduced by Nishi Amane in the 1870s, he barely understood its basic concepts. The early understanding of Western sociology is well illustrated by his explanation of the term "society."

> Society is to be translated as the cooperative way of life. The term society is literally applicable to the Japanese *sha* [group], but it seems to correspond better to the Japanese *to* [clique]. . . . The way of life of human beings means communal life within which people must be interdependent. Society, i.e., clique, refers to the life of clannishness that preceded the formation of the state or government.[1]

According to Nishi, the formation of the state and establishment of governments is based on the collective nature of human beings. Thus, there can be no clear distinction between the state and society. Although society or social life may arise first, the existence of the state or govern-

[1] Nishi Amane, entries in *Hyakugaku renkan, Nishi Amane zenshū* (Tokyo: Nihon hyōronsha, 1945), 1:239.

ment is equally a product of the collective nature of human beings. Here, in the natural state, human beings are conceived of as existing not individually but collectively.

Ariga Nagao, who in 1883 published the first Japanese book to use the term sociology in its title, cited the New Testament and criticized Western individualism in volume 3 of his *Shakaigaku* (Sociology) (1884). He cited the gospel according to Matthew, chapter 10; "For I have come to bring division, a man against his father, a daughter against her mother, a daughter-in-law against her mother-in-law; and a man's enemies will be those who belong to his own household. He who loves father and mother more than Me is not worthy of Me, and he who loves son or daughter more than Me is not worthy of Me." In Japan, society was analogous with the family. Therefore Aruga was surprised by these words and wrote:

> It is natural for Western people who believe such a creed that they do not treat their father as natural father, mother as natural mother, children as natural children. North American societies have had a history of about three hundred years, and during that time families which have the same origin and same name would number more than a dozen. But they do not have any contact with each other, as if they are strangers. There exists no close relationship between main and branch families in the West. People always are eager for wealth. To be rich, husbands and wives, fathers and sons, mothers and daughters, brothers and sisters quarrel with each other.[2]

In Japan the unit of society had been the household, not the individual. Religion was closely connected with the household, and even modern industrial organizations were regarded in familial terms. Thus all members of a business organization were expected to obey its head as if he were their real father. The traditional Japanese idea of society was quite different from the notion of civil society in the West.

Under such conditions, sociology in Japan could not be a popular discipline, if it were to be a discipline that makes the phenomena of civil society its object of study. In Japan, where the concept of civil society was undeveloped, the meaning of sociology was often distorted. Within sociology, studying the state to justify the emperor system always took precedence over studying civil society. Recognition of sociology in this first sense came not from the public but from the government. It has been said that sociology was officially accepted in the academic world when Tokyo Imperial University established courses in that field and created a standard curriculum in 1903. In a country where the people looked upon

---

[2] Ariga Nagao, *Zokusei shinkaron*, vol. 3 of *Shakaigaku* (Tokyo: Tōyōkan, 1884), pp. 281–82.

government officials as their masters, not as their servants, the imperial universities were much more prestigious than private universities. As in other fields, there remained the lamentable custom of *kanson minpi* (making much of the government and nothing of the people) in the academic world.

There were two sociologies: one was a discipline that served to support the ideology of the emperor system; the other was an authentic sociology that sought to analyze civil society independent from the state. Whereas government-school sociologists mainly introduced theories from Germany, such as Hegelian thought, and tried to establish a science of the state, sociologists without ties to the government introduced American sociology and stood very close to socialism. Therefore sociology was influential in the introduction of the labor and socialist movements at the turn of the century by those intellectuals who had studied in the United States.

Katayama Sen, one of the founders of the Japanese labor and socialist movements, claimed the modern labor movement began in the summer of 1897 after the war with China, and along with it the modern socialist movement. In 1897, a labor association organized for the purpose of setting up trade unions was formed by iron workers employed in the government arsenal and in railway workshops. In December 1897, the Iron Workers' Union was organized with more than one thousand members. This was the first trade union in Japan. Amid rising interest in social reform, there was eager discussion of the labor and socialist movements among intellectuals and progressive workers. Workers attempted to raise wages, shorten work hours, and create better working conditions. In the agricultural sector, tenants fought against landlords to lower land rents. At the same time, socialists and liberals organized an association to demand universal suffrage. Such trends were favorable for the development of sociology.

## Sociology in the Early Twentieth Century

During the first phase of the development of sociology, the felt need for a grasp of social theory, and for social action, was perceived both by scholars and by those engaged, or hoping to engage, in some form of social action. At first these two impulses seemed to work in tandem; but by the time of the First World War, the two streams of theory and practice, perhaps inevitably, moved apart. They were never again to join in so close a fashion.

The Shakai Gakkai (Sociological Society), the first sociological society in Japan, was founded in 1896. It started publication of a monthly journal, *Shakai zasshi* (with an English title, *The Sociologist*), in April 1897. This association was formed by nonacademic sociologists: journalists, ministers, social reformers, and socialists. Its constitution stated that the society's purpose was to study the principles of sociology, socialism, and social problems. The society's prospectus stated:

> Sociology is the foundation of all social sciences. It studies the laws of the historical development of mankind and of the evolution of society in general. It researches the actual social life of people and shows the course of social reforms in the future. In the Western countries, sociology has paid much attention to current issues, and it is said that in the social sciences, social problems are the main concerns. In Japan the gulf between rich and poor has come to be great indeed, and the poor are now confronted with serious problems. The problems of landownership arise from conflict between landlords and tenants, and labor problems arise form the struggle between capitalists and laborers. Under such conditions it goes without saying that we must study the principles of sociology and research actual social life to prevent or control social problems. Regarding social policies we must study the rise of socialism and the development of socialist parties.[3]

Interest in socialism and social reform resulted from the increasing social problems that accompanied the development of capitalism in Japan. During the late nineteenth century, Japanese sociology was very much influenced by American liberal sociology and by reformist ideas connected with Christian socialism and the social gospel.

The Sociological Society was dissolved and publication of *The Sociologist* was discontinued in August 1898. The dissolution of the society was closely related to the establishment of the Shakaishugi Kenkyūkai (Association of Socialist Studies). Influential members were Katayama Sen, Murai Tomoshi, Abe Isoo, Kōtoku Shūsui, and Kinoshita Naoe, most of whom were Christian socialists who had studied in the United States. Their association platform stated that the purpose of this new group was to examine whether principles of socialism could be made applicable to Japanese society. Membership in the association was open to all persons who agreed with this purpose regardless of their actual attitudes toward socialism; therefore, some liberal sociologists and social reformers were members of the Association of Socialist Studies and simultaneously members of the Sociological Society. Thus, after the Association of Socialist Studies was established, nonacademic sociologists who were not interested in socialism sought to establish a new sociology association.

It was in this context that the Shakaigaku Kenkyūkai (Association of Sociology Studies) was established in November 1898. Some of the influential members were Katō Hiroyuki, Takagi Masayoshi, Motoyoshi Yu-

[3] *Shakai zasshi* 1, 2 (May 1897).

jirō, and others. Katō was president of the association. Born in 1 his younger days he had studied Dutch and German. After servi official of the feudal government, he became a high official of the l..... of Education in the Meiji government. As an enlightened scholar, he joined with the famous reformer Fukuzawa Yukichi and others in forming a society called Meirokusha (The Meiji Six Society) in 1873. In the early Meiji period, he advocated the theory of representative government and equal rights of the people, but he changed his position after he became president of the Tokyo Imperial University. Through social Darwinism, he attacked the doctrine of the natural rights of man, insisting there were no equal rights in the jungle. Katō resigned as president of the Tokyo Imperial University in 1893. In the same year a chair of sociology was established at the university, to which Professor Toyama Shōichi was appointed.

When Toyama, a Spencerian, became president of the university, Takagi Masayoshi succeeded him as lecturer in sociology. Takagi was much influenced by scholars from Columbia University, especially by the work of F. H. Giddings. He therefore tried to introduce American psychological sociology to his students.

Motoyoshi Yujirō was born in 1858 and graduated from Tokyo Imperial University in 1881. After two years teaching English at Aoyama Gakuin, he went to the United States and studied psychology and sociology at Boston University and at Johns Hopkins from 1883 to 1887. He became a professor of psychology at Tokyo Imperial University in 1888. Thus many members of the Association of Sociology Studies were professional sociologists who held positions at the university.

The association began publication of the periodical *Shakai* (Society) in January 1899. The title was changed to *Shakaigaku zasshi* (Journal of sociology) in February 1902. The association's constitution stated that its purpose was to study the principles of sociology, social problems, and policies of social reforms. It should be noted that the word "socialism" disappeared and was replaced by the term "social policies." In the first issue of *Shakai*, the journals's editorial policy was announced as follows:

> We would like to organize a forum for the discussion of the ways to study and lead society. We can study society. Though the changing process of society is extremely complicated and any social trends develop, then disappear one after the other, once we attain insight into the essence of such phenomena, we can locate the immutable laws by which society is moved or changed. Thus society can be studied through scientific methods. We can lead society. Once we find the immutable laws of society, we can predict the movements and the changing processes of society. Thus, society can be led by sociologists.[4]

[4] *Shakai* 1, 1 (January 1899).

The difference in character between the Sociological Society and the Association of Sociology Studies is clear. Whereas the former insisted on close relationships between sociology and socialism, the latter tried to exclude socialism from sociology. Against the journalistic aims of the former, the latter insisted on academic perspectives in the study of sociology and social policies.

In January 1900, the Association of Socialist Studies was reorganized and renamed the Shakaishugi Kyōkai (Association of Socialists). The purpose of this association was to study the principles of socialism and apply them to Japanese society. Therefore, nonsocialist members who were merely interested in the academic study of socialism resigned, and only socialists remained. In the spring of the same year the Public Peace Law was enacted to prevent the working class from organizing themselves into unions. The law effectively prohibited industrial workers and tenant farmers from agitating against employers and landlords.

In May 1901, the Social Democratic Party, the first socialist party in Japan, was formed by Kōtoku Shūsui, Katayama Sen, Abe Isoo, Kinoshita Naoe, and others. They also published a socialist manifesto and a party platform. The manifesto stated, in part:

> How to abolish the gulf between rich and poor is one of the great problems of the twentieth century. The ideas of people's rights and freedom which spread in the West, especially in France, contributed to the realization of political equality. However, the development of productive forces created a new class antagonism between the rich and poor instead of between the aristocracy and plebeian. Economic equality is primary and political equality is second. Therefore, even if we could realize representative government and a democratic polity, the majority of the people would still be unhappy if we fail to eliminate economic inequality. This is why our party devotes all its efforts to solve economic problems.[5]

This manifesto reveals an up-to-date understanding of socialism and the work appropriate to a socialist party in the period. After the government suppressed the Socialist Party, the conflict between sociology and socialism became even clearer.

When the Russo-Japanese War began in 1904, socialists stood against the conflict and advocated world peace. Sociologists like Katō Hiroyuki and Tatebe Tongo supported the war, however, demanding that the government take drastic measures against Russia.

As mentioned earlier, Katō Hiroyuki had abandoned the theory of people's rights and freedom and had adopted the ideas of social Darwinism.

---

[5] Kawamura Nozomu, *Nihon shakaigakushi kenkyū* (Tokyo: Ningen no kagaskusha, 1973–75), 1:243.

By the turn of the century, however, he had relinquished the idea of the right of the strongest. His fear of socialism and communism distorted his interpretation of evolutionist ideas. Katō's theoretical emphasis was now not on conflict but on the harmony of society. In this context, Katō adopted the theory of the social organism and modified it to mean a state organism, to justify the status quo. To maintain the stability of the state organism, Katō stood against not only socialism and communism but also all liberal thoughts. He wrote:

> I support utilitarianism, but I do not support the doctrine of the greatest happiness for the greatest number. In the first place, the state is not a simple aggregation of individuals like a small hill of gravel, but an organic unity in which every institution and agent has organic and harmonious relationships. If the state is regarded as needing to pursue the greatest happiness for the greatest number, as in Bentham's theory, this proposition has to rest on the individualistic assumption that the state should be regarded as a mere aggregation of individuals, like a small hill of gravel.[6]

Thus the welfare of society was considered the equivalent of the wealth of the state, and patriotism was identified with loyalty to the emperor. If the state was to be a natural organism, the emperor was the nerve center. Since the emperor was a crucial organ of the state, he should be protected at the sacrifice of his "hands" and "legs."

When the Russo-Japanese War began, Katō published a book entitled *Shinkagaku yori kansatsu shitaru Nichiro no unmei* (Destiny of Japan and Russian in light of evolutionary theory) in which he predicted the victory of Japan based on the theory of the survival of the fittest. Japan was much stronger than Russia because Japanese society was firmly integrated under the emperor system.[7] Ironically enough, however, just when Katō's theory of the state organism was elaborated, the infrastructure on which the theory was founded began to collapse. It should be noted that the weaker the actual base of such a theory became, the more strongly it was put forward as an ideological concept.

Born in 1871, Tatebe Tongo graduated from Tokyo Imperial University in 1896. In his undergraduate days, Tatebe majored in philosophy. After two years of study in Europe, subsidized by the government, he became a lecturer in sociology at the university along with Takagi Masayoshi. After the opening of the department of sociology in 1903 he served as chairman of the department until 1922, when he resigned from the university. As a sociologist he styled himself the Comte of the Orient.

---

[6] Katō Hiroyuki, *Katō Hiroyuki kōen zenshū* (Tokyo: Maruzen, 1900), 3:240.

[7] Katō Hiroyuki, *Shinkagaku yori kansatsu shitaru Nichiro no unmei* (Tokyo: Hakubunkan, 1904), p. 85.

According to Tatebe, society was an organic, integrated body of the co-operative life of the people. He published the introductory volume of his *Futsu shakaigaku* (General sociology) in 1904, in which he argued the organic integration of Japanese society. Japanese society was to be adequately expressed by the concept of national polity. Tatebe called his position "sociocracy," but his vision represented nothing more than a desire to build the strong nation under the emperor's rule.

Tatebe was also strongly opposed to Russia. After the war, in 1906, he wrote a book on sociological studies of the war in which he attacked pacifism and socialism and supported the imperialism of Japan as a sociological fact.[8]

Other socialists organized antiwar propaganda and started a socialist weekly called the *Heimin shinbun* in February 1903. The following is a translation of their statement of principles.

> It is said that liberty, equality and fraternity are three cardinal principles of human life.
>
> In order to secure liberty among men, we support the principle of democracy, and desire to destroy all class distinctions and oppressions which grow out of the existing order.
>
> To bless men with equality we insist upon socialism, and we desire to make all the means of production, distribution, and exchange the common property of men.
>
> To favor men with fraternity, we adhere to a policy of peace and endeavor to bring about disarmament, to stop bellicose attempts without reference to distinctions of race and political divisions. We shall make every attempt, in realizing this ideal, to arouse public opinion and to allow all to act in conformity with the majority of men, provided our law will admit it; and we absolutely condemn man's rash attempt to satisfy his selfish enjoyment of the moment.[9]

When the Russo-Japanese War broke out, the socialists redoubled their efforts to fight for an early peace. On March 20, 1904, at a meeting in Tokyo, socialists voted to send a message of mutual comradeship to Russian socialists. In this letter they said that as social democrats they were neither nihilists nor terrorists, and therefore they objected absolutely to the use of military force, rather advocating struggle by peaceful means, by reason, and by discussion.

The *Heimin shinbun* was suppressed in January 1905. The Association of Socialists, mentioned above, was also suppressed and dissolved in 1905. The Nihon Shakaito (Socialist Party) was formed in February

---

[8] Tatebe Tongo, *Sensōron* (Tokyo: Kinkōdo, 1906), pp. 305–307.

[9] *Heimin shinbun* 1, 1 (February 15, 1903).

1906. On the first anniversary meeting of the party in 1907, heated discussions centered on questions of party tactics. It was suggested that the clause "we advocate socialism within the law" be stricken from the constitution. Kōtoku and others advocated a radical and fundamental change in the existing society through a resolution calling for direct action; Tazoe Tetsuji and others proposed universal suffrage and adoption of a policy of parliamentalism. The party now divided into two antagonistic factions.

In May 1910 the government began arresting socialists accused of plotting the assassination of the emperor. In a notorious show trial, twenty-four people, including Kōtoku Shūsui, were convicted of treason. Kōtoku and eleven others were executed. The so-called era of winter began as the socialists suffered severe suppression.

In October 1908, two years before the treason trial, an editorial article in the Nihon shakaigaku kenkyūjo ronshū (Bulletin of the Institute of Sociological Studies) entitled "On the Differences Between Socialism and Sociology" had pointed out that sociology was not based on radical ideas held to be dangerous to the body social but was a discipline for studying society without prior prejudice. According to this article, before the Russo-Japanese War, sociologists were seen to be dangerous persons who stood against the government and the national polity, because people confused sociology with socialism. After the war, sociologists who stressed close relationships between sociology and socialism were severely restricted and lost influence within academic society.[10]

## European-Derived Ideas of Liberal Sociology and Taishō Democracy

During the period following the end of World War I, a more concerted attempt was made to create an academic discipline of sociology in Japan. By now, a number of bright younger scholars had visited Europe, where they had become aware of the significance of the continental, particularly the German, example. The effort to bend European theory to the reality of Japanese specifics was in many ways heroic. Yet, as will be clear from the account that follows, the lack of a close fit allowed these European theories to be used to support a number of concepts, including those of the nationalists, never intended by their original authors.

In 1913 Tatebe Tongo and others established the Nihon Shakaigakuin (Society of Japanese Sociology). Tatebe was the society's first president and chief editor of its yearbook. In 1914, at the group's second congress,

[10] Kawamura, *Shakaigakushi*, 1:271.

Tatebe presented a paper entitled "The National Polity of Our Empire and the Disturbance of World War." According to Tatebe, the Japanese national polity was characterized by the idea that the prosperity of the imperial throne must remain as eternal as heaven and earth. To maintain the prosperity of the throne in the face of severe international competition, Japan must become a first-class nation. To be a strong nation, the Japanese population had to be increased to more than one billion. Thus Tatebe insisted that Japanese expansion must be one of the nation's priorities.

In 1916, the research committee of the Society of Japanese Sociology published an article entitled "The Fundamental Policy of Education in Japan." According to this policy, the purpose of education was to establish a strong nation. Emphasis was put on respecting the emperor and maintaining the prosperity of one's household. Individualism therefore represented a form of thought that might undermine the solid base of the national polity. The essential social unit of the nation was not the individual but the household. Tatebe commented on this fundamental policy, saying, "the values of society always oppose the values of the individual, therefore if the values of individuals increase, then the values of society will decrease."[11] Thus, Tatebe condemned scholars who assumed that the increase of individual values should result in an increase in social values, and who praised the recent conceptions of democracy. In academic sociology, the kind of nationalistic sociology that emphasized the unique national polity of Japan now became dominant. Thus the conservative sociologists who occupied positions in universities and institutions now became the leading faction in the Society of Japanese Sociology.

A few sociologists, however, took a more liberal standpoint. One of the most prominent liberals was Yoneda Shōtarō. He was born in 1873 of an outcast family. After completing a course of English study at a college in Nara prefecture, he went to the United States and Western Europe to study sociology. In the United States he studied the sociological theories of L. F. Ward, A. W. Small, and F. H. Giddings. He was much influenced as well by G. Simmel's formal sociology. Yoneda came back to Japan in 1902 and became a lecturer at Kyoto Imperial University. Because of his outcast background he remained a lecturer for a considerable time, but eventually he became the first professor of sociology at the university.

Yoneda criticized Tatebe's organic theory of sociology and defined society as the mental interaction between individuals. These ideas were taken from Simmel's concepts of sociology. He accepted Simmel's theories of formal social relationships. Following Simmel, Yoneda defined the

---

[11] Tatebe Tongo, "Teikoku kyōiku no konponhonshin ni tsuite," *Nihon shakaigaku nenpō* 4, 1 and 2, (1916).

object of sociology as *Formen der Vergesellschaftung* and focused on *seelische Wechselwirkung* among individuals. It is important that Yoneda grasped social relationships as form, not content, which was a result of Simmel's influences. Almost all important concepts and ideas of Yoneda's sociology were later adopted by his student Takata Yasuma, who would come to play a crucial role.

In 1919 Yoneda wrote an article entitled "The National Polity by the Emperor and Democracy," in which he argued that the emperor's sovereignty over the national polity in Japan could not be compatible with the people's sovereignty in a democracy, but that a form of democracy termed *minponshugi* could be introduced as a political system without respect to the problem of sovereignty. According to Yoneda, democracy as a political system should be realized in the form of universal suffrage and reasonable social policies. He insisted that a political movement based on more than these two goals was as dangerous as one that did not aim for both. Thus he stood against both socialism and conservatism.[12]

Yoneda contributed to the development of sociology not only in general theories but also in more specialized fields. He was the first scholar who studied specific social problems. In his book *Gendai chishiki kaikyū undō to narikin to demokurashi* (The modern intellectual class movement, the upstart millionaire, and democracy), published in 1919, he focused on the problems of the new middle class. He defined the intellectual class as those who do not have property and derive income through their technological or other knowledge. According to him, the intellectual class is almost the same as the new middle class. It is not an independent class but depends on either the bourgeoisie or the proletariat. Bourgeoisie and aristocrats alike until that time had protected intellectuals and assimilated them into their own classes. The number of intellectuals had increased, however, and the bourgeoisie could no longer assimilate them all. According to Yoneda, this was one of the greatest social problems of his day. Some intellectuals had come to identify with the proletariat, and their leadership and assistance would be needed if the working class movement could be developed in both organization and strategy.[13]

Takata Yasuma, born in 1883, graduated from Kyoto Imperial University in 1910. His supervisor in both undergraduate and graduate school was Yoneda. In his undergraduate days he was much influenced by socialist thoughts. He had been attracted by Kōtoku's study *Shakaishugi shinzui* (The quintessence of socialism), published in 1903, and believed that an enthusiasm for socialism could be satisfied by studying sociology.

[12] Yoneda Shōtarō, "Kunshu kokutai to minshushugi," in Ota Masao, ed., *Shiryō Taishō demokurashi ronsōshi* (Tokyo: Shinsensha, 1971), 1:135.

[13] Yoneda Shōtarō, *Gendai chishiki kaikyū undo to narikin to demokurashi* (Tokyo: Kōbundo, 1919), pp. 134–35.

Yoneda, however, dissuaded him from becoming involved in socialism. As a young scholar, Takata wrote some significant theoretical articles, including "On the Social Laws" (1911); "Nature of Theories of Social Evolution" (1912); "Theories of Social Laws" (1913); and "Nature of Social Laws" (1914).[14] He tried to isolate the universal laws of society and to exclude theories of social evolution from the field of sociology. He focused on "sociological laws" and was not interested in the laws of social development, or "historical laws." These ideas formed the basis for his famous theory of "the third view of history," which he expounded in 1925, and which represented a sociological-historical view. He attacked both idealistic and materialistic views of history, placing more importance on conscious social relations than on productive or economic relations.[15]

In 1919 Takata published a large volume, *Shakaigaku genri* (The principles of sociology). He accepted Yoneda's (and Simmel's) theories and defined society as the mental interaction between individuals. For Takata's sociology, the form of socialization is the most important element. In the era of Taishō democracy, he could for the first time define society as the mental interaction of individuals apart from the state and household. When compared with Simmel, however, Takata placed more emphasis on unity or bonds than on interaction. According to Takata, society is more than mental interaction; it is the mental unity of individuals. Unless each individual desires to live cooperatively within the social unit, society cannot exist. The will to coexist is important; society can exist only when people decide to live together. Still, the will for coexistence is not necessarily mutual. When, for example, the conqueror desired coexistence for his own sake and exploited the conquered, such a one-sided bond or unity was also wrongly defined as coexistence. According to Takata, society consists logically of individuals, but society is not a mere aggregation of individuals. Individuals are not only interacting with each other but are bound as well by external social forces. The forms of unity or bond are objective facts. Society is not merely interaction but is in essence a unity.

In his *Shakaigaku gairon* (General theories of sociology), published in 1922, Takata presented his view of the laws of social change, such as the "law of *Vergessellshaftung*" and the "law of constant quantity of total social bond." The former law refers to the tendency for social change to proceed along an axis from *Gemeinschaft* to *Gesellschaft*. He distinguished between two societies, one based on primitive, natural ties and the other based on secondary, cultural ties. The latter concept suggests that in any society, the totality of the social bond remains constant.

---

[14] These articles mainly appeared in *Tetsugaku zasshi*.

[15] Takata Yasuma, *Kaikyū oyobi daisanshikan* (Tokyo: Kaizōsha, 1925), p. 233.

Therefore, the more chances an individual has to come into contact with others, the less dense each social interaction will be. This he called the diffusion of social interactions.

In 1938 Takata argued in an article entitled "Nihon no tsuyomi" (The strength of Japan) that the spiritual strength of Japan existed in the social ties of the rural community. Accordingly, to protect the village community was to protect the strength of Japan. He once wrote, "I am a child of the village, and a child in a spirit of nostalgia."[16] According to Takata, the Japanese should not despise such nostalgia. Such attitudes led him to reconsider his former position of cosmopolitanism. In "The Strength of Japan," the emphasis was on the peculiar *gemeinschaftlich* character of Japanese society.

> Japanese society is still young because of its *gemeinschaftlich* character. People are simple and honest by nature and not selfish. Individualism is not yet strongly ingrained, and the individual is able to absorb himself in the collective of the social whole. . . . Because of this communal character, the Japanese can throw away his life for his country in complete earnestness. All Japanese, not only professional soldiers, are willing to sacrifice themselves for the sake of their country.[17]

Takata, recalling his younger days, wrote, "When I was writing my *Principles of Sociology* there was nothing but the concept of class in my mind. I was so influenced by such cosmopolitan ideas at that time that the concept of folk was insignificant for me. Since then, however, I have been aware of the meaning of folk."[18] It is a surprise indeed that such a prominent scholar of Western sociology could align himself with the ideology of "Japanism."

Takata predicted the direction of *Vergesellschaftung* as the course of social development. Yet in the spiritual world he was a child of the rural community. While he was living in an industrial urban area, he always yearned after rural life and sought *Gemeinschaft* in spirit.

In the field of family sociology, Toda Teizō was a leading scholar. He was born in 1887 and graduated from Tokyo Imperial University in 1912, taking a position as lecturer of sociology, there. He traveled to the United States and Europe, where he learned the method of social research and the theories of sociological positivism. He became an associate professor in the department of sociology in 1920 and was made a full professor in 1929.

[16] Takata Yasuma, "Shisō ruten no ki," in *Hinja hisshō* (Tokyo: Chikuma shobō, 1934), p. 21.
[17] Takata Yasuma, "Nihon no tsuyomi," in *Kaisōki* (Tokyo: Kaizosha, 1938), pp. 192–93.
[18] Takata Yasuma, *Hinja hisshō*, rev. ed. (Tokyo: Chikuma shobō, 1940), p. 21.

Toda published *Kazoku no kenkyū* (Studies of the family) in 1926. He analyzed data from the 1920 census, Japan's first modern census, and began a study of families on actual data. He predicted the transition of the family from institution to companionship in modern Japan. He analyzed relationships within the family from two perspectives: those between husbands and wives, and those between parents and children. He did not pay much attention to the institutions of the traditional household (*ie*). He pointed out that in the urban family at that time, the power of the family head was already weakened. Nor was the continuity of family line strongly emphasized. Of course, the *ie* institution remained a living concept among those families who had large amounts of land or property. He insisted, however, that poor urban families had nothing to do with the *ie* institution in their actual family life.

Toda acknowledged that in Japanese families, parent-child relationships were much stronger than those between husbands and wives. He also affirmed that, within a family, the male maintained a privileged position vis-à-vis the female, and insofar as primogeniture remained prevalent, the eldest son held a privileged position vis-à-vis other sons. Yet, he criticized the traditional pressure of the *ie* institution and supported civil freedom and independence for all members of the family. He concluded that self-realization by all family members, regardless of their sex, could occur through changes in conventional family relationships.

His perspective, however, was drastically altered during the war. For example, in his 1942 book, *Ie no michi* (The way of the household), he emphasized the importance of the patrilineal family. He wrote that all *ie* in Japan had the emperor's household as the main family; therefore, filial piety could consist of loyalty to the emperor. Each household could trace its line back to an ancestral father who was at the same time a god. The emperor could trace a direct line to an ancestral father through primogeniture. Toda emphasized that the way to expand *ie* was to establish in Asia a mutual prosperity sphere directed by the emperor. The peaceful order of Asia should be established against the aggression of Western countries being carried out under the mask of freedom. Society should be maintained like a large household.

In the 1920s, Takata, Toda, and other leading sociologists in Japan tried to establish liberal sociology. They did nothing more, however, than introduce modern Western sociological theories.[19] Most of them could

[19] Major sociological works translated into Japanese in the 1920s included, in 1921, G. Simmel's *Grudfragen der Soziologie* and C. H. Cooley's *Human Nature and the Social Order*; in 1922, Cooley's *Social Organization*; in 1923, L. H. Morgan's *Ancient Society* and J. G. Tarde's *Les lois de l'imitation*; in 1924, E. Durkheim's *Sociologie et Philosophie* and Tarde's *Les lois sociales*; in 1925, W. McDougall's *An Introduction to Social Psychology* and *The Group Mind*, and F. H. Gidding's *The Elements of Sociology*; in 1926,

not break through such limitations. In a sense they acted as importers. Therefore, when crisis came in the 1930s they easily converted their ideas to an obedience to the ideology of Japanese nationalism, or "Japanism."

## The Development of Indigenous Scholarship: Yanagita Kunio and Aruga Kizaemon

Meanwhile, new considerations coming to bear on sociological theory, often involving evidence taken from the specifics of Japanese society, were making themselves felt. Drawing on history and on the realm of traditional Japanese belief and social practice, a number of influential thinkers chose to develop a series of theories that grew out of what they took to be the bedrock of national experience. Their stance often proved influential, and the example provided by these thinkers has remained profound in postwar Japan. Yet their conceptions were brought with difficulties and dangers, some practical, some inadvertently ideological.

Yanagita Kunio, the most influential twentieth-century Japanese scholar of folklore, was born in 1875 in Hyogo Prefecture. He graduated from the faculty of law of Tokyo Imperial University and became an official in the Ministry of Agriculture. In his youth, Yanagita was a poet and a man of letters. Some of his close friends were Shimazaki Tōson, Tayama Katai, and Kunikida Doppo. Yanagita started his studies of agronomy around 1900. He published volumes entitled *Nōseigaku* (Agronomy) in 1902–5 and *Jidai to nōsei* (The age and agricultural administration) in 1910. In the latter study he stressed the important idea of the continuity of households (*ie*). Skeptical as to whether imported theories such as Marxism could explain the dynamics of Japanese society, he argued that indigenous theories were needed to explain indigenous social phenomena.

According to Yanagita, relationships between *oya* (parent) and *ko* (child) were social. He distinguished between concepts such as *oya* (one who takes the role of the fictive parent) and *umi no oya* (biological parents). Accordingly, a *ko* is not necessarily someone linked to an *oya* through blood lines, as is the case with natural parents and children. Although the term is now commonly used in a more limited sense, primarily to indicate such blood or family ties, Yanagita underlined the fact that the terms were originally used to indicate the leader-follower relationship within the social unit in which labor was organized. This social unit used to consist of a large household—the extended family. He pointed out that

M. Weber's *Wirtschaftsgeschichte*; in 1927, *The Complete Writings of Marx and Engels* and Simmel's *Uber soziale Differentzierung*; in 1928, R. M. MacIver's *The Elements of Social Science* and Tarde's *L'opinion et la foule*; and in 1929, Giddings's *The Principles of Sociology* and C. Bougle's *Qu'est-ce que la sociologie?*

these fictive kinship ties played an important role in social relationships among households. Within the network of fictive kinship, lineage groups did exist as important social units. Thus internal relationships within households decided the character of external relationships among households.

From these perspectives, Yanagita believed that Japanese folklore provided a rich source of inspiration for the development of an indigenous theory. His studies of local customs in various parts of Japan led him to evaluate the ability of the Japanese household to perpetuate itself. Much earlier Yanagita identified individualism as a deviant form of behavior that served only to undermine the value placed on lineage; furthermore, individual desires were seen as being unrelated to, or at least existing in a sphere totally separated from, the needs of the nation. In *The Age and Agricultural Administration* he argued that the uniqueness of Japanese culture was rooted in the fact that the Japanese people had lived and served the emperor as an institution for almost two thousand years. If there were no household system in Japan, the population could not understand how they could truly be Japanese.[20]

Although his was a very conservative ideological stance, Yanagita believed that modernization was imperative. He believed that continuity of the household, including the Imperial Household, was an important fact even after the Meiji Restoration of 1868. He realized that after 1868, the social character of landlords changed and they lost their traditional power over their tenants. A demand by tenants for the reduction of rice rent and the abolition of parasitic landlords seemed inevitable to Yanagita. In *Toshi to nōson* (Urban and rural society), published in 1919, he supported the demands of the farmer's union. But at the same time, he criticized the union because it had been organized only by tenant farmers. He pointed out that even if the present rice rent were to be abolished totally and tenants were to become owners of the land they farmed, they could be no better off than small farmers who now suffered debts. Therefore, the union should include owner-cultivators and should endeavor to find work for farmers.[21]

Yanagita insisted as well that communal ownership of land was the traditional custom in Japan. Cooperation of farmers in the process of agricultural production did not come from Western Communist ideas, but from the traditional way of peasants who could survive through mutual assistance in a village community. He believed that new capitalistic forms of agriculture would not be realized in Japan.[22] It should be noted that for him, opposition to the control of landlords did not mean promoting

[20] Yanagita Kunio, *Jidai to nōsei*, in *Yanagita Kunio shū* (Tokyo: Chikuma shobō, 1962–1964), 16:39.

[21] Yanagita Kunio, *Toshi to nōson*, in *Yanagita Kunio shū*, 16:345.

[22] Ibid., p. 378.

the capitalistic development of agriculture. Yanagita paid much attention to the communal way of living of the common people in rural as well as urban areas.

As Yanagita pointed out, the significance of ancestor worship is that it links social structure with religious values. The religious authority of a household head comes from the fact that he is a direct lineal descendant of the *ie*. In his article "Tamashii no yukue" (The abode of the departed souls), written in 1949, Yanagita wrote that in Japan the souls of ancestors do not go far from their native places. They always remain in the hills of their homeland and watch over the lives of their descendants. From respect for one's ancestors, one naturally respects the household head, who represents the link between ancestors and descendants.[23] In his 1927 article "Nōson kazokuseido to kanshu" (Rural household system and customs), Yanagita wrote that a household head had to celebrate festivals and to integrate his household members into such activities. He must do his best to ensure the prosperity of his descendants. Therefore, a head of the household feels he has failed his responsibilities to his ancestors if he fails to preserve his family's fortune. Yanagita said it would be harmful if the Japanese people came to attach little importance to the continuity of their households.[24]

Yanagita changed his field from agronomy to folklore after World War I. He combined folklore with history and elaborated an indigenous discipline of social history. His idea of folklore studies was expressed in the 1925 lecture titled "Seinen to gakumon" (Youth and scholarship):

> The goal of the study of the social study of our own country is to solve the problems of the common people. To understand the reason why we, the common people, still have to suffer the miserable conditions of our lives, we must study the history of our own country in order to clarify the relationships of ourselves to our own society, i.e., to Japan. To study history makes man wise. Heedless undertakings of the people would be dangerous in these days now that the people, who have long stood outside of political life, have voting rights. They have been left unlettered and have nothing to do but pray to the gods for mercy. Under the system of universal suffrage, public education should be emphasized. New scholarship should play an important role in enlightening the people to promote a better understanding of their present and future situation.[25]

On the subject of women's liberation, Yanagita expressed a unique opinion in his 1934 lecture entitled "Josei shigaku" (The history of Japanese women). He predicted the realization of women's suffrage in the

---

[23] Yanagita Kunio, "Tamashii no yukue," in *Yanagita Kunio shū*, 15:561.

[24] Yanagita Kunio, "Nōson kazokuseido to kanshū," in *Yanagita Kunio shū*, 15:356.

[25] Yanagita Kunio, "Seinen to gakumon," in *Seinen to gakumon* (Tokyo: Iwanami shoten, 1976), p. 16.

near future and said that, "as with men's suffrage, the assertion that woman should have her rights to share in decisions on national affairs is not refused by anyone insofar as the theory itself is concerned. One could object to it only on the pretext that it is still premature to talk about such an idea, or that the procedures to realize such an ideal have not yet been examined closely. Women today should be prepared to participate in national politics and to undertake social services that could be performed by women alone."[26] Yanagita pointed out the significant role of women in the traditional household, which required of all its members the communal way of *ie*. The status of the *okata* or *toji* (a wife of the head) in the household had once been very high. If to be a head of the household was a goal of young men, to be an *okata* was a goal of young women. In the traditional household, the work of the housewife was not simple; she had to make decisions on cooperative labor within a large family. Some domains of family affairs were left for her alone to decide, and even the head of the house could not intrude. Thus Yanagita expected that, in the communal epoch of the future, this traditional role of women would be reactivated.

As for women's education, he pointed out that it was difficult to bring up women of the traditional *okata* type in the modern educational system. Nor was it easy for parents to bring up their daughters to be docile and modest when they were new brides and to be gallant and dignified later, when they became *okata*. To be a good bride was not the same as being a good wife of the patriarch. As a new bride, a young woman was expected to obey her mother-in-law, but as an *okata* she was expected to manage household affairs. In his article "Daikazoku to shōkazoku" (A large family and a small family), written in 1940, Yanagita wrote that the modern education system was not suitable for contemporary Japanese women who were still expected to play the role of an *okata*. According to Yanagita, Japanese women now live in an age that requires unforeseen cooperative activities. Women are expected to perform important roles in a community, which often resembles a large extended family. Indeed, if the revival of communal types of society in a higher form in the near future could be foreseen, Yanagita's prediction of the coming large extended family need not be seen merely as a reactionary view.[27]

Yanagita as a folklorist gathered many materials concerning the life of the common people, but he was relatively indifferent to the construction of new theories. Aruga Kizaemon, who was much influenced by Yanagita's folklore, was a sociologist ambitious enough to build new indigenous theories of his own. He was born in 1897 in Nagano Prefecture and grad-

[26] Yanagita Kunio, "Josei shigaku," in *Momen izen no koto* (Tokyo: Iwanami shoten, 1979), pp. 253–54.

[27] Yanagita Kunio, "Daikazoku to shōkazoku," in *Ie kandan* (Kamakura: Kamakura shobō, 1946), pp. 144–45.

uated from Tokyo Imperial University's art history department in 1922. He started his studies as a folklorist and then changed his discipline to sociology. As the son of a large landlord, he felt no necessity to obtain a university position until the end of the war.

In his *Nihon kazokuseido to kosakuseido* (The Japanese family system and tenant system), written in 1943, Aruga argued that the origin of the relationship between landlord and tenant in Japan was that between *oyakata*, a kind of patriarchal leader, and *kokata*, indentured followers of the family, in the prefeudal period. Originally they were not separate enterprises but formed one *Interessengemeinschaft* in which each had different roles in conducting the cooperative management of agriculture. When he attacked the Marxists in these respects, Aruga stated that the independence of subordinate *kokata* was a characteristic of the feudal Tokugawa period.[28] He demonstrated that the parent-child (*oyakata-kokata*) relationship within the large extended family was a carryover from earlier times and had existed before the small landholding family gained its independence.

By the end of the Tokugawa period, however, economic differentiation among feudal farmers had brought serious problems. The upper classes began to accumulate arable land, becoming landlords, and the lower classes lost their land, becoming tenants. Thus new landlord-tenant relationships were established, colored, as Aruga emphasized, by lineage relationships. As both Yanagita and Aruga argued, social relationships between landlords and tenants were like those between parents and children. The relationship was one of mutual obligation and service. Tenants believed that they could make a living through the landlord's favor, even though almost half of their rice harvest was taken by the landlord as rent. Tenants owed certain services to the landlord as a means to express their personal subordination to him. For example, on the first day of the New Year and on All Soul's Day (O-Bon), tenants went to the landlord's house with presents and offered their services for domestic work. They assisted willingly on the occasion of marriages or funerals in the landlord's family. In the cases of corvée, domestic and ceremonial services were assigned as often as labor services. For example, Aruga described the relationships he observed between the *oyakata* and *kokata* of the Saitō family in Ishigami Village, Ninoe County, Iwate Prefecture in 1935. He witnessed services performed by the *bekke* (branch families) and *kokata* during O-Bon:

> The celebration of the festival began on the fourteenth of the seventh month. However, on the thirteenth day preparations were made for the arrival of the souls of the deceased by sweeping ancestral graves, and repairing and sweeping

[28] Aruga Kizaemon, *Nihon kazokuseido to kosakuseido* (Tokyo: Kawade shobō, 1943), p. 631.

the roads that passed through the village and led to the graves. The graves of
the *oyakata*'s ancestors were swept by the *bekke* and *kokata*. Early on the
morning of the fourteenth, the *bekke* and *kokata* went to the *oyakata*'s to do
*suke* [labor services]—the *kokata* cleaning the ground and the *bekke* decorating
the altar. When this work was finished, all went together to the grave, carrying
offerings. . . . Each night during the celebration, a faggot of pine was left burning in front of the gate as a welcome to the returning souls. On the sixteenth
the souls were seen off.[29]

For *oyakata* to be the head of a main family was atypical after the feudal period. Landlords in the Meiji period were often neither *oyakata* nor
heads of main families. The relationships between the main and branch
families did not always coincide with the relationships between landlord
and tenant established in the Meiji period. But ideological use of genealogical relationships by landlords was a different matter. The landlord
could control tenants by using traditional relationships between the main
and branch families. In cases where the genealogical status did not cor-
respond with the status based on the land-ownership and the landlords
were not actually the main families, they manipulated the records if at all
possible. For landlords in the Meiji period, the longer they had been established the better; however, this was not a necessary condition. In the
end, the rule of the landlord was based on his ownership of land. Lineage
relationships were simply an important means of legitimating his power
and evoking a spontaneous willingness among tenants to follow the landlord's dictates. Even in cases in which no landlords were involved, however, the ideas of the lineage group and the concept of the continuity of
the household would remain, especially among the households of owner-
cultivators. Without a connection to the landlord system, the festival of
O-Bon and other ceremonies were celebrated in different ways, in connection with the deceased household members.

In short, Aruga saw a peculiar character of the Japanese in the fact that
hierarchy is legitimated by lineage relationships. For instance, he observed that just as vertical relationships in Japan were characterized by
paternalism, and relationships between members of the family were hierarchical, so too were relations between main and branch families, or
between the emperor and "his people."[30] According to Aruga, the major
structural feature of Japanese society was its familistic principle of organization. This principle could be applied not only to the community, but
also to the state and to all organizations. As with Yanagita, it is easy
enough to criticize Aruga's conservative stance. Yet his arguments on the

[29] Ibid., pp. 638–39.
[30] Ibid., p. 726.

national character of the Japanese include many useful suggestions for further studies of the Japanese people, culture, and society.

If one can say that the essential character of family relations is not necessarily hierarchical, the familistic organization can be described as a horizontal relationship as well. As for the choice between egalitarian and hierarchical relationships, there is no question but that one would chose the former. Groupism as communalism has nothing to do with vertical social relationships, just as vertical social relationships do not necessarily result from groupism. The emphasis on vertical, rather than horizontal, relationships is only an ideologically biased use of traditional values. It is unlikely that in Japan, as in other non-Western pre-industrial societies, the complete independence of each individual could have preceded some kind of solidarity. Such mechanical distinctions between two stages of development do not seem relevant to Japan's experience.

## Final Observations

In 1908, an editor of a socialist journal on women's liberation in Japan wrote an editorial entitled "Kyōsanshakai no kazoku" (Families in Communist society), which suggested that in the future, "affections between the husband and wife and between parents and children will be the central forces in the family," but that in the present society, "love for one's sons, parents, wife, and oneself is rendered contradictory to one's love for others and for society." The author continued, "if one can love himself, his family members and relatives without contradicting his love for others and for society, then all these different loves can develop as admirable, beautiful, and true sentiments for all human beings."[31] The possibility of a revitalization of horizontal relationships and a solidarity among common people in traditional groups was seen as important in the early twentieth century. This description of family relationships remains accurate even now.

The story of the conflicting demands of theory, history, and culture during the interwar period in Japan is thus a complex one. A sense of struggle, in both academic social theory and social action must remain paramount in the minds of those who review the confusions and successes of the time. In retrospect, however, it certainly can be said that the struggles of Japanese intellectuals and socially concerned citizens alike did manage to allow both groups to reach an important level of awareness

[31] Cited in Arichi Tōru, *Kindai Nihon no kazokukan* (Tokyo: Kōbundō, 1977), p. 170.

about themselves and about the roles in which their society, in whatever terms that concept might be defined, had cast them. In that very important sense, much was accomplished. The postwar years brought other kinds of self-awareness, and new problems equally difficult to solve. But that, of course, is a different story altogether.

# 5

## Tsuchida Kyōson and the Sociology of the Masses

EUGENE SOVIAK

OF SOME celebrity in his own brief lifetime in intellectual-philosophical circles, Tsuchida Kyōson (1894–1934) passed into undeserved obscurity within a decade of his death. Perhaps the sheer quantity of the estimated forty-five volumes, fifteen of which have been published, that were produced in a relentless torrent in twenty years (under the compulsive goad of fragile health) may have intimidated the academically faint-hearted.[1] Perhaps, too, the astonishing range of his intellectual appetite (natural science, philosophy, religion, history, law, society, literature, aesthetics, poetry) and the synthetic virtuosity with which he manipulated this multiplicity of data dampens enthusiasm for him as a subject for any definitive study. This super-abundance of commentary, analysis, reflection, and polemic appeared in a restless succession of individually published volumes, serialized newspaper articles, journal essays in *Kaizō*, *Shin hyōron*, *Nijisseiki*—magazines of his own invention—*Bunka*, and *Jiyū daigaku zasshi*, and many years of regular lectures in his own "Free University" and elsewhere. Perhaps, above all, because of the formidable difficulties of classifying his intellectual stance in any facile or final way (he delighted in the contradictory labels that were showered upon him), he may have discouraged the appreciative scholarly post-mortem even the slightest acquaintance with his writing seems to justify.[2]

Reviled by the Marxists as a "fascist" and "bourgeois scholar," Kyōson was a laudatory purveyor of Marxist ideas but also one of the wickedest, most devastating critics of contemporary Japanese Marxism.[3] While im-

---

[1] *Tsuchida Kyōson zenshū*, 15 vol. (Tokyo: Seishinsha, 1982). Hereafter *Zenshū*.

[2] His current champion and resuscitator is Kamiki Toshiori. See his long article, "Tsuchida Kyōson to jiyū daigaku undō," *Shisō no kagaku*, no. 2 (1972): 70–98, and his more recent work, *Tsuchida Kyōson to jiyū daigaku undō* (Tokyo: Seibundō Shinkōsha, 1982).

[3] See his exposition in the debate with Kawakami Hajime, *Marukushizmu hihyō* (1930), *Zenshū*, 3:225–344, and also *Shakai tetsugaku genron* (1928), *Zenshū*, 2:155–268. Tsuchida observed, "While it doesn't matter whether I am regarded as a fascist or Marxist or whatever, being extremely free in my sensibility, I am not discomforted by this" (see Kamiki, "Tsuchida Kyōson," p. 72). He also noted, "Marxism taught me all my ideas on the connected relationship of everything that appears and disappears to single historical condition. As for myself, I have given life to the fundamental essentials of Marxist materi-

placably committed to philosophy as the ultimate intellectual mode he would, as I will show later, critically assault what to him were the inadequacies and failings of philosophy but never its aspiration to grand syntheses nor its intellectual techniques. Formally trained in philosophy at Kyoto University, he was steeped in the neo-Kantians, fell under the sway of Nishida, and reputedly did pioneering explorations in phenomenology.[4] Omnivorously, he read everybody; unhesitatingly, he used everybody; characteristically, he subscribed to nobody.[5] His academic mentors and intellectual associates and rivals were as varied as his interests and included university professors, Buddhist monks, socialists, union organizers, politicians, poets, playwrights, scientists, publishers, and educators. Only a small sampling of these would embrace personalities such as Miki Kiyoshi, Kawakami Hajime, Tanaka Ōdō, Mutai Risaku, Tosaka Jun, Takakura Teru, Ide Tadashi, Imanaka Tsugimaro, Kaneko Daiei, Hatano Kanae, Matsuzawa Kenjin, Tanikawa Tetsuzō, Oka Arajirō, Fukuda Tokuzō, Shimonaka Yasaburō, and Mizutani Chōzaburō. Even his obeisances to Nishida were more for the latter's gift of the habit and practice of "precision of thought" than for the specific contents of his philosophy, even when those contents could be and were employed to harry the Marxists in their dialectical heartland. The work that would most likely recall Tsuchida to mind for most—the faintly improbable *Contemporary Thought in Japan and China*—conveys the same noncommittal posture.[6] Here he is the informative but critical chronicler of the state of Japanese philosophy and intellectual history at the end of the twenties. Indeed, in its inclusiveness, the work might also be called a compendium of "intellectuals anonymous." But from out of Tsuchida's analytical ashes begins to rise his own philosophic phoenix, which he termed "Culturalism" and which represents his own peculiar tour de force of critical synthesis: an exhaustively reasoned reconciliation of anarchism and socialism that obsessively haunts almost all his works.[7]

---

alism and economics, and I think I have resolved the nineteenth-century historical limitations of these essentials. That is to say, in order to vivify Marxism in contemporary society, I have surpassed formalistic basic Marx" (*Marukushizumu hihyō*, introduction).

[4] His graduation thesis in 1918 was entitled "An Introduction to Contemporary Philosophy-Phenomenological Reflections on Cognition." This was followed by a published work in 1919 entitled *Symbolic Philosophy*, which apparently expanded the last section, on symbols, of the thesis. See Kamiki, "Tsuchida Kyōson," p. 77.

[5] Some said that he "was a philosopher who rushed to everything new," or that he was "a professional contractor of ideas." Tsuchida's reply was, "You cannot understand life squinting through a peephole," and "a fundamental requirement is to analyze questions which arise as you move from one thing to another." Ibid., pp. 70–71.

[6] *Contemporary Thought of Japan and China* (London: William and Norgate, 1927); in Japanese *Nihon Shina gendai shisō kenkyū* (Tokyo: Daiichi shobō, 1926), in *Zenshū*, 4:13–277.

[7] First expounded in his *Bunkashugi genron* (1921), in *Zenshū*, 2:269–450.

In the end it was as self-defined, self-appointed superlative "cultural critic" that Tsuchida conceived and idealized his intellectual role. That role he had envisioned and prepared for from very early in his intellectual development, and that ongoing develōpment was a continuous elaboration, enrichment and refinement of what he deemed the imperatives of such a role.[8] Much, both implicit and explicit, of his concern for an attempted fulfillment of those imperatives is evident in his long essay "Taishū no shakaigaku" (The sociology of the masses).[9] Inquiry into its closely argued "key-word" analysis of the concept of the "masses" (along with "crowd") reveals his central preoccupation with the concept of "society" and at the same time a retrospective commentary on the state of the social sciences, particularly sociology, from the vantage point of 1932.

This essay was one of his last works, yet it encapsulates many of the themes of his personal intellectual history as well as the ideological fixations of his historical milieu—the turbulent sociopolitical confrontations of Taishō democracy and early Shōwa nativism and accelerating political repression; in short, the already well-documented upheaval of political mass movements, tenant-landlord disputes, organization of the larger farmers' movement, labor unionization and strikes, universal manhood suffrage agitation, and ideological radicalization that energized and disrupted the later Taishō and early Shōwa periods. Considerable argumentative heat had already been expended and would continue to be generated over the ideological jurisdictions, proper content, scientific pretensions, and claims to historical finality of Marxism, socialism, and the social sciences which these historical spasms had invoked. And a luxuriant tangle of semantic confusion enveloped the vocabulary of discourse and the rhetoric or debate. For Tsuchida, as for the ferociously disputatious ideologues so embroiled, the critical focus and concept was "society"—its irreducible essence, its alleged laws, its political malleability, and its utopian potentials. While the inflamed polemical contenders flaunted their conceptual absolutes, historical certainties, and ideological dicta, Tsuchida would here probe the validity of their analytical credentials.

When the arguments in the essay are extended outward and conjoined with other themes in his intellectual "system," one discovers that for Tsuchida, the possessing and inescapable obligation of the ideal cultural

---

[8] In the introduction to a very early work, *Bummei shichō to shin tetsugaku* (Current ideas on civilization and the new philosophy) (1914). In 1914 he established a Cultural Studies Center, which from January 1920 to April 1925 produced fifty-four issues of a house organ, *Bunka*, written by Tsuchida. See Kamiki, *Tsuchida Kyōson*, p. 77.

[9] *Zenshū*, 15:236–46. Quotations in the following discussion are all taken from this work.

critic was to "sociologize" philosophy and "philosophize" sociology, or perhaps less clumsily, to make sociology philosophical and philosophy sociological.

For Tsuchida, the phenomena and forms of society are constantly shifting and changing. Mere novelty, the transient, are not basic social phenomena nor social form; still, sociology must take as its object, "just as it is, the content of actual social life, which is changing and shifting in this ceaseless fashion and analyze, record, and speculate upon this social life" (p. 236). Regrettably, from the outset, sociology seized upon all sorts of ready-made concepts. When it imposed these concepts upon this fluid social reality, all of its judgments were understandably fallacious or questionable.

In much the same fashion as social forms, the consciousness of social beings is correspondingly mutable and inconstant. Such social beings become indecisive in the ascription of value in this whirling milieu. Though, indeed, in one period there is value determinacy, in the next there may not be such fixity. "Because even such things as the content of the arts change by period, it cannot be concluded that only the content of certain art is absolutely the highest art" (p. 237). But despite the fact that these universal, and philosophically necessary, evaluations of the good and beautiful may no longer pertain as absolute standards, they may be significant in themselves, and they may be relevant to immediate social phenomena and their interpretation.

Even if it is conceded, Tsuchida proceeds, that social phenomena are to be confronted "just as they are," it is not sufficient simply to describe and accept these phenomena.

> Phenomena and forms go on changing and altering, but in these kinds of transformations there must be reasons for the changes themselves. In social life the past, present, and future are not things which are completely unrelated, and it probably goes without saying that thought must be given to all sorts of necessary relationships accompanying this historical progression. We accept actual social life which exists just as it is, but analyzing and probing its realities, we must reflect upon such questions as the reasons why new phenomena and forms come to develop from within the lifestyle of the past. Again, what is the meaning of these newly emergent phenomena and forms? Still again, in what ways will these things go on developing while intensifying their imprint on the future? In such things social concepts are not simply descriptive, and it becomes also a matter of searching out the relationships, significance, and essentials of phenomena. (p. 237)

To be sure, these new phenomena and forms can be glibly and mechanically subsumed within prefabricated assumptions. But such a priori certainties may merely distort such new configurations and inspire erroneous conclusions. "This is so-called formalism. And until now, how often we have been made to listen to the formalistic explanations from so-called Marxists" (p. 238). Yet even the Marxists must resort, at times, to revisionist adjustments in their explanations of social life. "Herein the contradictions between the obstinate formal theories of Marxism and actual social life arise, and probably the theories of Marxism itself must have a new formulation" (p. 238).

In precisely this fashion, "the masses" in contemporary Japanese society have come to acquire an important new meaning. And although the term had earlier (even Buddhist) currency, "there has probably been no time in which the 'masses' had such weighty significance as at present. It is possible that it would not be an exaggeration even if one said that the present is the age of the masses" (p. 239). Everyday language reflected the pervasiveness of this term in such expressions as "mass novel," "mass restaurant," "mass necessities," and "mass lifestyle." Initially, such usage seemed unnatural and obscure, but now, with its lively currency, it had accreted an apparently self-evident meaning. But exactly how was the word understood? Who or what were these "masses"? For some the concept was ambiguous if not meaningless. For others it was superfluous since the already domesticated concept of "society" either obviated or subsumed it. But neither of these responses was satisfactory, since the sources of the term's emergence, as well as its surprising vogue, were unaccounted for. Even if it were a subspecies of "society," the differentiation or identity of the two remained unexplored, and few had grappled with the sociology of the term. Given its current preeminence in the contemporary vocabulary, that variety of analysis could no longer be delayed.

But Tsuchida's analytical onion–peeling still had another layer to go before he reached the core, which would, of course, be an exacting definition of the "masses," but one dependent upon a definition of "society." The concept of "crowd" had already antedated and, perhaps more modestly, anticipated the appearance and circulation of the concept "masses." A single concept or general idea such as "crowd," Tsuchida argues, arises out of the context or background of a specific period. The term "masses" had also emerged to articulate the context of a specific period, namely, the present. In their etiology they were comparable, but in their particulars distinguishable.

Previously, the concept of the "crowd" had considerable visibility, and extensions of it, such as "crowd ethics" and "crowd sociology," had received considerable attention. That emphasis underscored the degree to which the concept embodied the milieu of the times. The use of the concept of crowd originated at a time when crowd movements disrupted the tranquility of Hibiya Park and energetically assaulted newspaper offices and even the National Diet. When these events generated published commentaries, these prompted heated public discussion of crowd ethics, which in turn provoked police detention of their authors and outcries against intellectual repression. According to Tsuchida "Even I, who was a student at that time, have recollections of these discussions of crowd sociology at the celebrated Student's Debating Conference. Now, however, the ethical and sociological study of crowds is not of this degree of importance, and beginning the sociological study of the 'masses' has become the necessity of the time" (p. 240).

Upon its appearance, even the term "society" was regarded as novel. And perhaps as significantly, when reference was made to the study of "sociology," this was construed as the study of socialism and radiated the latter's aura of subversive ideology. Even now any allusion to "society" triggered this stubborn and obtuse conception of the term as a dangerous and covert viewpoint: "Nevertheless, the perspective that sees our life socially is widely diffused. Abandoning this social frame of reference would make our life, particulary our urban life, unintelligible. Herein, the pervasiveness of the everyday word 'society' must be seen in the end as a reflection of actual [historical] circumstances" (p. 241).

And now, at last, the core exposed, Tsuchida begins his definitional gymnastics with the concept of the "masses." This delineation, not surprisingly, is submitted to the conceptual arbitration of the preexistent concept of "society": "Society has a single unitary organization, and those belonging to this society have the sense or awareness of belonging to this society. However, the 'masses' do not have such a clearly defined organization, and the masses do not have a clear awareness of belonging to the 'masses' " (p. 241). Mutual benefit organizations such as banks and churches exhibit such clarity and specificity of form, and their members' identification with them is unmistakable. Similarly, the self-conscious sense of inclusion of their participants in families and nations is axiomatic. And in this present time of the "masses," while mass movements proliferate (though they lack the definitive configuration of other social forms), they do nonetheless possess a kind of system of relationships. Otherwise, they would be indistinguishable as entities. Yet their lesser degree of organizational definiteness obviates the possibility of their participants' experiencing any pronounced recognition of being "masses." Habitués of mass dining halls might in some ways be classified as the masses, but the masses are devoid of intimate mutual relations, and such patrons lack any sensitivity to their mass status. In organizational configuration and the self-conscious identification of its members, "society" exceeds the masses, as it does also in its certainty of purposes and aims. Yet while the masses are bereft of such purposeful certainty, they are not completely purposeless, though their goals may be obscure.

In behavioral style, too, Tsuchida notes, "society" and the "masses" are disparate.

Because society is a body which even may be conceived of as encompassing blood relationships within the same group, this body is consciously aware of its objectives, and to realize these objectives, it carries on rational behavior. But because the "masses" do not have this conscious awareness [of objectives], their behavior is everywhere irrational and obscurely careless. (p. 242)

Society is fully capable of generating truly rational behavior or activity, but the masses, with their characteristic absence of total organization, are at pains to replicate such activity. Yet when their agitation reaches a certain level, it unleashes a collective momentum that expresses a powerful strength of will not easily deflected. But when that momentum achieves its momentary purpose, this group dynamism dissipates and the "masses" vanish. Thus, despite the typical contemptuous dismissal of the masses as amphorous and irrational, the masses can demonstrate an uncanny will power that is frightening in its intensity. It is this social configuration, the masses, that now looms large in society.

Once again the "crowd" is reintroduced into the analytical triangulation to align even more precisely the position of the masses. The masses, in Tsuchida's judgment, resemble the phenomenon of crowd that had previously aroused theoretical speculation. Rigorous scrutiny, however, revealed them to be similar but not identical social forms: " 'Crowd' now actually signifies a body of human beings who are assembled in a particular place and which has an external form visible to the eye, but the masses are not a group concentrated at specific spatial locations. Consequently, it [the masses] does not have a determinate form." (p. 243). Crowds have as their common purpose merely congregation at some locale, but the masses lack this conscious motive. And while the convening of crowds is invariably temporary or fitful, the existence of the masses is prolonged. But there are points of congruity as well. Crowds are spontaneous manifestations without apparent commitment to assuming the contours of formal group organization. In common with the masses, crowds admit no limitation to their collective, if often unstable and ill-defined, purposes.

It is a specific historical illustration of this dramatic self-assertion of the masses, the so-called Farmers' Movement, that makes it possible "to see clearly before our eyes the violent power of the rural masses" and brings Tsuchida to the final phase of his conceptual anatomy. The ultimate substratum that explicates the character and meaning of the social form masses also once again differentiates "society," and vice versa.

Society in the broad sense is something that was established on the basis of the mutual relations of human beings. If one takes this broad perspective, the masses are also, it goes without saying, one sort of "society." However, I think so-called society signifies something of somewhat narrower limits than this. Society among the mutual relationships of human beings in the narrower sense is something that was established containing a greater degree of conscious or rational [self-] awareness. (p. 244)

Communal societies and ethnic nations might be regarded as entities grounded upon lifestyles that incorporate the most basic emotions. But even in these, the rational group consciousness is not overridden.

> Human beings, I think, who are fundamentally and completely bound by emotional mutual relations may be divorced from such awareness of rational mutual relationships. If this is true in mutual human relations, then one must see that the coherence of the emotional life in the life of the individual is somehow more fundamental than the coherence of the rational life. (p. 245)

This coherence of the emotional life in human beings is everywhere deemed obscured because it is irrational and segregated from the intellect. Notwithstanding that, it is not something that eliminates the vital quality of mutual purpose. "That is to say, intellectually it is not purposeful, but it is irrationally purposeful" (p. 245). But there are other critical gradations in this emotional life. When mutual relations nurture collectively shared and sustained emotions, communal societies and ethnic nations are generated, and those mutual relationships are fully conscious. When that emotional life is not articulated with the self-consciousness of reciprocal interaction, then the social form "masses" appears.

Within society in the broad sense, thus, are embraced three social types. The first organizes rational, purposeful groups in mutual benefit associations. The second consists of communal associations constructed upon the foundation of the shared sentiment of the emotional life but in possession of a clear awareness of its reciprocal linkages. The third is premised exclusively upon the emotional life, lacks any systematic awareness of mutual interrelationships, and is designated the "masses." Of these, the least adequately comprehended and examined is the last.

The coda to this sociological etude begins and ends with a kind of polyphonic reworking of the emotional life motif hinting at uncomposed exercises yet to come.

> The more I reflect upon the social life of human beings, the more I must concentrate on the coherence of the emotional life that permeates the background of social life. One must see that what is more profound even than that which has previously come to be called communal society is the complex of emotional life that constitutes the relationships of human beings. Some of these mutual relationships do constitute communal societies. However, there exist great numbers of classes of people who have only the vaguest awareness of their mutual interrelationships. And such people become extremely powerful forces animating and impelling actual life (p. 246).

Indeed, the objective social life was not to be fully apprehended by merely charting its rational dimensions. For more penetrating exploration revealed that objective social forces could disguise their real bases in the obscure, irrational emotional life.

> In thinking about our social life, the masses represent one social form that cannot be neglected now. To make clear its essential features serves as probably no more than an introduction to reflection finally upon the still more specific form of our social life. Deeper analytical studies probing inner motives have been initiated within conventional psychology, which examines rational mental phenomena. So, too, with regard to society, a sociology that discusses the basis of its inner motivations must similarly be inaugurated. (p. 246)

Both directly and indirectly, this essay is an integral part and reflector of Tsuchida's total philosophic network and its recurrent and interlocked concerns with the deficiencies of academic philosophy, the complementary and therapeutic corrective of the social science, and the formulation of a new "social philosophy" as the responsibility of the cultural critic. What the cultural critic, by his prescription, of course, must and did do, Tsuchida did in this essay. He had demonstrated how a tentative "sociology of the masses" (or any other analytic venture into a major current social issue or phenomenon) might or should proceed—without formalistic theoretical presuppositions, in dogged pursuit of ultimate meanings and interrelationships, and even with the possibility of arriving at critical revelations—concerning the emotional matrix of the social, a state basic to the sociology itself. The compelling intellectual impulse here and everywhere in Tsuchida's work, I think, is his ambivalent esteem for the censure of academic philosophy and his persuasion that its redemption would come by massive infusions of social science. The agent of that therapy and intellectual reconciliation was already and would continue to be the cultural critic.

In Tsuchida's assessment, academic philosophers and philosophy had been unable or unwilling to contribute measurably to the advance of social philosophy in Japan.[10] While formidable social problems clamored for explication and resolution, philosophers seemed reluctant to proffer principles for their solution.

> Following the Great European War, great changes have occurred in Japanese society, and as a result of the heightening of social perspective on the masses, it

---

[10] Tsuchida, *Contemporary Thought*, pp. 113–14. These and the judgments that follow are widely scattered through his other works but are conveniently compressed and summarized sporadically in the *Contemporary Thought* volume. According to Tsuchida's own account, he already held these persuasions when he entered Kyoto University in September 1915.

has come about that all affairs are judged from a social perspective. But only philosophy has not yet received this baptism. I hope that hereafter philosophy will involve itself with the social problems that have emerged; and developing ideas that have this new perspective, philosophy, in consequence, will be able truly to animate the spiritual life of the masses.[11]

But perhaps even if such remedial precepts were forthcoming, such academic notables, with their chilly detachment from newly emerged popular aspirations and their conservative inhibitions, would hardly stir an enthusiastic reaction or consequential reflection among the people. "The people, on their part, also seem not to expect such a message from those academic philosophers concerning any principle for the solution of social problems. On that account the concrete principles of social reconstruction will flow from some other source."[12] Philosophy had not hitherto nor would hereafter take part in illuminating, guiding, or informing social development. "Just so far as those academic philosophers fail to take an interest in the concrete and social problems or fail to have any notion of the new demands among the people, they cannot hope to be philosophers for today and tomorrow even with their fine and strictly logical construction of thought" (pp. 181–82). Yet it was to be hoped that in their future evolution the academic philosophies would formulate such principles. Ironically, that function was not basically antagonistic to their previous practices and pretensions.

While Japanese philosophy had come to be strictly "scientific," which represented a commendable advance that it was hoped could be sustained, this scarcely tempered Tsuchida's discontent, since "those academic philosophies needed to have the flexibility to comprehend in the

[11] See Tsuchida Kyōson, "Shōwa shisō no shōrai," in Zenshū, 15:23 (originally in Sekai, February 1927). Nishida seems in part to have been exempted from the critical thrusts that follow: "Nishida's philosophy is something that touches on contemporary life, and though one might hear abundant criticism of it in contemporary society, in reality this is merely immature objective materialism, and is it not to be regretted that those who give ear to this have no doubts about it whatsoever? Nishida himself makes the contemporary problems his own problems." (See Tsuchida Kyōson, "Nishida tetsugaku no jidai-igi," in Zenshū, 15:234.) "But in his ideas regarding such points as his conception of the self, of an absolute other bearing down upon the self, and his conception of a concrete 'person' which contains irrational elements, he touches even more upon contemporary life. And probably even in the theoretical structure of Nishida one can detect the reflection of the period. On these points one can laud his contemporary significance." (Ibid., p. 233.)

"At the time the nature of the critical world which made American and English philosophy its key was very unsatisfactorily lifeless, and for myself, I more and more continually and carefully reflected upon this and dug down into life to its very depths. I wished, thus, to tie together precisely life and philosophy." (Kamiki, "Tsuchida Kyōson, p. 76.)

[12] Tsuchida, Contemporary Thought, p. 114. The following quotations are all taken from this work.

most comprehensive manner the new desires necessarily produced by real society" (p. 116). Almost universally, academic philosophers, by Tsuchida's account, were unequal to any perceptive grasp of current social thinking and ideals. None of these philosophic practitioners had espoused any social philosophy, and they all seemed supremely disinterested in new social movements. "But this course cannot forever be supreme in the future development of Japan: and furthermore the idea of the state among the people must, hereafter, by the aid of the new social sciences, be greatly revised" (p. 115). And though those social sciences were still rudimentary in their principles and often crude in their imposition of the causal laws of the natural sciences on the facts of history, "the necessity for the study of the state or history from the viewpoint of these social sciences cannot be denied forever, no matter how primitive their development may be today" (p. 115).

Moreover, those social sciences were progressively maturing in their sophistication.

> The fundamental reason for the misunderstanding of the original meanings of the state among the academic philosophers hitherto must be attributed, on the contrary, to their inadequate knowledge of these social sciences. Therefore, what is most necessary for them is the acquisition of such knowledge. In this way they will undoubtedly be able to rid themselves of many prejudices and individualistic tendencies and accommodate the people's constantly increasing desires. (p. 116)

The academic philosophies, almost without exception, pronounced that the end of the historism at which they all had arrived was the state, but that dogma was no longer convincing or empirically tenable. Independent inquiry into the meaning of the state and whether it was indeed absolute or not was of the utmost urgency. Certainly the state had been in the past a typical form of the community. Especially in instance of Japan, the state had been singularly skillful in retaining its form. "But the state itself is a form of the social body that makes its contents continuously vary; and the modern state especially has continuously been and still is varying its social function. We cannot therefore comprehend a conception of state as being absolute forever" (p. 117).

But even if philosophy could be so faulted for its aversion to or avoidance of the social sciences, the latter themselves were not above critical reproach. Tsuchida travels the argumentative circle in both directions. This circumnavigation takes the form of a composite prediction-recommendation approach. It was in essence the hope that social science researches would be grounded even more than previously upon the present, actual conditions in Japan.

To be sure, because scholarship should be built upon a universal foundation, that the theories of social sciences take universalistic methods is natural. But, nonetheless, the social sciences are all historical sciences. And because they are not natural sciences, if they lose their realistic historical basis their scholarly structure becomes impossible. Hitherto in Japan, however, the social sciences have been excessively grounded on universalistic foundations, and I think they have been deficient in theories that were based on the social realities of our country. For example, even in the theories of the development, maturation, and changes in capitalism in Japan, there must be theories that are based upon the realities of our country.[13]

Such investigations into the special features of capitalism in Japan would of necessity be centered upon the socioeconomic relations between city and countryside. Were Japan to seize the initiative in such researches in the international scholarly world, it could provide indispensable clarifications. In this same regard, such empirical endeavors would elucidate the interrelated quandary of population movement and density.

The problems that arise simply as workers' problems or simply as rural problems are not always of greatest importance, and concealed in the background are social relations problems between city and countryside. The more the industrial-commercial position of our country rises, the more the area of the city is expanded. . . . This comparative increase will bring the greatest threat to the society of our country hereafter. And, consequently, those who will solve this problem must be the social scientists of our country perforce taking up these problems. . . . As regards population scholarship, at the very least the social science world of Japan must become the leading world authority.[14]

The geographic scope of the social sciences must also inescapably widen. Japanese national isolation was no longer tenable, and the entirety of Asia must come within the purview of social scientific edification.

The reverse circling now concluding, above all else,

In the end the social sciences must on the one hand cooperate all the more with philosophy and on the other conjoin with ethnic historical studies. Just as today certain of the social scientists show contempt for philosophy, they are incapable of seeing the correct state of affairs. Some indeed criticize a philosophy that seeks a social perspective, but when philosophy obtains a social outlook, at the same time the social scientist must have a philosophical view. The reason for conjoining the social sciences with ethnography is that this will make all the more objective and realistic the researches of the social sciences. It is also ethnic history which will teach the many-sidedness of social analysis to social studies

[13] Tsuchida, "Shōwa shisō," p. 24.
[14] Ibid., p. 25.

that have been constructed only on an economic angle of vision. At the same time, because ethnic historical studies can be critiqued from a social science viewpoint, those studies will escape simplistic national essence–localistic points of view. And it will be possible to make their range of vision universal.[15]

To some important extent there had already emerged promising philosophical antidotes and alternatives to the academic varieties that Tsuchida so energetically indicted. These were the "critics of civilization" who had been and were occupying a more and more prominent position in the intellectual world. Not surprisingly, given the catalog of sins academic philosophy was guilty of, it was these "philosophies" that currently exerted the greatest sway over the people at large. The genesis of these "critics of civilization" (and, for Tsuchida, "cultural critics," among whom he naturally ranked himself) was to be found in what were related variations and reiterations of Tsuchida's critique of academic philosophies. These philosophies were not distinguished, in the estimate of outsiders, for their admirable commitment to a view of the unity of life that was originally the ideal of philosophical speculation. These philosophies were sadly lacking in vividness of thought, and in their criticism of life these philosophies were persistently formalistic and not focused upon concrete matters.

> What the people at large want to solve, as they are confronted by them and brought into conflict with them, are their own actual lives. . . . The least philosophical are the philosophers, because their criticism of life is not pertinent to events of the day. . . . They have in general but little social interest and have not been dynamic enough in their attitude. . . . This academic philosophy has, in a word, been far from possessing a humanistic interest. It really does, I think, deserve the discontent of their people.[16]

These newly arisen and instructive "critics of civilization" shared among themselves common foci of dissatisfaction. All of them inveighed against academic philosophy as excessively scholastic, ideologically uniform, and negativistic in its attitude toward life. Contrarily, the "critics" have aggressively declared the direct object of their researches to be the contents of actual life. And in their philosophical thinking they were invariably dynamic and functional. "It will be possible for the critic of the day's civilization to find out any inconsistency between the academic knowledge and the actual life that is on the point of being revealed, to survey this inconsistency and then apply the plummet to it."[17] Thus were philosophy and the social sciences chastised, reoriented, revivified, and

[15] Ibid.
[16] Tsuchida, *Contemporary Thought*, pp. 149–50.
[17] Ibid., p. 151.

only approved if they submitted to the admonitions and example of the "cultural critic." In the opening statement of Tsuchida's early work, *Current Ideas on Civilization and the New Philosophy*, he had already pontificated, as personal credo and perhaps all-inclusive dictum, that anyone who attempted cultural criticism must have a philosophy of his or her own, but there were no limitations on all philosophers becoming cultural critics.[18]

However much indebted to and even derivative from Marxist and socialist theories Tsuchida's thinking was, for him these were only instructive, if insightful, systems of social analysis and did not constitute the ultimate social sciences. Characteristic of his analytical assault on contemporary Marxists was his indictment that they were guilty of a common fallacy: that of identifying their so-called science of history and society with the verifiable absolutes and predictabilities of the natural sciences.[19] In the end, if even the vaunted certainties and laws of the natural sciences wobbled at times, how much more inconstant and insupportable were the "certainties" and "absolutes" in the social sciences. Repeatedly Tsuchida mercilessly dissected and dismissed the commonplace assumption that Marxism and socialism were synonymous with the social sciences.[20]

Not the academic philosophies (unless chastened by the social sciences), not Marxism (unless divested of its formalism and anachronisms), not socialism (unless it be Tsuchida's purified culturalist distilling of socialism and anarchism into a new social theoretical elixir), but the social sciences (and these in increasingly refined and perpetually self-critical form) could chart the route to convincing social interpretation, to persuasive social philosophies, to appropriate social reconstruction.

But was it sufficient unto itself for the cultural critic to grapple heroically with social reality, dutifully and meticulously comprehend the exigencies of the times, reconstitute philosophy through the illuminations extracted therefrom, and learnedly and beneficently furnish the didactic principles for "social reconstruction"? Or must the cultural critic become the activist architect and institutional pioneer of "social reconstruction" as well?

It would appear that the answer was already eloquently expressed in Tsuchida's almost self-destructively active origination and involvement

[18] Kamiki, "Tsuchida, Kyōson," p. 75.

[19] See his discussion of necessity in the natural and social sciences in the section "Kaizō no mokuhyō," *Nihon Shina gendai shisō kenkyū* (Tokyo: Daichi shobō, 1926), pp. 326–30.

[20] For example, see his dense philosophical exploration of the history and evolution of the concept of materialism and its limitation in Marxism, in "Marukusu ni okeru yuibutsuron no genkai," *Nihon Shina gendai shisō kenkyū*, pp. 513–44.

through the 1920s (and until the end of his life) in a kind of Japanese experiment in "Proletcult," but without the revolutionary paraphernalia. Apparently inspired by the tract of the same name of the English husband/wife team M. E. and C. Paul, he launched an extraordinarily ambitious "Free University Movement" in Shinano.[21] It was intended as an adult education enterprise for the university-deprived masses and encompassed the full curriculum of a formal institution.

Now belatedly reappreciated as a neglected but noteworthy development in the mass education experiments of Taishō democracy, Tsuchida's Shinano Free University was the actualization of his lifelong attachment to the aspirations of Proletcult. In a sense, too, it was the translation of his ongoing speculative sociology of the masses into the education of the masses, and no doubt this later essay was heavily informed by the pedagogical experience. It was also a playing out of Tsuchida's idealized "cultural critic" role, embodied and engaged, presciently identifying the crucial social phenomena of the time, the masses: responding creatively to their needs as he conceived and judged them; fulfilling the compulsions of social reconstruction; and weaving his won social philosophy tapestry as he proceeded.

In this later essay the historical preeminence of the masses and the unsatisfied urgency for a definitive sociology of those masses were still being reaffirmed. Quite probably the Farmers' Movement, which Tsuchida notes demonstrated the "violent power of the rural masses," had previously summoned forth this dedicated venture into adult education. In an already long history of rural disquiet, with antecedents in the early Meiji and Tokugawa periods, increasing tenancy conflicts since the beginning of the century and climaxing after World War I became the central focus of farmer agitation. These collective outbursts were fused into their first national organization in 1922 when the Japan Farmers' Union became the vehicle for coordinating tenant protest and the elevation of farmer status. While expanding quickly and overseeing rural agitation it succumbed to the typical ideological-personal factiousness that subverted much of the left-wing activism at the time. Constantly impeded by government repression and devastated by the rural depression, from the 1920s, despite an assortment of farmers' organizations, the movement's national direction remained fractured and ineffectual. By the 1930s national coordination was defunct, although a veneer of unity was feebly superimposed by right-wing theorists during the Pacific War. Quite

---

[21] See M. E. and C. Paul, *Proletcult* (London, 1921). The work dealt with the workers' cultural organizations in Russia designed to cater to the proletariat's spiritual life, which its founders Bogdanov, Gorky, and Lunacharsky saw as a third of the revolutionary movement. It flourished briefly in 1922, but afterward its influence persisted in the aggressive "proletarian" cultural groupings of the later 1920s.

clearly, Tsuchida considered himself singularly qualified among the ideological competitors for the tutelage of these energized and often badly
managed masses.

In embryo in the fall of 1920, Tsuchida's intellectual child, the Shinano
Free University, emerged in full panoply by the late summer of 1921. Its
whirlwind career until 1926, a year after ill-health drove Tsuchida into a
grudging but still paternally involved retirement, displayed all his organizational, administrative, pedagogical, and intellectual versatility.

In one way or another the other Free Universities that emerged rapidly
after the mid-1920s—Uonuma, Hakkai, Matsumoto, Sasanoi, Okatani,
Gumma, Kyoto, and Miyashiro—were all indebted to Tsuchida's imagi-
native didacticism. For these he was often progenitor, solicitous consul-
tant, intellectual goad, and moral preceptor. He served also these roles in
contributions to the pages of *Jiyū daigaku zasshi* (Free University journal) that chronicled and propagandized, as did the journal, these proliferating academies for the masses.

# 6

## Disciplinizing Native Knowledge and Producing Place: Yanagita Kunio, Origuchi Shinobu, Takata Yasuma

H. D. HAROOTUNIAN

Folklore must not be considered an
eccentricity, an oddity or a picturesque
element, but as something which is very serious
and is to be taken seriously. Only in this way
will the teaching of folklore be more efficient
and really bring about the birth of a new
culture among the broad popular masses, so
that the separation between modern culture
and popular culture of folklore will disappear.
  *Antonio Gramsci (1931–33)*

## The Problematic of Discourse

If it is true that folkloric study (*minzokugaku*) originated in Yanagita Kunio's objections to a series of political decisions leading to the administrative merger of shrines in 1908, it is also arguable that the conceptualization of a new social object—the folk and its place—and the subsequent formation of a discipline were sustained by a larger cultural discourse that was already contesting assimilated forms of new knowledge, developmental theories of history and institutions, and practices based upon industrial production and exchange. The prewar discussions on the category of "society" and the "social" were principally prompted by a profound distrust for the effects resulting from instrumental knowledge, its disposition to differentiate spheres of learning into specialized disciplines reflecting more basic social divisions, and a progressive conception of history that, for some, derived its "poetry from the future" to endow the present with meaning. At stake was a modern knowledge that constantly threatened to introduce "difference," as contemporary history was recording it, and eradicate all of those aspects of life—identity—that

Japanese had recognized as the Sign of irreducible sameness. What social critics like Yanagita Kunio, Origuchi Shinobu, Takata Yasuma, and Aruga Kizaemon detected in the vast spectacle taking place before them was the dilemma of social determinacy in which declining remnants of a precapitalist order coexisted in an antagonistic relationship to a capitalist society seeking to prevent the fulfillment of an uncompleted past. The cohabitation of earlier modes of economic and cultural production alongside newer industrial forms in the same social space, what Ernst Bloch called "nonsynchronicity," demanded a resolution of the question of social determinacy—the principles of social cohesion, if the survivors of the past were not to be subdated by capitalism and its theory of social relationships.[1] This meant finding a conception of the social that could best preserve received elements as a guarantee of order without discounting the vast changes that had already occurred in Japanese society. Ultimately, this would entail a rejection of the concept of society itself as an object characterized by distinct laws of motion and forms of sociation for its absence, a hermeneutic capable of recognizing the modes of interaction between specific groups, the content of daily life, and its meaning for the collectivity.

Social theorists saw the establishment of new forms of political organization and economic activity founded on the fundamental division between city and countryside as the direct outgrowth of a new instrumental knowledge. More often than not, it was this sense of a modern society, usually associated with the Meiji Enlightenment, that writers sought to overcome in the years before World War II. The problem that writers like Yanagita and Origuchi perceived, not to mention others like Watsuji Tetsurō, who were less interested in formulating a "science of society," was the ruination of the countryside, seen increasingly as the locus of authentic identity, and the sacrifices it was being forced to make for an entirely new kind of social order based on urbanization and massive industrialization. A further effect of this division between city and countryside, it was frequently noted, was the growing imbalance in the distribution of resources and its consequences for continuing public security. Many thinkers already willing to read the consequences of this historic shift as an amorphous "social problem" requiring immediate attention also recognized that social relationships, classes, which the reorganization of polity and economy had necessitated, were becoming the occasion for conflict and civil disobedience. The subsequent analysis of the current situation was therefore bonded to the conviction that the central problems endangering Japanese society had been produced by the state which, it was believed, had single-mindedly implemented and pursued a policy

[1] Ernst Bloch, "Nonsychronism and the Obligation to Its Dialectics," *New German Critique*, no. 11 (Spring 1977): 22–38.

pledged to industrial transformation.[2] Hence, the very quest to think the social and avoid the concept of society as a distinct object altogether was implicated in the process it sought to understand and even manage, while the task of social theory was to envisage ways to preserve older forms of relationship and practice before their elimination as a necessary condition for seeking a solution to the question of division, fragmentation, and conflict.

The ensuing struggle over identity and the terms of difference prompted writers like Yanagita Kunio and Origuchi Shinobu to enlist the earlier nativist narrative (*kokugakuron*) announcing subject positions for the folk and their "household duties" to combat a story-line that was upholding the march of modernization led by bureaucratic rationality serving the imperial state.[3] Yet, this invariably presupposed relying on a concept of what one might call "intransitive knowledge" as an alternative to instrumental rationality and its penchant for manipulation. By intransitive knowledge, I am referring to a mode of knowing that closes the distance between knowing subject and the object of knowing because, it is believed, knowledge is constituted from the life and custom of the knower. As a result, practice and hermeneutic became one and the same things. But it is important to add that this identification of subject with object not only managed to reaffirm the centrality of the category of an exceptional culture in the 1920s and 1930s, it insisted upon annexing politics to its authority by refusing to differentiate it as a separate or semi-autonomous sphere of activity. It was precisely this inflection that led to the readiness among thinkers to identify the folk with the state and the state's later appropriation of folkic thinking.

## Voiceless Narrative: Ethnography of the Other

Among thinkers and social theorists before World War II, none was more consistent than Yanagita Kunio in finding ways to integrate the self into the larger system of community by reinstating native knowledge—custom—as the Sign of place. At its beginnings, Yanagita's ethnological project was founded on two not always mutually reconcilable principles: literary form and scientific methodology. Aspiring early to be a writer, he relied on the form of narrative to tell the timeless story of the folk and to present his ethnological findings as an eventless tale. The collection of data was thus prefigured by the authority of narrative in his first major publication, *Tōno monogatari* (1910), which he had constructed, even

---

[2] Matsuzawa Hiroaki, *Nihon shakaishugi no shisō* (Tokyo: Chikuma shobō, 1973), pp. 8–47.

[3] This is the argument I have proposed in my *Things Seen and Unseen: Discourse and Ideology in Tokugawa Nativism* (Chicago: University of Chicago Press, 1988).

though later texts tried to show that custom itself told the tale, as it was lived and produced by the ordinary folk and inscribed in the very materials reflecting their daily life. This link between literary form and the folkloric program was later amplified by Origuchi Shinobu, who saw in national literature, as against historical narrative, what he called the "classics of life." Yanagita's account of the tales derived from the Tōno region was not, by his own acknowledgment, based on firsthand observation but rather was a reworking of stories turned over to him. While he would later embark upon a lifelong journey into the field, placing himself in the position of the traditional traveler, not the teller of tales but its listener, both to collect data and to secure the effect of being witness to the self-presence and timelessness of the folk experience, he remained faithful to the ideal of the writer who transcribes rather than originates. After all, it was his purpose to give expression or reflection to what was already there, and to efface himself as the mediator, in order to permit the voiceless experience to speak which, he believed, would tell its own story, rather than report the observation of the field worker. In this regard, ethnology, so constituted, came closest to nativism precisely at the point where both relied on narrative. For just as Tokugawa nativism constructed a narrative of the folk from "literary" fragments to demonstrate the timeless interaction between divine creation and the human necessity to reproduce the conditions of social existence (custom), so Yanagita sought to collect data to affirm the timeless history of folkic life and therefore to show how those elements that constituted the bonding of social solidarity survived into the present.

Yet Yanagita, at the same time, consistently upheld the claims of scientific rigor. Accompanying the production of *Tōno mongatari* was an insistence, in a number of other texts, that the procedures of the new ethnology must always be scientific and thorough. According to Origuchi, the new spirit of *minzokugaku* promised to complete the nativist program by introducing the element of "doubt," which had been so remarkably absent in the "moral certainty" associated with *kokugaku*. Now, he wrote, *kokugaku* could fulfill its purpose in a way never before imagined and assert its privileged knowledge by linking it to doubt. Hence, Yanagita positioned doubt as an enabling factor for discourse and proposed that it constituted the precondition of research and the guarantee of a more complete understanding of contemporary problems. But scientific skepticism was the entry point to investigating the "extremely interesting material" offered by country life, which should be approached "rigorously."[4] A corollary of this conviction was his belief that such a

⁴ Yanagita Kunio, "Gendai kagaku to iu koto," in Tsurumi Kazuko, ed., *Kindai Nihon-shisō taikei, Yanagita Kunio shū* (Tokyo: Chikuma shobō, 1975), 14:390.

science should lead to the development of an agricultural economics based not on Western practice, but on indigenous experience. In this way Japanese ethnology sought to detach itself from its genealogical past, nativism, and to ideologize it by drawing attention to the "unscientific" character of its "moral certainty."

While the retelling of tales from Tōno clearly made a story of a certain kind indistinguishable from the scientific study of the folk, the narrative signified a more complex statement concerning the nature of contemporary social and political life. The tales recounted incidents of ordinary folk in their daily encounter with the deities, ancestors, family, and friends.[5] Far from confirming official pieties and the new narrative of modernity, which was centered on the emperor and the primacy of veneration and filialism as safeguards of solidarity (referring to the ideology of the family state produced by the late Meiji reforms), the tales dwell on a different story manifested in examples of unfiliality, concerns for the ancestors who reside in the place of the village, the spirits, and the deification of things populating the daily life. Rarely do they mention the emperor, who, even in the writings of nativists, remained remote from the lives of ordinary people and probably counted for little in them. What seems significant in Yanagita's reworking of these stories was the effort to forge a natural relationship between the deities of creation, which he later valorized in studies concerning the importance of tutelary worship, and the ancestors and activities of daily life. In the context of late Meiji, he was able to offer another version of the life history of ordinary folk that claimed greater authenticity than the recent narrative announced by the state. Not only were the lives of the ordinary folk shaped and directed by certain religious beliefs, but as survivors from the past, they possessed a timeless authority capable of contesting the more recent appeals of state shinto and its "rational" identification of deities, emperor, and family as constituent elements of a civil religion.

It is important to note that the *Tales of Tōno* appeared two years after the Shrine Merger Act (1908) and Yanagita's own well-documented effort to counter the bureaucratic encroachment into the countryside. The impulse to preserve what increasingly was called the "natural village" (itself a fiction) before its elimination by the state in Meiji Japan inspired a number of people like Yanagita to established a science that was both authoritative and useful to contemporary affairs. A series of reforms culminating in the merger of shrines and the subsequent creation of the "administrative village" (*gyōseimura*) prompted him and the botanist Kumagusa Minakata to focus attention on the profoundly dislocating

[5] Yanagita Kunio, *The Legends of Tōno*, trans. R. Morse (Tokyo: Japan Foundation Series, 1975).

consequences of administrative acts seeking to destroy the ecology of the so-called natural village. According to Yanagita, the policy to merge shrines meant eliminating many more and served only to promote the interest of administrative centralization that promised to undermine the established centers of folkic worship which residents of locales had known from time immemorial. By concentrating on a natural and human ecological crisis, folklorists were able to find a critical language for talking about bureaucratic politics that was free from the conventional parties or even the radical idiom of socialists. Yet the critique that Yanagita enunciated was directed less toward political policy than to the occasion to identify the larger contest over deciding the true content of cultural form. In his thinking, modern political structures were insensitive to broader questions of culture and the determinants of social solidarity. Here, he shared a common ground with late Meiji socialists who, like himself, were very much concerned with envisaging a social imaginary free from the constraints of politics and the state.[6] While Yanagita's own involvement in the controversy over shrine merger was far less political than the commitment of Kumagusa, with whom he eventually broke over the question of action, it is evident that the issue offered the opportunity to shift attention from a preoccupation with the social to considerations of culture, and not to wage political warfare. But promotion of the "natural village" led him to conclude, with Nitobe Inazō and other likeminded ruralists, that the real problem was the confrontation between city and countryside which, it was generally acknowledged, had already inflicted irreparable damage on the latter in the interest of developing the former. The countryside, Yanagita observed, has always been the place of "dignity" and "honor." "Urbanites," he continued, "have to remember the liveliness and freshness of the countryside." Yanagita worried that the situation had worsened in recent years since no policy had yet been formulated that acknowledged the necessity of "training people to enlarge their interests in the countryside."[7]

Despite Yanagita's own determination to find ways to remove a number of conflict-producing practices between small cultivators and landowners derived from the feudal past, his principal interest remained Japan itself as a place. But the countryside he sought to privilege as the authentic Japan was made to function metonymically and call attention to the whole, that is to say, "one's native place" (kyōdo). If his implication in rural affairs revealed a politically ambivalent vision comprised of

---

[6] Matsuzawa, Nihon shakaishugi, p. 32.

[7] Haga Noboru, Jigatashi no shisō (Tokyo: NHK shuppan kyōkai, 1973), pp. 110–12. This is the subject of "Jidai to nōsei," which puts forth the argument that the countryside is imperiled and requires systematic attention in the form of a viable agrarian policy rooted in an understanding of Japan's peculiar circumstances.

trying simultaneously to improve the lot of small cultivators while devising ideological devices aimed at eliminating conflict in the countryside, it was nonetheless consistent with a view that always saw Japan as an agricultural place and the sanctuary of timeless values and verities that attested to collective purpose free from mere history. But this move was really no different from an earlier decision to juxtapose the power of the Meiji Restoration (the state) to the countryside, and pit rural energy against the city, an enduring native wisdom against new rationalities.

Yet, Yanagita's countryside was an imaginary, constructed from a discourse that alone promised to conserve and preserve traces of a lost presence.[8] Ethnology, as he came to formulate it, became the place or space of discourse, which he sometimes referred to as a "science," where he was able to constitute a timeless Japan that was "always, already there." Finding "Japan" in this way, in discourse, Yanagita was undoubtedly restoring an absent signified rather than a different signifier altogether, which might have opened the way to a play of difference and been mobilized to subvert the prevailing ideology of the state before the war rather than succumb to it. As a signified, Japan therefore became the content of a

---

[8] The concept of social imaginary has been advanced recently by Cornelius Castoriadis, *L'Institution imaginaire de la société* (Paris: Seuil, 1975), and Claude LeFort, *Les Formes de l'histoire: Essais d'anthropologies politique* (Paris: Gallimard, 1978). While Castoriadis and LeFort employ the idea of a social imaginary to refer not to a specular image submitted to reflection but rather to the indeterminate ways all societies must go about organizing the production of material goods and the reproduction of its members, I have emphasized the dimensions of both imaging and imagining in the practice of Japanese ethnologists who literally invented Japan as a signified, and, thereby, demonstrated the crisis of determinacy that they were trying to conceal. Regardless of my own inflection, the conception still calls forth the way society seeks, through diverse forms of signification, to endow itself with an identity sufficiently different from other societies and from chaos.

It is important to point out, in this connection, that when Yanagita sought to articulate a "science" of the native place in this *kyōdo seikatsu no kenkyūhō* (1935), the "method" was indistinguishable from the object it presumed to study, recalling nativist conceptions of learning founded in intransitive knowledge. Several years earlier (1931), the Marxist historian Hani Gorō published an essay entitled *Kyōdo naki kyōdo kagaku* (A science of the native place without a native place) in which he announced that even by his time, "nine out of ten people in the population had been banished from their native place and do not effectively have one. Those people who believe they possess a native place today will no doubt discover that they have been deceived. The apparent relationship we and others have to a native place has been destroyed, or it has been changed to a relationship of fetters that is difficult to endure." For this reason, Hani remarked, "a science of the native place today is a 'science without the native place.' " While Hani's purpose was to contest the already preponderant concern of the native place in the early Shōwa period, evidenced in the scholarly activity of people like Yanagita and Origuchi, he wanted to discount this view as nostalgic and romantic in order to show how capitalism had undermined the countryside and how the masses would, through such a "science," be able to defend themselves against "deception," "reaction," and "alienation" produced by the "distortions" of the ideology of the ruling class.

discourse, a specific place found only in discourse, characterized by fixed identities, instead of the radical neutral zone located in the center as imagined by late Tokugawa nativists. Where the discourse on Japanese ethnology seemed to depart from nativism lies in its presumption to establish a coherent and homogeneous subject, what Yanagita called the "ordinary and abiding people" (jōmin), as a condition for eliminating the Other, radical difference and history. The construction of a fixed identity shared by all Japanese was in fact designed to remove the presence of an Other whose existence as the locus of difference would jeopardize the stability of established subject positions. Yanagita was able to accomplish this by reducing the importance of reproduction—work—for forms of worship as a defining characteristic of the jōmin and thereby diminishing the relationship with the Other, which would have been a condition for ceaseless practice. The operation resulted in eliminating both the centrality of the body, working for the place of the Other, and the desire that compels people relentlessly to seek reunion with it. Failure to grasp the heterogeneity of the Other, the site of difference, meant that practice and activity were no longer emblems of the folk, since nothing was left to function as the object of desire. When Origuchi Shinobu proposed his theory of the "gods who rarely come" (marebito) as the irreducible source of difference and otherness, he seems to have gotten no further than Yanagita, even though it was his intention to displace the source of creativity to the place of the Other. For, he ended up specifying the Other in exceptional terms, particularizing it, in order to elucidate "national character" and the special characteristics of Japan's folk unconsciousness.

Instead of concentrating on reproduction and the activity of the body, Yanagita, confronting what he believed to be the spectacle of modernity and the devastating consequences of its division of labor, devoted his discipline to examining the problematic nature of the social bonds that united people in the hope of finding enduring forms of cohesion capable of guaranteeing lasting social solidarity. Fearful of failing to realize the prospect of social cohesion through the mechanism of difference, privileged by capitalism, individualism, and competition, he resorted to a logic of social likeness characterizing an older order that still persisted in the villages of Japan. Later, especially after the war, when signs of disintegration seemed to be everywhere and the necessity for national solidarity appeared to be more urgent than at any time in Japan's modern history, he appealed to native religious practices, especially tutelary and ancestor worship, to reinforce the structure of resemblance to link individuals more closely, directly, and harmoniously with society in order to secure the effect of making action and behavior spontaneous, unreflective, and collective. Here, it seems, is a possible explanation for the tragedy of Yanagita's immense achievements and the ethnological movement's inability to contest the state, apart from launching rather pallid campaigns protesting the consequences of unbridled industrialism on the environment, and why the state could easily appropriate the folklorist conception of a fixed identity attesting to sameness among all Japanese yet subvert it into official declarations announcing cultural exceptionalism and racial uniqueness. In this way, a social science of Japan became a Japanese social science.

Yanagita's discourse constituting Japan as a signified aimed to "forget" the eventfulness that had transported Japanese society into an industrial order since the Meiji era by constructing a new narrative. But this narrative centered a vanished place (in actuality a no-place, neither here nor there, past nor present, true nor false) and thereby projected the great antimonies of nature and culture, origin and presence, identity and difference. Recounting this history, not the history of politicians and generals, as he put it, promised to give expression to the story of society itself. Hence, his narrative of the ordinary and abiding folk functioned ideologically precisely in its promise to "forget" by intervening with the purpose of displacing into language the system of contradictions. In this way, the folkic narrative of place promoted the image of a sequential solution to the contradictions, and in discourse—the production of place—they became the fiction of synthesis, a harmonious order of reconciliation. This "transformation-in-the-telling constitutes the history of the group," which itself is constituted through and by the narrative of place. In Yanagita's texts, the telling—speaking for the voiceless folk, or being spoken by them—would seek to explain and "clarify what normally, in lived experience, remains opaque, uncertain and even dangerous. The original insurmountable antithesis of everyday activity is thereby explained." But within the discourse an even more important transformation was accomplished: the narrative of place guaranteed "the exchange of contradictory poles." What appeared to have developed along the trajectory of a storyline that is history is now transmuted into "the time of narrative discourse."[9]

History itself, Yanagita wrote, had repressed the voice of the folk and remained silent on their position. Historical narratives have "obscured the role of ordinary folk by concentrating only on wars and heroes." Even those records that disclose aspects of farming life in the past have invariably been written down by governmental officials and village officials. A three-thousand-year-old genealogy of the folk in Japan has scarcely been transmitted in writing. Because the contemporary historical view has

---

[9] Louis Marin, *Utopics: Spatial Play*, trans. Robert A. Vollrath (Atlantic Highlands, N.J.: Humanities Press, 1984), pp. 36–37. The preceding formulations derive from Marin's penetrating study of utopias.

placed so much weight on written materials, he remarked in an essay expressing hope for a history of the native place, the history of Japan appears as nothing more than a sustained account of war and politics,
"great events which relate the story of politicians and military struggle."
It should be noted that Yanagita was drawing attention to a historical
practice that had privileged the subject/individual as the author of action,
and value and eventfulness as the content of narrative.

Like nativists, Yanagita felt compelled to find a way of representing the
folk who did not write about themselves but, nevertheless, "actually
moved society until recent times." The practice of historical narrative invariably suppressed this fact, excluded the primary role played by the
folk, and remained adamantly silent on the details of the daily life. Nativists had shown that only reengagement of these activities will reveal the
genuine origins of society. In fact, it was writing itself, as a specific ideo-
graphic practice, that had effaced the memory of the folk and their ceaseless reproduction of custom. Before the formal development of ethnology
(*minzokugaku*), he observed, there had existed a history of place and the
daily life (*kyōdo seikatsu*) "always, already there," waiting to be rescued
from concealment. By rejecting written traces and the narrative story-line
they invariably embodied, Yanagita was able to turn away from signs for
things in order to hear that other language, in fact, the language of the
Other, without words or discourse, of sameness and identity that had
remained buried beneath the humus of historical writing. What he sought
to write was a "history" of the folk and their interaction with custom, to
create a new situation through the power of performance, speaking about
themselves, on their own authority, on the basis of their own experience,
and unmediated by another's language in order to avoid writing a "history" described from the other's language, whether it was reason or political power or both. "The history we have become acquainted with," he
wrote, "is repetitive" and appears as the unbroken record of daily life that
has been repeated over and over again.[10] In fact, he wanted to present this
account as a living narrative, as speech and performance, before it was
crushed beneath the language of historical progress, dominated, beaten
to the ground, a folk made into an object of otherness and exiled to mu-
seums. But when he embarked upon this project, he presumed the pose of
"methodical innocence" to speak from the place of the Other, the folk in
this instance, and presented himself as the traditional traveler, not the
teller or transformer of the tale, but its listener. His aim was to collect raw
data and achieve the effect of being a witness to the self-presence of the
folkic experience. Hence, Yanagita committed himself to the impossible

[10] Gendai Nihon Shisō Taikei, *Yanagita Kunio*, ed. Masuda Katsumi, (Tokyo: Chikuma
shobō, 1965), 29:20. Hereafter YK.

task of trying to speak for the folk outside of the very language of power and reason—history—which had concealed them from view. In this respect, he misrecognized his task and failed to see that the misfortune of the folk, the "interminable misfortune of their silence" and their own failure to secure representation for themselves, lay precisely in the fact that when one attempted to convey their silence from their place, "one had already passed over to the side of the enemy," the side of history, writing, and reason, "even if one fights against" it by calling its claims into question.[11]

Regardless of the paradox of this misrecognition, Yanagita's program of developing a discipline devoted to immediacy and self-presence, aimed at retrieving an absent signified, seemed to match a desire to make this "science" useful to the present. "The first objective of studying the native place," he wrote in 1935, "is, in a word, to know the past of commoners . . . to know ourselves."[12] This path was not historical progression but genealogical succession. "The footprints of the life of the people's past has never stopped," and the concrete, material practices involving food, shelter, clothing, yearly rituals, and beliefs constitute enduring forms of life immune to historical change. Even those practices and material artifacts that have originated in a distant past invariably appear as new manifestations when contemporaries embrace them in their daily lives. According to this vision, history is eventless and consists of sediments piled on top of each other to resemble the imperceptible growth of a large icicle.[13] Yet, the manifold layers function palimpsestically to disclose the shapes of earlier forms of practice gleaming beneath the surface. "Although straw rain coats (*mino*) are repeatedly made anew every year," he observed, "it is still the same rain coat as was made in the past."[14] By diminishing the division between past and present in vital activities related to daily life, Yanagita believed he had found a way to validate the practical purpose of his discipline. The search for knowledge from a variety of "real facts of life that exist before us" would result in "supplementing common sense."[15]

Yanagita's disclosure of a new "history" signified by the "study of place" aimed at discounting synthetic conceptions of the world of human

---

[11] This kind of criticism was leveled by Jacques Derrida against Michel Foucault's *Folie et déraison: Historie de la folie a l'age classique* in *Writing and Difference* (Chicago: University of Chicago Press, 1978), p. 36.

[12] YK, pp. 279–80.

[13] Tsurumi Kazuko, "Yanagita Kunio's Work as a Model of Endogenous Development," *Institute of International Relations Research Papers* A-26 (Tokyo: Sophia University, 1975), pp. 13–14; also, *Hyōhaku to teijū to* (Tokyo: Chikuma shobō, 1977), pp. 86 ff.

[14] YK, p. 283.

[15] Ibid., p. 19.

species that overlooked the particularity of unrecorded custom. But it was critical of all those evolutionary schemes that emplotted the development of society according to criteria of scientific and technological progress. Commenting on H. G. Wells's *History of the World*, Yanagita observed that despite the claim of a general history, "there are peoples who are not in this world history." The reason for this exclusion was the absence of writing systems among many peoples, while others, like the African bantu, have been represented by their conquerors.[16] In this way, he condemned the paradox of a historical discipline that remained silent on those principal aspects of Japanese life that were embedded in the repetition of practices and constituted the ordinary life.

Ultimately, Yanagita concentrated on the central role of the "abiding and ordinary folk" (*jōmin*) whose lives were regulated by intersubjective relationships inscribed in customs and things.[17] While this interest no doubt stemmed from his concern for the cause of rural relief and the search for a method capable of avoiding class conflict, it was also prompted by a profound conviction that when ties binding people disappear, the expected consequence will invariably produce conflict and disharmony. The effect of his reconceptualization of classes into *jōmin* was to emphasize a neutral association over a socially specific referent in order to establish the conditions for a fixed common identity, rather than differences corresponding to class membership.

This concern for a supraclass identity, social solidarity, the guarantee of stable relationships between people, led Yanagita to religion itself. The idea of folkic religious practices was inherent in any consideration of one's native place. As Origuchi Shinobu explained, Yanagita had always been interested in the deities and ancestors and shared with the great nativist scholar Hirata Atsutane a life-long conviction that coupled religious practices with social solidarity.[18] Where they differed was over the function each delegated to the deities and ancestors. For Hirata, the call to the hidden world, the governance of Ōkuninushi and the ancestors beyond, was a way of emphasizing the role ordinary folk were supposed to play in the great cosmic narrative, which was reproducing the conditions of social existence as a form of repayment to the blessings of the gods. With Yanagita, reproducing the means of life lost its primary importance to considerations that viewed the native religious system as an irreducibly Japanese inflection, because the spirits of the dead (*shinrei*) always return to the "native place" to repeat the process of watching over their descen-

16 Ibid., pp. 283–84.

17 Tsurumi, "Yanagita Kunio's Work," pp. 7–13, for a convenient summary of meanings related to the term *jōmin*.

18 Origuchi Hakushi Kinenkai, *Origuchi Shinobu zenshū* (Tokyo: Chūō kōronsha, 1956), 20:349–50.

dants from their "unseen" mountain perspective. Proposing this meaning in his *Senzō no hanashi* (Talking about the ancestors), Yanagita remarked that the idea of people becoming spirits after death and remaining rooted in the place of their former life conferred significance on the life of the living and offered the necessary bonding for community relationships. As for the idea of the afterlife among the Japanese, he wrote, the spirits reside in the national soil forever. The belief that they do not go to a distant place has been deeply rooted since the time of antiquity and has persisted continuously down to the present.[19] By emphasizing the role of the ancestors and their relationship to the household and clan deities, he believed he had found a way to bring about the reconstruction of the native place in modern times. Ultimately, this religious view permitted him to conceptualize an alternative to the modern state and its social imaginary which, he believed, caused conflict and struggle owing to its privileging of power relationships, individual interest, and difference. In its place he envisaged the tutelary shrine as the form of a stable order that was more religious than political. Here, his study of the native place was applied to elucidating the spiritual topography of Japan's religious inheritance, with its centering of a communitarian consciousness produced by the household and forms of worship guaranteeing its continuity, which, he observed in 1931, distinguished the Orient from Western rural society.

After World War II, Yanagita expanded the role of common worship in a series of three essays that might more appropriately be called "Discussions on the New Nativism" (*Shinkokugakudan*): "Considering National Holidays" (*Saijitsukō*), "On Mountain Shrines" (*Sangūkō*), and "Clan Deities and Parishioners" (*Ujigami to ujiko*). While the "new nativism" had already been articulated as early as 1935 when he called for a new method to study the native place, it was now employed to explain to a defeated nation how the folk might restore the country's well-being and their good fortune. Predictably, his assurances for recovery relied on the willingness of the people to reinstate in their lives the characteristic religious beliefs of Japan, which meant expanding the tutelary shrine system beyond its prewar level. War and defeat demonstrated the calamitous nature of the modern state, he argued, reaching a conclusion already advanced by Marxists for different reasons. But the effort to resuscitate tutelary worship as the foundation for national renewal aimed at establishing a communitarian order that might, in some way he never really explained, replace the structure of the state altogether yet secure the guarantee of social solidarity, a view still held by his *epigoni*, the historian Irokawa Daikichi and the poet Yoshimoto Takaaki.

Recalling Tokugawa nativists and their own discussions concerning ag-

[19] YK, p. 273.

ricultural beliefs, Yanagita explained that the word for tutelary—*ubu-suna*—derived from remote antiquity and referred not simply to the place of one's birth but more broadly to the names of the deities associated with a specific locale. Actually, he wrote, the term means the "place of the deities" and connotes both the gods of a locality and the locality itself. As a result of this association, place became an object of worship. Because it acquired the status of a sacred sanctuary, people were required to make the appropriate acts of respect. "The place occupied by the folk is that of the tutelary gods or clan deities. It is not erroneous to use both terms interchangeably."[20] Worship of these sacred places was performed in common by large numbers of people who lived in the village or locale where the shrine had been erected. But, he warned, this regional associations never meant to exclude outsiders from religious participation at the shrine. It was for this reason, Yanagita observed, that people in Japan were eventually identified according to place rather than blood ties or even landownership. Yet the effect of this proposition concerning place was to show that any place or region was as good as another, and all or each could easily substitute for Japan, the "native place of one's birth," and vice versa. Japan as an expanded tutelary shrine where all pay their respect to the place of birth promised to secure both guarantee of commonality and the lasting relationships capable of insuring social cohesion. "The space of the deities," he noted, "was really the place of the village," and worshipping the clan or guardian god was really making observances to place and its inhabitants, the "ordinary and abiding folk." "When referring to the *kamisama*, the gods, which is the language of our commoners, and speaking of temples and shrines, what these mean are our villages and households. They are the same words for father and mothers."[21]

By invoking the relationships and associations implicated in tutelary belief, Yanagita was certain that he had discovered the necessary authority for a logic of likeness capable of reintegrating Japanese society in the immediate postwar years. He also believed that he had effectively clarified the question of respect for the communal deities, which had been so recklessly manipulated by the prewar state, as a preparatory move to replacing the discredited state shinto with a renewed veneration of the *kami*, who are bonded to the household, village, and place. A revitalized conception of kami respect, now stripped of its debilitating associations with the state and public power, might reveal itself in the regular visitation of large numbers of people to shrines of place and thereby illuminate the intimate relationship between folk and the gods. Yanagita hoped that the

[20] Haga Noboru, "Yanagita Kunio to Origuchi Shinobu," in Furukawa Tetsushi and Ishida Ichirō, eds., *Nihon shisōshi kōza* (Tokyo: Yuzankaku, 1977), 8:223.
[21] Ibid., p. 225.

present was appointed to fulfilling this immense task of reviving the more simple and authentic form of kami worship akin to ancestor veneration and to eradicating definitively the memory of the state's cynical appropriation of shintō for "moral" mobilization. "To preserve the space of the kami," he wrote, "we must once more restore a view that advocates the idea of the sacred place as it had existed in an earlier age."[22] Convinced that the renewed belief system was synonymous with communal and household worship, he called this act of society worshipping itself a "confidence of plenitude." Defeat seemed to offer the Japanese a second historical opportunity to restore this basis of social solidarity, which the earlier commitment to modernity had nearly destroyed, and reinstall a worship of the deities, which, as a result of the "confidence of plenitude," would secure for all time the self-presence of place.

## The Place of Literature

If Yanagita's discourse was devoted to identifying the ties of social cohesion stemming from a logic of likeness, and centered place and worship of it to constitute the voiceless narrative of the "ordinary and abiding folk," Origuchi Shinobu (1887–1953) sought to locate the origins of this narrative in a preliterate orality and the production of a "literature" that had existed prior to literature and which attested to the enduring sense of plenitude, self-presence, and immediacy. Yet despite his own effort to distance his discourse from Yanagita by emphasizing its "scientific" rigor, Origuchi's concerns rarely strayed from considerations of identity and social solidarity. At the heart of this theory identifying the production of "literature" with a specific place was the earlier nativist presumption that only the ancients had achieved a perfect correspondence among word, thing, and intention, which the subsequent adoption of writing had destroyed. Origuchi's reformulation of this idea led to an explanation of how literary consciousness had erupted in archaic times as a result of an interaction between the first Japanese and the ordinary things of their placement. To recover this trace of authenticity, he turned to a "scientific" study of literature as the most authoritative expression of this lapsed experience which, regardless of the domination of writing since earliest times, remained inscribed in the folk consciousness.

A self-proclaimed follower of Yanagita Kunio, Origuchi fixed Hirata's brand of nativism as the indisputable source of folkic studies in Japan.[23] It was his conviction that nativism represented the beginning of Japan's

[22] Ibid., p. 224.
[23] Origuchi, *Origuchi Shinobu zenshū* 20:348 ff.

entry into the modern world and thus constituted a vital stage in the development of an ethnological discipline. But while nativism had concentrated on the question of origins and ethical practicality—the necessity of
daily life—folkic studies were first and foremost rigorously scientific and
empirical. A social science made in and for Japan alone was no science at
all but only sentimentality if it failed to develop a method capable of application elsewhere. To make good this claim, Origuchi expanded his research agenda by carrying on field work in surrounding areas like the
Ryukyu Islands. But his interest in Okinawan shamanism was prompted
most by a desire to find in the present enduring examples of archaic Japanese practices. Because folkloric studies derived from nativism, the discipline was unable in the end to shake off those particularistic associations that could only compromise its claims to a science.

In an essay entitled "The Tradition of Hirata Nativism," Origuchi insisted that Hirata was, above all else, a scholar devoted to integrity who
possessed a broad learning that was always characterized by moral intensity and a deep and abiding love for scholarship.[24] More than any other
thinker of his day, Hirata single-handedly liberated learning from a reliance on Chinese knowledge. And it was precisely this critical moment
that Origuchi claimed to have detected in Hirata's later texts that qualified *kokugaku* as a proto-science of ethnology. In its exploration of language and later religiosity, nativism constituted a "backbone" discipline
that successfully uncovered the authentic image of ancient history and its
moral structure. "A nativism without this dimension," Origuchi wrote,
"cannot exist." What this signified was the development of a new style of
learning that "must be passionate" and even sensuous. For, he continued,
"it is not sufficient merely to acquire knowledge meditatively, because it
must also be endowed with elements of activity." Nativism, he believed,
had been the learning of active and practical belief. "Today," he urged at
the outbreak of World War II, "the time has arrived to act according to
[this] exercise of moral passion. While we must always aim for the accomplishment of this goal [practice], the time is ripe for us to act."[25]

Origuchi believed that "Japan, since antiquity, has been at a standstill,"
which now must be overcome if the folk is to be united with its original
purpose. Yet, the "history of Japan is filled with examples of believing in
miracles."[26] The miracle he apparently was referring to was the basic belief system the Japanese disclosed first in antiquity and to which the present is destined to return for renewed inspiration. While Origuchi appeared more patriotic than scientific during the war, he had always

---

[24] Ibid., p. 331.
[25] Ibid., p. 318.
[26] Ibid., p. 319.

insisted that a scientific ethnology, consistent with its own origins, depended upon the active dissolution of the framework authorized by narrative historical time, much in the manner of the ancient histories he and
nativists examined. The aim of his own approach was to "give expression
to a new nativism. The point is to look at the origins of ancient beliefs,
which have been rationalized and modernized. . . . This new nativism derives from ancient practices, from the study of social and personal affairs,
and instructs us on how and why we must make a fresh start."[27] Neither
philosophy nor religion was adequate to an understanding of these remote facts. But he acknowledged that the fresh start he was envisaging as
a project had already been inaugurated by Yanagita and folkic studies,
which was promising renewal in the present. If such an inquiry were made
from a perspective opposed to conventional narrative, it would enable an
experiencing of past and present or past in present without encountering
the discontinuous differentiations demanded by historiography. For Origuchi, such a move required abandoning rationality in order to become
steeped in the particularistic rationalities of the ancient Japanese rather
than the logic of the Greeks. Contemporaries who study national consciousness and the folkic spirit invariably come up against the blind alley
of "utility," "rationality," and "reason." The prayers from antiquity and
the oral poetry of the epics are the "originating place of folkic theory,"
which he called the "logic of the gods" that would provide the surest
entry to a place that existed before and beyond reason.[28]

If the power of rationality failed to grasp the shape of the past, here
was sufficient reason to employ an alternative method of retrospection.
Origuchi was convinced that remote antiquity was "transhistorical" and,
therefore, functioned as a kind of transcendental signified. As a result, he
believed he needed to find a method capable of securing retrospective certainty, or, as he explained, a means that might permit a "regression" to
this concealed place of unreason. This regressive method required an exercise of "actual sensation" (jikkan), which, thereby, would enable the
empathic observer to live actively the past in the present and the "heart/
mind (kokoro) to know correctly the relationship between all kinds of
things."[29] Actual sensation, as imagined by Origuchi, summoned more
than a passing resemblance to Motoori Norinaga's conception of "knowing mono no aware" as it was now resituated within the idiom of Dilthey's more accessible hermeneutic (since Japanese romantics were already praising its claims) based on empathetic reenactment (erlebnis,

[27] Kindai Nihon Shisō Taikei, Origuchi Shinobu shū, ed. Hirosue Tamotsu (Tokyo: Chikuma shobō, 1975), 22:6 ("Kodai kenkyū" tsuigaki).

[28] Ibid., p. 368.

[29] Ibid., p. 369. Also, this is the method he employs in Okina no hassei; see ibid., pp. 77,
79, 92.

*einfühlung*). Looking back years later (1950), he referred to this conception of "actual sensation" as the "expressive method," which, for him, had the same feel as the "method of representation." Because representation itself appears limited to the level of form alone, he said, "I have used the term 'expressive method' because I have aimed at the place where form and content interact."[30]

As a consequence of this methodological shift, Origuchi was convinced that his "expressive method" would be able to chart a detour around conventional historical narrative and open a direct way to reaching antiquity through the activity of "grasping local life." By dehistoricizing antiquity it was, he believed, possible to make it accessible to contemporaries as a living experience. The operation would transform the ethnologist into a poet. As a result, Origuchi appeared driven by two seemingly paradoxical agendas: He wanted to pursue the study of folk beliefs in the present, yet he was simultaneously interested in looking at the past as a condition for understanding the real present. It was for this reason that he embarked upon a program of field work in the Ryukyus, especially Okinawa, where he believed the transmitted legends were still enacted and "revealed the shape of ancient Japan. In the contemporary life of the Ryukyu Islands, especially its interior life, we are able to see the life of men from the time of the *Man'yō* as it was."[31] When he declared his intention to transcend conventional historical time to reach a place that had existed before time and reason, a vision he insisted appeared only "intermittently" in folk memory, he was referring to a past that had not yet been fixed or defined by the establishment of emperors, dynasties, and chronology. It came close to resembling a place of radical heterogeneity. Here, Origuchi turned against historians for their "unfortunate endeavor" of "slicing up time according to months and years." The past he wished to rescue could not be measured by time or fixed by political markers. What he envisaged was a perspective that deprivileged historical content for the elevation of timeless form. Empathetic understandings offered reunion with antiquity, the Other, and the prospect of living among the ruins of antiquity as if they existed in the present. Accordingly, antiquity was spirit as it acquired manifestation in the survival of artistic forms and skills.

While Origuchi acknowledged the difficulties encountered in distinguishing between history and legend, he doubted the veracity of the so-called historical method to actualize the "logic of antiquity." "Since the results of historical discourses (*shiron*) are supposed to be realized in the

---

[30] Ibid., p. 370, from "Nihon bungaku keimō," quoted from an article by the editor of this volume.

[31] Ibid., p. 376.

concrete," he observed, "I think that the novel must be advanced anew in order to discover the shape of the (human) drama. In this, I have used the form of the novel as the expressive means to study tradition and legend."[32] Literature, then, and especially the novel, by which he undoubtedly meant classic verbal fictions, permitted direct engagement of the concrete real as no historical method could. Yet, it was precisely this move that had led him to favor ethnology (*minzokugaku*) over history, which he came to describe variously as an "assisting discipline to the study of national literature" or as a "classic of life."[33] The former called attention to the intimate connection between literature and folklore, while the latter aimed to translate the folk into a living text. After all, he wrote, "literature aims at excavating the theories of social life. Since the human legends are solely things that illuminate the individualistic causes of folk character, the study of national literature must depart from the same place where the study of ethnology makes its goals."[34] Hence, ethnology is the authentic reflection of national life and prompts people to recall the "seduction of older forms of life." In the "customary" of unknown origins, Origuchi believed he had located the "classics of life." Elsewhere, he supplemented this sentiment by proposing that *minzokugaku* consists of the "affairs transmitted from antiquity, whether they relate to households or religion" and consequently functions as a "prior knowledge" (*sendai no chishiki*). Antiquity escaped becoming a stage in the passage of historical time because ethnology was able to reenact the archaic life in the present and resuscitate it not simply as relics but as living reminders of the continuity of forms. "In our life," Origuchi remarked, "because we have proceeded on two paths, one whose meaning lies in the past, the other oriented toward the future, the fixed traces of the former have been passed on to us in ethnology and folklore." But, he noted, an ethnology so constituted could never be limited to mere study and research. "Its actualization is not realized as knowledge alone but reached through the contents of one's life."[35] It is, in fact, a performative.

In his seminal essay *Kokubungaku no hassei* (The production of national literature), published in 1924, Origuchi turned to showing that a real break existed between contemporary literary practice in Japan and its starting point in a time before "literature" and writing. He complained that contemporary literary practice had long departed from the aims and

---

[32] Quoted in Hasegawa Masaharu, "Origuchi Shinobu no 'gaku' no kōzō," in Takahashi Tetsu, ed., *Origuchi Shinobu o "yomu"* (Tokyo: Gendai kikakushitsu, 1981), p. 90.

[33] Origuchi, *Origuchi Shinobu zenshū* 16:483–92.

[34] Ibid., 15:24–25.

[35] Ibid., 16:491. See Kindai Nihon Shisō Taikei, *Origuchi Shinobu shū*, 22:386–89, for Origuchi's argument for realizing the past in the present from the "perspective of one's heart" and his conception of a transhistorical antiquity.

goals of literature that attended the genesis of its production. In fact, the presumption of uniformity of forms and goals between antiquity and the present is the product of later development and "literary conventions." The appearance of prose and its "power of representation" came rather late in the history of the folk. Yet prose, even though it managed to "tame" speech, had no reason for existence outside of conversation, which stemmed from the daily usage of the folk. Prose developed in order to transmit "great eventfulness," which speech, owing to its immediacy and self-presence, could not accommodate or preserve. Composition, writing down sentences (*seibun*), suppressed the motive power behind poetry and obscured its links to daily speech, which Origuchi acknowledged was no longer accessible even though its founding source lay in "words of the gods."[36] What he hoped to demonstrate with this critical observation is how modern literary consciousness had misrecognized the profound discontinuity between the two moments, past and present, performance and prose, presence and absence, and failed to see that archaic "literature" constituted a site of genuine difference. For Origuchi, recalling archaic difference was reaffirming life over death. No conventional scientific method could reach this place. But an empathetic "leap" over the forms authorized by written literature would deliver one to this "distant place." "The so-called folk memory," he wrote as early as 1916, is "revived intermittently throughout the ages."[37] This unending process of recall and repetition reveals "an emotional and imagined recollection" pointing to the "mother country," a "yearning for the distant land." This place of otherness was the land of "wealth" and "good fortune." Folk memory, he argued, constantly returns to search for this place, which in archaic times was called the "land of eternal night" (*tokoyo*). In time, this world of dreaded gods who lived in permanent darkness was changed into the place of "good fortune" and "wealth," and its godly tenants were transformed into deities who would make periodic visits from the "distant place." For Origuchi, this revelation from folkic memory recalling a distant land not only offered an explanation for real difference, thereby illuminating the reason why folklore was the "classic of life," but also showed the real origins of arts, skills, and literature. Ultimately, literature appeared as the site of the Other, and place became text.

In the context of this argument, Origuchi introduced his controversial conception of the *marebito*, the men-gods who came yearly from the distant land to incant prayers related to communal agricultural cultivation. At this juncture, it should be observed that Origuchi's marebito diverged widely from Yanagita's "spirits," who were the departed ancestors of the

[36] Kindai Nihon Shisō Taikei, *Origuchi Shinobu shū*, 22:129.
[37] Ibid., p. 21.

living. While Yanagita's "spirits" or "ancestors" had once lived in the
world of the living and continued their links with the household as a result of ritual observances accorded to them by their descendants, the
marebito were gods who resided in the Other World (takai) and were
called to make periodic visits to enrich the human community. These
marebito were men-gods who were distinguished from the deities on
high. "The original meaning of the marebito," he explained, "refers to
the gods who come at appointed times, from the sky and from beyond
the seas, to certain villages. They bring about bounty in a number of
things, wealth and good fortune, and it was believed by villages that such
accomplishments were godly deeds. These gods were not the product of
a religious imagination since the villagers of antiquity had heard the
marebito, at the time of their annual visitation, pushing against the doors
of houses."[38] They were guests, Origuchi explained, and even "strang-
ers," whose visitation coincided with the yearly cycle of "village production" and whose prayers and recitations invoked abundant harvest and
good fortune. It was for this reason that the later "traveling teller of tales"
(kataribe) sung songs and told stories about planting, production, and the
continued good fortune of the community. Moreover, the kataribe aimed
at recounting in prose poems the relationship among the gods, the household, and the land. In time, the form of recitation changed into more
"mature" genres and finally into historical narratives and verbal fictions.
In this inflection, Origuchi noted a similar evolution of political forms
from the village to the state, which seemed to accompany the passage of
literary form from orality and speech to writing and settled representation. Inscribed in this formulation was the assumption of an original link
between literary production and utterance, "godly words" and "good
deeds" to constitute the most fundamental form of expression, recalling
both nativist considerations of language and prayer and the even more
important suggestion of desire for the distant land, the place of radical
difference. Folk memory had designated this place as the site of difference
and hence the object of desire that is reached only in the last instance,
which never comes.

Origuchi further specified that tokoyo, in its old usage, came close to
meaning "constancy" (kōjō), "unchanging" (fuhen), and "absolute" (zet-
tai) more than mere longevity or even eternality, to supply an argument
for the primacy of spatiality over temporality, permanence of place over
the changes of time.[39] For the ancients, the distant land was a far-off place
separated by sea, out of sight to villagers who stood on the shores and
tried to visualize the destination of ancestral spirits. In the end, only the

[38] Ibid., p. 37; also p. 138.
[39] Ibid., p. 167.

dead went there. The archaic spirits had revealed this truth, but since that time "belief in the deities of earth has receded." Still, there appear "flashes" of this archaic spirit in *minzokugaku* and the promise of releasing its light in the present. Origuchi had recognized that ancient folk traditions had gradually perished in modern Japan, but he also believed that there was still time enough to redeem them because of the inheritance of an "unusually ancient spirit." Yet the critical ground Origuchi seems to have gained by resorting to a "science" that displaced the source of creativity to the place of the Other was invariably lost by specifying the Other, an "absent signified," in exceptionalist terms to elucidate "national character" and folk consciousness. It was for this reason that Origuchi's own discourse never succeeded in rising above considerations of social solidarity and failed to transform a Japanese social science into a social science of custom. For in the end, his project to identify folkic studies with timeless life forms simply reaffirmed a hermeneutic whose task was to uncover what was always there as essence, self-presence, and irreducibly Japanese.

## "Folkism"

Between the two world wars, Japanese social thinkers could easily agree with Max Scheler's dim description of the concept of society as "only the *remnant*, the *rubbish* left by the inner decomposition of communities" and applaud his unequivocal denunciation of contractual arrangements that signify the end of unified communal life and the unleashing of a "completely unorganized 'mass' portending worse things to come." But they could also draw reassurance for their own critical programs in this authoritative insistence that "society" is not the inclusive concept, designating all the "communities" that are united by blood, tradition, and history.[40] To this end, Yanagita Kunio and Origuchi sought, each in their own way, to rob the social of its commanding role as a principle (and principal) of determinacy and to illuminate, by appealing to folk and the meaning of their enduring customs, precisely those aspects of life that had not yet been assimilated to modern society. Here, ethnology was formulated to challenge a conception of society based upon exchange and contractual arrangements necessary to the development of capitalist forms of economic activity, by calling attention to a social image that had prevailed prior to the organization of contemporary society and whose fundamental elements continued to persist uneasily in the present. The ur-

---

[40] Max Scheler, *Problems of a Sociology of Knowledge*, trans. M. S. Frings (London: Routledge and Kegan Paul, 1980), p. 8.

gency of their project was undoubtedly provoked by Marxists who, in the same years, were providing their own critique of capitalist exchange values, the "inevitable" decomposition of the social order, and offering their own versions of the daily life drawn from a future not yet envisaged. Both Yanagita and Origuchi, as has been seen, employed a hermeneutic they believed was capable of extracting meaning once discourse fixed in narrative a relationship between place and folk, in order to demonstrate how the folkic experience and custom had remained immune from the caprices of historical change or the laws of necessity. While Yanagita situated ethnology in the contemporary scene to combat ceaseless change by offering the prospect of stability in its disclosure of enduring folkic custom, Origuchi moved to exhume for the present the lost meaning of folk *mentalités* from the "poetry of the past." This difference was further sharpened by the contrast provided by Yanagita's concern for the "ancestral spirits" and Origuchi's articulation of the marebito. Yet this disparity was not as great as it appeared, since society seemed to vanish altogether in both programs as a result of the narrative identification of place and folk. In fact, Origuchi's conception of the "gods who rarely come" constituted a crucial supplement to Yanagita's image of a community (*kyōdōtai*) authorized by an appeal to the ancestral spirits. For it should be noted that the archetype of a social group worshipping its ancestors was ultimately expressed in the form of a familistic community—the *kyōdōtai*—that is indistinguishable from place. By contrast, the marebito, since they belonged to the Other world—another community and place (*tokoyo*)— were not in a position to be responsible for originating community. What characterizes the group that celebrates the marebito is therefore not identical with the familial or clan unit that offers respect to its departed ancestors. It is important to recall that marebito were called for visitation not to supply abundance to any particular familistic group but to offer "good fortune" to humans who organize the communal unit itself.[41] As a result, the texts of Yanagita and Origuchi managed to accomplish an account of social origins that was, in fact, present to itself and to imagine a conception of community whose existence persisted in the repetition of practices associated with a specific place. In this way society as an object was exiled to become the *not-said* in the subsequent articulation of an ideology that privileged the presence of place, spatiality, and atemporality, to live a fugitive life as a negative image of all those declarations that have insisted upon the irreducible communalism of the Japanese.

This ideologeme, which bonded folk to place, dominated discourse in the 1930s and was invariably employed to counter Marxian claims, dramatized in the powerful debate over the nature of Japanese capitalism,

---

[41] See Komatsu Kazuhiko, *Ijin* (Tokyo: Aonisha, 1985), pp. 178–90.

and the philosophic critiques of thinkers like Miki Kiyoshi, Tosaka Jun, and Katō Tadashi to establish the authority of their own reading of capitalist society and what needed to be done to install a more genuinely human order. It was this contest of claims, rather than the prevalence of capitalism, that drove non-Marxian social thinkers like Takata Yasuma (1883–1956) to shift their own interactionist perspective toward forms of essentialism that closely resembled Tönnies' description of *Gemeinschaft*. This thinking conformed to the program of Yanagita and Origuchi, not to mention others, insofar as it shared their distrust of society as a core object of social science for one that now proposed harmony and solidarity (*ketsugō*) as the essence of social arrangements. In Takata's thinking, the apparent reason for this intensification of an essentialist social science was the growing influence of Marxian modes of social inquiry, especially its explanation of social conflict and the volatile nature of social relationships, and his growing desire to "protect the folk." "While I have always admired the socialization of interest in the progress of society," he conceded, "I am still a child of the village in spirit," acknowledging at the same time how he "adored the fresh vitality of village life, its communitarian society." "Even though I live in the midst of a society," he continued, "my heart has pursued *Gemeinschaft* ceaselessly. Doesn't this show that the native place—Japan—is a broad community (*kyōdō*)?"[42] What attracted Takata most to the communal mode was its "simple and honest human nature" attesting to a binding emotionality governing human interaction absent in urban life. Takata's heart also told him that a modern society, founded on the clash of interest, was no different from Marxism, which saw in the murderous competition of claims the necessary motor of social change. With this fear in mind, Takata developed in the late 1920s a nervous critique of Marxism (and capitalism), which he eventually called "The Third View of History."

Accordingly, the third view of history referred to the scientific effort to explain history by accounting first for the nature of social relationships. It differed from both the "first conception of history," called the idealistic view, which saw the origins of historical development in the movement and manifestation of the spirit, and the second conception of history (Marxism) which envisaged social change as effects of shifts in the economic base. His third view aimed to show that the determining cause of historical development is society itself, that is, the nature of relationships that bind people together. Where Takata believed he differed from Marxists was in his promotion of a conception of "social power" as the force that determines human interaction and accounts for sociation. Through the mediation of this concept he was able to explain that class, or any

[42] Kawamura Nozomu, *Nihon shakaigakushi kenkyū* (Tokyo: Ningen no kagakusha, 1973), 2:33.

form of social differentiation, originated, not in productive forces, but from fundamental divisions between the powerful and powerless based on the acquisition of talent and ability. It is important that Takata, like Yanagita and Origuchi, sought to separate production—economic activity—altogether from the social in order to argue that the relations between people constituted an independent variable.

At the heart of social relationships was what Takata called the "aggregative composition" of society. "The sociological historical view (third view of history)," he explained, "establishes an aggregative composition of society as an initial explanation. This [factor] refers to the quality and quantity of charter members of society who enter into social relationships. In a word, it is the form of social structures seen from the perspective of population density and the heterogeneity of society, and it becomes the base that determines the relations of mutuality among humans, relations of union and division. These social relationships also determine the content and change of all other social phenomena."[43] In this scheme, then, the extent of population density functioned as a first principle that made possible, in descending order, subsequent social relationships such as the fixed organizations of society (political and legal systems), the economy, and spiritual culture (collective consciousness). Envisaging social forms independent of the forces of material production, and therefore history itself, drew Takata closer to a discursive kinship with contemporaries such as Yanagita, Origuchi, and the younger Aruga Kizaemon, as well as all of those cultural critics of the 1930s who had already embarked upon the effort to show how cultural form manifested self-presence.

Under the sanction of this third view of history, Takata was emboldened, in the early 1930s, to call for the construction of a "Japanized" social science, quite in contrast to Origuchi, who had started from the reverse premise but ended up in the same place. Such a social science should emphasize the special characteristics of "Japaneseness" (*Nihonteki na mono*) and be employed to counter the hidden injuries inflicted by a mistaken acceptance of class and social relations of production as viable principles of social determinacy. As he saw it, the problem before his generation was to implement a transformation from "anthropologism" (as he called it) to "folkism" in order to explain the unity of the folk and its capacity for "self-defense."[44] By this time, Takata's interests had turned to the "folk problem," which he believed had been provoked by concerns over the future of the folk and the rural crisis of the 1930s caused by the process of subordinating villages to the necessities of urban industrialization. Yet this concern was informed by a prior conviction that only the

---

[43] Odō Yasujirō, *Takata shakaigaku* (Tokyo: Yuhikaku, 1953), p. 161.

[44] Kawamura, *Nihon shakaigushi*, 2:33.

folk dwelling in a place for a long time constituted the "unbreakable" bond of solidarity. In contrast to modern society, which constantly illustrated the fragility of bonds that tie—"break-off," as he put it—nothing is more resistant to dissolution than the community of land ties that originated in the remote past. The strength of Japan is therefore in the village, not the cities; it is spiritual, not material; form, not content. Hence, "to protect the village is to protect spiritual strength."[45] Uniqueness resides in folk life and is signified even today by a "communal society that has constituted an exceptionally intimate solidarity." The true tradition of Japan is simply consciousness of the ordinary peasant who, over the long duration, has managed to sustain harmonious social relationships as the indisputable condition for communal order. In a sense, the peasant represented a living reminder in the present of the veracity of the "third view of history."

Takata's intense commitment to the folk stemmed from the conviction that no modern bond equaled the example of a folkic group identified with past and place. But owing to a scheme that privileged social relationships derived from a folkic order of the past and saw politics as an effect of this principle of determinacy, he could not adequately differentiate folk, or nation, from the state. Yet by the same token, Takata easily conflated the expansion of the group ego, as he called it, with imperialism. But folkism, he urged, should not be understood as simple imperial expansion but rather as the natural necessity of the group to transcend "certain limits." "The formation of Manchukuo," he wrote, "had nothing to do with capitalism but rather resulted from the needs of the Japanese folk."[46] The solidarity characterizing the folkic community had originated from the traditions of Japanese particularity, which his earlier theory of "aggregative composition" had already prefigured and authorized. The meaning of group solidarity validates the continuity of a fixed identity of being Japanese rooted in a specific place, which reaches back to remote times (social relationships as form) to authorize an anamnesis toward the origins of culture itself, still full and self-present, yet stretching forward to the future. At this juncture the discourse on folk and place promised to become the ideological instrument of domination.

## Cultural Overdetermination and Reimagining the Japanese

The disciplinization of native knowledge was never far from the very presumptions of state power it sought to avoid. Once the program to estab-

[45] Ibid., p. 246.
[46] Ibid., p. 247.

lish a social science of place was envisaged as a corrective to an ideology masquerading as the truth of history, the terms of difference were assimilated to the claims of an essential similitude authorized by the idea of a cultural totality. But when the "totality" is no longer the "conclusion" but an "enabling axiom," the possibility for theoretical and practical social criticism is foreclosed. In Japanese social thought, this totality was inevitably represented by the folk fixed to a specific place. Meaning was possible only within this horizon. The folk, it was posited, possessed a natural-organic unit prior to all social differentiations, classes, and interest groups. As a result, culture (the folk) was made to join nature. The whole, like nature itself, constituted both the sum of the parts and the unit that functioned as a precondition for their fulfillment. Hence, it is not surprising to see from this discussion how the primacy of the whole, made possible by eliding the distinction between culture and nature, presupposed forms of production and reproduction of life as "given" and "general." Moreover, this conception of the whole was relieved of economic and even social content (Takata's insistence that the social was an independent variable), from any real, concrete mediations that would have specified it historically.[47] Even Aruga Kizaemon, responding to Marxian accounts of the practice of tenancy in the Tokugawa period, rejected explanations that attributed its "substance" to feudal managerial/serf relations (history) for one that "had passed through several stages of historical development but remained, in essence, unchanged." As for these relationships—which Marxists attributed to domination—Ariga proposed that they must be grasped as a "general cultural phenomenon." Accordingly, the character of tenant relationships transcends chronological meaning because the oyakata/kokata relationship is fixed in the folkic substrate of the extended family (dōzoku).[48] Yanagita's earlier formulation of the jōmin, representing the combination of all classes, was supposed to overcome struggle and conflict. According to Herbert Marcuse, this kind of vision inverts prevailing theories of utopia insofar as it proposes a classless society, or, at the very least, one whose hierarchical distinctions were produced by nature, not history, but only at the price of imagining this arrangement within the framework of existing class society.

Ethnology sought to project a narrative in which the folk constituted a "primal given," natural and prior to the artificial system of society. Culture, now posing as nature, became the great antagonist of history. A

[47] Herbert Marcuse, Negations, trans. J. J. Shapiro (Boston: Beacon Press, 1968), p. 23.

[48] Kawamura Nozomu, Nihon bunkaron no shūhen (Tokyo: Ningen no kagakusha, 1982), p. 114. For an interesting expression of "kinship" between Ariga's and Yanagita's conception of folk as culture, see Ariga Kizaemon, Itsu no Nihon bunkaron (Tokyo: Miraisha, 1981), pp. 125–30.

central tenet of social thinking before the war was its disposition to enforce a "natural" identity between the folk and a timeless nature. What
folk and nature shared was a process that endlessly reproduced the forms
necessary to the continued survival of their respective species into an indefinite future. As nature, what Aruga referred to as "restoring humanity
and nature," the folk served as the substructure of history, and their
forms of life the eternal and permanent constant in the continual flux of
economic activity and "civilization." This similitude could be found in
the way nature was mirrored in the spirit of the folk. But it should be
pointed out that the folk as nature "does not appear as a factor of production" or even as a condition of production, much less as the historical
basis of human history.[49] The transmutation of culture into nature invariably resulted in an overdetermination of texts which culminated in
what Marcuse has called the "depravation of history" and its reduction
to a merely "temporal occurrence external to the real principles of determination," which many believed to be the permanent totality.[50] Dehistoricization, as has been seen, was the necessary presupposition for devaluing time in favor of space and vanished place and elevating the static
over the dynamic. Just as nature knows no time, so folk life resembles
interminable repetition. Yet the overdetermined production of texts insisting on the elimination of history—the site of both difference and production—for the privileging of place failed to conceal its own blindness
in the interest of stabilizing a particular condition of life that evidently
could no longer be justified in the present historical circumstances.

It is important to recall that Yanagita's efforts to constitute the folk as
the subject of an ethnological discourse required their "voicelessness" as
an indisputable condition for representing their timeless life. Moreover, it
is equally significant to recognize that this operation apostrophized the
folk's absence from written history in order to emphasize the primacy of
performance (orality) and presumably production as against mere representation (writing) and the domination it imposes on the represented. Yet,
Yanagita managed only to recuperate representation of the folk on his
terms, that is, reading/writing, rather than theirs, which was performance, speaking, doing. Silence, therefore, is what made the folk eternal
and abiding. The native place was where the folk had always carried on,
silently, but we must remember that this place was the site of discourse.
A voiceless community, as Yanagita and Origuchi envisaged it, was like
an orality that leaves no traces and was never far from a *politically silent*
community. Silence, in short, guaranteed political assent and even indifference. So, while Yanagita's program to re-present the voiceless narrative

[49] Marcuse, *Negations*, p. 23.
[50] Ibid., p. 24.

of the folk aimed to challenge "civilization" and "rationality," promising heterogeneity for systematic homogeneity, it was purchased at a price of establishing a community of silence that, because of its natural endowment, would refrain from participating in politics. When Origuchi equated orality with village simplicity and writing with the development of political forms, he was instating in the present an antique unpoliticality as the fundamental condition for life and art. Both managed to forfeit the very heterogeneity (difference) their discourse was supposed to install for a newer and even more dangerous homogeneity, by reimagining what it might mean to be Japanese. In the interest of trying to rescue a form of otherness, imperiled as an endangered species, yet simultaneously prevent the instance of massive disorder by making the folk voiceless once again, ethnology transformed identities from class to supraclass, culture to nature, and thereby set the stage for a new national subjectivity.[51]

Beneath the overdetermination of ethnologic and social scientific texts was the problem that had already posed the question of political and social order, which the privileging of culture was supposed to answer. Moreover, this discussion to culture would mean that all subsequent discussion of politics and society could take place only within the framework of an essentialized and normative conception of culture. The installation of culture as an unproblematic category represented a recognition among intellectuals and academics of all persuasions of the futility of embarking upon purposive forms of action leading to transformation. Culture came to represent natural and internalized values made manifest in form, and thus it functioned to preclude acting in the external world. True action, it was believed, was realized only in the endless externalization of these values of spirit. This mediation, suppressing the difference between essence and existence, led only to acceptance, not action, representation and its interpretation, not production and practice. A theory that seized upon creativity and its interpretation as equivalence could easily be appropriated to confirm the received order to things, if not the spiritual mobilization of the masses by the state. The ideological effect of this cultural hermeneutic, undoubtedly founded on the fear of individual interests, competition, and conflict, dissolved determinate classes into the larger classification of a folk unmediated by history. In the end, a dehistoricized culture replaced a historical society, folk was substituted for class, and the production of place supplanted the place of production.

[51] This is certainly the argument of Murakami Yasusuke, Kumon Shunpei, and Sato Seizaburō, *Bunmei to shite no ie shakai* (Tokyo: Chūō kōronsha, 1979), pp. 257–58.

# Part III

MARXISM AND CULTURAL CRITICISM

MARXISM, both as a philosophy and as a call for social action, has had a powerful effect on various aspects of Japan's political and social history. Much of this influence has been studied and explicated with skill and understanding by Western scholars. The importance of Marxism as a form of cultural criticism as practiced by Japanese writers and thinkers, however, has as yet drawn less attention. Recent interest in England and the United States in such continental figures as Lukács, Adorno, and Benjamin suggest that it may be time for an examination of the important Japanese figures who used their understanding of Marxist ideas and ideals to help shape the contours of modern Japanese thought concerning the nature of culture. In those terms, the philosopher Miki Kiyoshi (1897–1945) and the novelist Miyamoto Yuriko (1899–1951) remain among the most significant figures of their period, yet no significant study of their lives and works has been published in any Western language, nor could essays on their work be included in the present volume. Foreign students of modern Japanese culture are thus missing one of the major strands of thinking that went into its formation.

Commentators on modern Japan have often speculated on the reasons for the appeal of Marxism to interwar Japanese intellectuals, who attempted to use these concepts as a means to understand developments in their own society. Those who did so often sought the kind of international and "scientific" model that European Marxists proposed to present. Japanese Marxist thinkers looked neither to a model such as the folk, proposed by Yanagita, nor to traditional neo-Confucian sources of value inherited from older traditions. They wished rather to begin with the reality of the sort of rapidly urbanizing society they found around them. The doctrines of Marxism provided them, they felt, both a means to analyze that society and a plan for action. Marxist ideas seemed to clarify the inevitability of capitalist exploitation and helped explain as well the rise of a militaristic state. In this sense, Marxist cultural criticism as practiced in Japan was as attractive to Japanese intellectuals as European Marxist criticism during the same period was to their counterparts in France, Germany, Hungary, and elsewhere.

Writers interested in using Marxist concepts to analyze Japanese cultural facts were faced with a series of particularly difficult challenges. Marxism, as a European system of thought, had grown out of a long tradition of philosophical analysis, the assumptions of which were, on the whole, unfamiliar to all but a relative handful of Japanese intellectuals.

The writings of such leading European cultural critics as Lukács or Benjamin might have provided useful examples of how such a critical stance should be put to use, but their works were not widely known or translated into Japanese until the 1950s and after. A thinker like Miki, who himself studied in Germany in the 1920s, working with such eminent thinkers as Rickert and Heidegger, helped serve in his own writings as a conduit for certain of those modes of thought. Still, the details of Marxist dialectic remained elusive for many sympathetic to their general thrust. The work of Miki and others provided a powerful impetus for many intellectuals to open up to the social dimensions of the political and social situation in which they found themselves. Appeals for the development of social conscience and social action by such important figures as the poet Ishikawa Takuboku (1885–1912) at the time of the Kōtoku Shūsui affair now took on a renewed vigor and significance.

Marxist writers during the interwar period, in their analysis of Japanese culture and society, often found the weight of the Japanese tradition served as a particularly problematic burden; they did not fail to point out the means by which the continuing appeal of older cultural forms served to mask new changes in society. Such methods of analysis required in turn an informed sense of Japanese cultural history. Some intellectuals, in their attempt to use the data of Japanese history to analyze contemporary problems, found that Japan's past put its experience in parallel with other nations where Marxist analysis was found to apply. Others, however, came to the conclusion that the experiences of Japan had been too special. These intellectuals began to question the universality of the Marxist principles with which they had begun; some, as Germaine Hoston illustrates in her study of Sano Manabu, went so far as to believe that the corpus of Marxist ideas with which they were working represented a kind of Western cultural imperialism aimed at Japan, which, as a nation outside the European tradition, should develop its own modes of thought and analysis. Whatever the range of responses, however, the Japanese encounter with Marxism in the cultural sphere was of crucial and sustained importance in the formation of modern Japanese thought.

The need remains for Western scholars to examine this rich corpus of writings in order to give this thought its appropriate place in the larger patterns of modern Japanese intellectual and cultural history, in contradistinction to political history. Nor is the topic of mere academic or historical interest. The work of a number of writers active during the interwar years, such as Nakano Shigeharu (1902–1979) and Haniya Yutaka (born 1910), as the essays of Brett de Bary and Miriam Silverberg point out, finds resonances with contemporary Japanese readers who locate in the thinking of these artists important clues to understanding the shifting dilemmas of a modern world and the nature of Japan's place in it.

# 7

# Marxism Addresses the Modern: Nakano Shigeharu's Reproduction of Taishō Culture

MIRIAM SILVERBERG

> ... that the soft water's movement will
> conquer the strongest stone, in time. You
> understand: the hard ones are undermined.
> *Bertolt Brecht*

ANY ATTEMPT to provide a biographical context for the legacy of Nakano Shigeharu must be prefaced with a qualification recently awarded his contemporary, Langston Hughes: "Who he was is a smallish part of what he was."[1] Nakano Shigeharu's autobiographical fiction on coming of age in the closing years of the Meiji era, his account of provincial student life, his chronicle of the agony of a youth drawn to an incomprehensible ideology in a hostile city, and his rendering of the emotional costs of betraying the cause of the Japanese Communist Party have received the respectful hermeneutical exegesis accorded the Confucian classics. The novels have thereby greatly contributed to the reconstruction of who Nakano was, and yet there are glaring omissions in the fictions. These absences, along with the emphasis on institutions rather than ideas in the histories of prewar Japanese revolutionary culture, have prevented a full understanding of what he was. Of course the complexity of *what* a poet was cannot be reduced to a single label or a solitary goal, but a close reading of the words of Nakano Shigeharu written during the closing years of the Taishō era reveal a dimension to the man almost unmentioned in autobiography and therefore repeatedly absent in biography. Nakano's writing tells the reader that during the second half of the 1920s he was a Marxist critic of contemporary mass culture.[2]

---

[1] Gwendolyn Brooks, review of *The Life of Langston Hughes*, by Arnold Rampersad, *New York Times Book Review*, October 12, 1986, p. 7.

[2] See *Nashi no hana* in *Nakano Shigeharu zenshū*, vol. 6 (Tokyo: Chikuma shobō, 1977) [*Shinchō* 1/57–12/58], hereafter cited as *NSZ* with original date and place of appearance of text under discussion in brackets; *Uta no wakare*, *NSZ* 5:1–95 [*Kakushin* 4, 5, 7, 8/39]; *Machi aruki*, *NSZ* 5:99–121 [*Shinchō* 6–7/40]; *Muragimo*, *NSZ* 5:123–404 [*Gunzō* 1–7/

A recapitulation of dates and places along with organizations and publications can only detract from the power of Nakano's simple language and the vision preserved in his works. Nevertheless, for the record, the student of modern Japanese literature has read who Nakano Shigeharu was. In the histories of the prewar Culture Movement he was the brash young activist from the Imperial University who harnessed his talents as a lyric poet to the dictates of Leninist political organizing. He engaged in highly polemical debate and published acclaimed fiction documenting the life of the cultural revolutionary before and after imprisonment. The chronology is not wrong, for the leading Japanese writer, Nakano Shigeharu, was born in a small coastal village in 1902, attended the elite Fourth Higher School in Kanazawa, and then moved on to Tokyo, where he engaged in labor and literary organizing activities during the mid-1920s. By 1932, the year marking the dissolution of the organized movement of left-wing Japanese artists, he was being canonized in anthologies as a leading poet, leading modern writer, and leading proletarian writer. After the war he maintained his position as political and literary leader, organizer of a revived literary movement, editor of the Communist newspaper *Akahata*, and representative of the Japanese Communist Party in the National Diet from 1947 until 1950. After expulsion from the party in 1964 he would edit his own revisionist journal. There and elsewhere he provided scathing commentary in ironic terms, covering such fronts as world affairs, the use of the Japanese language in postwar Japanese society, and his own prewar past. At the time of his death in 1979, he was engaged in editing the second edition of his twenty-eight-volume oeuvre.[3]

Nakano's essays and poetry of the prewar era confront the twentieth-century phenomenon of the overt appropriation of the mass media by the state. But what is important in the context of Nakano's critique of Taishō culture is not so much his awareness of the power of overt state control through censorship or the imprisonment of intellectuals, but his awareness of the more subtle, but in no way less powerful, ways in which mod-

---

54]; and *Mura no ie*, NSZ 2:64–89 [*Keizai ōrai* 5/35]. For an annotated bibliography of the proliferating scholarship on Nakano, refer to Sugino Yokichi, *Nakano Shigeharu no kenkyū* (Tokyo: Dasama shoin, 1979).

While the Taishō era is officially bracketed between 1912 and 1926, years of a decidedly nonillustrious imperial reign, there has been much discussion of where and how to demarcate the era, usually in the context of the definition of "Taishō Democracy." Herein Taishō refers to an era in cultural history, the decade following the earthquake of 1923 and ending soon after the invasion of Manchuria in 1931. The time corresponds to the emergence of a consumer culture, to the lifetime of the Japanese Culture Movement, and to the moment of Nakano Shigeharu's prewar literary production.

[3] For the most complete chronology of Nakano's achievements, see the standard *nenpu* in the second edition of the complete works, NSZ 28:259–83.

ern forms of culture can dominate the producers and consumers of such mass-produced cultural commodities as literary works and newspaper photographs. As a Marxist, Nakano Shigeharu was concerned with the reproduction of culture as it took form in his own society. He wrote about the packaging of Japanese tradition for domestic and foreign consumption. As a Marxist, he also alerted his readers to a new culture of reproduction made possible by modern technological advances. These two aspects of his Marxist critique of Taishō culture are explicated and translated herein in order to interpret better what was no small part of the legacy of Nakano Shigeharu, his profound appreciation of the cultural forces at work in Taishō society.

## The Reproduction of Culture

In February 1927, Nakano Shigeharu published a three-part poem entitled "Train" in *Roba*, the nonsectarian literary magazine founded by a group of progressive young writers who were backed by such Taishō luminaries as Nakano's mentor, the poet Murō Saisei, and Akutagawa Ryūnosuke.[4] While Nakano never associated his turn to Marxist thought with his work for the journal in any of his autobiographical writings, from its inception in April 1926, *Roba* had provided the forum for him to work through his study of Marx in his own way. The words must speak for themselves.[5] For example, the third part of "Train" can be read as Nakano's rephrasing of Marx's concept of simple reproduction, the process whereby social relationships are created and recreated under capitalism:

---

[4] Nakano, "Kisha," *NSZ* 1:515–17 [*Roba* 2/27]. The citations are from the original versions of the poems in *NSZ* 1. All translations are my own.

[5] For an extended discussion of Nakano Shigeharu's discovery of Marx's thought within the context of Taishō culture, see my *Changing Song: The Marxist Manifestos of Nakano Shigeharu* (Princeton: Princeton University Press, 1990). Nakano rarely cited Marx, never mentioned his work in his poetry, and provided no narrative about his discovery of Marx. My discovery of Marx in Nakano, therefore, is premised on my reading of Nakano's texts. What is important as context for my analysis is not the documentation of Nakano's intention but an awareness of the popularity of Marx's writings in Japan during the 1920s and the complexity of Nakano's own ideology as preserved in his works. To place my method, I defer to Dominick LaCapra. LaCapra centers textual analysis by noting that "the rhetoric of contextualization has often encouraged narrowly documentary readings in which the text becomes little more than a sign of the times or a straightforward expression of one larger phenomenon or another. At the limit, this indiscriminate approach to reading and interpretation becomes a detour around texts and an excuse for not really reading them at all." Dominick LaCapra, *Rethinking Intellectual History: Texts, Contexts, Language* (Ithaca: Cornell University Press, 1983), p. 14.

### III

Bye Bye Bye Bye
Good-bye Good-bye Good-bye Good-bye
We saw that
We heard that
A hundred factory girls alight
Where a thousand factory girls ride on

What are factory girls?
What are mill factory girls?
What are companies factories chimneys dormitories?
What does it mean that the girls are wrung out
What does it mean that they are wrung out like wet towels?
And what is New Year's?
What is New Year's break?
Ahh—the girls have been thoroughly wrung out
And pushed out—in the name of New Year's
And we saw that
A hundred factory girls alight where a thousand factory girls ride on
And we saw that
Fathers and mothers and brothers and sisters come out from the snow
Atop their oil-papered raincoats
Atop their capes
Atop their wraps the white snow collecting
And their straw shoes wet all the way along up
And we saw how they and the girls embraced
And we saw that
They and the girls stroking each other
They and the girls stroking each other's heads and faces and shoulders
And how the snow kept falling on

Bye Bye Bye Bye
And the girls knew
That only for a while they were able to embrace
Only just a while for giving pats receiving pats
Ah—the girls knew
Who they themselves are
Where their villages are
And what sorts await in the village

The girls were pushed out   in the name of New Year's
The girls were thoroughly wrung out
And in the villages new buyers for them making all the rounds
Leaving those small stations

Through the snow
The girls are returning to the buyers there in ambush
This they all knew

Bye Bye Bye Bye
Good-bye Good-bye Good-bye Good-bye
That there was Etchū
That there the land of special treats for the rich
Atop the dirt floor exposed to the wind in that small station
Daughters and parents and brothers and sisters each patted the other
The parting words of those who sit and those who keep riding
Of the girls probably to be bought and rebought up again by different
    factories
Of the mill factory girls probably never to meet again
The chorus of their thousand voices
Spun round and round that never stopping sky of snow

Marx had introduced his concept of simple reproduction in the first
volume of *Capital* (which had first appeared in Japanese in 1919), by
emphasizing the simultaneous, intertwined nature of the process of production and reproduction. The premise for change was thus repetition:

> Whatever the form of the process of production in a society, it must be a con-
> tinuous process, must continue to go periodically through the same phases. A
> society can no more cease to produce than it can cease to consume. When
> viewed, therefore, as a connected whole, and as flowing on with incessant re-
> newal, every social process of production is, at the same time, a process of
> reproduction.[6]

According to Marx, the working class is reproduced in its relationship
to the capitalist class. This reproduction is concealed from the worker
because of the constant change of employers and in the wage commanded
by the employment of his labor power, both of which bestow an illusion
of freedom and of change and chance. The unity of the process is thus
broken apart into the kaleidoscope of shifting pairs, but the nature of the
components remains constant, and the worker is at first unable to break
out of this existence wherein he is made into a thing or a commodity. He
is not aware that he is living a dehumanized life; moreover, he is unaware
that this condition is shared with others. But reproduction is not merely
repetition. It is also accumulation—of both the proletariat and capital.
The process leads to the accumulation of misery, ignorance, and degra-

---

[6] Karl Marx, *The Process of Capitalist Production*, vol. 1 of *Capital* (New York: International Publishers, 1967), p. 566.

dation while at the same time augmenting wealth for the capitalist class, wealth based on the labor power of the class that produces.[7]

The last segment of "Train" expresses the repetitive nature of capitalist reproduction. In the opening lines of his verse, the sounds "Bye Bye Bye Bye / Good-bye Good-bye Good-bye Good-bye" introduce the idea of this aspect of reproduction via the dulling rhythm of the words of the young factory girls arriving home on New Year's break from their labors in the textile mills of Taishō Japan.[8] Here, then, is the process of reproduction as played out in the Toyama countryside. By following the girls off the train, to the scene of family reunion, the poet captures the notion of the production and reproduction of the working class. Capitalist society is in constant, repetitive movement, just like the train, which stops, only to start again, along the northern coast of Japan to deposit its load of young girls. These girls will soon return to new employers on the same train. They will reenter the same life that Nakano sketches with his blunt question. This query, "What are companies factories chimneys dorms?" is made up of a series of questions, just as the system of capitalism comprises innumerable units of production. The parts are merely part of a nonvisible whole. In addition to exposing the structuring of capitalism, Nakano draws attention to the historical place of capitalism. He implies a historical transition by relating the journey of the factory girl as a transition from factory and the chimneys symbolizing the modernity of industrialization, home to Etchū, the premodern term for Toyama Prefecture.

Nakano says that the factory girls "know" their true situation. Yet ultimately he conveys the message that the girls are only conscious of the actual process of reproduction—of their transport between work and family and between successive work-sites. While he implies that capitalist production hurls the factory girls from the organic unity of family ties into a new community of horizontal linkages with women workers and of confrontation with managers within a new city life, Nakano does not take the poem in the direction of a new working class culture.[9] This is because he is more interested in the appropriation of traditional culture for an unprecedented purpose. While the factory girls are ostensibly sent home to be reunited with their families, this is merely a momentary break in the process of their reproduction. The old conceals the new, because the observance of a traditional cultural practice is merely an excuse to reproduce a new, capitalist social relationship.

[7] Ibid., pp. 578, 613–14, 645.

[8] The Japanese words are *sayonara* and *sayōnara*.

[9] Nakano did acknowledge the importance of examining the consciousness of the worker, its complexity, and its availability in language and material culture, as I determine in *Changing Song*.

Nakano's account of the ride of the factory girls did say more about the reproduction of socioeconomic relationships under capitalism than about the dynamics of changing tradition, but in another poem in *Roba* he was more direct about this process of the reproduction of culture in Taishō Japan. "Imperial Hotel" made it clear that in his society it was not sufficient to understand the relationship between old and new.[10] The domination of West by East must also be factored into any theory of contemporary Japanese capitalist culture:

**Imperial Hotel**

I

This is the West
The dogs use English

This is the proper West
The dogs invite me to the Russian Opera

This is the West A Western Exposition
The Japanese marketplace for kimono and shop-worn curios

And this is a prison
The guard jangles his keys

This is a dreary, damp, dank prison
Neither the prisoners nor the wardens trade words with a soul

And the prisoners are called by number
And the guards stand in the exits/the entranceways

And then this is a cheap dive
The old fat guy is roaring drunk

And also this is a cheap whorehouse
The women walk naked

And this is a hole
Black and Fetid

II

A large hole
A large whorehouse
A large saloon
A large dampish prison
A big and seedy sample Japanese marketplace
Undestroyed even by the earthquake

[10] Nakano, "Teikoku Hoteru," *NSZ* 1:510–11 [*Roba* 11/26].

> In the center of Tokyo
> Over our heads
> Squats, letting loose a stench

While *Capital* has been cited as the source for the concept of reproduction found in "Train," Marx's *Communist Manifesto* was a resource for Nakano's interrogation of the reproduction of culture. In this work (available in Japanese since 1906), Marx had charted the reproduction of capitalism via empire, into other parts of the world and into the cultural realm of society, in the following terms:

> In place of the old wants, satisfied by the production of the country, we find new wants, requiring for their satisfaction the products of distant lands and climes. In place of the old local and national seclusion and self-sufficiency, we have intercourse in every direction, universal interdependence of nations. And as in material, so also in intellectual production.[11]

The poem "Imperial Hotel" illustrates how culture does indeed move in more than one direction. Just as contemporary European culture is reproduced in commodity form to be sold in Japan, so is Japanese culture broken into profit-producing units to be sold in the market. While the opening lines suggest a rejection of the West and of the Japanese urban citizenry's desire to adopt its cultural fashions, the poet does not retreat into a nativist tradition. Here, his intent is to do battle with the bourgeois values of capitalism, which are responsible for the deformation of human beings into things or numbers, and for the transformation of the site of everyday intercourse into a marketplace. The Imperial Hotel, playground for the Japanese nouveau riche, stands for Tokyo, and for the nation as a whole. By 1926, Japan had become the source of antiquarian objects, its culture a warehouse. Simultaneously it was a place where the European bourgeoisie sold its own cultural commodities.

Nakano has reworded Marx's argument in *The Communist Manifesto*. The bourgeoisie covers the globe in search of locales in which to expand its market and thus gives a cosmopolitan character to production and consumption throughout the world. This class forcefully introduces into other nations what is termed civilization, creating "a world after its own image." Marshall Berman's reading of this part of Marx's text is a most appropriate paraphrase: "Culture becomes an enormous warehouse in which everything is kept in stock on the chance that someday, somewhere, it might sell."[12] The Japanese poet's method of interpreting Marx

---

[11] Karl Marx and Frederick Engels, *Manifesto of the Communist Party*, trans. Samuel Moore (Chicago: Charles H. Kerr, 1985), p. 17.

[12] Marx, *Communist Manifesto*, 1:18. Marshall Berman, *All that Is Solid Melts into Air: The Experience of Modernity* (New York: Simon and Schuster, 1982), p. 162.

is to strip the veneer of civilization from the hotel, revealing the freedom of movement in the corridors to be confinement and the items for sale only objects that will pretend to satisfy vulgar cravings. The second part of the poem is devoid of human actors; it retains only the metaphors for the hotel. The conclusion to the poem reveals an eroticism gone sour in an urban world offering no real ties between humans beings, while continually promising new excitement through the reproduction of new commodities. This culture provides constant new images and texts and conceals a reality wherein "no words are traded."

In "Train," Nakano Shigeharu touched on the uses of culture when he disclosed how the reproduction of New Year's rites concealed the new within the old. "Imperial Hotel," produced during the same era, was about the commodification of tradition. During the next several years, the closing years of the 1920s, Nakano moved beyond the ideal of Marx. He would ground his writing in a Marxist conception of historical change and of the figuration of human relationships governed by commodities under capitalism, to aim his anger at a modern capitalist phenomenon that first confronted Marxists in the twentieth century. This was the political power of the media. Nakano's concern with the reproduction of Japanese cultural artifacts for capitalist consumption was now replaced by his indictment of a cultural process capable of homogenizing human experience and thus obliterating all historical and cultural distinctions. Nakano was concerned with new forms of culture, for he was aware that just as the reproduction of premodern culture could conceal economic and social change, the terms could be reversed. That is to say, the twentieth-century mass culture, while celebrating continual innovation, concealed the repetitive and nonprogressive aspects of social and economic reproduction; the ostensibly new hid the old. All of the elite Japanese subcultures that had made Nakano who he was—the Fourth Higher School culture of male bonding, the rigorously ideological society of the "New Man Society" or Shinjinkai at Tokyo Imperial University, and even the bohemian literary culture to which the young man belonged as a revolutionary writer during the mid-1920s, had been colored by new and old indigenous traditions.[13] But in his critique of Taishō mass culture, Nakano would address cultural phenomena that did not recognize borders between countries or cultures.

Nakano's twofold approach to Taishō culture as both the reproduction of culture and the culture of reproduction is best summarized in the exegesis of the twentieth-century thinker Henri Lefebvre, who has applied Marx's conception of reproduction to the revolutionizing of tradition in the modern age:

[13] See my discussion in *Changing Song*.

Underneath its pretended and pretentious newness, *modernity* conceals the te-
dium of the repetitive, its self-satisfied cud-chewing and regurgitation, the re-
dundancy which would have us believe in the intelligibility of this world. The
redundant brilliance and the appearance of newness in everyday cultural repetition conceal total reproduction. Conversely, the reproduction of the old in the
modern conceals the current society which is renewing and reproducing itself.[14]

Nakano Shigeharu, half a century before Lefebvre, criticized that dual
nature of the reproduction of culture whereby cultural innovation conceals social continuity and the appropriation of cultural tradition ob-
scures the emergence of new relationships in society. In sum, "Train" and
"Imperial Hotel" had both been about the reproduction of the old in a
modern context; Nakano would next turn to new forms of culture offering an illusion on constant change.

## The Culture of Reproduction

Nakano had alluded in "Imperial Hotel" to the commodification of culture into items for profit, but he was more explicit in his prose response
to the suicide of Akutagawa Ryūnosuke over a year later. The miscellany,
"On Akutagawa and Other Matters," which appeared in the January
1928 issue of *Bungei kōron*, the popular magazine of letters, comprised a
series of ostensibly unrelated segments.[15] The work included Nakano's
version of his one meeting with Akutagawa, which at the time was rapidly
being enshrined in the literary world as the moment when the mantle was
passed down from disillusioned modernist to young Marxist,[16] along
with biting commentaries on such topics as hero worship in Meiji Japan,
theatre, and the fad for translation in the Japanese academy. The final
two segments, "Advertisement No. 1" and "Advertisement No. 2," identify the contemporary Japanese man of letters as an actor in the marketplace. In a blunt short-hand the author made note of how capitalism in
Japan threatened to engulf art into a system of commodity exchange.
Nakano hinted that the intellectual, not unlike the proletarian, is a producer forced to sell the products of his labor in order to survive. But
whereas the worker sells his labor power, thus creating surplus value for
the capitalist, the man of letters supplies cultural objects created by himself or others. Nakano's two "advertisements" provide an unmasking of

[14] Henri Lefebvre, *The Survival of Capitalism: Reproduction of the Relations of Production*, trans. Frank Bryant (London: Allison and Busby, 1978), p. 34.

[15] Nakano, "Akutagawa shi no koto nado," *NSZ* 9:102–12 [*Bungei kōron* 1/28].

[16] On this phenomenon see Kurihara Yukio, *Puroretaria bungaku to sono jidai* (Tokyo:
Heibonsha, 1971), pp. 18–28.

this new order of things. The reader of "Imperial Hotel" should recognize that the poet was commenting on the complexity of Japanese culture, which had incorporated foreign works of art within its system. The first document, segment XIX, reads as follows:

XIX. Advertisement No. 1

I need some change so I want to sell the following two things. You can subtract some from the price. If those interested will write to me I will show the items to you.

*Complete Works of Heine* (Hoffman und Kampe, ed., published 1861–63, all 20 volumes, 100 yen). Korai Doll, one (4,000 yen).

You just can't find the Heine in Japan. Can't even get it in Germany. I just put a name on the Korai doll—it's an earthenware piece. Small. Maillol can't compare.[17]

Nakano has fixed a price on poetry by pricing the Heine. Moreover, the Korean doll is posited within a world market by the comparison to the French object. The two items, so different in quality, in history, in form, and in use (or use value) have had their differences obliterated as they are both means to an acquisition of money. These commodities comprise the first part, or the first "C" of Marx's formula for the exchange of commodities, C-M-C, presented in the first volume of *Capital*. A commodity is sold so that a producer can purchase an item of equal value. In Marx's words, "The exchange becomes an accomplished fact by two metamorphoses of opposite yet supplementary character—the conversion of the commodity into money, and the reconversion of the money into a commodity."[18] In other words, Nakano will sell these commodities to make money, which he in turn will spend on an item advertised for in the last stanza of "On Akutagawa and Other Matters":

XX. Advertisement No. 2

Looking for benevolent person to build a bedstead. (Apparently Kaji Wataru wants one also, but he's already got one made of tangerine boxes or something.) One that's sturdy and simple would be good.[19]

The two advertisements when combined comprise the opportunity for behavior appropriate to a mercantile economy. Nakano, in other words, is interested in spending his money on an item for its own use. But the advertisements are an ironic exercise of the poet's imagination, for its author and his readers live within a capitalist and not a mercantilist society which bases its economic behavior on Marx's final formula: M-C-

[17] Nakano, "Akutagawa shi," p. 112. The term Korai refers to an ancient Korean kingdom.

[18] Marx, *Capital*, 1:105.

[19] Nakano, "Akutagawa shi," NSZ 9:112.

M. As Marx explains in his chapter "The General Formula for Capital," in the earlier circuit C-M-C, the same piece of money changes its place twice. The seller receives it from the buyer and pays it to another seller. The circuit, he continues, begins and ends with a commodity, and the satisfaction of wants or "use value" is the end of the transaction. Under the capitalist system, however, it is the commodity and not the money that "changes its place twice." Industrial capital is money that is changed into commodities to be sold and thereby reconverted into more money. Therefore, the leading impetus for this process is not use, but exchange value.[20]

Nakano developed his analysis of Japanese capitalism from a position within the system of commodity circulation, by viewing himself as a producer, along with the other members of the Japanese literary elite who made literary objects that were resold in the press. He was to provide an even more explicit analysis of how culture could be packaged and sold two years later, in "The Selling of Writing and Other Matters," published in *Shinchō*, a magazine catering to a new middle class. The article opened with a sharp caveat: a poet was qualified to talk about money because those possessing nothing (here the producer of culture was portrayed as proletarian in nature) were more capable of talking on the issues than those possessed of wealth. The issue he wished to raise, as a producer who had sold his writings to the newspapers for financial gain, was the literary style sought by the media. Nakano took on as a metaphor one of the most widely advertised items of late Meiji and Taishō Japan, sen-sen or *Jintan*, and placed it within an analogy from prison life.[21] A prison culture with its own set of rituals and artifacts was in fact being institutionalized by the late 1920s in Japan at the same time as capitalist culture appeared to offer the public an ever-increasing choice of items for consumption, and Nakano managed to strike at both in deadpan fashion.[22] He did not mention the sweeping nationwide arrests of intellectuals on March 15, 1928, and April 16 of the following year, nor did he personalize the subject by even mentioning his own brief incarcerations in 1928 and 1929. Instead he quietly introduced into his work the topic of everyday life in prison. But the real subject under consideration was not the overt repression of

[20] Ibid., pp. 148–55.

[21] Nakano, "Bunsho wo uru koto sono hoka," *NSZ* 9:264 [*Shinchō* 9/29]. The patent medicinal mint *Jintan* was made famous after the Russo-Japanese War in full-page newspaper advertisements giving it the lead over other advertisements, and it maintained its prominent position during the Taishō era, after the introduction of billboards. A social history of the Japanese advertising industry compares the advertising costs incurred during the final years of Meiji, 120,000 yen per annum, to the fee paid to sell Japanese sen-sen in 1923, an amount exceeding one million yen. Yamamoto Taketoshi, *Kōkoku no shakai shi* (Tokyo: Hōsei University Press, 1984), pp. 60–61, 195.

[22] Nakano, "Bunsho wo uru," p. 264.

incarceration. Nakano was talking about the much less direct, hegemonic aspect of cultural control in the free marketplace of late Taishō Japan:

> In jail even if you get sick they won't buy you medicine. Sometimes they will buy you just Jintan. That's because Jintan can't be "either poison or medicine." The reason that Jintan is sold so widely is this characteristic of convenient usefulness. Probably writing that is like Jintan sells quite well. That sort of writing probably has as good an effect as Jintan. And I have the utmost faith in the efficacy of Jintan.[23]

Clearly, Nakano does not really accept the value of writing he has likened to the glittering, uniformly round pellets of silver-coated mint so easily reproduced in quantity for the market. Jintan is a literary conceit allowing him to attack literature produced for profit. In a passage that can only be read as a reworking of the opening section of the first volume of *Capital*, Nakano claimed that "to sell writing is to produce it as a commodity. Commodities, as everybody knows, are produced for the market and not so they may be used by people. The truth is the opposite of this."[24] Exchange value, in other words, is substituted for any use value, as implied in Nakano's two advertisements.

Nakano's "Jintan culture," whose bland uniformity panders to the needs of the capitalist press, appears under another name in the writing of Walter Benjamin, who, like Nakano Shigeharu, would claim that in the late 1920s and early 1930s the author had become a literary producer of cultural commodities. In an address to the Institute for the Study of Fascism delivered in Paris on April 27, 1934, Benjamin opened with what he termed a new question.[25] Rather than positing a work in relation to its attitude toward the social relations of production of an era, he was concerned with the function of a work within the literary relations of production. Benjamin stated what Nakano had already explored during the 1920s: Society was "in the midst of a mighty recasting of literary forms" epitomized by the unprecedented literary position of the newspaper. It was not sufficient for a left-wing intellectual to feel solidarity with the proletariat; he must experience comradeship as a producer within a process of production and cooptation controlled by a bourgeois "apparatus of production and publication" that was constantly assimilating revolutionary themes. This apparatus could be turned against the bourgeoisie, in a revolutionary direction, if authors would take control of the means of production of this modern culture.

[23] Ibid.

[24] Ibid., p. 265. Cf. Marx, *Capital*, 1:35–83.

[25] Walter Benjamin, "The Author as Producer," in Peter Demetz, ed., *Reflections: Essays, Aphorisms, Autobiographical Writings*, trans. Edmund Jephcott (New York: Harcourt Brace Jovanovich, 1979), pp. 220–38.

In Benjamin's language, mass culture is examined within the category of "the work of art in the age of mechanical reproduction." In an essay by that name first published in 1936, the Frankfurt School thinker narrated how historically the work of art has been transformed because its *mechanical* reproduction is an historically unprecedented development, isolating the object—now a product—from its history, and thereby depriving it of authenticity. Art has been emancipated from tradition; it now serves politics, and not ritual. The German thinker's conclusion underscores the political ambiguities inherent in the new cultural context. The modern technology allowing for mass reproduction can in fact be used for politically antithetical purposes: just as fascism aestheticizes politics, so communism responds by politicizing art.[26]

The writings of Nakano Shigeharu had not actually circulated westward, nor had Nakano been privy to the ideas of Benjamin. The historian must conclude that the reality of the capitalist culture in which each man worked provided the material pushing both thinkers beyond Marx's theory of the reproduction of commodities as set forth in *Capital*, to write, in their differing languages, of a culture of reproduction. While Nakano was undoubtedly selling his writing to make a living, his decision to place his revolutionary energies within the cultural sphere through the production of mass-marketed articles and poems published in revolutionary and nonrevolutionary media is proof that he recognized the potential of technology to aid in the revolutionary transformation of society. Nevertheless, his poems about culture in the age of mechanical reproduction emphasize the first part of Benjamin's equation. His poetry attacked the aestheticization of politics by focusing on the homogenization of history and politics in the mass media, in the name of culture. By the time Nakano's essay containing the sen-sen metaphor appeared in 1929, he had already produced a series of poems recording the abuses of technological reproduction by the photograph. While the sen-sen metaphor is graphic, these poems are the most revealing expression of Nakano Shigeharu's analysis of the Taishō culture of reproduction. In such works as "Picture of the Arrival of the Newly Appointed Ambassador to the City," "Journalist," and "The Photograph in the Newspaper," texts almost unmentioned in the vast secondary literature on Nakano, the Japanese

[26] Walter Benjamin, *The Work of Art in the Age of Mechanical Reproduction*, ed. Hannah Arendt, trans. Harry Zohn (New York: Schocken Books, 1978), pp. 217–42. The process whereby Walter Benjamin's fascination with urban culture was sharpened into a Marxist analysis of commodity culture can only be understood within the context of the influence of Bertolt Brecht and Theodore Adorno. On Benjamin see Susan Buck-Morss, *The Origin of Negative Dialectics: Theodor W. Adorno, Walter Benjamin, and the Frankfurt Institute* (New York: The Free Press, 1977), pp. 151–61, and Richard Wolin, *Walter Benjamin: An Aesthetic of Redemption* (New York: Columbia University Press, 1982).

Marxist politicized art by bringing into question the innocence of the press.[27] More specifically, he asked his readers to take a second look at the photograph, a modern medium that Benjamin would term the "first revolutionary means of reproduction."[28] Nakano's confrontation with the press began when the following poem appeared in *Roba*:

### Picture of the Arrival of the Newly Appointed Ambassador to the City

That man's photo appeared in a hundred newspapers this morning
He'd brought along his wife and daughter
Surrounded by police and officials
What, I wonder, has he planned to do here?
Most likely he plans to tell lies here
Here again and again he probably plans to tell lies
And I wonder for whose sake he's going to tell those lies
And I wonder what path those lies will take
How I wonder how will those lies echo back to us

That liar's photograph
Surrounded by wife and daughter and police and officials
Appeared all at once in a hundred newspapers this morning.

The poem contained the theme of cultural exploitation coated by foreign friendship and diplomacy,[29] but these lyrics introduced an unexamined aspect of contemporary cultural manipulation into Nakano's analysis. The poet was not merely pointing to the political machinations of the new diplomat. In addition, he wanted to investigate and expose the medium of the lying, which had appeared "at once in a hundred newspapers." Walter Benjamin would raise the same issue when he decried how man "is increasingly unable to assimilate the data of the world around him by way of experience."[30] The German theorist declared that newspapers purport to organize this information for the edification of their readers, but in fact they isolate the reader from understanding. The form of the message is as responsible as its content, in its abuse of the truth. According to Benjamin, "The principles of journalistic information

---

[27] Nakano, "Shinnin taishi chakukyo no zu," *NSZ* 1:507 [*Roba* 7/26]; "Shimbunkisha," *NSZ* 1:511–12 [*Roba* 11/26]; and "Shimbun ni notta shashin," *NSZ* 1:519–20 [*Puroretaria geijutsu* 7/27].

[28] Benjamin, "Work of Art," p. 224.

[29] Nakano may have been referring to the arrival in Japan of the French ambassador, Paul Claudel, who was called the "poet-ambassador" in the Japanese press. See *Tokyo asahi shinbun*, January 16, 1922. Nakano would take on the diplomat in a poem published in the January 1927 issue of *Roba*. For discussion of "Paul Claudel" as a critique of Orientalism see my *Changing Song*.

[30] Walter Benjamin, *Charles Baudelaire: A Lyric Poet in the Era of High Capitalism*, trans. Harry Zohn (London: NLB, 1973), p. 112.

(freshness of the news, brevity, comprehensibility, and above all, lack of connection between the individual news items) contribute as much to this as does the makeup of the pages and the paper's style."[31]

Benjamin continued by citing the contention of Karl Kraus that newspaper linguistic usage has "paralyzed the imagination of readers." He then argued that the data provided by the newspaper did not enter tradition because of its appearance in large editions. Shared information, in other words, is not perceived as privileged and is thus not passed on. It is available to all, at once, without any transmission among readers, until the next news item cancels out the previous edition's revelations.[32] In this poem about the picture Nakano wished to freeze this process of the constant production of items by the press in order to reveal that the picture is the product of a history, and that because of this one photograph (which would not be seen or mentioned in the following morning's newspaper, or ever again), an ideologically saturated history could be constructed in a twofold fashion. First of all, there would be additional layers of deformation resulting from mistranslation, misquotation, or misrepresentation by the press. Second—and this is the real subject of the poem—there would be the impression left by the photograph, naturalizing the official as a given entity. The newspaper coverage would not question either his past or his future intentions.

Nakano knows that the meaning given to a photograph is constructed within a given culture at a certain moment. The viewer must recognize that the picture is not a transparent reflection, but a representation of a highly problematic historical reality. In the poem about the picture of the newly arrived ambassador, Nakano's seemingly naive questions (the litany in "Train," beginning with "what are factory girls," comes to mind) are his way of voicing his sophisticated insight that a photograph, like any other cultural text, must be read with a critical eye for what is not overtly articulated. A culture contains unquestioned presumptions about the place of photographs and about how a photograph should be read, as one part of the ideology it reproduces in order to give shape to its history. Benjamin warned his readers to turn their attention away from the question of whether photography was an art to the issue of the transformation of a work of art within the photograph.[33] But, like Nakano, he was interested in a certain sort of photographic image, the picture that was com-

---

[31] Ibid.

[32] Ibid., pp. 112–13.

[33] Walter Benjamin, "A Short History of Photography," *Screen* 13, 1 (Spring 1972): 22. This essay first appeared in 1931; Benjamin would raise the issue a second time five years later, when he noted an absence in the discourse on the photograph: "The primary question—whether the very invention of photography had not transformed the entire nature of art—was not raised." Benjamin, "Work of Art," p. 229.

modified and captioned for sale in the illustrated press. Benjamin remarked on the expansion of the marketplace after the invention of the photograph: "it offered on the market, in limitless quantities, figures, landscapes, events which had previously been utilizable either not at all, or only as pictures for one customer."[34] He recognized that just as the press could create personalities, it could appropriate ideas originally produced, to bring into question the capitalist culture encouraging the commodification of words and images: "the bourgeois apparatus of production and publication can assimilate astonishing quantities of revolutionary themes, indeed, can propagate them without calling its own existence, and the existence of the class that owns it, seriously into question."[35] The journalist was central to this process, for he created truncated, isolated occurrences, which appeared as arbitrary, historically unmediated events. Five years earlier, in 1926, Nakano had already concurred, for the position of the newspaperman as a producer who works against the production of any historical consciousness was the subject of Nakano's second poem about the world made by the newspaper. The following verse, which appeared in *Roba* in November 1926, was obliquely worded but clearly captioned:

### Journalist

Did you know
We were "talking"
You came on in
You saw me and were shocked
You took heed of me in front of the whiteman
You asked the whiteman
Does he speak English
No that he does not
You were relieved
I see I see hm hm
Ahh your chatter was ultra-leftist

You knew
That I speak no English
But did you know
That I understand a small amount of English

Did you know
What you asked of that whiteman
What you forced that foreigner to say

[34] Benjamin, *Charles Baudelaire*, p. 163.
[35] Benjamin, "The Author as Producer," p. 229.

In front of me
From that whiteman of my circle
What you robbed from him and how

And do you know?
When you flew out like a crow
What that whiteman said to me
That whiteman said it
Dringend neugierig!
And the base of my ears turned red

But worry not
We'll probably talk tomorrow
About you
About newspaper journalists
About Japanese newspapers in general
And we'll probably laugh jovially
Ahh—Fatty
You be loyal to your work
That itself can be the topic of our talk

The narrator and a German friend who appears to be a fellow revolutionary seem to be visiting a cafe when their conversation is interrupted by an aggressive journalist whose "chatter" is leftist. He is a poseur, possessing no real understanding or interest in revolution. Instead of recognizing the bond of friendship between Nakano and the foreign man (the crude term *ketō* has been translated as "whiteman" herein to denote its vulgarity) that transcends the Japanese poet's inability to communicate in English, the journalist affects a conspiratorial, cosmopolitan air and immediately presumes an intimacy with the German man. The dialogue is sketchy; the reader knows no details of the exchange between the German and the reporter, and even a translation of the German phrase reveals only that "Dringend neugierig" means "insistently curious." But the poem is an angry, assured statement of the author's rejection of Taishō mass culture, which has coopted and packaged Taishō revolutionary fervor. The "topic of our talk" is the work of a new historic personality, the "loyal" Japanese newspaperman. His journalism is sensationalist, relying on the instant creation of news or a "happening" before the writer can rush on to create his own subjective shaping of a situation in another instant article.

Nakano knows full well that the profession of journalist, along with the photography industry, has been well established since the closing decades of the Meiji era, but he also knows that "Journalist" is being read in the midst of a major newspaper war among the leading dailies for con-

trol of a vastly expanded readership that expects to be entertained.[36]
"Journalist" illustrates Benjamin's view that the press has replaced politics with a curiosity that cannot even be sustained, but must keep alight-
ing on new objects and new topics. In the newspaper, fact is inseparable
from fiction, because the newspaper incorporates advertisements, serialized novels, and any other pieces of writing that can be indiscriminately
utilized to present the experience of novelty to the reader. There is no other
organizing principle to journalism, other than "that imposed on it by the
reader's impatience." But this very role placed on the reader, that of organizer of ideas, can be used to insert politics into the news. The reader
can become a writer, capable of prescription and not merely description.[37]

By the summer of 1927, Nakano was beginning to shift his attention
away from the culture of reproduction explored in the pages of *Roba*
toward a poetry celebrating revolutionary violence in a series of violent
scenarios reporting class conflict in the cities and the countryside of early
Shōwa Japan. Two years later, in 1929, his poetry and essays would take
yet another turn as his revolutionary fervor was marshalled against the
state's control of culture. The Jintan metaphor in "The Selling of Writing
and Other Matters," which went on sale in 1929, has been cited herein to
demarcate his analysis of consumer culture, but it also marked the beginning of a shift in his language away from this concern. While the essay
explained how culture was bought and sold, thereby providing a label for
his critique of the reproduction of culture, by the time Nakano Shigeharu
wrote those words, *where he was* was no longer within a society of producers and consumers of culture. By then the Marxist writer was in battle
with a repressive state that was actively moving to prevent him and his
colleagues from expressing their anger publicly. By 1932 the Culture
Movement would be shattered, its journals abolished, its leadership si-
lenced.

The histories tell us who Nakano Shigeharu was in 1926 and 1927
when he wrote "Imperial Hotel," "Journalist," and "Train." And indeed
he was a young university graduate, a literary man, and a political activist
destined to become editor and leader of a series of revolutionary forums,

---

[36] The expansion of the press is reflected in the following statistics: in 1912, 200,000
copies of the *Osaka mainichi shinbun* were sold; four years later the figure rose to 460,000;
and by 1926, when "Journalist" appeared, the number had soared to 1,230,000. For these
figures see Minami, *Taishō bunka*, p. 121. The sales of the *Osaka asahi* and the *Tokyo asahi*
also doubled during the Taishō era, the former going from 342,386 in 1918 to 782,709 in
1926; the latter, from 221,434 to 431,811 during the same period. Yamamoto Taketoshi,
*Kindai Nihon no shinbun dokushazō* (Tokyo: Hōsei University Press, 1981), p. 410.

[37] Benjamin, "The Author as Producer," pp. 224–25. This sentiment was reiterated elsewhere when the author pronounced that "the distinction between author and public is
about to lose its basic character. . . . At any moment the reader is ready to turn into a
writer." Benjamin, "Work of Art," p. 232.

beginning in the summer of 1927, when Akutagawa Ryūnosuke committed suicide and "The Photograph in the Newspaper" appeared in the new
magazine *Puroretaria geijutsu*, published by the Japan Proletarian Arts
League. But what the works examined here have recorded is that, in the
closing years of Taishō, Nakano Shigeharu was a Marxist critic engaged
in a struggle to tell his people how images were being sold to them and to
show them that they had the power to see through such lies if they would
only look.

Nakano Shigeharu did not meet Langston Hughes. Nor was Nakano
among the Japanese revolutionary writers who were arrested while waiting to meet with the black American poet during his stay at the Imperial
Hotel in the summer of 1933, for he had already been imprisoned since
the spring of the previous year.[38] He could not have read either the lines
of Brecht cited in the opening to this essay, or any of the writings of Walter Benjamin during the closing years of Taishō and the first years of
Shōwa. Nakano and Benjamin were not friends. There were no exchanges
between them, but their shared grounding in Marx's concepts liberated
them to challenge an historically unprecedented means of oppression. Images were dictating actions in films and photographs, in Tokyo during the
late 1920s just as in Berlin and Paris during the early 1930s, and for both
writers it was not a foregone conclusion that the state would consolidate
control over the power of representation.

Benjamin's interpretation of the poem written by his colleague Bertolt
Brecht, quoted at the beginning of this essay, brings Nakano Shigeharu
and Walter Benjamin together, highlighting how the two men emerging
from radically different traditions in the third decade of the twentieth
century made some very similar decisions. Concluding his discussion of
the poem wherein Lao Tze and his page are waylaid by a customs official
on their way into exile—a poem about friendship, as he explains it—Benjamin ends with a message: "the lesson or advice here is never to forget
about the inconstancy and changeability of things, and to align oneself
with those things which are inconspicuous and sober and inexhaustible,
like water," or like the cause of the oppressed.[39] Nakano Shigeharu's re-

[38] About his stay in Japan, Langston Hughes wrote, "You may be killed, but you'll never
be bored." On the encounters of Langston Hughes in Tokyo, see Arnold Rampersad, *The
Life of Langston Hughes*, Vol. 1: *1902–1941, I, Too, Sing America* (New York: Oxford
University Press, 1986), pp. 272–75.

[39] Walter Benjamin, *Understanding Brecht*, trans. Anna Bostock (London: NLB, 1973),
p. 74.

Elizabeth Young-Bruehl, whose translation of the Brecht lines is used here, relates how
the "Legend of the Origin of the Book Tao Te Ching on Lao Tzu's Way into Exile" was a
means to friendship and a source of sustenance for Hannah Arendt's husband, Heinrich
Blucher, when he was interned in France along with hundreds of other German nationals in
the summer of 1939: "Walter Benjamin had been to visit his friend Bertold Brecht in Den-

production of Taishō culture teaches this lesson. In his struggle against injustice, like Langston Hughes and Bertolt Brecht, he chose to align himself with poetry. In verse, he reproduced the culture of his time and place to show how new traditions could continue to deny the inconstancy and changeability of the Japanese social order. He chose to turn the culture of reproduction against itself to challenge a system offering things for sale to its citizens instead of an honest accounting of history. Benjamin would be dead within little more than a decade, Brecht's poems would be written in exile, and Nakano Shigeharu's poetry would end with the beginning of the Shōwa era, several years after his release from prison in 1934. But his words would continue to appear—sober and inexhaustible in prison letters, in essays, and in novels about imprisonment. The legacy of Nakano Shigeharu is in no small part his critique of the reproduction of Taishō culture, but in large part his legacy is also a challenge to any state that would silence its poets and all others who deny that the way things should be are the way they always have been.

---

mark the preceding spring and returned with an unpublished poem. Hannah Arendt learned it by heart, and Blucher took their copy with him to Villemalard, where he treated it like a sacred talisman with magical powers: those of his fellow inmates, who when they read it, understood it, were known to be potential friends. Brecht's 'Legende von der Enstehung des Buches Taoteking auf dem Weg des Laotse in die Emigration' was 'like a rumor of good tidings,' Hannah Arendt remembered; 'it travelled by word of mouth—a source of consolation and patience and endurance—where such wisdom was most needed.' " Elizabeth Young-Bruehl, *Hannah Arendt: For Love of the World* (New Haven: Yale University Press, 1982), pp. 150–51.

# 8

## "Credo Quia Absurdum": *Tenkō* and the Prisonhouse of Language

BRETT DE BARY

STUDIES of the development of structuralist and poststructuralist thought in the West often emphasize the role of the avant-garde text in challenging realist literature's ability to represent a "vraisemblable," or accepted natural view of the world. Rosalind Coward and John Ellis, in introducing their study *Language and Materialism*, for example, observe that it was "in analyzing texts by Mallarmé, Lautréamont, Joyce," and others "that semiology's assumptions about the speaking subject (parole) and its relation to language (langue) became increasingly untenable."[1] In Japan, too, the short-lived claim to preeminence of Naturalist-style realism had been challenged, by the early 1920s, by the production of avant-garde texts by writers affiliated with "modernist" (most notably the New Perception School) or Marxist philosophies, and the appearance of these texts had fueled debate within critical discourse as well. Critic Senuma Shigeki sees, around the time of the Kantō earthquake in 1923, the beginning of a protracted crisis of Japanese "modern" literature which, in contradistinction to "modernist" literature, may be characterized by a mimetic mode and what Senuma defines as a thematics of the "individual ego" (*kojinteki jiga*). Within the late Taishō context of economic instability, social unrest, and the emergence of revolutionary working class movements, the notion of the "individual" in literature began to disintegrate: according to Senuma, the doctrine of "class consciousness" in proletarian literature and the overturning of "common sense perceptions" in the early work of such writers as Hirato Renkichi, Kawabata Yasunari, and Yokomitsu Riichi promoted this dissolution.[2]

In chronological periodizations of modern Japanese literature, the active periods of proletarian literature (1918–23; 1928–33) appear brief; "modernism," as a visible literary movement (as opposed to the experiments of individual writers) flourished even more briefly during roughly

[1] Rosalind Coward and John Ellis, *Language and Materialism* (London: Routledge and Kegan Paul, 1977), pp. 5–6.

[2] Senuma Shigeki, *Teihon Shōwa no bungaku* (Tokyo: Tōjusha, 1976), pp. 5–27.

the first half of the decade of the twenties.[3] Alternatively, both Marxism and modernism are often seen as early "phases" along the path to maturation of individual writers who eventually "reverted to older styles."[4] In their effort to trace the lengthening of the shadows of war over society in the late 1930s and the withering effect of censorship on cultural production, historians of Japanese literature have often failed to recognize, in such post-1933 phenomena as the appearance of the conversion novel (*tenkō shōsetsu*), the genre novel (*fūzoku shōsetsu*), and the debate over the "literature of angst," the continuity of theme with an earlier, more cosmopolitan period.[5] In fact, the debate about the status of the realist text, initiated by the Marxist and modernist movements in the late Taishō and early Shōwa, was not eclipsed but rather permutated and intensified as the nation was drawn into the widening vortex of war. Avant-garde texts, fewer in number and often highly esoteric because of the necessity for circumventing censorship restrictions, continued to play a role in this process.

Haniya Yutaka's *Credo Quia Absurdum* (*Fugōri yue ni ware shinzu*, or I Believe Because It Is Absurd) is one such text. Published in serial form in the little magazine *Kōsō* (Conceptions) between 1939 and 1941, the work reveals not only that radical challenges to the realist text continued to appear throughout the "dark valley" years, but that the debate over realism was profoundly implicated in the political developments of the time. Haniya acknowledges that his text, despite its nonnarrative, iconoclastic form and the fact that it was written five years after his release from imprisonment as a Marxist, is a conversion novel or *tenkō shōsetsu*. The majority of works in this genre, which proliferated after the conversions of Communist Party leaders Sano Manabu and Nabeyama Sadachika, took the form of ex post facto narratives of justification for confessional "documents" signed under duress by imprisoned Marxists. While incorporating, through the motifs of confession and personal testimony, key elements of the I-novel form (*watakushi shōsetsu*), which has been seen as the hallmark of Japanese literary modernity, the conversion novel often subverted that form, with its claims to mimetic authenticity, by exposing the author's historical or "real" confession to have been in-

[3] This periodization for Japanese proletarian literature is followed by Tatsuo Arima in *The Failure of Freedom* (Cambridge: Harvard University Press, 1969).

[4] Donald Keene, *Dawn to the West, Japanese Literature in the Modern Era: Fiction* (New York: Holt, Rinehart and Winston, 1984), p. 630.

[5] For one summary of the evolution of these genres and the accompanying literary debates, see Senuma, *Teihon Shōwa no bungaku*, pp. 5–45. A provocative analysis of the Japanese literary scene after 1933 from a Marxist perspective may be found in Miyamoto Yuriko's "Kyō no bungaku no tenbō," written in 1939 and published posthumously. The essay is included in *Miyamoto Yuriko zenshū* (Tokyo: Shin Nihon shuppansha, 1980), 11:261–312.

complete, a subterfuge, or a mere empty convention. The effect of the state's suppression of the Proletarian Literature Movement was, in this sense, not so much an interruption as a transposition of the terms of the debate over realism. Nevertheless, in the case of well-known conversion novels like those of Shimaki Kensaku, Tokunaga Sunao, and Hayashi Fusao, the challenge to the realist text remained implicit, and critical reception of the works tended to invoke rather than question the well-worn criteria of "authenticity" and "sincerity." Miyamoto Yuriko, writing in 1939, was quick to spot this contradiction, suggesting that it was largely because of "the mood of the time" that the tenkō novelist's confession of "worthlessness" and "pangs of conscience" was seen as "honest, human, and guileless."[6] Because their challenge to realism was implicit and easily ignored, such novels laid no claim to the status of the avant garde.

In Haniya's *Credo Quia Absurdum*, by contrast, the implicit internal contradiction of the tenkō shōsetsu, that of confession invalidating confession, has been elevated to an explicit thematic and compositional principle. The result is a radically iconoclastic text that rejects the form of the linear narrative, directly attacks the cause-effect logic upon which it is based, and systematically calls into question language's ability to refer to or represent the very experience of conversion in which the text itself appears to be grounded. In that "both the given material environment and the given social relationships" are "radically excluded from its form," *Credo* displays many of the characteristics of the subjective expressionism described by Raymond Williams as a response to the crisis of high naturalism in early twentieth-century Europe.[7] But the abstraction of this work was also directly linked to its inquiry into the nature of language. Even the graphic surface of the text heightens one's sense of the precarious and arbitrary nature of the signifying process: each page consists of a small block of print suspended in, and almost overwhelmed by, blankness. One may imagine a voice uttering the words on the page (a voice that is sometimes addressed by other voices in the text), but this voice is unidentified and never takes on the configuration of a character. Although the blocks of print allude indirectly to a narrative, which one may construe as a narrative of conversion, Haniya himself has described the form of the text as "aphoristic." Blocks of print that seem to be in dialogue with each other on two interfacing pages constitute a single "aphorism" (fifty-five in all). Each aphorism presents a riddle or enigma, a text that appears to be incoherent or unintelligible if one relies on conventional assumptions about language to decode it.

When Credo first appeared in 1939, Haniya Yutaka was a well-posi-

[6] Miyamoto, *Miyamoto Yuriko zenshū*, p. 263.

[7] Raymond Williams, *Culture* (London: Fontana Paperbacks, 1981), p. 175.

tioned but not well-known writer. As a little magazine, *Conceptions* was not widely circulated, and the obscurity of meaning of the text discouraged comment. (Haniya later referred to this lack of response, or more accurately of "resistance" [*tegotae*], when he described the initial publication of the work as "throwing a black ball into blackness.") It was not until the postwar period that the group of literati who had coalesced around *Conceptions*—Haniya, Ara Masato, Sasaki Kiichi, Hirano Ken, Odagiri Hideo—emerged as leading figures in the literary world, with the founding of the journal *Kindai bungaku* (Modern literature). The members of the Modern Literature Group, who were to remain among Japan's most influential literary critics throughout the three decades following the war, reissued *Credo* in the journal in 1946. A few months later, Haniya began publication of the monumental *Shirei* (Ghosts), the eight-volume work "in process" until 1985, which commands almost forbidding respect among Japanese intelligentsia. The two works, together with other short fiction and numerous essays on culture and politics, have made Haniya a seminal figure in postwar avant-garde thought, whose work has been interpreted and reinterpreted during successive phases of postwar history. After a brief description of the text, I will consider it in relation to its first, and most influential, early postwar reader, Tsurumi Shunsuke, who, in turn, presents *Credo Quia Absurdum* as a prewar *tenkōsha*'s reading of Immanuel Kant.

> After tormenting myself over the magic of the predicate, I dimly sensed myself approaching a mystery.
>
> "And now, the ceremony . . ." in my soul's secret depths I thought I heard a voice whisper. A being, like a shadow, offered me the ritual cup.
>
> "All assertions are false. It is not true that a thing can be the same as itself and yet expressed by something else."[8]

Describing the composition of *Credo Quia Absurdum* retrospectively, Haniya wrote that he attempted to fuse "logic" (*ronri*) and "free verse poetry" (*shi*) in the work.[9] Ordinarily, one might assume that the choice of the term "logic" was intended simply to invoke the broader notion of "philosophy" or "philosophical inquiry" in general. Certainly the broad-ranging allusions to philosophical works in the text, most notably to the thought of Immanuel Kant, the Greek Sophists, and early Buddhism, orient *Credo Quia Absurdum* to the realm of philosophical inquiry just as strikingly as many of its literary techniques draw on the avant-garde

---

[8] Haniya Yutaka, *Fugōri yue ni ware shinzu*, in *Haniya Yutaka sakuhinshū* (Tokyo: Kawade shobō shinsha, 1971), 2:8–9.

[9] Haniya Yutaka, "Ronri to shi to no kon'in," cited in Sugaya Kikuo, "Romanesku no hango," in Shirakawa Masayoshi, ed., *Shireiron* (Tokyo: Yosensha, 1985), p. 228.

works of Hagiwara Sakutarō, Kajii Motojirō, Arthur Rimbaud, James Joyce, and others. Still, the opening lines of *Credo*, cited above, make it appear that Haniya's choice of the term "logic" was quite deliberate. From the start, whether underhandedly or openly, the text ensnares one in logical traps. Grammar is used to subvert grammar, as in the sentence using "magical" (therefore, illusory) as the attribute of the attribute, a textual opening that uses sentences to disavow faith in the act of sentence-making, or predication itself. Other statements construct logical antino-mies, sentences in which subject and predicate rely on each other for their logical meaning and yet cancel each other out. (If "all assertions are false," this assertion, too, is invalidated, and thus the statement is "true" and "false" at the same time.) Logic, then, and quite specifically the un-likely theme of logic's twisted relationship to grammar, is taken up at the beginning of this unusual text. The narrative thus adopts a deliberately self-contradictory stance from the outset. Language is used to subvert lan-guage; language is turned back against itself. The text might be seen as applying to itself the type of analysis elaborated by Paul de Man in his *Allegories of Reading*. It sees as highly problematic the series of relation-ships usually assumed to be continuous and symbiotic: that among gram-mar, logic, and rhetoric. De Man, for example, holds in question our "common-sense" understanding of "the passage from grammar to prop-ositions, as being relatively unproblematic: no true propositions are con-ceivable in the absence of grammatical consistency."[10] The continuity of the relationship between grammar and rhetoric, in its turn, has been chal-lenged by "theoretical and philosophical speculations" both "recent" and "age-old." De Man cites the example of Kenneth Burke. Kenneth Burke mentions *deflection* (which he compares structurally to Freudian dis-placement), defined as "any slight bias or unintended error," as the rhe-torical basis of language, and deflection is then conceived as a dialectical subversion of the consistent link between sign and meaning that operates within grammatical patterns; hence Burke's well-known distinction be-tween grammar and rhetoric.[11]

Frederic Jameson has observed that "we read every text through sedi-mented layers of interpretation," and this is particularly true of *Credo Quia Absurdum*, which, in a sense has been "discovered" and "rediscov-ered" throughout the postwar period. When the text was reprinted in *Kindai bungaku* shortly after the war, Haniya's own associates were con-tent to exclaim over its obscurity rather than to interpret it; credit for introducing the text, and perhaps initiating the postwar fascination with Haniya, goes to sociologist Tsurumi Shunsuke and the influential two-

---

[10] Paul de Man, *Allegories of Reading* (New Haven: Yale University press, 1979), p. 7.
[11] Ibid., p. 8.

volume *Tenkō* (Conversion), published in 1959. It was Tsurumi who suggested, among other things, that *Credo* might be seen as a prewar Japanese reading of Kant's *Critique of Pure Reason*, which Haniya read in his prison cell. While other commentaries on *Credo* have emphasized its affinity for what might be called "deconstructive" impulses in Kant's thought, Tsurumi's reading, strongly shaped by the early postwar search for universal values and individual autonomy, is positivistic, historicist, and pragmatic. In fully exploring the relationship between *Credo* and Haniya's tenkō, and in pointing to "root metaphors" in the text that were to persist in Haniya's postwar writings, especially *Ghosts*, Tsurumi's essay has had a lasting influence on the reception of Haniya's work.[12]

Haniya's tenkō, as shaped by Tsurumi's interpretation, is both "paradigmatic" and crucial to later developments in postwar thought. It is paradigmatic in that Haniya represents a generation of Japanese intellectuals whose late Taishō and early Shōwa education, according to Tsurumi, "had Western philosophy as its axis"; and in that it represents the "collapse of faith" of these intellectuals in the possibility of sudden, revolutionary transformation of Japanese society (p. 289). Tsurumi's commentary on the centrality of Haniya's tenkō to postwar thought reflects his own concerns as a postwar intellectual with autonomy and the creation of a Japanese ethos based on universalistic, as opposed to particularistic, values. In *Credo Quia Absurdum*, therefore, Tsurumi emphasizes the importance of an "experiential" (*jikkanshugi*) methodology whereby Haniya, by hewing closely to the isolating experience of tenkō, develops a stance of critical independence from the collective identities of the Japanese state and the Communist Party. His analysis accordingly emphasizes a concept of autonomous selfhood. *Credo Quia Absurdum* becomes a stripping away of identities and a drastic paring down of narrative focus to the bare essential of the self. Tsurumi claims the narrative for "history"; but Haniya's is a "history of the self" tensely poised between, and maintaining its resistance to, cooptation by "Japanese history" and "Communist Party history." Tsurumi thus frequently moves to assert, perhaps paradoxically, the unique ("one time only") nature of Haniya's conversion, which in turn becomes a correlative of his unique individuality, and, finally, the basis for a "universalistic" and therefore critical perspective. In the categories it invokes to explicate and affirm Haniya's literary praxis, the following quotation is typical of Tsurumi's manner of argument:

[12] Tsurumi Shunsuke, "Kyomushugisha no keisei: Haniya Yutaka," in Shisō no Kagaku, ed., *Tenkō* (Tokyo: Heibonsha, 1959), 1:290–296. Tsurumi traces the imagistic treatment of eight important conceptual categories in *Credo*: thought, being, space, time, logic, ethics, aesthetics, and ideology.

Haniya is creating literature based on a history of the self and trying to make this a standpoint from which both state and party versions of history can be judged. Haniya takes the self's unique experience—a "conversion" which happened only once—and by analyzing it . . . attempts to construct a towering fortress. Documents of the state, in the form of reports from the Metropolitan Police Office or statements from the Imperial Headquarters, or in whatever form they accumulate as years and months pass, cannot drag Haniya's narrative from its fortress. Nor can the party, with its Comintern Theses and its Akahata articles. (pp. 298–99)

It was through this type of analysis that Tsurumi was able to transform the interpretation of a small number of tenkō shōsetsu from that of narratives of shame to narratives of resistance, and thus to consolidate, from within the tragedy of the war itself, a starting point for Japan's postwar culture. "Haniya's aphorisms," he writes elsewhere in the essay, "are rooted in an experience of conversion that happened once and once only; yet they have grown into a mighty tree from which we can envision the future" (p. 296).

The "principle of identity" (jidōritsu) Tsurumi mentions refers to a pivotal phrase in Haniya's text: "Roses, humiliation, the principle of identity. . . . When it comes right down to it, that's all I am."[13] Elsewhere one finds the phrase, "the unhappiness of the principle of identity" (jidōritsu no fukai), and the term "unhappiness" is given prominent, refrain-like repetition that suggests it is being used to characterize the human condition in a manner similar to Kierkegaard's use of the term "angst." Differing interpretations of this concept seem to be the key to divergent readings of Credo Quia Absurdum. Tsurumi's positivistic reading identifies the "principle of identity" as one of the principles of Aristotelian logic ("A thing cannot be itself and something else at the same time"), a rule that, in the Critique of Pure Reason, is used to distinguish a priori (or what Kant terms transcendental) knowledge of the "I" or "subject" from empirical knowledge.[14] Tsurumi points to the particularly close relationship between the section on Transcendental Dialectic in the Critique and Haniya's text. In this section, Kant stresses that the "logical identity of the I" is a necessary but purely logical entity that gives us no bridge to an empirical knowledge of the self. "The identity of the person by no means follows from the identity of the I," Kant states (p. 261). Kant's argument is complex in that it both elevates logic, which he often defines as the "formal conditions of thought," to the realm of the transcendental and exposes the limited and circular nature of logical knowledge. He writes,

[13] Haniya, Fugōri yue ni ware shinzu, p. 19.

[14] Immanuel Kant, Critique of Pure Reason, trans. Max F. Muller (New York: Doubleday, 1966), p. 249.

for example, "The identity of my consciousness at different times is therefore a fixed condition only of my thoughts and their coherence and proves
in no way the identity of my subject . . . *in spite of the logical identity of
the I*" (p. 259).

Tsurumi's juxtaposition of *Credo Quia Absurdum* and Kant on the
transcendental dialectic is highly productive. Tsurumi correctly traces the
way in which Kant's analysis of logic extends into a critique of language
and here, too, finds meaningful parallels with the Haniya text. He cites
the essay "Naze kakuka" (Why write?), published in the journal *Gunzō*
in March 1949, in which Haniya told of his excitement, in prison, in reading Kant's discussion of "the logic of *scheinen*" (literally, the "logic of
appearances," elsewhere referred to as the "transcendental illusion of
pure reason," etc.). Logic, according to Kant, can itself be a source of
illusion, as we can see from our ability to construct "transcendental pa-
ralogisms," or logical problems that drive us to formally false conclusions. "A paralogism," Kant writes, "depends . . . on the very nature of
human reason, and produces an illusion which is inevitable, though not
insoluble" (p. 248). The act of predication fundamental to language,
moreover, is logically false, since it contradicts the principle of identity,
which maintains that a thing can only be itself. Kant used this discrepancy
to topple the Cartesian formula "cogito ergo sum," which saw the existence of thought as guaranteeing the possibility of empirical knowledge
of the self. Kant compared his attack on Cartesian philosphy to the Co-
pernican revolution in the natural sciences because it amounted to a reversal of the subject-object relationship and a radical insistence on the
*representational* nature of all knowledge, including knowledge of the self.
" 'I think,' " Kant writes, "cannot contain any but transcendental predi-
cates; the smallest empirical predicate would spoil . . . its independence
of all experience" (p. 249). The problematic relationship between "I" (the
subject) and the predicate, which results in the representational nature of
self-knowledge, is strikingly depicted in the following passage from the
*Critique*. Kant refers to the

> perfectly empty, representation of the *I* of which we cannot even say that it is a
> concept, but merely a consciousness that accompanies all concepts. By this *I*,
> or *he*, or *it* (the thing), which thinks, nothing is represented beyond a transcen-
> dental subject of thoughts = x, which is known only through the thoughts that
> are its predicates, and of which, apart from them, we can never have the
> slightest concept, so that we are really turning around in a perpetual circle,
> having already to use its representation before we can form any judgment about
> it. (p. 251)

Other, substantive portions of the *Critique* demonstrate that the formal
conditions and circular quality of our knowledge of the self inhere in our

knowledge of the phenomenal world in general. "They [phenomena] cannot, as phenomena, exist by themselves," writes Kant, "but in us only" (p. 36). Therefore, "even if we could see to the very bottom of a phenomenon, it would remain forever different from knowledge of the thing by itself" (p. 37).

Kant's perception of the representation of the "I" as essentially "empty" presages the critique of the subject in twentieth-century European semiotic and poststructuralist theory. While other critics of *Credo Quia Absurdum* have emphasized ways in which the text incorporates such "deconstructive" insights in the *Critique*, Tsurumi's analysis is ambivalent. He reads *Credo* as a text that thematizes the problem of "radical skepticism" (which he also calls nihilism) without acknowledging the extent to which the text renders *itself* problematic as representation. This gives rise to contradictory impulses in Tsurumi's own argument, which affirms the radical skepticism that enabled Haniya to declare his independence from party and state, but then attempts to "fix" and idealize this gesture as the basis for a postwar individualism. Tsurumi, for example, uses *Credo* as biography in observing that "in a reaction against the absolute faith of Haniya, the twenty-year-old Communist Party member, the twenty-two-year-old Haniya, awaiting sentence in prison, gave himself over to a logic and rhetoric of thorough-going skepticism" (p. 294). Even when Tsurumi insightfully describes *Credo* in terms of a "rhetoric" of skepticism, however, he gives primacy to the categories of biography, personality, and psychology in establishing the motivation for such a rhetoric. Thus, in Tsurumi's own influential commentary on Haniya's "principle of identity" one sees vacillation between a biographical approach, which refers unproblematically to Haniya's "life" as a means of decoding the text, and a rhetorical approach, which emphasizes the text's inability to tell the truth about that life or anything else.

As a biographical critic, Tsurumi grounds *Credo Quia Absurdum* in what he calls the "true facts" (*jijitsu*) of Haniya's conversion as narrated by Haniya himself in his book *Mucha to koma* (The whip and the spinning top). The fact that conversion statements were obtained through coercion was crucial to the definition of tenko developed by Tsurumi and his colleagues affiliated with the journal *Shisō no kagaku* (The science of thought) in conducting their path-breaking research. In writing about Haniya, Tsurumi also developed the notion of conversion as involving a "violence to language." He cites as an illustration Haniya's description of the process through which his deposition was obtained in prison.

The examiner worked quickly to produce my document. His work proceeded smoothly and without a hitch, as if he were deftly unwinding a ball of string in his palm. This was the origin of the "deposition" which later I laughed and

cried over within myself. Until that moment I had dimly conceived of a deposition as a record that followed the course of an investigation point by point, a
faithful record of the dialogue between two people alone in a room. But when
I became a character *within* a deposition, I was astonished at the way in which
this unique process of recording diverged from what I had imagined. Not a
single deposition I know of is the record of words exchanged between examiner
and suspect; they record only the statements of the examiner himself. The examiner presents the suspect with a question, and then, surprisingly enough, has
the question entered in the document as if it were the actual answer of the
suspect. The method was probably first adopted as an economy of time and
then became routinized, but, in keeping with it, the examiner simply proceeded
forward from within what he already knew and never went beyond that framework. He would say, for example, "What you have written is a violation of the
divinity of the Emperor, as you know. Now, this was written seriously (you
meant it when you wrote it), wasn't it? That's alright, you can give me any
answer you want. You certainly didn't write it in jest, so it must have been
serious. . . . alright, now, since you wrote it seriously, it was your aim to criticize the emperor system. . . ." The investigator would simply ramble on like
this. The person being examined had no chance to initiate his own statements,
and generally sat in virtual silence, without giving any answer except for an
occasional monosyllabic comment in a low voice. This was a negative attitude
that inevitably arose out of the prisoner's passive state but was also a protective
stance aimed at saying as little as possible; the person being examined would
surmise what the investigator knew and try to avoid until the very end revealing
anything he did not know. . . .

When the investigator who had been facing me finally stopped talking and the
clerk had had time to record our conversation up to that point, he produced
this laughable record:

Question: "Tell me about the essay you wrote."
Answer: "Yes. I humbly submit that I wrote this essay in order to damage the
prestige of the emperor. I wrote it in all seriousness. My aim was to criticize the
emperor system. This was certain."

Our parts in the conversation were systematically reversed in the final version.[15]

Tsurumi notes that this passage in Haniya's writing gave his research
group a crucial indication of the unreliability of the prison records of
interrogation, which comprised a major part of the materials investigated
in their study of tenkō. He goes on to suggest that the young Haniya
turned to "literature" after experiences like the one recounted above shattered his belief in the truth-telling claims of "histories" and bureaucratic

---

[15] Haniya Yutaka, *Muchi to koma* (Tokyo: Miraisha, 1957), pp. 99–100.

documents. Yet Tsurumi proceeds, characteristically, to posit literature
as a category that can be exempted from, or even seen as transcending, Haniya's "thorough-going" skepticism. Literature, according to
Tsurumi, is a receptacle of "truth," moreover a "fixed" (*teichaku shita*)
truth, because it is rooted in the integrity of the individual personality.
Thus Tsurumi can claim that Haniya "discounts both the state's and the
party's 'history' concerning conversion" and "declares that the only fixed
truth abides in literature, *literature that is based on that which the self
alone knows through experience*, elaborated on through various suppositions" (p. 298). Here again, Tsurumi tells the tale of Haniya's breakdown only to salvage intact the notion of an independent subject as the
source of narrative.

Tsurumi's provocative characterization of Haniya's method in *Credo
Quia Absurdum* as that of the "violent use of the copula" (*hinji no bōr-
yokuteki na shiyōhō*; the phrase is taken from the work itself) presents
the text as a symbolic reenactment of the author's tenkō as violence
to language (p. 306). The text is an allegory, as it were, which depends
for its meaning on the referential reality of Haniya's life. According to
Tsurumi, as Haniya the author experienced coercion and saw violence
done to language in prison, so Haniya the author will do violence to language in his own text. Tsurumi's ambivalence is most conspicuous on this
point, for his grounding of *Credo Quia Absurdum* in Haniya's lived experience leads to some of his most radical insights into the text as a commentary on language and "truth." The following passage, for example,
contains Tsurumi's influential decoding of Haniya's "principle of identity" as autobiography. Tsurumi claims that in the line, "Roses, humiliation, the principle of identity. . . . When you come right down to it, that's
all I am," the image of "roses" represents the "rose-colored illusion of
absolute faith in Communism," "humiliation" stands for "conversion,"
and the "principle of identity" refers to individual "identity" as well as
to logic. But this autobiographical mode of interpretation, as one can see
below, quickly leads to a logic that deprives the text of all of the claims
to truth and leaves one with only "deliberate falsehood."

> The experience of conversion—to have one's will subjugated through force—
> gives birth to paranoid delusions. One cannot speak of "rose-colored" illusions
> after this; one resolves to speak only of what is truly certain. But what is cer-
> tain? Only the cycle of thought which begins from the self and returns to the
> self. Only these propositions, whose validity is guaranteed by the principle of
> identity, remain: "I am I" or "This A which is my thought is this A which is my
> thought." But one hesitates to say even this. . . .
>
> Even in solitary confinement, where one can, in a sense, do nothing more than
> constantly verify the principle of identity, there is the sky, seen through the

skylight, and light from the outside world shines into this indirectly. Through imagination, one can become the light and explore the world outside.

When we think about speaking, and try to choose a word, we can hesitate momentarily between subject and predicate while countless words other than the one we must choose clamor for our attention. Should we sacrifice the logical certainty of the principle of identity and make the leap to one of these words? But each of the assertions we make in this way becomes a falsehood as soon as we utter it; this we know immediately. This gives rise to a method where we resolutely tell lies, knowing that they are lies. This method [discovered in prison and explored in *Credo*] became the basis for Haniya's postwar *Ghosts*. (p. 294)

Here, once again, Tsurumi forges links between Haniya's conversion, *Credo Quia Absurdum*, and Haniya's stance as a postwar intellectual. Haniya's use of language, his self-styled "violent use of the copula," is defined by Tsurumi as the method of "resolutely telling lies, knowing that they are lies," a method grounded both experientially in tenkō and in a perception of the nature of language itself. For Tsurumi, this lays the foundation for Haniya's postwar literature (p. 294). By thus interpreting it, Tsurumi indeed construes Haniya's literature as a "towering fortress" of postwar thought. He grants the maximum revolutionary potential to Haniya's "method." By asserting, through reference to Kant, the "internal necessity" of logic as a precondition of thought, Tsurumi can present logic (and its relationship to speech) as a kind of tyrant against which *Credo Quia Absurdum* stages a rebellion. By paralleling this with revolutionary political praxis in the "external realm," Tsurumi is able to describe Haniya's method as a "gesture of secession" in the internal realm.

We can secede from the inevitability that permeates external reality by constantly considering the realm of possibilities in a framework larger than external reality, and by "assembling" these possibilities to create events outside of reality. But what about necessity in the inner realm (the necessity of logic)? Here, too, one can doubt the rules of speech and destroy them, and each time one does so one will be making a gesture of secession. Haniya called this "the violent use of the copula." (pp. 306–307)

In the end, Tsurumi's argument plays with the paradoxical concept of *conversion as consistency*. That act of turning or betrayal which had been seen as the Japanese intelligentsia's badge of shame is transformed, through Tsurumi's rhetoric, into something both revolutionary and enduring. The act of violently using the copula is seen as a steadfast stance that links the prewar *Credo* with the postwar *Ghosts*. By stressing that this gesture of secession is directed toward both the party and the state, Tsurumi emphasizes Haniya's autonomy, and, in the ultimate step of his postwar logic, that this autonomy is itself "revolutionary." In the section of his essay called, significantly, "The Communist Party as seen from the midst of conversion," Tsurumi compares Haniya's independence of attitude with that of other tenkōsha. "The weakness of many tenkōsha" Tsurumi writes, "is that they moved too quickly from tenkō itself" (p. 300). For example, many who attained a lucid insight into the weakness of the prewar Communist Party quickly moved to a position of unqualified support for the state. The productive nature of Haniya's thought lies in the fact that "Haniya did not try to distance himself quickly from tenkō but sat rooted to the site of the tenkō process" and from this position developed a sustained critique of prewar Japanese communism. To Tsurumi, Haniya's critique was "revolutionary" and has remained revolutionary throughout the postwar period. This stance drew on Haniya's prewar anarchism, a philosophy he embraced prior to his commitment to the Communist Party; as Marx inverted Proudhon's *Philosophy of Poverty* to the *Poverty of Philosophy*, so did the young Haniya envision an anarchist revision of Lenin's *State and Revolution* entitled *Revolution and the State*. Tsurumi sees Haniya after his tenkō as reviving his anarchist philosophy. Although some tenkōsha rejoined the Communist Party in the early, liberal era of the U.S. Occupation, Haniya did not. He rather sought to "open up a new perspective on Marxism by critiquing it from an anarchist standpoint" and emphasizing the anarchist dimension of the communist vision (p. 301). Haniya believed that "the essential principles of communism were correct," but that one should judge "every case in terms of a distant future when party leadership would disappear" (p. 303). Thus Haniya became well-known in the postwar period for the paired figure, in *Ghosts*, of the "walker" (*hokōsha*) and the "sitter" (*zasha*, emphasizing contemplative sitting as in *zazen*), who represent the need for the integration of revolutionary praxis and a revolutionary theory based on "unflinching contemplation of the future" (p. 303). The notion of "revolutionary criticism," as well as of "perpetual" or "ongoing revolution" (*eien na kakumei*), also plays a prominent role in Haniya's postwar writing. Tsurumi notes that in 1951, at the time of intense divisiveness between the "internationalist" and "mainstream" factions within the Japan Communist Party, many young Communists, disenchanted with the party, turned to Haniya's writings. In a later development, partly anticipated by Tsurumi's essay and partly, perhaps, created by it, New Left intellectuals who broke with the established opposition parties at the time of the Anti–Security Treaty Struggle in the early 1960s again turned to Haniya.

(I've never known a man as slippery as you! You can find reasons for anything.)

The woman's features are imprinted, oppressively, on my memory. Ah, but it is not just her image. When I observe her consciousness stealthily, I become entangled in its mysterious power—subtle, invisible, inescapable.

"No matter what we are, we are different from that."

Let me tell you the story of a certain recluse. Searching for the self, he first cut off his feet. "There must be more," he told himself, and he cut off his hands. Finally he had carved himself away until no trace, no shadow remained. "But listen, I can still hear a voice muttering. There! A voice coming from some place very still, very uncertain. . . ." Truly, there is no logic without falsehood.

—*Credo Quia Absurdum*[16]

Tsurumi Shunsuke's reading of *Credo Quia Absurdum* locates a thematics of radical skepticism in the text but fails to acknowledge the degree to which the text problematizes itself as representation. In the same manner, Tsurumi seems unaware of the extent to which his own interpretation of Haniya relies on a forced reading: the notion of "conversion as consistency," to which even the concept of Haniya as an advocate of continuous revolution can be traced, depends on a contradictory, literal reading of an expression that is essentially figurative, that of Haniya "sitting in" or remaining somehow permanently "in the midst of" conversion (p. 300). In his quest for a vision of Japan's postwar culture, Tsurumi himself has been seduced by the "magic of the attribute," constructing metaphorical descriptions of Haniya, only to treat them as reality.

[16] Haniya, *Fugōri yue ni ware shinzu*, pp. 8–9.

# 9

## *Ikkoku Shakai-shugi*: Sano Manabu and the Limits of Marxism as Cultural Criticism

GERMAINE A. HOSTON

IN JUNE 1933, Sano Manabu and fellow imprisoned Japanese Communist Party (JCP) leader Nabeyama Sadachika repudiated their Communist affiliations, thereby launching a massive wave of tenkō (conversions) by Japanese Marxists to the "national cause." As imperial officials coopted the movement to engineer public unity in support of the war against China, tenkō engulfed the Left and finally culminated in the collapse of the Japanese Communist movement by 1935.[1] That Sano's and Nabeyama's recantation had such a great impact is in large part attributable to their status as leaders of the Communist movement. Sano (1892–1953) was a graduate of Tokyo Imperial University and lectured in economics at Waseda University before joining the newborn JCP in 1922. He became a member of the party's Central Committee the following year. Nabeyama (1901–79) was a laborer with only a secondary school education but, like Sano, he became involved early in the JCP. In 1926 he was the Japanese representative to the Profintern (Red International of Trade Unions) and a delegate to the Comintern. When the two men were arrested for their JCP activities in 1929, they led the effort to use the joint public

The author wishes to express appreciation for the assistance of Benjamin I. Schwartz, John D. Montgomery, Patricia Golden Steinhoff, the late Ukai Nobushige, Maruyama Masao, Ishida Takeshi, Baba Hiroji, Takahashi Masao, Tsukagoshi Tsutako, and Constance Rosemont, and for the helpful comments of Thomas Rimer and other participants in the workshop. Research support was provided by the International Federation for University Women, the National Endowment for the Humanities, and the Social Science Research Council.

[1] See Patricia Golden Steinhoff, "*Tenkō*: Ideology and Social Integration in Prewar Japan," Ph.D. dissertation, Harvard University, 1969; and Germaine A. Hoston, "*Tenkō*: Marxism and the National Question in Prewar Japan," *Polity* 16, 1 (November 1983): 96–118. This essay discusses Sano's tenkō and his objections to orthodox Marxism-Leninism in the context of the workshop's consideration of Marxism as a vehicle of cultural criticism. Other aspects of Sano's thought, particularly the role of nationalism and attachment to the Imperial Household, have been treated in comparative perspective in my article "Emperor, Nation, and the Transformation of Marxism to National Socialism in Prewar Japan: The Case of Sano Manabu," *Studies in Comparative Communism* 18, 1 (Spring 1985): 25–47.

trial of JCP members as a forum for JCP propaganda. They were sentenced to life imprisonment in October 1932.[2]

Sano was joined in tenkō by thousands of other Marxists, but unlike most of his fellow tenkōsha, he ventured beyond the mere renunciation of his Communist ties to evolve his own Marxian doctrine of socialism-in-one-country (*ikkoku shakai-shugi*). Professing a return to what he considered the essence of Japaneseness, Sano offered his national socialist doctrine as a superior version of socialism, one that was based on traditional "Eastern" (*tōyō-teki*) perspectives on man and society yet retained orthodox Marxist tenets concerning social change.

In the years after the war, Sano elaborated these ideas as the basis for a new vanguard socialist party and established his own Nihon Seiji Keizai Kenkyūjo (Japanese Institute for the Study of Politics and Economics) to disseminate them. His intense efforts to promote his "Oriental" brand of Marxian socialism failed to gain widespread popular support. Nevertheless, Sano's extensive writings chronicling his return to Eastern philosophical traditions, a critique of the Marxist theory of the state that was echoed by other tenkōsha, and the articulation of his national socialist thought offer an opportunity to weigh the appeal of Marxism against its limitations as a vehicle of cultural criticism in prewar Japan.

As Sano's case indicates, not all tenkōsha jettisoned Marxism itself along with their Communist ties. Indeed, it is useful here to distinguish between two kinds of tenkōsha: those who repudiated the JCP, particularly in opposition to its subordination to Soviet leadership and Comintern policies, and those who abandoned the Marxian framework as well to return to an indigenous philosophical or spiritual tradition like Buddhism or *kokutai* (national polity) thought.[3] Unlike many tenkōsha, Sano rejected the vision of violent socialist revolution advocated by the Comintern and JCP and revived Buddhist and kokutai elements of Japanese tradition, yet he retained crucial elements of Marxism in his new thought.

Sano was not the only Japanese Marxist who endeavored to adapt Marxism to the Japanese context by transforming it into a nationalist and statist variety of socialism. Takabatake Motoyuki, the first to produce a Japanese translation of the three volumes of *Das Kapital*, had propounded a *kokka shakai-shugi* (national or state socialism) doctrine as early as 1919; by 1927, Takahashi Kamekichi had earned the disdain of

---

[2] *Nihon shakai undō jinmei jiten* (Biographical dictionary of Japan's social movement) (Tokyo: Aoki shoten, 1979), s.v. Sano Manabu, s.v. Nabeyama Sadachika.

[3] Takahashi Masao, personal letter, April 4, 1984. According to Takahashi, even among members of the dissident Rōnō-ha (which had seceded from the JCP in late 1927), there was a split between those who accepted the validity of the October revolution as a true socialist revolution, and those who rejected it as "utopian" and "non-Marxist." (Interview with Takahashi Masao, Tokyo, Japan, May 5, 1984.)

peers in the proletarian movement when he adduced a Marxian analysis of Japanese economic development to support Japan's military expansion onto the Asian mainland; and in 1929, a group of imprisoned JCP members around Mizuno Shigeo (the so-called Kaitō-ha or "dissolutionist faction") prefigured the tenkō movement when they abandoned the JCP and advocated a system of socialism based on the Imperial Household.[4] Finally, after the Manchurian Incident, Akamatsu Katsumaro adopted an explicitly national socialist program.[5] Among these thinkers, only the Kaitō-ha and Akamatsu openly couched their positions in terms of a return to Japanese "national character," but neither the considerably junior Kaitō-ha nor the continually vacillating Akamatsu wielded the authority of Sano in his leadership of the JCP's prison Central Committee; and neither produced as voluminous writings on the fundamental conflicts between Soviet-style Marxism and indigenous Japanese thought.[6]

As has been argued elsewhere, the phenomenon of tenkō itself reflected

[4] See Germaine A. Hoston, "Marxism and National Socialism in Taishō Japan: The Thought of Takabatake Motoyuki," *Journal of Asian Studies* 44, 1 (November 1984): 43–64; Tanaka Masato, *Takabatake Motoyuki: Nihon no kokka shakai-shugi* (Takabatake Motoyuki: Japanese national socialism) (Tokyo: Gendai hyōronsha, 1978); Hoston, "Marxism and Japanese Expansionism: Takahashi Kamekichi and the Theory of 'Petty Imperialism,'" *Journal of Japanese Studies* 10, 1 (January 1984): 1–30; Hoston, "State and Revolution in China and Japan: Marxist Perspectives on the Nation-State and Social Revolution in Asia," Ph.D. dissertation, Harvard University, 1981, 4:954–62. In addition, Takabatake Michitoshi has named fifteen individuals who espoused some form of national socialism after tenkō. See Naimushō Keihōkyoku, *Shakai undō no jōkyō* (The situation of the social movement), 1935 and 1942 eds., cited in Takabatake Michitoshi, "Ikkoku shakai-shugisha—Sano Manabu–Nabeyama Sadachika" (One-country socialists: Sano Manabu and Nabeyama Sadachika), in Shisō Kagaku Kenkyūkai, ed., *Tenkō* (Conversion), (Tokyo: Heibonsha, 1959, 1965), p. 193.

[5] See George O. Totten, "Akamatsu Katsumaro: Political Activist and Ideologue," in Peter Berton, Paul F. Langer, and George O. Totten, trans. and ed., *The Russian Impact on Japan: Literature and Social Thought—Two Essays* (Los Angeles: University of Southern California Press, 1981).

[6] Only two years before his tenkō, Sano had denounced the Kaitō-ha as "social fascists" and reasserted the official Comintern-JCP line on the need to abolish the emperor system. See Sano Manabu, "Sano Manabu jōshinsho—Kaitō-ha ni tsuite" (Sano Manabu's written statement—on the Kaitō-ha [Dissolutionist faction]), February 1931, handwritten manuscript, Institute of Social Science, University of Tokyo, pt. I, pp. 5–7, 10–13; and Kobayashi Morito, *Tenkōsha no shisō to seikatsu* (The thought and lives of tenkōsha) (Tokyo: Daidōsha, 1935), pp. 11–12. Sano's prison statement remains a key source for the ideas of the Kaitō-ha, the writings of whose members—with the sole exception of Mizuno Shigeo—are virtually impossible to locate in any major Japanese research library. Mizuno Shigeo's account of the faction's thought appears in "Jōshinsho" (Prison statement), January 28, 1929; "Kansō" (Reflections), pts. 1 and 2; and "Nihon Kyōsantō dattō ni saishi tōin shokun ni" (To party members on the occasion of the dissolution of the Japanese Communist Party), May 22, 1929, handwritten statement, [Tokyo Chihō Saibansho Kenjikyoku Shiso-bu Saku], May 24, 1929.

the continuing power of the traditional kokutai myth in the Shōwa era.[7] Dominated by an emperor system, the physical and emotional power of which was heightened in the atmosphere of crisis that followed the Manchurian Incident, traditional ties and perspectives on the Japanese nation and state conflicted with and finally overwhelmed the appeal of Marxism-Leninism among both imprisoned and free Communists. A closer examination of Sano's post-tenkō thought, however, reveals the potentialities as well as the limitations of Marxism as a vehicle of cultural criticism in prewar Japan. On the one hand, Marxism's claim to scientific truth and universality empowered Japanese intellectuals to launch a critique of their own society and culture from without. Other imported perspectives based on Buddhism and Confucianism had been selectively and eclectically incorporated and neatly intertwined with native Shintō into a holistic package; this made it difficult for one to adopt a coherent stance within this philosophical framework on the basis of which to criticize separate aspects of Japanese culture and society. Thus, for example, even constitutional scholar Minobe Tatsukichi's emperor-organ theory, which did not fundamentally challenge the Meiji framework, was harshly repudiated as culpable of lèse majesté by the Diet, the very institution it was designed to bolster.[8] Under the dominance of the kokutai conception (as enforced under the Peace Preservation Law), there was simply no legitimate means to criticize the existing power structure without appearing to question Japaneseness itself, or the very standards one was using to launch such a critique.

Marxism was appealing in this context not only because its interpretation of politics and economics helped to explain many of the unfortunate realities of Taishō and Shōwa politics, but also because Marxism offered an alternative philosophical basis (buttressed with organizational support) for one to step outside the dominant philosophical and cultural framework in order to criticize its separate components fully. An analogy might be made to Marx's observation in nineteenth-century Germany that as long as the Young Hegelians, of whom he himself was one, remained constrained by the bounds of the Hegelian philosophical system, they could never launch an effective critique of Hegel.[9]

Yet Sano Manabu's treatment of Marxism illustrates that it was precisely in this strength of Marxism as a basis for cultural criticism from without that we find its vulnerability in the context of Taishō and espe-

[7] See Hoston, "Tenkō," passim.

[8] See the more detailed discussion of the dominance of kokutai thought in Hoston, "State and Revolution in China and Japan," chap. 1; and Ishida Takeshi, Meiji seiji shisō shi kenkyū (Studies in Meiji political thought) (Tokyo: Miraisha, 1954), pt. 1.

[9] See the analysis in Robert C. Tucker, Philosophy and Myth in Karl Marx, 2d ed. (Cambridge: Cambridge University Press, 1961, 1971), especially chaps. 4, 6.

cially Shōwa Japan. Particularly in its Soviet incarnation as Marxism-Leninism, when it appeared that the JCP's formulistic solutions to Japan's social problems were being imposed by the distant authority of Comintern officials who were remarkably ignorant of Japanese conditions, Marxism appeared to be a foreign, even alien system of thought.[10] Conceived on the basis of the Western European experience, where different values and customs had defined the context of social change, its historical schema might or might not be applicable to Japan.[11] Might not the Japanese intellectual who nevertheless attempted to impose that framework in order to reinterpret and criticize Japanese society and culture be subjecting himself (and Japan) to "cultural imperialism"?[12] Might not some indigenously conceived theory of social and cultural change be more applicable to Japanese realities, and therefore preferable to Marxism as the basis for cultural criticism?

In the early 1930s, as the possibility of war became more imminent, a heightened sense of national pride rendered Marxism more vulnerable than ever to such doubts as these. In this period, the effectiveness of Marxism as cultural criticism was increasingly vitiated by the conflict between fundamental elements of its method and assumptions and the complex of indigenous values and ideas about the nature of man, society, and polity prevailing among Japanese at the time. Ironically, it is in the work

[10] Sano's nephew has made this charge explicitly. See Sano Hiroshi, "Kakumeika Sano Manabu" (Sano Manabu, revolutionary), *Kokumin hyōron* (National review) (June 1953): 111–27.

[11] The debate on Japanese capitalism (*Nihon shihon-shugi ronsō*) from 1927 to 1937 was a strenuous effort by Japan's Marxists to dispel these doubts. See Hoston, *Marxism and the Crisis of Development in Prewar Japan: The Debate on Japanese Capitalism* (Princeton: Princeton University Press, 1986). Both Takabatake Motoyuki and Takahashi Kamekichi, Sano's predecessors in injecting nationalistic elements into their Marxism, expressed such concerns. Takabatake saw Marx's view of the state as flawed by his tendency to read Western "bourgeois values" back into all human history and rejected his historical materialism. Similarly, Takahashi commented on the inadequacies of Western economic theories for understanding Japan, where economic customs differed. See Takabatake Motoyuki, *Marukusu-gaku kenkyū* (Studies on Marxism) (Tokyo: Daitō-kaku, 1919), pp. 37–41; Takabatake Motoyuki, *Marukusu-gaku kaisetsu* (An explication of Marxism) (Tokyo: Kaizōsha, 1928), pp. 78–79; and Takahashi Kamekichi, *Takahashi keizai riron keisei no rokuju-nen* (Sixty years of the formation of Takahashi [Kamekichi's] economic theory) (Tokyo: Tōshi keizaisha, 1976), 1:60–61.

[12] The issue of "orientalism" (to borrow Edward Said's term) in Marxism, suggested by the notion of "cultural imperialism," is not treated here. Sano was not as concerned with Marx's normative view of the East and its implications for the acceptability of Marx's overall historical schema, partly because he felt that Japan was unique in Asia in that it combined features of both East and West. (See below and Sano Manabu, *Minzoku to kaikyū* [Race and class], Minshu shiriizu [Democracy series], no. 3 [Tokyo: Kinrō jihōsha, 1949], p. 13.) On orientalism, see Edward W. Said, *Orientalism* (New York: Random House, Vintage Books, 1978, 1979), introduction.

of one who endeavored to synthesize Marxism with "Oriental" and Japanist perspectives that these antagonistic features are most starkly illuminated, for Sano's critique of Marxism was heavily dependent on an analysis of cultural disparities. The discussion that follows will focus on the two most prominent themes in Sano's critique: (1) the perception that Marxism, as Western materialistic *ideology* (in the Marxist sense of that word), was normatively and methodologically alien to the tradition of Eastern spirituality; and (2) the challenge that Japanese exceptionalism posed to Marxism's claim to universality.

## Eastern Spirituality versus Western Materialism: Marxism as Alien Ideology

Immediately after his tenkō, Sano Manabu embarked on a rigorous review of Marxism in an effort to systematize his critique of Marx's historical materialism and to explicate a new socialist theory that could reconcile the culturo-philosophical conflicts that had prompted him to tenkō. The main theme of this process became the differences between Eastern and Western ethics and philosophy, an issue that had been the subject of an intense controversy among Chinese intellectuals a decade earlier.[13] These differences, in Sano's view, made Marxism, as a Western philosophy, inappropriate as a blueprint for social revolution in an Eastern environment. Sano wrote: "We are Orientals, Japanese. Our socialism must be something appropriate to the Oriental, Japanese environment. No matter how cosmopolitan a character Western Europe's socialism has, it is something that Western European peoples created in conformance with their special social environment, so it is unreasonable to try to transfer it wholesale as it is. To Orientalize, to Japanize, Western European socialist principles is most important of all."[14]

Sano felt that his identity as an Asian was crucial to his repudiation of Soviet-style Marxism in tenkō, and an essential aspect of his critique of Marxism as an alien ideology was his reawakening to "Oriental" culture. Thus, in his prison dairy, Sano asserted:

[13] See Chow Tse-tsung, *The May Fourth Movement: Intellectual Revolution in Modern China* (Cambridge: Harvard University Press, 1960), chap. 13. The cofounder of the Chinese Communist Party, Chen Duxiu, addressed the subject in an essay entitled "Dong-Xi genben sixiang zhi chayi" (The differences in the basic thought of Eastern and Western peoples), in Chen Duxiu, *Duxiu wencun* (Collected writings of [Chen] Duxiu, 2 vols., 3 quan (Hong Kong: Yandong tushu gongsi, 1965), 1:35–40. For a conservative opinion echoing Sano's views on the superiority of Oriental philosophy, see Liang Souming, *Dong-Xi wenhua ji qi zhexue* (Eastern and Western cultures and their philosophies) (Taibei: Wenxue chuban she, 1977).

[14] Sano, *Minzoku to kaikyū*, p. 10.

I believe that deep concern for Asia was a correct element that I have continued to maintain since the time of tenkō. The specialness of Asian society and culture; [the view] that the elimination of the conservatism of India and China are the conditions for the progress of world history; the necessity that Asia be liberated from the capitalism of Europe, America, and Japan; [the conviction] that the formation of a socialist league of Japan, China, and Korea first, rather than a vague internationalism, is possible and, furthermore, a necessary aim have been [my] beliefs since that time. In prison, I endeavored to study thereafter the history, social structure, and culture of the Orient and to raise my self-consciousness as an Oriental man.[15]

On the basis of his newly awakened consciousness of being "Oriental," Sano found that many fundamental aspects of Marxian thought conflicted with traditional "Oriental" approaches to man and society. First among these was an epistemological issue: for as he looked back to the turn of the century, Sano observed that in uncritically accepting Marx's theory of revolution, intellectuals of his generation had fallen victim to a superficial "intellectualism." Since the Meiji period, in the defensive quest for Western knowledge, young Japanese had found themselves not only accepting Western ideas that were contrary to Oriental traditions, but also despising their own homeland for its lack of comparable wisdom. But "Western knowledge is knowledge of phenomena, knowledge of cause and effect, mere recognition alienated from volition and sentiment," Sano lamented. By contrast, "Oriental knowledge is intuitive knowledge, essential knowledge [gained] by the operation of intelligence fused harmoniously with volition and sentiment; instead of looking at the object from without, [it] grasps it from within as something linked with itself. Thus, [in the East] intellect is fused with deed, faith, and love."[16] The cold intellectualism of an "objectivist view of history [such as one found in Marx's historical schema] could not lead man to true self-consciousness and joy," Sano claimed.[17]

Thus, it was unfortunate that young Japanese intellectuals in the Meiji and Taishō periods had been seduced by Western-style abstract knowledge estranged from the Japanese national experience. "Alienated from its own people's life and instinct, it [Marxist thought] naturally became formula without creativity," reflecting Western and not Eastern reali-

[15] Sano Manabu, "Gokuchū-ki" (Prison diary), in Nabeyama Sadachika and Sano Manabu, Tenkō jūgo-nen (Fifteen years since tenkō), Rōdō minshu shiriizu (Labor democracy series), no. 7 (Tokyo: Rōdō shuppan-bu, 1949), p. 97.
[16] Sano Manabu, Waga gokuchū no shisō henreki (The course of my thoughts while in prison) (Tokyo: Shihōshō keisei-kyoku, 1944), pp. 12–15.
[17] Sano Manabu, "Atarashii shakai-shugi no sekai-kan" (The world-view of a new socialism), in Sano Manabu chosaku-shū (Collected writings of Sano Manabu) (Tokyo: Sano Manabu chosaku-shū kankōkai, 1958), 2:965.

ties.[18] Egoism and individualism were the products of this wholesale importation of Western-style learning, of which Sano himself had partaken, and Marxism too was part of this package of Western learning. Distant from the real requirements of the Japanese people, Marxism taught materialism, "a nonspiritualistic fatalistic view of history that erases from history mankind's creative will and activity, a mechanistic schematism in the theory of the base and superstructure of society, and a conceptual game." It presented an atomistic view of individual men, the hedonistic pursuit of comfortable clothing, food, and lodging as the highest ideals, antinationalism, suprastate internationalism, a preoccupation with the specter of socioeconomic classes in constant conflict, the denial of the role of great men in history, and a violent but utopian theory of social revolution.[19] Indeed, Sano came very close to asserting what Takabatake Motoyuki had suggested earlier about Marxism as ideology in the Marxian sense, meaning "false consciousness": like the ideologies of Thomas Hobbes, John Locke, and G.W.F. Hegel, Marxism, particularly in those aspects that were alien to the East, simply reflected the Western bourgeois-capitalist society in which it had been born.[20]

At the core of Marx's thought, for example, was the theme of class struggle, an emphasis that Sano rejected as excessive and inapplicable to Oriental society. The manner in which Marx originally dealt with the subject of class struggle served to emphasize its incompatibility with the "Oriental experience." As John M. Maguire has noted, "Not only does Marx present class relations . . . as merely alienated individual activity; he also argues that they emerged historically from interregnum periods in which individual activity achieved a temporary, transitional freedom from class conditions."[21] This individualism or egoism was precisely, it will be recalled, the element of capitalism most repugnant to Meiji socialists like Kawakami Hajime, as well as to Sano and Nabeyama.[22] Indeed, the Marxian emphasis on individualism and the pursuit of profit as the bases of capitalism buttressed Sano's conviction that capitalism was alien to the Orient, as well as that orthodox Marxism, as a response to Western

---

[18] Sano, *Waga gokuchū no shisō henreki*, pp. 12–15.

[19] Ibid., pp. 6–7; cf. Kobayashi, *Tenkōsha*, pp. 7–8.

[20] See Takabatake, *Marukusu-gaku kenkyū* (Studies in Marxism) (Tokyo: Daitō-kaku, 1919), pp. 79, 82.

[21] John M. Maguire, *Marx's Theory of Politics* (Cambridge: Cambridge University Press, 1979), p. 17.

[22] See Kawakami Hajime, *Jijōden* (Autobiography) (Tokyo: Iwanami shoten, 1952), 1:204–206; Gail Lee Bernstein, *Japanese Marxist: A Portrait of Kawakami Hajime, 1879–1946*, Harvard East Asia Series, no. 86 (Cambridge: Harvard University Press, 1976), chap. 4; and Nabeyama's view that capitalism caused a degeneration of morality, in Nabeyama Sadachika, "Kokoro no sokuseki" (The footprints of my mind), in Nabeyama and Sano, *Tenkō jūgo-nen*, pp. 16–18.

capitalism, was not applicable to the East. Nonetheless, Sano was optimistic that a socialism might be reformulated by combining elements of both East and West: "in the Orient, cooperative social characteristics based on natural spontaneous human love are stronger than profit or intellect [as motivations for human behavior]. . . . If we adopt the self-consciousness of the Western European individual and reintegrate into this, then we can show to the world a new social form that Western Europeans must consider." Contributions from the East could also include, for example, "the attitude that does not separate the philosophy of life or moralism or knowledge from action."[23]

As Sano's critique of Marxism evolved, he became more and more convinced that despite its deficiencies vis-à-vis the West, "there are . . . aspects of Oriental civilization in philosophy and religion that are superior to Western Europe." In many respects, Sano's evaluation of the Orient shared much in common with Marx's pessimistic and often derogatory views.[24] Like Hegel and Marx, Sano observed that "the ancient civilization of the world began from the Orient, and until the middle ages, the Orient also frequently dominated the West." Since the sixteenth century, however, the Orient has "lagged behind Western Europe in social organization and culture," and the current phenomenon of European imperialism also placed the Orient in danger of losing its few remaining spheres of superiority. Interestingly, the catalog of the Orient's deficiencies presented by Sano resembled very closely Marxist depictions of the Asiatic mode of production: Asia was dominated by "small-scale irrigated agriculture," backward development of industrial capital, the "remarkable subordination" of women, "a fatalistic ideology," which caused "the freedom of spirit to be curtailed and [the attainment of] fresh, lively knowledge about nature and humanity to be hindered," and "a despotic political order [that] rules and restricts the freedom of the individual." These characteristics, Sano concluded, had resulted in the "so-called Asiatic stagnancy within the societies of Oriental peoples, most of whom had therefore fallen into the status of colonies or semicolonies.[25] This plight made Sano's task of devising a nationalist form of socialism that could liberate the peoples of the East that much more urgent.

Despite this recognition of the weakness of the East, in articulating this new "Orientalized Marxian socialism," Sano placed far greater weight on the superior aspects he found in Eastern culture. Having completed his critical reexamination of Marxism, Sano endeavored to reinforce his re-

[23] Sano, Minzoku to kaikyū, pp. 15–17.

[24] These are best expressed in Karl Marx, "The British Rule in India" (June 10, 1853), in Robert C. Tucker, ed., The Marx-Engels Reader, 2d ed. (New York: W. W. Norton, 1978), pp. 653–58.

[25] Sano, Minzoku to kaikyū, pp. 11–13.

awakening to consciousness of his "Oriental" and "Japanese" character by immersing himself in Eastern classics. Over a two- to three-year period, Sano "read and learned thoroughly the *Kojiki*, the *Nihon-shoki*, *norito* (Shintō ritual prayer), the *Man'yōshū*, *senmyō* (ancient imperial proclamations)," and other classics including works from the Heian, Kamakura, Ashikaga, and Tokugawa periods. While he found the classics "simple, crude, objective, and artistic as well, but nowhere logical and speculative," Sano did extract from them the following philosophical characteristics:

1. "The affirmation of life."
2. "Pantheism," "a philosophy of life" that was "more sentimental than Western pantheism." "A great life flows in the universe, and all nature and mankind expressing that are viewed as alive and beautiful."
3. "*Seisei-shugi*" (creationism): "Stagnation is death."
4. "*Kō-shugi*" (activism), which "grasps . . . the unity between nature and man premised on the activity of mankind."
5. "Realism: the ancient Japanese liked to emphasize the present moment to put their spirit into it."

Furthermore, Sano discovered that "in the ancient state there were no private ownership and class divisions as in later ages; consequently, there were not yet the anxiety and pessimism that arose therefrom."[26]

Since Sano's objective was to know himself as an Oriental man, he studied the Chinese classics as well, and these writings supported his interpretation of Eastern philosophy. (Although he intended to study Indian writings, he was never able to do so. On India he read only secondary materials: "about twenty of the major classics of Buddhism, Max Weber's study of religious society, and the research of Japan's [scholar] Ui Hakuju.") He studied the thirteen Confucian commentaries, the *Book of Poems*, the *Book of Changes*, the *Analects*, the *Doctrine of the Mean*, and the *Great Learning* as essential sources for classical Chinese political thought. Sano found legalist thinkers Guanzi, Shangzi, and Han Feizi "to stand at the pinnacle of the world's ancient political studies," while in "Mozi's altruistic socialism" Sano found the key "source of Chinese humanism." He also perused Qing histories as well as such classic novels as *Dream of the Red Chamber* and *The Scholars*. On the basis of this work on China, Sano penned a study of "Ancient Chinese society and thought," and an eight-volume *History of Qing Society*, which was eventually published. More importantly, Sano gained what he believed to be an understanding of "the essence of the Chinese spirit":

[26] Sano, "Gokuchū-ki," pp. 111–13.

1. The notion of the unity of heaven and man: "a pantheism that brims with the unity of nature and man, with the concept of heaven as mediator."

2. The notion of the "moral empire" and government by philosophers "based on democracy and regarding making the people's livelihood secure as paramount."

3. The notion of self-denial (*kokuji*).

4. The "unity of thought and action."

5. "Empiricism (represented by [the philosophy of] Han Feizi)." "He understood the state as the organization of power, saw law as a concrete means of power, as something of primary importance, and advocated certain punishment and sure rewards."

All these elements were to be reevaluated by Chinese as well as Japanese in the interest of a new future for the Orient.[27]

These aspects of Eastern philosophy offered to Sano an important corrective to aspects of Marxism that the tenkōsha like himself had found offensive. For example, Marx's and Lenin's narrow and prejudicial views of the state as a mere instrument of exploitation were unacceptable to those who saw the state (whether viewed in Confucian, Buddhist, or kokutai terms) as a locus of positive moral value. Marx's notion of the state, like that of Western political theorists from Machiavelli to Hegel to Marx to Lenin, had been authoritarian and (with the exception of Hegel) amoral, Sano asserted.[28] Moreover, as he looked further into this authoritarian core of Marx's thought, Sano discovered assumptions that were in contradiction with indigenous Japanese beliefs about state and society. First, Marx's notion of authority was based on violence: its content was armies, prisons, and other organs of violence and repression. As a result, Marx not only overlooked the purely nonviolent leadership or organizational functions of the state; but, because of this narrow perspective on political power, he also failed to see the potential for nonviolent revolution. A related difficulty with this view of the state lay in the analysis of the state "exclusively from a class perspective": such an interpretation was too simple. The state did not, in fact, exist only because of classes: consequently, "to say that in a socialist society, with the disappearance of classes, the state will experience a natural death cannot be but an elegant illusion. The state as the organization of power training mankind will probably continue to exist for a long time."[29] The hope of the "withering away of the state" ignored the fact that "the state is the most real-

---

[27] Ibid., pp. 115–18.

[28] Sano Manabu, "Marukusu kokka-ron to sono hihan" (Marx's theory of the state and its critique), in *Sano Manabu chosaku-shū*, 1:543, 569; cf. Sano, "Gokuchū-ki," pp. 121–22.

[29] Sano, "Marukusu kokka-ron," 1:570–73; and Sano, "Gokuchū-ki," pp. 120–21.

istic condition of human society. Civilized man cannot live apart from the state."[30]

It was only because Marxism had been derived from an analysis of Western capitalist society that Marx had identified the state so fully with class exploitation. By contrast, having returned to his Eastern philosophical roots, Sano found that it was "because capitalism became predominant that elements such as egoism, profitism, materialism, and classism became powerful, the public leadership character that formed the essence of [state] authority became weak, and the danger that [state] authority would be above and removed from social life became more serious than in any previous age."[31] The state was not inherently exploitative and oppressive.[32]

Finally, the third, and perhaps most important, weakness of Marx's view of the state, for Sano, was its emphasis on classes and on economic causation to the neglect of any appreciation of the nation or people. "Politics, economics, and culture" interacted mutually to form human society; historical materialism with its notions of surplus value and class differentiation was incorrect in its single-minded emphasis on economic factors.[33] Such an emphasis on classes, Sano argued, was also the result of certain characteristic tendencies in Western philosophy. "Classes are certainly major real elements of history, and in particular, their significance and functions have increased in the modern age, when status-system garb has disappeared; but to absolutize this [class] as Marx [did], to try to explain the life of the state on the basis of class factors" can be said to be the product of "bringing into sociology anew Western philosophy's peculiar antagonistic concepts of 'subject [actor] and object.'" Moreover, the absolutization of economics, the exaltation of the role of economic classes in human history, rendered Marxism a mechanistic theory by which economics conditioned politics. This, in Sano's view, was a "schematic idealism characteristic of German academics."[34]

Finally, Sano argued that his previous obsession with materialistic Western philosophy, including Marxism, had obscured an essential aspect of socialist revolution that was readily apparent from the perspective of Eastern philosophy: the need for a spiritual revolution as well as a radical change in the economic institutions of society. Here Sano found

[30] Sano, "Marukusu kokka-ron," 1:525.
[31] Sano Manabu, "Kenryoku to rōdo" (Authority and labor), in Sano, Sano Manabu chosaku-shū, 2:1001.
[32] Cf. Takabatake's critique of Marx's treatment of the state. (Hoston, "Marxism and National Socialism in Taishō Japan," pp. 54–55.)
[33] Sano, "Marukusu kokka-ron," 1:576; and Sano, "Gokuchū-ki," pp. 119–20.
[34] Sano, "Marukusu kokka-ron," 1:573, 575. And on classes, cf. Takabatake, "Marukusu-gaku kenkyū," p. 82.

great potential in Buddhism, as a religious spiritual basis for resolving social problems. "Buddhism," Sano argued, "is not content only with a superficial institutional resolution [of the problem of 'exploitation'], as is ordinary socialism, but endeavors to resolve [it] in relation to a revolution in human nature." The struggle for socialism was above all a moral struggle between good and evil, and socialist society in which the state provided the essential conditions not for exploitation but for "cooperative labor" was possible only on the basis of a "spiritual revolution."[35] Drawing on Confucian and Buddhist thought, Sano saw that in such a revolution men would constantly strive for self-denial in order to achieve a true resolution of the social problems plaguing Japanese society.

This call for spiritual revolution as a requisite for social revolution bears comparison to the ideas of Chinese Marxists Li Dazhao and Mao Zedong, both of whom argued that reforms directed at socioeconomic arrangements alone were not sufficient to realize meaningful social change. For both men, a spiritual and cultural revolutionary process was essential. For Sano, as for Mao and Li, Confucian conceptions concerning spiritual self-cultivation and moral regeneration became essential components of the adaptation of Marxism to the East Asian context.[36] Similarly, all three moderated Marx's notion of class conflict, reflecting Sano's view that Marxism's emphasis on class not only was divisive in the wars of national liberation that were essential to the survival of Asia, but was also antithetical to the presumption of natural harmony that was characteristic of "Oriental philosophy." Sano argued that as an ideology of liberation, Marxism failed to value the *minzoku* (nation or people), even as international imperialism increasingly made the nation and economic class coincide. It was here, in the discussion of Marx's neglect of ethnicity

[35] Sano Manabu, "Bukkyō to shakai-shugi" (Buddhism and socialism), in Sano, *Sano Manabu chosaku-shū*, 3:732.

[36] Ibid., passim. See Li Dazhao, "Jingshen jiefang" (Spiritual liberation), February 8, 1920, in Li Dazhao, *Li Dazhao xuanji* (Selected writings of Li Dazhao) (Beijing: Renmin chubanshe, 1962), p. 309; cf. Maurice Meisner, *Li Ta-chao and the Origins of Chinese Marxism* (New York: Atheneum, 1979), especially chaps. 5 and 6; and Hoston, "State and Revolution in China and Japan," 4:1061–63. This was also a major theme of Mao Zedong's *On New Democracy* (Peking: Foreign Languages Press, 1967), passim. In this respect, Sano, Li, and Mao exhibited nonmaterialist proclivities in their thinking about socialist revolution that can be analyzed fruitfully in comparison with similar tendencies in Latin American "liberation theology" and in "Black liberation theology" in contemporary South Africa. I have explored this theme of spiritual revolution in more detail and drawn such comparisons in an article entitled "A 'Theology of Liberation?' Perspectives on Spiritual Cultivation and Socialist Revolution in Chinese and Japanese Marxism," in Paul A. Cohen and Merle Goldman, eds., *Ideas Across Cultures: Essays on Chinese Thought in Honor of Benjamin I. Schwartz* (Cambridge: Harvard University Press, under the auspices of the Council on East Asian Studies, 1990), pp. 165–221.

and nationalism, that Sano moved beyond the East versus West dichotomy to address the issue of Japanese exceptionalism and its challenge to Marxism as a universally valid theory of social change.

## Japanese Exceptionalism versus Marxism's Claim to Universality

Despite the substantial emphasis that Sano devoted to the East-West dichotomy in making his critique of Marxism-Leninism, his view of Japan as unique lay at the very core of his decision to tenkō. Sano wrote in his prison diary, "[I] felt painfully the negation of being a Japanese who had forgotten being a Japanese. . . . That it was necessary to open up a unique path to socialism with the strength of our own national people was the first reason for my tenkō."[37] Indeed, in later years, Sano pointed to the inability of Marxism in its Comintern-JCP form to respond to Japan's realities as one of the major reasons that Marxian socialism had encountered such resistance in Japan. "In Japan there are still quite a few people who feel distrust toward the word 'socialism,' " Sano noted. "This is because, hitherto, socialism has placed too much emphasis on class and economics, and did not suit the mood of the masses, because it has ushered in Western socialism in its existing form without looking back at Japan's real conditions and traditions."[38]

As Sano formulated his own ideal of socialism-in-one-country, the emotional content of this motivation in his tenkō was reflected in his treatment of antagonism between the alleged universalism of Marxism as formulated in Western Europe and the particular characteristics of the individual Japanese people to which any vision of socialism must be adapted. Late in his life, Marx had once protested to the Russian *narodnik* (populist) N. K. Mikhailovsky that his schema of social development was never intended to be "an historico-philosophical theory of the *marche générale* imposed by fate upon every people, whatever the historical circumstances in which it finds itself."[39] Nevertheless, the assertion that he had derived his schema on the basis of a "scientific" analysis of the historical laws governing socioeconomic development implied a claim to its universal applicability. But Sano and his imprisoned fellow Marxists suddenly recognized that even the epistemological and methodologi-

[37] Sano, "Gokuchū-ki," pp. 87–89.

[38] Sano, "Bukkyō to shakai-shugi," pp. 735–36.

[39] Karl Marx to the editor of the *Otyescestvenniye zapisky* (Notes on the Fatherland), in Karl Marx and Frederick Engels, *Selected Correspondence*, trans. Dona Torr, Marxist Library (New York: International Publishers, 1942; reprint ed., Westport, Conn.: Greenwood Press, 1975), 29:354.

cal bases of Marx's schema came into conflict with the intuitive foundations of Eastern and especially Japanese culture and philosophy. The
reality of war with China taught Sano and his peers that by accepting this
alien ideology and following the Comintern line on violent revolution and
abolition of the emperor system, they were committing treason against
the kokutai.[40] Once awakened to love of one's own people in prison—to
the realization that "[t]he nation is not only something sentimental,
but . . . a concrete reality, an active, living political force and a deep
moral force"[41]—Sano was able to cast aside the alien premises of Marxism and return to Oriental first principles.

For Sano, the nation or people had a far greater historical role than
Marx had attributed to it when he proclaimed that in the era of socialist
revolution, class superseded nationalism. Contrary to Marx's view, the
nation and the state would play crucial roles in the liberation of man
through socialism. "Mutual love" was the basis for the nation, Sano observed, which in turn formed the foundation for the cooperative society
that was socialism. "Patriotism is the emotion of loving one's own country, . . . loving one's own people through the medium of the form of the
state," Sano argued, asserting, as had Takabatake Motoyuki before him,
that Lenin was such a patriot. Finally, "patriotism forms the spiritual energy of socialist construction."[42] Yet Sano felt that the conflict between
his view of the primacy of the nation and Marx's emphasis on classes
could be reconciled, for "the core of the nation is laborers." Moreover,
the nation and nationalism would be the essential vehicle by which the
conflict between "haves" and "have nots" in the international sphere
would result in the socialist liberation of the East from the yoke of Western imperialism.[43]

More importantly, Sano stressed the inherent superiority of the Japanese nation, a superiority that not only would enable it to achieve state-
ness and thereby socialism, but would also enable it to be the leader of
national liberation through socialist revolution for all of Asia. In tenkō,
Sano and Nabeyama recognized that state and nation were not analyti-
cally separable, as Marxist theory presumed them to be: "Japan's state
organ was absolutely not a creature of the bourgeoisie, but was a creature
of the whole of the masses, a fraternity."[44] The Japanese state was a cooperative community, and not the product of intense class conflict.
Clearly, the Japanese experience with statehood had been different from
that of the West. As Sano wrote:

[40] Sano, *Waga gokuchū no shisō henreki*, pp. 6–7.
[41] Sano, "Gokuchū-ki," pp. 96–97.
[42] Sano, *Minzoku to kaikyū*, pp. 34–36; and Sano, "Marukusu kokka-ron," 1:571–72.
[43] Sano, *Minzoku to kaikyū*, pp. 31–34, 21–29.
[44] Kobayashi, *Tenkō-sha*, pp. 19, 31.

The basis of the three-thousand-year history of the Japanese Empire is essentially different from Western history. Modern Western materialism is so far different from Japan's tradition. In the West, society is the basic datum, but for the Japanese, the state is the basic datum. Liberalism, communism, and individualism, which are more or less antistate fundamentally, cannot possibly occupy a basic position in Japan. The national spirit of Japan—which is cheerful, cooperative, and loves symmetry and harmony—could not long endure the lowly people's spirit that moves through individual benefits, struggle/conflict, and hatred and envy. . . . Sparked by the Manchurian Incident, the self-confidence of the empire became stronger, national sentiments arose among workers and peasants with a surging force, and the "class interests" and "class struggle" that were the amulets of communism were pushed far afield.[45]

Here Sano stressed elements of Japan's orthodox kokutai thought, which posited the family-state headed by the emperor as a locus of positive value. Sano envisaged a socialism premised on an "emperor system," which, through spiritual revolution, returned to the noble traditions of the Meiji state, under which the kokutai conception had been systematized as state orthodoxy. On the basis of that kokutai, Sano's Japanese socialism, based on the emperor system, would be unique and superior to any other form of socialism.

In the countries of other peoples, state and society are in antagonism, and God and the state are not compatible; by contrast, in Japan, God, state, and society form a complete union. To die for one's country is the greatest service to *kami* [God], the greatest loyalty to the emperor, and also the highest way of life as social man. The subjects of His Majesty regard dying for one's country as the greatest joy.[46]

Nevertheless, Sano's national socialist vision was not designed for realization within the existing bounds of the Japanese state. In Sano's view, these bounds and indeed the very notion of the nation-state itself were, like Marx's theory of the state, imposed from without by the West. Sano believed that the Japanese people were inherently superior. Among their many superior attributes were their independence, their "capability as rulers," and, most importantly, their "accumulation of the essence and purity of Oriental culture."[47] Thus, Sano's quest for a socialism-in-one-country was an effort to define not a socialism that was merely Japanese, but one that was "Oriental." As a Japanese thinker, he would formulate

[45] Sano, *Waga gokuchū no shisō henreki*, pp. 19–20.
[46] Ibid., p. 100.
[47] Kobayashi, *Tenkōsha*, pp. 24–25; cf. Sano, "Gokuchū-ki," p. 97.

for Japan, Taiwan, and Korea (which he regarded as part of Japan),[48] Manchuria, and China, what thinkers of these other Asian countries could not formulate for themselves. It was his express hope that the Pacific War, the war for the Greater East Asian Co-Prosperity Sphere, would evolve into a war of national liberation for all the peoples of the Orient.[49] Presumably, the national peculiarities of Korea, Taiwan, Manchuria, and China—"the amount of population, geographic position, natural resources, the extent of the development of the forces of production, the form of culture, historical traditions, and differences of temperament, etc."[50]—were not of sufficient significance that these countries should be permitted to develop their own indigenous national forms of socialism.

Thus, Sano's view of Japanese exceptionalism played a major role in his transformation of Marxism to national socialism. Japan was destined to play a special role in this process because it alone, of all Oriental countries, shared both Western and Oriental characteristics. Moreover, its emperor system was, first and foremost, evidence that Japan's unique indigenous characteristics had enabled it to build a strong nation and state.[51] This combination of qualities made Japan uniquely capable of developing socialism indigenously—for Japan alone had "pass[ed] through the same feudal system as Western Europe's middle ages" and "cultivate[ed] Western European social life and thought through the importation of capitalism since the Meiji."[52]

In the early years of the Pacific War, Sano saw proof of the Japanese potential to lead the rest of Asia in this enterprise. As the defeatism of the JCP perished with the party in tenkō, "the glorious future of [the Japanese Empire, as] an absolutely invincible and leading country in the world, [became] apparent."[53] Sano's socialism-in-one-country, in short, like Takahashi's "petty imperialism" notion, accommodated the military vision of a Greater East Asia Co-Prosperity Sphere to a revolutionary ideal that maintained some Marxian elements: industrialism, proletarianism, and socialism. But unlike the Marxism of the JCP, Sano's vision was fully compatible with that of the Japanese military in that both endeavored to

[48] Sano, *Waga gokuchū no shisō henreki*, p. 25; and Sano Manabu and Nabeyama Sadachika, "Kyōdō hikoku dōshi ni tsuguru sho," (Letter of proclamation to fellow defendants), June 8, 1933 in Sano, *Sano Manabu chosaku-shū*, 1:16.

[49] Ibid., p. 14. Sano subsequently felt that his support for the war had been "a kind of adventuristic opportunism" ("Gokuchū-ki," pp. 142–44), and after the war he urged the reformation of the "militaristic" and "class"-based *tennō* into a truly democratic basis for his national socialism. (See Sano, "Tennō-sei to shakai-shugi," in Sano, *Sano Manabu chosaku-shū*, 2:381.)

[50] Sano, *Minzoku to kaikyū*, pp. 10, 9.

[51] Kobayashi, *Tenkōsha*, pp. 24–25.

[52] Sano, *Minzoku to kaikyū*, p. 13.

[53] Sano, *Waga gokuchū no shisō henreki*, pp. 3–4.

resolve Japan's social and economic crisis on the basis of Japan's unique and unchanging kokutai.

## Conclusions: Marxism and the Problem of Cultural Imperialism

Sano Manabu's tenkō and efforts to articulate a nationalistic and "Oriental" variety of Marxian socialism illustrate the difficulties Japanese intellectuals encountered in using Marxism as a basis for social criticism. If the initial impulse to tenkō was based on somewhat sentimental and emotional factors, as Sano engaged in a sustained critique of Marxism after his tenkō, this impulse was translated into logical and rational terms. Clearly the Soviet component of the ideology and organization of Marxism-Leninism dominating the JCP was a major factor alienating Japanese intellectuals (and common citizens as well) from the left-wing movement. Indeed, as early as 1927, the issue of foreign domination by the Soviet-led Comintern had helped to precipitate the split between the Rōnō-ha (see note 3) and the orthodox JCP. The outbreak of full-scale war with China, then, helped to trigger the tenkō movement of the 1930s; but even well before the outbreak of hostilities the issue of cultural imperialism was a negative element affecting the popularization of Marxism in Japan.

Sano's response to the issue was not to reject Marxism completely, but to continue to use it—particularly after the war—to update or restructure elements of indigenous Japanese culture in preparation for the birth of socialism. Most significantly, Sano established an amalgamation of Marxist and indigenous "Oriental" values and philosophy as the basis for his new socialist vision. Nevertheless, Sano never managed completely to escape the dilemmas inherent in the application of Marxism as cultural criticism beyond its birthplace. On the one hand, there remained the question of the validity of the application of essentially alien values and methods of analysis to advocate fundamental change in Japanese society. When measured against the often antithetically different European context, would not Japan always be judged to fall short of the ideal? Was it therefore legitimate to use Marxian political economy to recommend changes in "Eastern" values and institutions so that Asia might no longer "lag" behind the West? On the other hand, if one used "Oriental" values and philosphical references as a basis for discarding unpalatable aspects of Marxism, what happened to the fundamental appeal of Marxism itself? It was attractive as a comprehensive and scientific theory of social development at the outset; but stripped of many of its essential elements, could it still be a useful and attractive tool in explaining and predicting social change?

Interestingly, throughout Sano's voluminous post-tenkō writings, the

"Oriental" and Marxist components of his vision never appeared to be fully integrated into a cohesive theory; and neither his fellow Marxists nor the Japanese public were convinced. His strenuous efforts notwithstanding, Sano remained constrained by the fundamental dilemmas inherent in the application of Marxism to foreign soil that he had originally revealed in tenkō.

# Part IV

## JAPAN IN ASIA

As SOPHISTICATED intellectual methodologies inspired by European models became increasingly assimilated in Japanese thought, the various means used to develop a modern and self-conscious understanding of the true nature of Japanese culture helped generate in turn a renewed understanding of the nature and importance of historic and contemporary Japanese ties with Asia. In the case of China and Korea in particular, these connections, at various points in history, had certainly been as important culturally and intellectually as the European ties had become to Japan by this century. Now, ironically, these Asian bonds were to be renewed both by geographical proximities in an age of more rapid travel and by Japan's new experience as a participant in the movement toward a modern Asian imperialism.

Among those who felt that the realities of modern Japanese culture might draw on a new synthesis of Japanese and Western values, some realized that Japan's Asian roots and connections needed new explications at a time when Japanese cultural patterns were rapidly changing. As a result, Japanese scholars and intellectuals now adopted European methodologies of studying cultures in order to help examine and define the nature of Japan's Asian relationships. In the interwar years the Japanese themselves began to play a powerful political role in Asia, which added special complications, and a peculiar poignancy, to the work of those attempting to think through and reevaluate a different set of connections between Japan and the continent of Asia than had pertained in the past.

In any case, whatever the pattern of historical change involved, contemporary Asia now constituted a political force with which Japan would seek renewed relationships, in both practical and intellectual terms. Some Japanese, as Thomas Burkman shows in his essay, attempted to play a role in this process though official diplomacy and by means of personal relationships with other Asians. William LaFleur's study of the shifting assumptions of the philosopher Watsuji Tetsurō (1889–1960) shows that others attempted to study Asian traditions using methods to some extent consonant with their own historicized and now Westernized mentalities. Similar mentalities, as Jackie Stone points out in her study on Buddhism in the interwar years, were to govern a whole new means of interpreting the Asian religious past.

Many commentators, even at this remove, would insist that the Japanese intelligentsia, more than forty years after the Pacific War, still remain

estranged in a profound sense from the truth of Japan's historical relationships with Asia during the past hundred years. Many issues were involved during the interwar years, however, and, in hindsight at least, the
range of understandings and apprehensions remained too broad to admit
any simple resolution.

# 10

## Nitobe Inazō: From World Order to Regional Order

THOMAS W. BURKMAN

A SUBJECT as broad in its scope, as high in its aspirations, and as delicate in its operations as foreign policy must be discussed in its various aspects—geographical, political, economic, cultural, and intellectual. Ideas are crucial determinants in diplomacy, and diplomatic historians often stress the intellectual foundations of foreign policy decisions. Thus, standard treatments of the Spanish-American War or the annexation of Hawaii devote much attention to such doctrines as social Darwinism, the White Man's Burden, and navalism as bases for American action abroad at the turn of the century.

Studies of Japanese diplomacy between the world wars, however, give less emphasis to the role of ideology in the shaping of policy. In fact, some authorities argue outright that Japanese diplomacy is idea-less (mushisō)—since, it is said, the Japanese respond to concrete needs and set no value on transcendent principles. Japanese conciliatory policies of the 1920s are pictured as products of party government, the personal influence of Hara Kei and Shidehara Kijūrō, and an effective system of disarmament. On the other hand, aggressive behavior in the 1930s is seen as a derivative of the Depression, the demise of party government, the threats of nationalism and communism in China, and a bogey called militarism—which is portrayed as having a life of its own. That these phenomena are real and important is not to be denied. But the field of interwar diplomacy needs to be minded again to uncover conceptual patterns.

Such patterns clearly emerge when one compares Japanese world views of the 1920s and the 1930s. One obvious position can be called international accommodationism. According to this stance, the nation's security and prosperity are best achieved by relating harmoniously to the global power structure, which at the time was centered in the Anglo-American

Research for this study was partially funded by grants from the College of Arts and Letters of Old Dominion University.

powers. This view asserted itself in force in the latter months of World War I and was the dominant impulse in Japanese foreign affairs throughout the 1920s. Though it suffered a disabling blow at the time of the Manchurian crisis, it continued to be voiced from time to time by frustrated internationalist intellectuals until the mid-1930s. A significant counter-impulse is regionalism. Regionalism is the notion that the nation's security and prosperity are best achieved through the creation of a stable and hospitable political, economic, and cultural order incorporating neighboring lands, in Japan's case East Asia. This view gained adherents from the mid-1920s onward, displaced accommodationism in the 1930s, and culminated in the declaration of the New Order in East Asia in 1938. In the case of accommodationism, regional predominance defers to upstanding world citizenship; in regionalism, international isolation is deemed an affordable price to pay in the quest for local powerhood.

This essay seeks to interpret various expressions of international accommodationism and regionalism from 1918 to 1938. Some of the voices heard are those of intellectuals; others are those of diplomats and politicians. The study focuses particularly on the world-order views of Nitobe Inazō (1862–1933).

Nitobe stands among those rare prewar Japanese individuals who attained a world reputation. During the 1920s and early 1930s he was known in Europe and North America for his writings explaining East Asian culture to the West. His book *Bushidō* is still read in the Occident by those in search of traditional Japanese values. Son of a wealthy samurai from Morioka, he studied economics and agriculture at Johns Hopkins University and at Halle University in Germany. His career included stints as a colonial administrator in Taiwan, headmaster of the prestigious First Higher School (Ichikō), and professor of colonial policy at Tokyo University. He converted to Christianity with the Sapporo Band, married a Philadelphia Quaker, and traveled widely in Europe and North America. Nitobe served from 1920 to 1926 as Under-Secretary General of the League of Nations and thereafter as an officer in the Institute of Pacific Relations. Few Japanese of his day acquired such thoroughgoing credentials of world citizenship. Not surprisingly, he tried to teach the West diplomatic as well as cultural concepts. Much of his didactic writing and public speaking had to do with world order and Japan's rightful place in it.

Nitobe's career reflected both accommodationism and regionalism. Widely known for his advocacy of internationalism, Nitobe was in fact a spokesman for regionalism in the latter years of his life. His disciples continued to articulate his regionalist views after his death in 1933. The transition in Nitobe's case occurred in the midst of global experience surpassing that of any other well-known Japanese. It also took place well before the Manchurian crisis. Nitobe's tenkō was not an isolated experience but, as will be shown, is illustrative of conceptual changes occurring throughout the intellectual world of Japanese diplomacy in late Taishō and early Shōwa. Nitobe was also a thoroughgoing humanist, to whom cultural understanding was the key to world peace. A probing of his—and others'—ideas on world order will shed light on the question of whether shifts in Japanese diplomatic posture were rooted in changing views on culture.

## Japan in the World

During World War I Japan encountered the circumstance Japanese foreign policy makers feared most: diplomatic isolation. By the time of the Armistice, policy mistakes at home and uncontrollable events abroad seemed to have opened a yawning gap between Japan, on the one hand, and its Western allies and its Eastern neighbors, on the other. Japan was viewed abroad as having challenged the powers and crossed the line from "respectable imperialism" to bald aggression in the Twenty-one Demands and the Siberian Intervention. Japanese tactics of threat under the Katō Kōmei cabinet created for Chinese nationalists an antiforeign cause celebre that burst forth in the May Fourth Movement. Suspicion was pervasive among Entente leaders that Japanese sympathies lay with the Central Powers. The Bolsheviks abrogated the 1916 Russo-Japanese Alliance, while British officials were heard to say that the Anglo-Japanese Alliance had served its purpose. Absent from the front line of the war, Japan did not keep abreast of the breathtaking advances in armament implemented in the battlefields of Europe. In 1918 Japan emerged from the Great War diplomatically suspect and militarily insecure.

The dire state of diplomatic isolation made the repair of Japan's image abroad a matter of utmost concern to all thoughtful Japanese. Anxiety over Japan's predicament coupled with a fleeting affair with Wilsonian idealism gave rise by the war's end to a surge in internationalist thinking. The ascendancy of internationalism is evident in the press and in pronouncements by new liberal societies, and it is reflected in government policy in the postwar period. Internationalists argued that Japan's interests could be best secured if the nation expanded its international role beyond the confines of the East Asian subsystem and played an active part in global affairs. As determinants of policy, Japan should balance regional concerns with worldwide trends, and national self-interest with the collective interests of humanity. In short, internationalists promoted a consciousness of "Japan in the world"—a phrase used repeatedly by Prince Saionji Kinmochi.

The rise of internationalism cannot be dissociated from the movement of "Taishō democracy," which reached its peak in 1919 and whose central figure was Yoshino Sakuzō. The social upheaval and intellectual ferment associated with rapid industrial growth during the war did much to swell the ranks of the Taishō democrats. Ultimately concerned with domestic matters, spokesmen in the movement became intensely interested in world affairs as the war neared its end. Making the widely held hope for a new age of justice and democracy their own self-fulfilling prophecy, they reasoned that Japanese affirmative participation in global affairs would facilitate the enactment of such internal reforms as universal male suffrage, recognition of labor unions, and reduction of arms expenditures. Yoshino, a Tokyo University professor of political history and theory, was a formidable exponent of social democratic thought, a tireless organizer of liberal societies, and a prolific contributor to leading journals of the day. Apparently repentant of his earlier vindication of the Twenty-one Demands, he called for a redirection of Japan's foreign policy and democratizing reforms at home that would enable "a special mission for Japan on the world stage" to lead nations to greater freedom and cultural progress. He warned that Japan could not afford to risk isolation from emerging global political and economic systems.[1] The Taishō democracy intellectuals were the first to stir public interest in a new world order, but they had no direct influence on government policy. The movement lacked a popular rank-and-file and preferred the stimulation of intellectual debate to the rough-and-tumble of political organization. Political elites' endorsement of internationalism was usually more guarded and qualified. "Internationalism is as inevitable as gravitation," opined Prime Minister Hara Kei, but "the road to a sound internationalism lies through a healthy nationalism."[2] More important than Hara's verbal equivocation are his deeds: under his leadership Japan cooperated in the Four-Power Consortium, joined the League of Nations, and prepared for disarmament at the Washington Conference.

A term ubiquitous in the rhetoric of Japanese internationalism is *taisei*

---

[1] Mitani Taichirō, "Taishō demokurashii to Amerika" (Taishō democracy and America), in Saitō Makoto, ed., *Demokurashii to Nichi-Bei kankei* (Democracy and Japanese-American relations) (Tokyo: Nan'undo, 1973), pp. 126–37; Bernard S. Silberman, "The Political Theory and Program of Yoshino Sakuzō," *Journal of Modern History* 31, 1 (March 1959): 319–20; Yoshino Sakuzō, "Gurē kyō no 'kokusai dōmei ron' o yomu" (upon reading Lord Grey's League of Nations idea), *Chūō kōron* 33, 7 (July 1918): 61–62.

[2] Hara Kei, "Through Nationalism to Internationalism," *The Outlook* 125, 7 (June 16, 1920): 316.

*junnō* (conformity to world trends).[3] The concept occupies a prominent place in the history of Japanese diplomacy since the Meiji Restoration, but it is particularly conspicuous in diplomatic documents of the World War I settlement. The Japanese envoys to the Paris Peace Conference were formally instructed by the Foreign Ministry to act "in unison with the allies in accordance with general world trends" on such questions as secret diplomacy, freedom of the seas, and disarmament. The delegation defended its acquiescence to the British-proposed mandate system by explaining that the United States, Australia, New Zealand, and South Africa were disposed to accept the plan. After Versailles, War and navy Ministry research reports on arms limitation were replete with the thinking and language of *taisei junnō*. They advised that Japanese League of Nations representatives conform, within prudent limits, to the trends of League disarmament talks.[4]

Around the time of the Armistice strong arguments for international accommodationism began to be heard in the Foreign Ministry. A November 30, 1918, memorandum by Komura Kin'ichi, European section chief of the Ministry's Political Affairs Bureau, is a case in point. Komura, son of famous Foreign Minister Komura Jutarō, argued forthrightly for a redirection of Japan's China and peace conference policies and, more important, for Japan to lift its eyes beyond its regional environs and see the implications of global trends for its national destiny. The section chief's statement began with a list of revolutionary changes taking place in world society. Pacifism, humanism, labor unrest, global economic centralism, and political radicalism had gained worldwide momentum and "could not be stopped." Moreover, each of these ideological developments could act as a threat to Japanese national sovereignty and national interests. Japan, argued Komura, had underrated their significance and prepared for the postwar settlement with its eyes blinded to everything but Shandong, the Pacific Islands, and Siberia. Japanese leaders had naively as-

[3] For more extensive theoretical treatments of diplomatic conformity, see Michael K. Blaker, *Japanese International Negotiating Style* (New York: Columbia Univesity Press, 1977), pp. 19–21; and Mushakoji Kinhide, "The Cultural Premises of Japanese Diplomacy," *Japan Interpreter* 7, 3–4 (Summer–Autumn 1972): 282–92.

[4] Uchida to Chinda, December 26, 1918, in Japanese Foreign Ministry, ed., *Nihon gaikō bunsho* (Documents on Japanese foreign policy), 1918, 3:667; Makino telegram quoted in Kobayashi Tatsuo, ed., *Suiusō nikki* (Suiusō diary) (Tokyo: Hara shobō, 1966), p. 387; "Kokusai renmei kaku gundaihyōsha ni ataru kunrei no ken" (draft of instructions to the several military representatives at the League of Nations), September 16, 1920; Kaigunshō (Navy Ministry), "Kokusai renmei kankei jikō kenkyūkai no okeru gunbi seigen mondai ni kansuru kenkyū narabini ketsugi" (Research and resolutions on the problem of limitation of armaments prepared by the committee for the study of matters related to the League of Nations), August 5, 1920, in Japanese Military Documents, U.S. National Archives, microfilm items T1207, T1208.

sumed that global issues of an ideological nature had no bearing upon the nation's future. On the contrary, argued Komura, Japan was particularly vulnerable to current tendencies because of its racial and religious minority status among the powers, and because Japan had fallen out of step with the world by pursuing "expansion by military means," a style of behavior now repugnant to the world. Unless Japanese foreign policy were immediately reformed, the peace conference would impose restraints upon the empire. The Komura memorandum counseled that Japan should actively promote the principles of equality and world peace, and take deliberate steps to reform its China diplomacy. As concrete measures to implement the latter, he advised that Japan take the initiative in abandoning extraterritoriality and spheres of influence, withdraw all troops from China, and support the Four-Power Consortium, which the United States was promoting at the time.[5] Makino Nobuaki, newly appointed as a plenipotentiary to the postwar peace conference, took up Komura's theme of accommodationism in advocating before the Gaikō Chōsakai (Diplomatic Advisory Council) a diplomacy responsive to world trends and supportive of the League of Nations.[6]

The widespread voicing of international accommodationism at the end of the First World War reflected Japanese elites' shared perception of their nation's vulnerable position as a secondary power. While apprehensive about the roadblocks that the status quo order of the League could erect in the path to regional power, they agreed that an empire inferior in power and prestige to the leading Western countries should, at this stage of its development, eschew autonomy and acquiesce in the world program of the powers. The Seiyūkai cabinet of Prime Minister Hara, the business community, and the Foreign Ministry understood that to stand aloof would raise further suspicions among the powers. Moreover, they were attracted to the prestige that a permanent seat in the League Council would afford Japan. Thus Japan swallowed its misgivings and joined the European victors of the war in charter membership in the League of Nations. In doing so it opted to enter a multilateral, world-scale system of international order. This choice initiated the cooperative posture Japan would maintain at the Washington Conference and throughout the following decade.

In the aftermath of the Paris Peace Conference, Japanese dignitaries seemed to vie with each other to voice the ideal of "Japan in the world."

[5] Komura Kin'ichi, "Kōwa kaigi no taisei ka Nihon no shōrai ni oyobusu eikyō oyobi kore ni shosuru hōsaku" (A policy to deal with trends of the peace conference and their effect on Japan's future), November 30, 1918, Makino Nobuaki Papers, National Diet Library, File 322.

[6] Gaikō Chōsakai, meeting of December 2, 1918, in *Suiusō nikki*, pp. 323–28; meeting of December 8, in ibid., pp. 333–34.

Upon his return to Tokyo in August 1919, Chief Plenipotentiary Saionji declared to the emperor that "Japan ranks among the five Great Powers of the world and has passed the threshold that allows it to take part in the affairs of Europe."[7] When peace treaty ratifications were exchanged at Versailles the following January, Prime Minister Hara warned that "the condition of the world no longer allows independent action for any country in international affairs, and it will be necessary for all countries to maintain harmony and cooperation with each other. It is desirable that the Japanese should pay due attention to this phase of the new order of things."[8]

But amidst the heralding of the universal order, voices less sanguine were heard. Spokesmen unimpressed by the claims of new diplomacy cautioned that the global system was fundamentally inhospitable to Japan, and that ultimately the nation would have to seek its true interests in Asia. Reflecting upon the peace conference's refusal to incorporate the principle of racial equality in the League of Nations Covenant, journalist Kawakami Kiyoshi spoke for the cynics:

> As far as Asia is concerned, the League is not likely to be a harbinger of glad tidings. . . . The Far Eastern peoples, then, must not, under the new regime, expect much brighter days, but must be prepared to trudge along the same thorny path as heretofore, making the best use of their own resources, and endeavoring not to trespass upon the domain monopolized by the great Powers of the West, even if they have to trample upon one another within their own sphere in the sheer struggle for existence.[9]

## Universal Humanity

As the permanent machinery of the League of Nations was set up following the Paris Peace Conference, it was assumed that Japan would be asked to nominate one of its own for appointment as Under-Secretary General. Japan sought a candidate fluent in Western languages, a pleasing personality of international reputation, and someone unassociated with government. The perfect candidate was found in Nitobe Inazō. At Paris in 1919, Baron Makino pushed for Dr. Nitobe's appointment to the League Secretariat, knowing that such a genuine internationalist could serve the League wholeheartedly. The plenipotentiary also believed that the placement of so cultivated and well traveled a Japanese in the world eye could

---

[7] Saionji report to Emperor, August 27, 1919, in ibid., p. 692.
[8] Hara statement translated in *Japan Advertiser*, January 14, 1920, p. 1.
[9] Kawakami Kiyoshi, "Japan and the World Peace," n.p., n.d., p. 61.

ɔ to refurbish the Prussian image Japan had acquired during the war years.

Service in the secretariat enabled Nitobe to apply in action the principle of global understanding that guided his entire career. Nitobe believed that lack of true knowledge was the primary cause of international conflicts. While lecturing for the Carnegie Endowment in Baltimore in 1912, Nitobe had told his Hopkins audience that "a fuller and deeper understanding" of one another would enable Japan and America to forgo the sword. There were no real bases for Japanese-American animosity, he reasoned, and war-talk was merely the product of the greed of munitions makers and newspaper publishers.[10] All through his life Nitobe pressed the conviction that true knowledge brings peace, confident that, if given the facts, the League of Nations could accept Japan's Manchurian policy and Henry Stimson could affirm Manchukuo. To understanding, Dr. Nitobe added tolerance. James T. Shotwell, an organizer of the International Labor Organization, summarized Nitobe's message as "there should be more thoughtfulness in the judgment that we make concerning others." The sympathetic heart was, to Nitobe, the essence of the Geneva spirit and a requisite for the functioning of world order.[11]

Nitobe viewed his appointment to the secretariat as a means to fulfill his lifelong mission to be "a bridge across the Pacific Ocean, over which the ideas of the West and those of the East could travel back and forth unimpeded."[12] The concrete product of his efforts was the International Committee for Intellectual Cooperation, the forerunner of today's UNESCO. Nitobe solicited the participation of twelve savants of world reputation, including French philosopher Henri Bergson, who served as the committee's first president. The ICIC sought to facilitate contacts between teachers, artists, scientists, and authors, and to establish ties between universities in different countries. An even more ambitious goal, never achieved, was to encourage nations to involve intellectuals in the foreign policy making process. Nitobe viewed scholars as an untapped reservoir whose influence in support of international political cooperation might be very great.[13]

At the heart of Nitobe's tolerance and internationalism lay his concept

[10] Nitobe quoted in *Baltimore Sun*, January 12, 1912, p. 8; William Robert Carter, "With the Nitobes in America, 1911-1912," chapter of unpublished thesis draft, pp. 22, 26.

[11] James T. Shotwell, "An Appreciation," *Pacific Affairs* 6, 8 (November–December 1933): 547.

[12] Nitobe, in *Tokyo nichi nichi*, April 2, 1929, p. 2.

[13] On the ICIC, see F. P. Walters, *A History of the League of Nations* (London: Oxford University Press, 1952), pp. 190–94; Charles Hodges, "The World Union of Intellectual Forces," *Current History* 24, 3 (June 1926): pp. 411–15; Unno Yoshirō, *Kokusai renmei to Nihon* (The League of Nations and Japan) (Tokyo: Hara shobō, 1972), pp. 107–13.

of universal human commonality. He elaborated on this doctrine in a book, *Japanese Traits and Foreign Influences*, which he penned before resigning his League office in 1926. "Fundamentally human nature is identical," he wrote, and "if one be scratched only deep enough he will show common humanity." This commonality applied in intellect, morals, religion, and art. He spoke of universal genius, of "the global character of the moral world," and of the demise of religious barriers in the light of modern scholarship. His assertion of a "universal standard of beauty transcending all technical canons of national aesthetics" recalls Ōnishi Yoshinori's application of Western aesthetic analysis to the concepts of *yūgen*, *aware*, and *sabi*. Nitobe saw in Christ, his chief mentor, an example of "universalism of spirit." Hope for man lay in "his growing more universal in knowledge and in sympathy, in broadening his education so as to embrace the East and the West." Here the nature of Nitobe's internationalism is clarified: it was cultural internationalism, not political internationalism. The basis for any world order was the cultural unity of mankind. Nitobe assured readers of *Japanese Traits* that Japan was stirring to the spirit of world community: "The new pioneers of our education feel a fresh throbbing of the pulse. There are abundant and tangible proofs of the awakening of the new international spirit in our education—proofs that the chauvinistic wine-skin is tearing, proofs that the new receptacle to receive that spirit is to be the spacious world itself."[14] Even in his later years, when the Manchurian crisis awakened his nascent nationalism, Nitobe did not undergo the cultural return to Asian heritage evidenced by Watsuji Tetsurō in his *Koji junrei*.

Unlike the community of Taishō Buddhist scholars described by Jackie Stone, Nitobe did not posit any one philosophical system—be it Japanese Buddhism or his own Christianity—as the primary repository of truth. His cultural internationalism abhorred ethnocentricity. Enlightenment, to him, emanated neither from the West nor from Japan, but was common to all humankind. Nitobe's eclecticism parallels efforts by Nishida Kitarō and Watsuji Tetsurō to integrate Western philosophy and Buddhist thought. His vision of Japan as a bridge between East and West was akin to that of Takakusu Junjirō, a Buddhist savant who engaged in comparative religious studies and explored parallel concepts in Buddhism and Christianity. One of Quakerism's primary attractions to Nitobe was its mysticism, productive as a link between Oriental thought and Christianity.[15]

---

[14] Nitobe, *Japanese Traits and Foreign Influences* (London: Kegan Paul, Trench, Trubner, 1927), pp. 9, 175, 189–206, 216.

[15] Kiyoko Takedo Cho, "The Christian Encounter with the Traditional Ethos of Japan: A Study of Nitobe Inazō's Ideas," in International Christian University, *Asian Cultural Studies* 5 (October 1966): 125.

Nitobe's thought system did not rule out Japanese political and territorial expansion on the continent. In fact, it was very hospitable to imperialism. Educated in New-Manifest-Destiny America, Nitobe believed in the irrepressible, onward march of superior civilizations. In Nitobe's Asia, the agent of progress was Japan, the civilizer of Taiwan. He allegorized Japan's outward thrust in terms of legendary Momotarō's mission to subdue the southern Island of Ogres. He regarded the Chinese as incapable of republicanism or any organized government. Later in life, at the time of the Manchurian crisis, Nitobe would argue that "Japan's advance . . . , in search of a life-line, is as irresistible an economic force as the westward march of the Anglo-Saxon empires."[16] Thus within Nitobe's internationalism there was, from the start, a secure place for expansionism. In this regard he falls within the mainstream of Taishō period internationalism.

From December 1924 Nitobe spent eleven weeks on furlough in Japan. His time was devoted to lecturing on the League and assessing the state of Japanese attitudes toward international organization. The detailed report he complied for Secretary General Sir Eric Drummond on his return to Geneva provides evidence of Nitobe's continuing support for global order. It also shows the Under-Secretary's dismay at the discovery of widespread cynicism concerning the efficacy of international organization as a means to secure Japanese national interests. Nitobe found that Japanese zeal for the League was confined to "the educated youth," while "the older generation as represented in the higher governmental service, the parliament, the larger business circles, and the professions is lacking in enthusiasm except in a few instances." Though the press had dutifully reported debates in Geneva on the protocol and the opium question, "the League looked so far off, and its work touched the country so lightly. . . . Many studied the League, but few knew it." Among the specific complaints Nitobe encountered at home was the allegation that the League had failed to achieve universality. The complaint that the United States was outside its domain was voiced even by Prince Regent Hirohito when Nitobe lectured at the palace. Some Japanese viewed the League as Eurocentric and asked whether League participation was profitable for Asian nations. Nitobe confessed that the question of universality was the hardest to answer satisfactorily. His reply to Japanese questions concerning the practical value of League membership is a classic statement of international accommodationism: "Japan will find in a few years that the

---

[16] Miwa Kimitada, "Crossroads of Patriotism in Imperial Japan: Shiga Shigetaka (1863–1927), Uchimura Kanzō (1861–1930), and Nitobe Inazō (1862–1933)," Ph.D. dissertation, Princeton University, 1967, pp. 276, 345; Nitobe, "Japan, the League of Nations, and the Peace Pact," radio broadcast, May 8, 1932: Nitobe, *The Works of Inazō Nitobe* (Tokyo: University of Tokyo Press, 1972), 4:247.

wisest course for her to pursue in her diplomacy is to bring it in line with the world's public opinion as mirrored in the League. Such a course, far from being a passive obedience to a supernational body, as some ultra-nationalists fear, can rightly be viewed as an active utilization of the League on the part of Japan." The under-secretary informed Drummond that any serious consideration of the League of Nations in the schools of Japan evoked fears of compromising national polity. The former First Higher School headmaster and Tokyo University professor noted that the educational system was thoroughly grounded in the theory of the absolute sovereignty of the state and the exalted position of the throne, and "the educational authorities are exceedingly jealous of any doctrine or opinion that may possibly infringe upon their sacred dogmas." While the textbooks proudly represented the League as a "quasi-philanthropic 'Parliament of man'" to which Japan adhered of its own accord for the welfare of the world, the official mind was afraid that "the interest and dignity of the nation may be compromised by affiliation with a supernational organization." Nitobe was conscious that a struggle between nationalism and internationalism in Japan—"The World" versus "The Country"— could be perilous. He regretted that the authorities were wary of people who philosophically or professionally upheld the claims of the world in opposition to those of the state. Nonetheless, he took heart in signs that leading educational institutions had recently opened their doors to the activities of the League of Nations Association. Nitobe ended his report with an appeal for more and better communication between Tokyo and Geneva. In direct response to his urging, the secretariat established a branch information office in Tokyo in 1926.[17]

In late 1926 Nitobe retired from the League with a sense of accomplishment. He had helped to organize the secretariat and had watched the elevation of its international reputation. His frequent appearances on behalf of the League had won him and his nation respect and had lent credence to the myth of the organization's universality. As his Geneva years closed, Nitobe's support for Japanese adhesion remained strong. True, the earlier assurance was somewhat dimmed, and he was more apt to state the League's failings and limitations. But he believed Japan had no better alternative. Back in Japan, he summed up a lengthy defense of Japanese membership: "The League of Nations has now been in operation for eight years. In these years Japan has lost nothing by her membership. The imponderable advantages she has gained more than justify her presence in that parliament of the world."[18]

[17] Nitobe, "The League of Nations Movement in Japan (a Report on the Trip to Japan)," April 9, 1925, in League of Nations Archives, Geneva, Box 572.

[18] Nitobe, in *Japan Times*, quoted in *International Gleanings from Japan* 3, 10–11 (October–November 1927): 8.

## Japan in Asia

During his seven years in the secretariat Nitobe had occupied an ideal vantage point from which to evaluate the progress of universal order. Germany's admission to the League in 1926 pleased him, but he was troubled by the continuing refusal by the United States to join. Moreover, with the Soviet Union a nonmember, it was obvious that the League was not universal in scope. Despite conscientious Japanese involvement in its activities, the League remained preoccupied with European issues. While Nitobe's Japanese colleagues in the secretariat returned home on furlough, they found frequent references in the press to the League as a European club. Anti-Japanese discrimination in California, capped by the U.S. Immigration Act of 1924, which vexed the under-secretary, called into question the efficacy of universal morality.[19]

The course of European diplomacy during Nitobe's Geneva sojourn gave strong evidence that the powers were prone to circumvent the League in matters of vital self-interest. The 1923 Corfu Incident involving League members Italy and Greece was settled by a conference of ambassadors rather than League machinery because Italy refused to accept League jurisdiction in the case. In 1925 a set of significant political, military, and territorial accommodations with Germany was concluded by Britain, France, Italy, and Belgium at the Locarno Conference. Though elaborate efforts were made to harmonize the Locarno Pact with League procedures, it was obvious that the European powers were presenting the League with a fait accompli and using the organization as window dressing for understandings forged elsewhere. The League was clearly secondary in the European power game. Despite clear evidence that the League of Nations was not measuring up to the universalistic ideals that inspired its founding, Japanese spokesmen continued in the mid-1920s to support the principle of universality and to discourage the formation of regional peace machinery to displace the League of Nations. Japan's leaders believed that the publicity and status benefits to be derived from international organization were dependent upon the extent of its inclusiveness. The full acceptance of Japan as a world power could be achieved best in an international system that was truly global in scope. The continuing quest for racial equality would be meaningless in an Asian forum from which Europeans and North Americans were absent. At a session of the Seventh Assembly, which convened September 1926, Ishii Kikujirō rose to congratulate Germany on its entry into the League and then warned

[19] Furukaki Tetsuro, "Le Japon et le Société des Nations," March 21, 1927; Harada Ken, "The Visit to Japan," October 9, 1924; in League of Nations Archives, Box R1573. Nitobe stated publicly that he would not visit his second homeland again until the United States repealed the offensive immigration legislation.

against the tendency to address problems on a regional basis: "In general, groups formed on a continental basis or on the basis of religion or race are, in our opinion, by no means to be encouraged, since they would necessarily have a sectarian or regional tendency, however praiseworthy their original purpose. True world peace can only be achieved after every barrier erected upon continental, religious, or racial consideration has been broken down."[20] In the same year Brazil withdrew from the League of Nations. The *Osaka asahi* voiced apprehension that this move would expedite the formation of an American league of nations and cause the League in Geneva to devolve into a European organization. The government-subsidized Japan League of Nations Association adopted a resolution in the same vein:

> While admitting the technical possibility of organizing some kind of local or continental league within the League of Nations, the League of Nations Association of Japan cannot acquiesce in such organization, provided that it creates, in respect of the countries concerned, such rights and obligations as are directly in conflict with those already existing by the Covenant of the League of Nations, or calculated to lead to racial or economic estrangement or to produce discord among nations challenging the very authority of the League of Nations.[21]

Soeda Juichi, the association's vice-president, admonished his country in a speech in the House of Peers in 1928 to "see faithfully and loyally that the League will not suffer from divided interests or regionalism."[22] While leaders in government sought to sustain the global order of the League of Nations, Nitobe Inazō was beginning to break ranks with universalism. His reversal became public at the Third Conference of the Institute of Pacific Relations (IPR).

In 1929 Nitobe was named chairman of the Japanese Council of the IPR, a position he held until his death four years later. The internationally minded intellectuals who made up the Japanese Council were already known to be "apostles of the Nitobe faith." At the center were such First Higher School graduates as Takagi Yasaka, Tsurumi Yūsuke, Takayanagi Kenzō, and Maeda Tamon, who regarded Nitobe as their personal mentor. The Japanese Council of the IPR was truly an extension of Nitobe's shadow.[23] In 1929 he headed his country's delegation to the institute's Third Conference, which convened in Kyoto.

[20] Ishii, quoted in Matsushita Masatoshi, *Japan in the League of Nations* (New York: Columbia University Press, 1929), p. 167.

[21] Ibid., p. 168.

[22] Soeda, quoted in ibid., p. 169.

[23] Nakami Mari, "Taiheiyō mondai chōsakai to Nihon no chishikijin" (The Institute of Pacific Relations and Japan's intellectuals), *Shisō* (February 1985): 106.

As delegates from the Pacific states gathered, a reassessment of all options for international order was compelled by unsettling developments in East Asia. The world Depression had hit, the Nationalists had reunited China, and the Soviet Union was emerging as a power after a decade of domestic instability. In his opening address Nitobe referred to Geneva as "that world capital, the Mecca of international peace and cooperation," and called the League of Nations "indispensable for the future of our species." But more telling than his benediction was Nitobe's call for a regionally based mechanism to supplement the Geneva order:

> As the League grows in membership and geographical dimensions, it will presumably be compelled to conduct some of its business in regional congresses. For, though theoretically and ideologically the concern of one nation is the concern of the whole world, there are, in practice, international questions that affect only restricted areas. Questions of this character can be best discussed by the parties interested in a regional gathering, under the general direction or oversight of the central body.[24]

Roundtable discussions among the IPR delegated scrutinized in depth the notion of peace machinery for the Pacific, and in the parley the Versailles order as then constituted came up wanting. Japanese delegate Rōyama Masamichi depicted existing systems as incapable of enforcing such multilateral arrangements as the Nine-Power Pact and the Kellogg-Briand Pact, which had replaced the more effective bilateral agreements preceding Versailles. "It will be very necessary," he said, "to consider means of developing a proper organization for their full enforcement in order that international relations in the Pacific in general, and in the restless regions in particular, may be regulated and adjusted in harmony with the provisions and intent of these more comprehensive agreements."[25] The Chinese delegation articulated widely held views when it expressed frank suspicions concerning the fairness of League procedures and the relevance of the system to Asia. China had just received both injustice and neglect; the League was too far away, too absorbed in European affairs, and too much under the domination of the great powers. Other delegates added that the League, with its successes mainly in Europe, might in fact be regarded as a European regional organization. In the Pacific, practical advance had been made mainly by regional conferences outside the League.[26] The Kyoto conference provides ample evidence of a shift in Nitobe's world order view well before Mukden. His universalistic principle

[24] Nitobe, "Opening Address at the Kyoto Conference of the Institute of Pacific Relations," October 28, 1929, in Nitobe, *Works*, pp. 355, 356.

[25] Rōyama Masamichi, "Japan's Position in Manchuria," in J. B. Condliffe, ed., *Problems of the Pacific, 1929* (Chicago: University of Chicago Press, 1930), p. 536.

[26] Condliffe, ed., *Problems of the Pacific*, pp. 227, 241.

that the concern of one nation is the concern of the whole world was now displayed by regional schemes and bilateral approaches. Significantly, Nitobe's book *Japan*, published in 1931, stated that the 1922 termination of the Anglo-Japanese Alliance had been a mistake.[27]

Fast-paced events following the September 1931 Manchurian Incident would bring Japan's relationship with the League of Nations to a bitter end. The struggle between the League and the empire over Manchuria was the most frustrating dilemma of Nitobe's internationalist career. In the midst of heated exchanges between Tokyo and Geneva, the Fourth Conference of the IPR convened in Shanghai. Nitobe again headed the Japanese delegation. As in Kyoto two years before, the question of diplomatic machinery for the Pacific was the central political issue, and the immediacy of the Manchurian crisis made the discussion all the more poignant. Nitobe's direct input on this question is not recorded, but Takayanagi Kenzō, a professor of the Law Faculty of Tokyo University, made a formal presentation of the Japanese delegation's position in which he tackled the universalism-regionalism problem head-on:

> It seems to me that the conception of universalism—the League as a universal organ, to deal with all disputes arising throughout the world—is a very valuable one. There should not be too many competing organs. There is much justification for that argument. But that conception may well be reconciled with an attempt to set up here in the Pacific an organ to investigate in a realistic way the conditions in China and Japan, and ultimately to solve the international difficulties in the Pacific area. Arrangements may be made in such a way that such an organ will not do away with the idea of the universality of the League.

Takayanagi then took up the issue of Manchuria, contending that a League without American and Soviet representation could not deal adequately with such complex matters as Chinese nationalism and Soviet designs on the region. His conclusion was a clear challenge to existing League machinery:

> My main thesis tonight is that Geneva is too far away to appreciate the complex conditions obtaining in the Far East. Members of the League Council may fall into the error of judging things by superficial observation of events and the mere study of the provisions of the treaties contained in MacMurray. A permanent body, either a part of the League or an independent unit affiliated with the League, and with America and Russia cooperating, is highly desirable for dealing, not only with the Manchurian question, but with questions relating to the whole international situation in the Orient.[28]

[27] Nitobe, *Japan: Some Phases of Her Problems and Development* (London: Ernest Benn Limited, 1931), p. 160.

[28] Takayanagi Kenzō, "The Application of Existing Instruments of Policy," in Bruce Las-

The following April, Nitobe embarked on a personal mission to the United States and Canada to explain Japan's course of action in Manchuria. Though this mission was consistent with his conviction that understanding is the route to peace, it turned out to be the most frustrating experience of his life. His message was not well received or understood. As he crossed the continent giving lectures, radio addresses, and press interviews, he advocated Asian solutions to Asian problems. He tried to place Japanese policy in perspective—not only the perspective of the real circumstances of Asia, but also the perspective of the regional hegemonic impulses that had shaped the historical development of the United States. Citing the case of Panamanian nationhood, he defended the helping role of an outside power in the birth of Manchukuo. Why, he asked, should such action be right in one place and wrong in another? How do you Americans respond to disturbances in Nicaragua and El Salvador? He chafed, "We have learned many things from America, especially in dealing with neighboring unstable governments, and when we put the lessons into practice we are severely criticized by our teacher."[29]

In North America the former under-secretary had much to say about mechanisms for world order. For a New York radio audience he listed among fatal drawbacks to a Japan-League relationship the nonmembership of the United States and the Soviet Union and the lack, until the current case, of issues at Geneva involving Japan as a principal party: "The twelve years Japan has sat there she has largely been a spectator of European events that concerned her little." As for the Kellogg-Briand Pact and its application in the Stimson Doctrine, Nitobe warned that to clamp the treaty rigidly on a nation whose self-preservation was at stake would destroy the treaty: "Nations will not offer themselves for martyrdom for an interpretation of a pact," he said. China and Japan must be left to work out their differences without third party interference, be that third party the United States or the League of Nations. Nitobe warned that if the League refused to "recognize the justice of our claim which involves our honor and our very existence as a nation," Japan would withdraw and "carve out, unaided and alone, her own destiny." On occasion he praised the League as a noble creation and voiced the hope that Japan would remain in Geneva, but his message in the present case was clear: no amount of international favor was worth accommodation of League

---

ker, ed., *Problems of the Pacific, 1931* (New York: Greenwood Press, 1969), pp. 233–36. "MacMurray" is a reference to the standard compilation of China treaties, published in 1921.

[29] Nitobe, "The Manchurian Question and Sino-American Relations," November 21, 1932, in Nitobe, *Works*, 4:232; *New York Times*, August 14, 1932, VIII, p. 2, and July 29, 1932, p. 11; Nitobe, "Japan and the United States," November 28, 1932, in Nitobe, *Works*, 4:256.

directives.[30] The clash between League and Japan's assertion of predominant regional power in East Asia exposed the paradoxes in Nitobe's complex character and ideology. In February 1933 Matsuoka Yōsuke led the Japanese delegation out of the League of Nations. Within six months Nitobe Inazō, sad, tired, and deteriorated in body, passed away.

## Blueprints for Regional Order

Knowledge that in Manchuria Japan was taking on the League of Nations and the major powers caused considerable anxiety in Japan. Behind strident allegations of the League's malfeasance lurked the fear of international condemnation and isolation, which had troubled thoughtful Japanese after World War I. The present circumstances were even more unsettling due to the absence of the Anglo-Japanese Alliance. The Four-Power Pact, which had supplanted it in 1922, could hardly be depended upon to secure Japanese interests since the creation of Manchukuo. Japanese knowledgeable in foreign affairs groped for a new mechanism that would fill the security gap created by departure from Geneva and, at the same time, be amenable to the realities of Manchukuo and Japanese aspirations for predominance in East Asia. From 1932 to 1938, several models were proposed for peace machinery in the Far East.

### Locarno Pact for the Far East (1932)

Japanese greeted the Locarno Pact favorably when it was signed by European nations in December 1925. Aside from provisions for mutual security, arbitration, and French evacuation of the Rhineland, the accords that constituted the Pact paved the way for German entry into the League of Nations. Upon the initialing of the treaties, the Japanese delegate to Geneva, Ishii Kikujirō, acknowledged that the Versailles Treaty alone "could not give the world genuine peace."[31] Speaking to the Diet, Foreign Minister Shidehara Kijūrō welcomed Germany's return to the family of nations and praised the Locarno signatories for forgetting old scores. He saw a brighter future for the League in the light of the new agreement.[32] The positive reaction of the Japanese public was evident in the press. The *Hōchi* declared, "The peace of Europe was nominally restored by the Ver-

[30] Nitobe, quoted in *New York Times*, July 29, 1932, p. 11; Nitobe, "Japan and the Peace Pact," radio broadcast, August 20, 1932, in Nitobe, *Works* 4:240–50; Nitobe, "Japan and the League of Nations," radio broadcast, May 8, 1932, in Nitobe, *Works*, 4:234–39.

[31] Ishii, quoted in Société des Nations, *Journal Officiel* 6, 2 (November 1925): 1715–16.

[32] *International Gleanings from Japan* 3, 1 (January 31, 1927), pp. 1, 5.

208 THOMAS W. BURKMAN

sailles Treaty, and it has now been effectively assured by the Locarno Pact." The pact was more realistic, said the editorial, than the "defect-ridden treaty of peace." The *Kokumin* attributed the pact's potential effectiveness to its local nature.[33] Locarno was attractive to many Japanese because it seemed to be concrete rather than idealistic, political rather than moralistic, and regional rather than universalistic. Dino Gandi, a diplomat of another aspiring middle power, Italy, voiced sentiments strikingly akin to those of the Japanese when he described the framing of Locarno:

> They corrected, or at least they aimed at correcting, those deviations from reality inherent in the universality of the League and in its abstract and ideological character. They sought to remove the League from the world of prophecy to the world of hard facts, from purely theoretical and universal affirmations to the immediate guarantees necessary to satisfy the craving for safety and protection—those are the very words of the Locarno Treaty—that animate the countries who were victims of the war scourge of 1914–1918.[34]

As noted earlier, in the mid-1920s the potential benefits of universalism restrained Japanese leaders from plunging headlong down the path of regionalism. But the events of 1931–32—coupled with a shift in Japan's trade distribution toward Asia—brought a renewed interest in the model of Locarno as a lodestar of international order. The major sponsor of the Asian Locarno concept in 1932 was Ashida Hitoshi. Ashida was a diplomat-politician who resigned from the Foreign Ministry in 1931 on the basis of his antimilitarist views. In November 1932, when he published an article in *Gaikō Jihō* calling for a Locarno Pact for the Far East, he had just been elected to the Lower House of the Diet.

Suspicious of any status quo order "outside the law of mutation," Ashida dismissed the Versailles-Washington system as incapable of coping with issues such as the Manchurian Incident, which arise with the passing of time. If the powers persisted in refusing to recognize Manchukuo, Manchuria would remain a "chronic disease," perpetually fouling Japan's relations with other major nations. A solution, wrote Ashida, was a Locarno Pact for the Far East (Kyokutō Rokaruno), an instrument for the pacific solution of disputes just like the system developed in Central Europe in 1925. It should comprise Japan, Manchukuo, the Soviet Union, and China. Such a mutual security agreement had already been adopted by Japan and Manchukuo. Though Chinese Nationalist leaders were not likely to go along at first, Ashida saw signs of a more favorable climate

---

[33] *Hōchi* editorial, December 4, 1925; *Kokumin* editorial, October 17, 1925.

[34] Dino Grandi, "Italy," in Council on Foreign Relations, ed., *The Foreign Policy of the Powers* (New York: Harper and Brothers, 1935), pp. 88–89.

among "the Chinese as a whole." American acquiescence could be expected from "practical statesmen in the United States who are aware of the real situation in Manchuria, Japan's position, and the realities of China." The support of such Americans for Japan's continental policy would grow over time as Japan demonstrated that it harbored no territorial ambitions beyond the borders of Manchuria.[35]

### Security Pact of the Pacific (1933)

At the Fifth Conference of the Institute of Pacific Relations at Banff in August 1933, Takagi Yasaka and Yokota Kisaburō presented a detailed proposal for a Security Pact of the Pacific. Takagi had been a pupil of Nitobe at First Higher and an intimate associate thereafter. He had accompanied his teacher and mentor to the Kyoto conference of the IPR and now to Banff, Nitobe's final parley. At the time Takagi was professor of American institutions at Tokyo University. Yokota was professor of international law at the same school. Yokota had attended the 1930 London Naval Conference and defended the disarmament agreement against its Japanese critics. He had also publicly criticized Japanese actions in Manchuria after 1931.

The Takagi-Yokota report explained that the absence of the United States, the Soviet Union, and Japan from the League of Nations severely handicapped the organization in dealing with Far Eastern questions. Recent events in the area had made the inadequacy of existing peace machinery "particularly conspicuous." Existing international organization had not solved the problem of economic inequality among nations. But the League might still act constructively in Asia. As a starter, it might organize international economic conferences in the Pacific region. These conferences should operate under their own secretariat.

The Tokyo University professors called for the conclusion of "Pacific Agreements." Contracting parties should include Japan, China, the USSR, the United States, Great Britain, and France—a group more far-ranging than that proposed for Ashida's Locarno Pact. But like Ashida, the authors cautioned that the new mechanism, unlike the prevailing world system, must not perpetuate the status quo, but "must now shift its emphasis to that of change and development." Change and evolution in the Pacific

---

[35] Ashida Hitoshi, "Kyokutō Rokaruno no teishō" (Advocacy of a Far Eastern Locarno), *Gaikō Jihō* 671 (November 15, 1932): 27–33. After World War II Ashida would serve briefly as foreign minister and prime minister.

area, they argued, are "inevitable, and indeed desirable."[36] They insisted
that "it is absolutely necessary to devise some procedure to modify peace-
fully the status quo and to adjust the existing economic inequalities and
political injustices."[37] They referred to the provision in Article 19 of the
League Covenant concerning "the consideration of international conditions whose continuance might endanger the peace of the world" as a
basis for the avoidance of a status quo order. Would the new Pacific order
compete with the League of Nations? On the contrary, it might ultimately
be incorporated into the world organization—"possibly after certain
modifications in the League."

Takagi and Yokota then proceeded to lay out an actual draft treaty
with provisions for security, nonaggression, and arbitration. To encourage international acceptance of their scheme, they deliberately borrowed
wording from the League's Model Treaties, the Four-Power Pact, the
Locarno Pact, the Kellogg-Briand Pact, and the Stimson Doctrine. The
contracting parties, they said, should find no difficulty ascribing to provisions to which they were already committed in substance.[38]

Nowhere in the proposals of Ashida or Takagi and Yokota are there
any references to common culture as a basis for Pacific order. In fact, the
latter attribute unrest in the region to circumstances of heterogeneity—
divergence of national traditions, national outlook, and pace of development.[39]

### Greater Asia Federation (1933)

Greater Asianism (Dai Toa shugi) was promoted by pan-Asianists, who
based their system on cultural affinity. This tradition in Japan had a long
history institutionalized in the Genyōsha (1881), the Kokuryūkai (1901),
and the Dōbunkai (Common Culture Association) founded in 1898 by
Konoe Astumaro. Atsumaro's son Fumimaro served as vice-president of
the Dōbunkai from 1922 and president from 1936. Japanese pan-Asianists believed that China and Japan should formulate common goals so
that Asian civilization could flower in China under Japanese guidance.

On March 1, 1933, a new organization, the Dai Ajia Kyōkai (Greater

[36] Takagi Yasaka, "Some Considerations on the Future Reconstruction of Peace Machinery in the Pacific," in Takagi, *Toward International Understanding* (Tokyo: Kenkyūsha,
1954), pp. 22–23, 27, 31; Nakami, "Taiheiyō mondai chōsakai," p. 112.

[37] Takagi Yasaka and Yokota Kisaburō, "A Security Pact for the Pacific Area," in Bruno
Lasker and W. L. Holland, eds., *Problems of the Pacific, 1933* (Chicago: University of Chicago Press, 1933), p. 442.

[38] Ibid., pp. 442–50.

[39] Takagi, "Some Considerations," p. 23.

Asia Association), was formed to promote the ideal of East Asian regional unity. Among the charter members of the group were Konoe Fumimaro and Yano Jin'ichi. Yano was a prominent Sinologist and historian at Kyoto Imperial University and one of the major spokesmen for the concept that China was not a nation but a culture. General Ishiwara Kanji frequently attended the meetings of the Dai Ajia Kyōkai and formed his own Tōa Renmei Kyōkai (East Asia League Association) in 1939 to further the idea of a Japan-China-Manchukuo axis.[40]

The Dai Ajia Kyōkai advocated a Greater Asia Federation (Dai Ajia Rengō) reflecting the *wang dao* (great way) that Sun Yat-sen had advocated in Japan in 1924 as a basis for regionalism. The group viewed such a federation as a defense of East Asia against cultural conquest by Occidentals, represented most threateningly by Soviet communism. The association's charter clearly stated its purposes:

> In culture, politics, economics, geography, and race, Asia is a body of common destiny. The true peace, prosperity, and development of Asian peoples are feasible only on the basis of their consciousness of Asia as one entity and an organic union thereof. . . . The heavy responsibility for reconstruction and ordering of Asia rests upon the shoulders of Imperial Japan. . . . Now the Manchurian Incident has provided another opportunity in human history for a great turning point. Imperial Japan has, happily, expanded the world-historical meaning of the Russo-Japanese War, and now is the time for Japan to concentrate all its cultural, political, economic, and organizational power to take one step toward the reconstruction and union of Asia. . . . The formulation of the Greater Asia Federation is the historical mission facing the Japanese people today.[41]

As the 1930s wore on, Asian culture was accorded unprecedented attention in government. In a deliberate effort to expand cultural relations, the government in 1934 established a semi-official agency, the Kokusai Bunka Shinkōkai (KBS). This office encouraged the study and knowledge of Japanese culture.[42] Within the Foreign Ministry, Shigemitsu Mamoru became a spokesman for doctrinaire pan-Asianism. Vice-minister from 1933 to 1936, he advocated excluding all Western nations from the set-

[40] Mark R. Peatie, *Ishiwara Kanji and Japan's Confrontation with the West* (Princeton: Princeton University Press, 1975), pp. 281–82, 322.

[41] Shimonaka Yazaburō Den Kankōkai, ed., *Shimonaka Yazaburō jiten* (Encyclopedia of Shimonaka Yazaburō) (Tokyo: Heibonsha, 1965), pp. 242–43; see also Miwa Kimitada, "Japanese Policies and Concepts for a Regional Order in Asia, 1938–1940," IIR Research Paper A-46 (Tokyo: Institute of International Relations, Sophia University, 1983), pp. 3–7.

[42] Robert S. Schwantes, "Japan's Cultural Foreign Policies," in James W. Morley, ed., *Japan's Foreign Policy, 1868–1941: A Research Guide* (New York: Columbia University Press, 1974), pp. 179–80.

tlement of Asian problems.[43] In 1938 the Shōwa Kenkyūkai (Shōwa Research Association), the unofficial brain trust of Prime Minister Konoe Fumimaro, formed its own Cultural Problems Research Group under philosopher Miki Kiyoshi. Miki believed that military power alone would not defeat China; Japan had to triumph in thought and culture as well to achieve a permanent victory. Japan had to create a new ideology that would allow China to transcend "simple nationalism" and join the new order with Japan. Miki's group concluded that intellectuals had to forge principles for a new East Asian culture of international significance, comparable to Hellenistic culture, which had united the Western world. An East Asian bloc established by Japan would be premised upon an ideology of cooperation for the welfare of the whole community that would discard the West's defective notion of individualism, which had produced a culture marred by the "evils of capitalism" and needless "class struggle."[44]

### Far Eastern League of Nations (1933)

In 1933 internationalist scholars were disconcerted by Japan's severance of ties to the prevailing world order. Such thinkers as Tokyo University professors Rōyama Masamichi and Kamikawa Hikomatsu harbored affection for the ideals of the League of Nations and, at the same time, fear of the consequences of unrestrained nationalism. They promoted regionalism as a practical middle course between universalistic internationalism and atavistic nationalism. Eventually, they would lend their intellectual muscle to the creation of the New Order in East Asia, which they rationalized as the awaited appearance of the Far Eastern League, designed to unite East Asia against the twin evils of Western imperialism and Chinese nationalism.[45]

Kamikawa was a diplomatic historian who during the 1920s had been an idealistic supporter of the League of Nations. In a May 1933 lecture at Tokyo University, later published in Kokka Gakkai zasshi, Kamikawa

[43] Akira Iriye, "The Role of the United States Embassy in Tokyo," in Dorothy Borg and Shumpei Okamoto, eds., Pearl Harbor as History: Japanese-American Relations, 1931–1941 (New York: Columbia University Press, 1973), p. 112.

[44] Miles Fletcher, The Search for a New Order: Intellectuals and Fascism in Prewar Japan (Chapel Hill: University of North Carolina Press, 1982), pp. 62, 110–13. Miki's concern for Japan's contribution to world culture elicits comparison to Watanabe Kaigyoku's urging, documented by Jackie Stone, that Japan have an impact on world civilization through Buddhist studies.

[45] Mitani Taichirō, "Changes in Japan's International Position and the Response of Japanese Intellectuals: Trends in Japanese Studies of Japan's Foreign Relations, 1931–1941," in Borg and Okamoto, eds., Pearl Harbor as History, pp. 580–89.

issued a critique of Greater Asianism, which he identified with pan-Asianism. Pan-Asianism, he said, was based on shared culture and race and common antagonism toward alien cultures. In the Asian setting it would not flourish, he said, without a sense of confrontation with the West. This spirit was contrary to the principles of the League of Nations—principles that ought to be appropriated in any worthwhile regional order: "Even though Japan has withdrawn from the League of Nations of Geneva, it must not completely abandon the principles of the League. The very idea of the Far Eastern League is to implement those principles in the region of the Far East and to bring to realization a Far Eastern League of Nations." Kamikawa warned that Greater Asianism would eventuate in a disastrous racial war. Moreover, Greater Asianism as espoused by the recently established Dai Ajia Kyōkai was an impractical course in view of the hostility the powers would inevitably show toward such a stance. Kamikawa's admonition is evidence that accommodationism was still lurking in the mind of one regionalist. Kamikawa's counter-proposal to Greater Asianism was a Far Eastern League of Nations (Kyokutō Renmei). It was to act not as an expression of pan-Asianism, but as a regional administrative unit of the League of Nations. He pointed to a recent call by the president of Uruguay for an "American League of Nations"— based on equality and not dominated by the United States—as evidence that the time was ripe. Kamikawa's raising of the issue of international equality reflects sentiments deeply harbored by Japanese since Japan sought unsuccessfully to implant the principle of equality in the League of Nations Covenant at the Paris Peace Conference. The Far Eastern unit would comprise Japan, Manchukuo, China, Siam, Siberia, and the Philippines. To make the Far Eastern League feasible, it was necessary to heal the Sino-Japanese conflict as soon as possible.[46]

A similar view of regional organization was held by Matsuoka Yōsuke, former League of Nations delegate who later negotiated the Tripartite Pact with the Axis. In 1946 he told his American interrogator:

After Geneva I began to think that the League of Nations that tries to gather all the nations in one conference was impossible, and that the world should have leadership in each region and establish a kind of league of nations of that smaller and separate sphere. For instance, America to lead the Western Hemisphere and Great Britain to lead the nations she is closely interwoven with, and then Soviet Russia to lead Soviet Russia and some neighboring countries, and Japan to lead the Far East, etc. And then these regional leagues to be joined roughly, so that from time to time they can exchange their opinions and views.

[46] Kamikawa Hikomatsu, "Ajia rengō ka kyokutō renmei ka?" (Asian federation or Far Eastern league?) *Kokka Gakkai zasshi* 47, 7 (July 1933): 90–100.

In such a way, only in the then prevailing conditions of the world, can we contribute toward world peace.[47]

## New Order in East Asia (1938)

By the time full-scale Sino-Japanese war erupted in 1937, regionalism had degenerated into a one-sided imposition of the Japanese will upon China. Nonetheless, much idealism and intellectual discussion went into the New Order in East Asia (Tōa Shinchitsujo) proclaimed by Prime Minister Konoe on November 3, 1938. The New Order was a program of political, economic, and cultural cooperation among Japan, China, and Manchukuo.

Rōyama Masamichi was an important member of the premier's Shōwa Kenkyūkai. He saw the New Order as a "new international organization," a regional bloc similar to that being created in Central Europe under German leadership. The New Order would introduce a new epoch of cooperativism to replace the artificial concept of nationalism, which had been imposed by the "old imperialists" at Versailles. When war erupted in Europe, Rōyama would urge a more unified domestic political structure at home to enable more efficient effort for building the New Order abroad. Thus he called for the disbanding of political parties that had arisen, he said, under the "cooperative diplomacy" with the Anglo-American powers.[48]

When Prime Minister Konoe went on the radio to announce the New Order, he made it clear that the East Asian system he envisioned was designed to supplant the Versailles structure in Asia:

> What the world needs today is the establishment of peace, justice, and equality. It cannot be denied that the past various rules have maintained the unbalanced condition. It is well known that international agreements such as the League of Nations Covenant already have lost their dignity, because of irrational principles. There must be brought about a new peace system based on realities, covering trade, immigration, resources, culture, and other fields of human life.[49]

It is no coincidence that Konoe's proclamation came just twenty-four hours after his government severed all remaining ties with the World Court as well as the humanitarian and social agencies of the League of Nations. All strings connecting Japan to universal order were now cut.

[47] Interrogation of Matsuoka Yōsuke, March 29, 1946, in U.S. National Archives, IPS Records, Entry 319, Case No. 118 (Courtesy Prof. Awaya Kentarō of Rikkyo University).

[48] Rōyama Masamichi, The Foreign Policy of Japan, 1914–1939 (Tokyo: Japanese Council of the IPR, 1941), p. 169; Fletcher, The Search for a New Order, pp. 81, 138–39, 145.

[49] Konoe, translated in Japan Times and Mail, November 4, 1938, p. 1.

## Conclusion

A tension between accommodationism and regionalism as approaches to international order is found in Japanese diplomatic thinking during the years between the world wars. Regionalist proclivities and internationalist tendencies were present in varying proportions throughout the two decades. One impulse, dominant in late Taishō, sought the advantages of an international voice and full equality within the League of Nations. A second, in ascendancy in early Shōwa, groped for security through leadership in East Asia. These imperatives are not unique to Japan. Every power reflects the behavior that Karl Deutch has labeled the "schizophrenic concept of foreign affairs—to wit, to assert equality when the nation is weak, and predominance when it is strong.

Curiously, some of the empire's most prominent diplomatic leaders officiated at Japan's rites of initiation into both orders. Foreign Minister Uchida Yasuya in 1918 instructed the plenipotentiaries departing for Paris to conform to world trends on the issue of the establishment of the League of Nations. In 1933, again as foreign minister, he ordered Japan's Geneva representatives to quit the League in clear defiance of world opinion. Matsuoka Yōsuke and Konoe Fumimaro were both part of the Japanese entourage at Paris. Fourteen years later Matsuoka would lead the Japanese delegation out of the League Assembly, while Konoe as prime minister in 1938 would proclaim a regional New Order to replace universal order in East Asia. Educator, intellectual, and renowned internationalist Nitobe Inazō would similarly be associated first with universal order and then with regional order. As under-secretary general of the League of Nations, he was a major publicist for the philosophy that the concern of one nation is the concern of all. His ideal of universal mankind provided the intellectual framework for his efforts for tolerance and global understanding. As an officer in the Institute of Pacific Relations and apologist for Japan in its struggle with the League over Manchuria, he promoted the solution of Asian conflicts through regional peace machinery. The very continuity of actors in these seemingly contradictory scenarios suggests the strong probability of underlying elements of similarity in the diplomatic thought of the 1920s and 1930s. These need further exploration.

Intellectually speaking, did Japan abandon universalism in the post-Taishō *tenkō*? It is significant that several of the architects of schemes for regional order—Yokota, Takagi, and Kamikawa, for example—openly based their proposed regional peace machinery on principles and even wording borrowed from the League of Nations. They argued for localized systems, not to displace the League, but to operate within an expanded

League framework to make the global organization more realistic and effective. Most proposals for regional order envisioned a Pacific community incorporating such non-Asian entities as the Soviet Union and the United States. The Far Eastern Locarno plan drew inspiration from an arrangement presumed successful in Europe. In nearly every regional framework, the ghost of universalism can be detected. One is reminded of the common explanation for the rise of feudalism in medieval Europe and *bakufu* Japan: the memory of the universal empire of the past helped determine the shape of the decentralized order that displaced it. Similarly, the vestiges of universal order lay entrapped in the hearts of the drafters and woven into the blueprints of regional systems of the 1930s. Nor did Japan after 1931 cherish a so-called autonomous diplomacy. Japanese foreign policy did cease to be accommodationist; but Japan quickly sought new colleagues, at first in Asia and after 1936 in the fascist power of Europe.

Finally, was the retreat from international accommodationism a cultural reversion to Asia? This much can be ventured. Cultural affinity was a basis for only one stream of regionalist thought—the pan-Asianist stream—and was distinctly absent in other streams. The prolific writings and utterances of Nitobe, which clearly document his own shift, show no evidence of an accompanying Asian culturalism. Pan-Asianist ideals became influential in diplomatic thought as the 1930s wore on and were an important intellectual ingredient in the New Order in East Asia. But pan-Asianist ideas began to appear in prominent discussions of regionalism only after the Manchurian Incident and after Japan's estrangement from the League of Nations. In this light, it seems difficult to argue a cultural basis for imperialism. Asian culturalism seems rather to gain prominence as a means of adjustment to and consolidation of established regional power.

# 11

## A Vast and Grave Task: Interwar Buddhist Studies as an Expression of Japan's Envisioned Global Role

JACKIE STONE

Ui HAKUJU (1882–1963), Buddhologist and scholar of Indian philosophy during the Taishō-Shōwa periods, in reviewing the achievements of his own generation of Japanese Buddhist scholars, wrote the following in 1951:

> By now, with respect to Buddhist studies, we may say that we have reached a point where ours excel those of any other nation. . . . Thanks to the lifetime zeal of many Buddhist scholars, Buddhist studies in our country have developed and advanced as Japanese Buddhist studies, producing something unique and not to be found in either India or China. From the broad standpoint of culture as a whole, Japanese Buddhist studies form our contribution to the development of the culture of humanity, and are the crystallization of the efforts of our countrymen. It therefore cannot be denied that our Buddhist studies are no mere import, but something we have thoroughly integrated and absorbed.[1]

Three decades later, Japan's accomplishments in the world of Buddhist studies still far surpass those of any other nation, not merely in the area of Japanese Buddhism, as one might expect, but also with respect to the Buddhism of India, China, Tibet, and Central and Southeast Asia. Japan attained its present eminence in Buddhist studies—and at the same time self-defined its role as the disseminator of Buddhism to the world—during the Taishō and early Shōwa periods, that is, in the interval between the world wars.

At least three distinguishing characteristics of Japanese Buddhist studies may be found during this period. First, the new field of Buddhology emerged as an academic discipline independent of the Buddhist clergy and traditional sectarian Buddhist studies. Second, there was a complete absorption of modern Western scholastic methods, including philological and historical studies, textual analysis, and the interpretation of Bud-

---

[1] Ui Hakuju, *Nihon bukkyō gaisetsu* (Tokyo: Iwanami shoten, 1951), p. 217.

dhism in the light of such new disciplines as psychology, sociology, archaeology, and comparative religion. Third, there was a massive effort at integration and systematization, including the collating, editing, and translating of texts, attempts to systematize various Buddhist doctrines and developments within an overreaching framework, as well as a search for a single underlying truth in which the whole of Buddhism might be subsumed. These three developments together enabled Japanese Buddhist studies of the interwar period to emerge as the foremost in the world. I believe it is possible to see them all as expressions of broader intellectual trends operating at that time, including an effort on the part of Japanese intellectuals in the post-Meiji years to define the position of their country with respect to Asia, the rest of the world, and history. I will attempt here to begin drawing some connections between these general trends and specific developments in interwar Buddhist studies, referring where necessary to the background of the latter in the Meiji period.

The Buddhist establishment in post-Restoration Meiji Japan faced an immediate crisis. More than two hundred years of patronage by the Tokugawa regime had bred widespread moral and financial corruption. Now, suddenly deprived of their state support, temples and priests lost a major source of revenue, and in addition, Buddhism came under attack for its foreign origins, an opposition that reached its extreme in the short-lived but violent *haibutsu kishaku* movement, described in William La-Fleur's essay, in which art treasures were destroyed and temples and lands seized. As Japan hastened to Westernize, Christianity posed still another threat. Younger intellectuals, crediting Western religion in part with the remarkable rise of Western science and technology, tended on the whole to turn away from Buddhism. Here and there, however, a few voices could be heard asserting that, far from being an archaic foreign import, Buddhism had by centuries of association become something uniquely Japanese and might therefore contribute to Japan's prestige among foreign nations. "Only in our country of Japan do we have the sects and texts, as well as the people who understand the profundity of the One Vehicle," observed Inoue Enryō (1858–1919), one of the most influential of the new Meiji Buddhist scholars.[2] Writing as early as 1887, he declared:

Buddhism is now our so-called strong point. . . . Material commodities are an advantage of the West; scholarship is also one of their strong points. The only advantage we have is religion. This fine product of ours excels those of other countries; the fact that its good strain died out in India and China may be considered an unexpected blessing for our country. If we continue to nurture it in

[2] Quoted in Kathleen M. Staggs, " 'Defend the Nation and Love the Truth': Inoue Enryō and the Revival of Meiji Buddhism," *Monumenta Nipponica* 38, 3 (Autumn 1983):271.

Japan and disseminate it some day in foreign countries, we will not only add to the honor of our nation but will also infuse the spirit of our land into the hearts and minds of foreigners. I am convinced that the consequences will be considerable.[3]

I have quoted this passage because it prefigures an identification of Buddhism with Japan's unique role in the world community, which was to emerge fully during the Taishō period. In this respect, Inoue proved to be far-sighted. It is probably safe to say that most of his contemporaries active in the Meiji Buddhist revival movement did not view Buddhist studies as a means of enhancing Japan's global prestige but hoped merely to purify the Buddhist establishment, restore Buddhism to its former power and influence, and enable it to emerge and survive as a modern religion. With this aim in mind, leaders within the various sects sent promising young priests to England and Germany to absorb the latest developments in European Buddhist scholarship. First among those to go abroad was Nanjō Bun'yū (1849–1927), who in 1876 journeyed to England where he would study Sanskrit with F. Max Müller (1823–1900), the great Orientalist and one of the founders of the science of religion. What these students brought back would alter irrevocably the configuration of Buddhist studies in Japan.

Until this time, Japanese Buddhist studies had been based almost exclusively on the Chinese texts that had been gradually brought into Japan since the introduction of Buddhism via Korea in the sixth century. These texts were generally divided into three major categories: the sutras (regarded as the direct preaching of the Buddha); the treatises, or discussions of the Dharma written by "bodhisattvas" such as Nāgārjuna or Vasubandhu; and the commentaries, or exegeses on the sutras and treatises, written by the enlightened human teachers of past ages. Doctrinal studies were for the most part carried out within the framework of each sect's *kyōhan* or "comparative classification," a ranking of the various Buddhist teachings in some systematic order, usually designed to emphasize the supremacy of one's own school. In short, traditional Buddhist studies in Japan were sectarian in orientation and indissolubly welded to Buddhist faith and practice, carried out within a circle of people who were themselves Buddhists and who all accepted the same body of scriptures as a faithful record of the Buddha's word.

Into this closed system now came the innovations of modern Western scholarship, with its emphasis on historical studies and textual analysis and its demand for academic objectivity. The young priests who had studied in Europe in the first decades of the Meiji era brought back not only these disquieting new approaches, hard to reconcile with the old sectarian

[3] *Bukkyō katsuron jōron*, cited in ibid., p. 271.

and pietistic system, but what their elders must surely have regarded as an unseemly fascination with a body of Buddhist texts that had never formed a significant part of the Japanese Buddhist tradition—namely, the Pali canon. Most of these young men had studied in London, where F. Max Müller was supervising the editing of the ambitious *Sacred Books of the East* series and T. W. Rhys Davids (1843–1922) had founded the Pali text society. For European scholars of the day, Buddhism generally meant Indian Buddhism, and the more ancient the form, the greater the orthodoxy it was assumed to possess. Theravada or southern Buddhism was at first regarded as the oldest, "purest" form of Buddhism. The Pali scriptures, the Theravada canon, represented a tradition contemptuously dismissed for centuries by Japanese Buddhists as "Hinayana," yet this was the very body of texts now being intently scrutinized by the Europeans, who seriously hoped to find in it the direct words of Śākyamuni himself. More of this later, but for now, suffice it to say that conflict between the traditional and the new approaches to Buddhist studies was inevitable and violent. Murakami Senshō (1851–1929), an important Meiji Buddhist historian, was divested of his Jōdo Shinshū priesthood for some years over an essay published in 1901 in which he asserted that the Mahayana sutras did not represent the direct preaching of Śākyamuni Buddha.[4] Nor was this an isolated instance. Inexorably, lines were being drawn between those who wished to retain the old sectarian mode of Buddhist studies and those who opted for the Western academic approach. By the beginning of the Taishō period, the schism was complete. The new paths in Japanese Buddhist studies would be blazed by a group of young lay scholars centered around Tokyo Imperial University. Most of them had studied extensively in both England and Germany and were thoroughly competent to deal with both Pali and Sanskrit Buddhist texts, as well as the Chinese *tripiṭaka*. Their financial backing came not from the Buddhist establishment but from the Imperial government; as faculty of the Imperial University, they by definition held civil service rank in the Ministry of Education. And while some counted themselves devout Buddhists, they embraced a different set of aims, assumptions, and motivations than any previous generation of Japanese Buddhist scholars.

Buddhist studies at Tokyo Imperial University chiefly centered around the department of philosophy in the College of Liberal Arts. This department had established a chair of Sanskrit studies in April 1901, held by the

---

[4] The intensity of this reaction can be appreciated more clearly when one realizes that Murakami was in no way suggesting that the Mahayana scriptures be discarded. He continued to regard himself as an adherent of the Mahayana doctrines, which he considered more profound and sophisticated than those of Hinayana. His point was purely and solely historical; modern textual studies clearly demonstrated that the Mahayana sutras did not represent the Buddha's direct preaching.

great India and Buddhist scholar Takakusu Junjirō (1866–1945); a chair
of the science of religion in 1905, held by Anesaki Masaharu (1873–
1949), who had studied for three years in Germany; and a chair of Indian
philosophy in 1917, held by the above-mentioned Buddhologist Murakami Senshō. These individuals and their students formed the nucleus of
the new Buddhist studies at Tokyo Imperial University. The major in Indian philosophy in particular often entailed a chiefly Buddhist emphasis.[5]
The curriculum reflected the changing orientation: In addition to Hindu
and Buddhist texts and the Sanskrit and Pali languages, students were
required to study the science of religion, Western and Asian philosophy,
and English, French, or German, as well as to choose electives from such
diverse fields as psychology, metaphysics, Chinese philosophy, ethics, aesthetics, and sociology.

When plans to establish the chair of Indian philosophy at Tokyo University were announced in 1916, Watanabe Kaigyoku (1872–1933), one
of the leading Taishō Buddhist scholars and reformers, offered the following response in an editorial:

This, the highest educational institution in the empire, should from the outset
have possessed a chair for the teaching of Mahayana and Hinayana, Sacred
Way and Pure Land, and exoteric and esoteric teachings. This is but a matter
of course in terms of our history, the present state of scholarship, and our prestige with respect to foreign universities. That we have lacked it until today must
be termed our greatest grievance with respect to imperial education, and the
utmost shame for this outstanding institution. But now, the time having gradually ripened, the grievance and shame of these years are on the way to being
resolved. . . .

The [Japanese] Empire is the leader of peace in Asia and must also be the
forerunner of her culture. In this sense, the establishment of this chair of Buddhist studies[6] at the Imperial University will surely draw a favorable response
from China, on the one hand, and from Siam, India, and Manchuria on the

[5] A similar situation existed at Kyoto Imperial University where, even before the formal
establishment of a chair of Buddhist studies in 1926, Buddhist texts, history, art, and so
forth were taught under the rubric of "Indic studies" by Matsumoto Bunzaburō, who held
the chair in that field, and his assistants. It is estimated that the greater part of those students
pursuing an Indic studies major were in fact engaged in Buddhist studies. See Kyoto Daigaku
Nanajū Nenshi Henshū Iinkai, ed., *Kyoto Daigaku nanajū nenshi* (Kyoto: Kyoto University,
1967), p. 284.

[6] Though Watanabe refers specifically to a "chair of Buddhist studies" (*bukkyō kōza*), the
*Tokyo Teikoku Daigaku gojū nenshi* (Fifty-year history of Tokyo Imperial University)
makes no reference to a chair of Buddhist studies established at this institution during the
interwar period. Because the dates coincide, and because Watanabe mentions that the chair
in question was established largely through the efforts of Murakami Senshō, I have assumed
that he refers to the chair of Indian philosophy inaugurated in 1917, to which Murakami
was appointed.

other. . . . Indeed, the establishment of this chair will be of the profoundest significance for the peace of Asia.[7]

I have quoted these somewhat rhetorical remarks because they adumbrate several attitudes that were to characterize interwar Buddhist scholarship. First, we note Watanabe's reference to "Mahayana and Hinayana, Sacred Way and Pure Land, and esoteric and exoteric teachings." These pairs denoted the broadest and most fundamental lines of sectarian division under the old *kyōhan* system. Grouping them together in this fashion was a traditional way of indicating "the whole of Buddhism," and I suspect that, in using this expression here, Watanabe is suggesting that Buddhist studies conducted at the Imperial University should be comprehensive and not bound by the earlier sectarian concerns. Indeed, Buddhist studies from this point on would succeed in breaking the confines of the earlier, sectarian orientation and attempt to grasp Buddhism as a single, integrated system. Second, we note the competitive consciousness with "foreign universities"—a new but very powerful impetus in the advance of Buddhist scholarship at this time, as Japan, having eagerly absorbed a great mass of Western influences in the preceding decades, now set about asserting its own identity. Third, Buddhist studies are seen here as a means of defining Japan's relationship to the rest of Asia, both linking it to the long tradition of the Asian continent and helping to qualify it for the leadership of Asian culture, however such leadership might be defined. This, too, would become a recurrent theme in the Buddhist scholarship of the interwar period. Fourth, one sees expressed the hope, often voiced in the tumultuous years following World War I, that Buddhist studies might, by illuminating the basis of human culture, somehow serve the cause of peace.

Watanabe himself—Buddhologist, educator, Jōdo, priest, and initiator of many social welfare projects—was outstanding among the new breed of interwar Buddhist scholars. From 1900 to 1910 he had studied in Germany at the University of Strasbourg (the University of Kaiser Wilhelm II, now in French territory), where he devoted himself to Sanskrit, Pali, Tibetan, and other languages relevant to Buddhist studies, as well as to comparative religion. During this decade, he also developed a keen interest in the relationship between religion and social issues, which fueled his desire to revitalize Mahayana Buddhism (in a broad, nonsectarian sense) as a force for social betterment and positive contribution to the nation. This determination underlay his many later efforts for the relief of impoverished workers and similar undertakings, which won him widespread

[7] Watanabe Kaigyoku, "Teikoku bukkyō kōza no setchi," *Kogetsu zenshū* (Tokyo: Kogetsu zenshū kankokai, 1933), 2:232–33.

praise as "a modern bodhisattva."[8] On returning to Japan, he was appointed professor at both the University of Religious Studies (Shūkyō Daigaku) and Tōyō University, and he served as editor-in-chief of *Jōdo kyōhō*, the journal of the Jōdo sect's educational establishment.

By the beginning of the Taishō period, Watanabe had clearly grasped the current state of Japanese Buddhist scholarship vis-à-vis that of Europe, and the directions it would have to pursue in order to rival comparable endeavors in the West. In 1918, he published a book of about two hundred pages entitled *Ōbei no bukkyō* (Buddhist studies in Europe and America), outlining recent advances in Western Buddhist scholarship. A pioneering work, especially with respect to esoteric and Tibetan Buddhism, this book made a tremendous impact on Buddhist circles and became a model for subsequent works of similar type introducing the achievements of Western Buddhist studies. The book also seems to offer considerable insight into the attitudes motivating academic Buddhist studies in the interwar period. In its introductory section, Watanabe advances three reasons why self-respecting Japanese intellectuals should bend their efforts toward overtaking Western Buddhist studies. They were, first, to establish independence in scholarship; second, to promote the development of Asia; and third, to contribute to the culture of humanity as a whole. Concerning the first reason, Watanabe states:

> Our nation, which so indiscriminately imports the ideas of other nations, remains in utter ignorance of Buddhology, which is now truly becoming one of the world's foremost disciplines. This casts the utmost discredit upon our people. . . . Our country has now truly become the focal point of Asia. In keeping with the dignity of this position, those who study the writings of the East have a duty to conduct independent research. Yet even with respect to the literature of China, no sooner does the least difficulty arise than they turn immediately to Western writings. . . . The hegemon of Asia, ranking among the world's leading nations, has no independence whatsoever when it comes to scholarship. Our outlook is that of a small businessman with limited capital, relying on the wholesalers or middlemen of Europe for their studies. How pathetic! Not only with respect to their philosophy but in terms of such disciplines as [Western] medicine and the physical sciences, which shine with originality and invention, we have yet to be liberated from our slave-like condition. And in the areas of Asian studies, especially the study of Buddhism, this lamentable state of affairs represents a tragedy of the first order. Whether in Pali or in Sanskrit, in archaeology or history, the progress of Buddhist studies in our country lags far, far behind. With respect to this situation, it is vital that the people of our land— who have a particular bond with Buddhism and who hold for it a special sym-

---

[8] Serikawa Hiromichi, *Watanabe Kaigyoku kenkyū: Sono shisō to kōdō* (Tokyo: Daitō shuppansha, 1978), p. 2.

pathy and interest—arouse at this time the most burning indignation and reflect on their position![9]

One notes immediately the economic metaphor. Japan's most urgent task as a nation in the first several decades of the modern era was, of course, to gain economic and political footing with the advanced Western capitalistic economies in order not to be exploited by them. Scholarship—especially Buddhist scholarship—Watanabe evidently considered fully as essential to national independence as advances in economics, science, and industry. Heir to the views of Inoue Enryō, who had looked upon Buddhism as "this fine product of ours," Watanabe too regarded Buddhism as something uniquely Japanese that could help Japan achieve independence and prestige with respect to other nations.

Closely allied to this was his second reason for promoting Buddhist studies: They would aid in the "development" of Asia. Noting that before he and his contemporaries were born, Russian scholars at the University of Kazan had made efforts to collect Mongolian Buddhist texts and pursue the study of Tibetan Buddhism, he attributed the Russian "success" in Mongolia largely to the long-term efforts on the part of Russian scholars to familiarize themselves with the language, customs, and religion of the people there and thus gain the confidence of the native priests. "Our scholars today should note how the Russians in this way appeased and pacified the Lamas, gradually making them their tool, gaining influence inch by inch and yard by yard, until at last, they imposed on Mongolia its present state," he wrote. "In terms of our awakening to [our role] in the development of Asia, what inducements are offered us by Western Buddhist studies!"[10]

How far the rather imperialistic tone of this section reflects Watanabe's own views may be open to question. He makes clear that he is here addressing "politicians, businessmen, statesmen, and others in the real world" (i.e., the people who sponsor scholarly endeavors), enjoining them not to dismiss lightly Buddhist studies as irrelevant to their practical concerns. The third point, on which he elaborated at the greatest length, was that Buddhist studies would constitute a major avenue of Japanese contribution to world culture. Here Watanabe outlined what he saw as the impact to date of Buddhism upon European civilization, citing not only the contemporary interest in Eastern religion and philosophy but what he regarded as the indirect influence of Buddhistic elements—introduced via Indian thought and literature in general—on the poetry of Goethe and Heine, the philosophy of Schopenhauer, and even the music of Richard Wagner. "This being the general trend of Europe, those thinkers

[9] Watanabe, *Ōbei no bukkyō*, *Kogetsu zenshū*, 1:8–9.
[10] Ibid., p. 11.

and writers of Japan who wish to make some worldwide contribution will
find the most appropriate, effective, and direct route in research and publication relevant to Buddhism,"[11] he concluded. He then proceeded to
enumerate those areas of Buddhist studies toward which Japanese scholars would do well to turn their attention: Pali textual studies, Sanskrit
textual studies, Chinese Buddhism, Tibetan Buddhism, Buddhism as illuminated by general Indic studies, and the material relevant to Buddhist
studies yielded by archaeological excavations in Central Asia.

What Watanabe does for his readers in this essay is to cast Buddhist
studies as a crucial link between Japan and the world, one that would not
only help delineate Japan's unique identity with respect to other nations
but enable it to assume leadership in Asia, and also exert an impact on
the West. Watanabe's discussion of the *existing* Buddhist influence upon
European culture, setting aside the question of how deeply this influence
had actually penetrated,[12] deserves attention for the shift of perspective it
suggests concerning Japan's relationship to Europe. Japan—for several
decades the passive recipient of Western enlightenment—is here shown to
have a unique bond with the Buddhist thought that has already perme-
ated the cultural basis of Europe. The view of Buddhist studies as a
unique vehicle for Japan's contribution to world culture seems to have
heavily influenced the advances in that field during the interwar period.
Just how strongly Watanabe's views resonated with those of his fellow
scholars may be seen from subsequent developments: Within two decades, Japan had surpassed Europe in virtually every major area of inquiry enumerated by Watanabe.

One of the leading figures in this achievement was Watanabe's long-
time associate Takakusu Junjirō, mentioned above, who for twenty-seven
years held the chair of Sanskrit studies at Tokyo Imperial University. In
1890 he had gone to Oxford University armed with a letter of introduction from Nanjō Bun'yū to F. Max Müller, who influenced him in the
direction of Indic studies and urged him to master Sanskrit and Pali. After
graduating from Oxford, Takakusu studied at other European institutes,
including the universities of Berlin, Kiel, and Leipzig and the College du
France, where he came to know the French Buddhologist Sylvain Lévi.
During this period, he produced an English translation of the *Kuan wu-
liang-shou ching* (Jap. *Kanmuryōjukyō*) under the reconstructed Sanskrit

---

[11] Ibid., p. 13.

[12] For an evaluation of the influence of Buddhism upon Schopenhauer, Wagner, and
Nietzsche, see Guy Richard Welbon, *The Buddhist Nirvana and Its Western Interpreters*
(Chicago: University of Chicago Press, 1968), pp. 154–93. Wagner's interpretations of Bud-
dhist concepts are further discussed in Dorothea Watanabe Dauer, "Richard Wagner and
Buddhism: *Tristan and Isolde* and *The Victors*," *The Eastern Buddhist* 9, 2 (October 1976):
115–28.

title *Amitāyurdhyāna sutra* and other works. On returning to Japan in 1897 he became an instructor at Tokyo Imperial University and a full professor two years later. From 1900, he concurrently headed the Tokyo School of Foreign Languages, and he was appointed to the chair of Sanskrit studies in 1901. He also became interested in Buddhist education for women, and after retiring in 1927, he served as president of Musashino Girls' School, which he had founded in 1924. From 1931 to 1934 he was dean of Tōyō University and taught as guest professor at the University of Hawaii from 1938 to 1939.

Takakusu, together with Watanabe Kaigyoku, was responsible for the colossal undertaking that first brought Japanese Buddhist scholarship to world attention: the *Taishō shinshū daizōkyō*, or simply the "Taishō *tripiṭaka*," the most complete collection of the Chinese Buddhist scriptures ever before assembled. Takakusu conceived the plan and sought Watanabe's assistance in implementing it. Formally launched in 1922, the project eventually ran to a full hundred volumes, published between 1924 and 1934. With its arrangement of the sutras in probable chronological sequence of their compilation and the treatises according to their school, and with Sanskrit or Pali etymology provided for technical terms, the Taishō tripiṭaka represents the most thorough, well-organized collection of the Chinese scriptures to date, "marking a considerable advance over all precedents, as much for the wealth of sources employed as for the critical erudition that informs the arrangement of the text and the convenience of its presentation,"[13] as the foreword to a French-language index praises it. The Taishō tripiṭaka received the Stanislaus Julien Prize from France's Académie des Inscriptions et Belles-Lettres in 1929 and the prize of the Tokyo Imperial Academy in 1933. Journals in the United States, Germany, and France hailed its publication. This single work placed Japan prominently on the map of world Buddhist scholarship, and its fame at present is such that a single capital T in a footnote will identify it to students of Buddhism anywhere in the world. Interestingly enough, it is the "Taishō" rather than the "tripiṭaka" that is thus immortalized.

In the foreword to their magnum opus (actually written by Watanabe), professors Watanabe and Takakusu state in part:

> The completion of the way of benevolence and love, the ultimate principle of perfectly endowed truth, permeates the ten directions and pervades the three existences, encompassing all things and unfolding in all phenomena. How vast and great is the true teaching of the sage Śākyamuni! Moreover, this complete and wondrous teaching which he left behind is transmitted and set forth in our tripiṭaka. In this immense work with its more than eight thousand fascicles, its

[13] Sylvain Lévi and Takakusu Junjirō, eds., "Fascicule Annexe: Tables de Taishō Issaikyō," in *Hōbōqirin* (Tokyo: Maison Franco-Japonaise, 1931), p. i.

hundred million and many tens of thousands of words, the true reality of the universe is thoroughly expounded and the conclusion of life made clear. . . . Truly it is the fountainhead of wisdom and virtue for humanity and the great treasury of the world. . . . Yet apart from us, the Buddhist scholars of Japan, who can clarify and spread its teachings? The responsibility of propagation rests on our shoulders. All the more so, after the great world war, when the need to seek the truth presses most urgently upon us, when the study of Buddhism is now on the rise in Europe and America, and when we see so few scholars versed in the Chinese scriptures! The Buddhist scholars of our nation must realize how vast and grave our task has become.[14]

Here again one glimpses the peculiar juncture of the universal and the particular that characterizes interwar Japanese Buddhist studies. Buddhism is seen as the absolute truth transcending time and space and capable of bringing peace and enlightenment to all people, but the Japanese are the ones preeminently capable of interpreting it to the world. Buddhist studies at this time evidently contributed to the Taishō-period transformation of the national self-image: Japan, recipient of Western enlightenment in the Meiji period, becomes the country that shall bring enlightenment to the world.

Publication of the Taishō tripiṭaka was accompanied by a veritable flood of similar collections compiled and edited during this period. Among the most important are *Nihon daizōkyō*, a collection of Japanese Buddhist texts published in 48 volumes between 1914 and 1921; the *Dainihon bukkyō zensho*, another collection of Japanese Buddhist texts published in 150 volumes between 1912 and 1922; the *Kokuyaku daizōkyō*, a Japanese translation of important Chinese sutras and other texts, published in 30 volumes between 1917 and 1928; the *Kokuyaku issaikyō*, comprising two collections in Japanese translation, one of Indian Buddhist texts, published in 155 volumes between 1930 and 1936, and another of Chinese Buddhist texts other than those included in the *Kokuyaku daizōkyō*, published in 66 volumes between 1936 and 1944; the *Seizō daizōkyō sōmokuroku*, a complete index to the Tibetan tripiṭaka published in 1934; and the *Kokuyaku nanden daizōkyō*, a Japanese translation of Pali scriptures that had circulated in Sri Lanka, Burma, Thailand, Cambodia, Laos, and other Southeast Asian countries, published in 65 volumes between 1935 and 1941, also under the editorial supervision of Takakusu Junjirō.

This mammoth effort to assemble, translate, and systematize texts formed the basis for a parallel effort to integrate the concepts and doctrines contained in those texts into a coherent framework. This attempt

[14] Takakusu Junjirō and Watanabe Kaigyoku, eds., *Taishō shinshū daizōkyō sōmokuroku* (Tokyo: Taishō shinshū daizōkyō kankōkai, 1924), pp. 1–2.

at synthesis stands out in sharp contrast to earlier sectarian studies: Among the new publications of this period, one finds some dealing with isolated works or schools but a great many dealing with the overall history of Buddhist thought as well as fundamental doctrines (Emptiness, dependent origination, liberation, the Middle Way, etc.) that serve as threads of continuity among the various schools and phases in Buddhism's development. The search for continuity extended even so far as to attempt to uncover some single underlying truth common to the whole of Buddhism, if not to the entirety of religion and human culture. This distinctive feature of interwar Buddhist studies in Japan would seem to stem from several factors. One, I suspect, may have been the reaction of the new generation of Meiji Buddhist scholars to the discovery of the Pali canon.

I have already mentioned that the first wave of Japanese students of Buddhism to go abroad found European Buddhologists absorbed in study of the Pali scriptures, in which they initially hoped to find the direct words of the historical Buddha. The Mahayana scriptures, on which the Japanese Buddhist tradition is based, were widely regarded at this time as a later corruption. The introduction of this view to Meiji Japan, coinciding as it did with the nation's general identity crisis, wreaked temporary havoc in Buddhist circles. Several scholars raised a cry for a return to "original Buddhism" (*genshi bukkyō*) or "fundamental Buddhism" (*kompon bukkyō*), believing, along with their European counterparts, that in the Pali canon they might discover the true preaching of Śākyamuni. Anesaki Masaharu (1873–1949), for example, writing in 1910, said, "East Asian Buddhism is the flower, and Southeast Asian Buddhism, the leaves and branches. To be dazzled by the color of the blossoms and forget the root, for leaves and branches to flourish futilely, alienated from their source—surely this describes the state of modern Buddhist studies!"[15] Such, he said, was his conclusion based on comparative studies of the Pali canon and the Chinese tripiṭaka.

This trend to seek the "fundamental Buddhism" in the Pali scriptures for a time placed the entire Japanese Mahayana tradition in a rather ambiguous light. I suspect, however, that as Japan emerged from the period of almost indiscriminate Westernization and began the process of redefining its own role, Buddhist scholars similarly began to feel a need to reclaim the Japanese Buddhist tradition. In any event, works soon began to appear suggesting that intensive textual study would uncover some fundamental truth common to both Hinayana and Mahayana. An early pi-

[15] Anesaki Masaharu, preface, *Kompon bukkyō* (Tokyo: Sankōdō, 1910); revised in *Anesaki Masaharu chōsaku shū* (Tokyo: Kokusho kankōkai, 1982), 8:1.

oneer in this attempt was Murakami Senshō, who states in the foreword to his *Bukkyō tōitsu ron*:

> My aim in taking a unified approach in my research was to make known the unified oneness of the Buddhist ideals, which hitherto have been represented in so fragmented a fashion. . . . No matter what points of difference or friction might exist among the various sects, when one views these points from the perspective of their depths, they all prove without exception to be develop-ments of thought concerning nirvana, the great enlightenment of Śākyamuni.[16]

This search for the underlying truth of Buddhism expanded and gained momentum in the Taishō period. It may have been aided on its way by the progress of European historical and philological studies, which even-tually yielded the discoveries that even the Pali canon scriptures show marked layering and had not begun to be recorded until at least two to three hundred years following Śākyamuni's death. With these new in-sights, it became clear that the Pali canon could in no way be said to derive in its entirety directly from the Buddha himself. One may easily imagine that such discoveries gave confidence to the next generation of Japanese Buddhist scholars, seeking to validate their own tradition.

In their effort to uncover truths common to both Hinayana and Ma-hayana traditions, the Japanese scholars of Pali and Sanskrit soon found they possessed an unexpected advantage over their European colleagues: their familiarity with the Chinese tripiṭaka and the East Asian Buddhist tradition. During the Taishō period, research based on comparative stud-ies of Chinese and Pali, Sanskrit, or even Tibetan texts flourished, and in this area the Japanese had no rivals. Among the pioneers in this area were Takakusu Junjirō and two of his most brilliant pupils, Ui Hakuju and Kimura Taiken (1881–1930). In 1914, Takakusu and Kimura together published *Indotetsugaku shūkyō shi* (A history of Indian philosophy and religion), a detailed study of the development of Indian religion based on exhaustive study of the Vedas, Brahmanas, Upanishads, and Buddhist su-tras, one of the first works to attempt to grasp Indian Buddhism within the overall historical framework of Indian religious thought. In 1922, Ki-mura alone published *Genshi bukkyō shisō ron*, a systematized discus-sion of early Buddhist thought based on his study of the Pali canon, the *vinaya-piṭaka* and the Chinese *āgamas*. In this work he denied the long-standing view that equated the Pali *āgama* sutras with Hinayana and re-garded Mahayana as a later development; Hinayana and Mahayana alike, he argued, had a common base in the Pali *āgamas*. Kimura also translated into Japanese major works of *abhidharma* literature, including

---

[16] Cited in Nakamura Hajime and Takeda Kiyoko, eds., *Kindai Nihon tetsugaku shisōka jiten* (Tokyo: Tokyo shoseki, 1982), p. 555.

the *Abhidharma-mahā-vibhāṣā-śāstra*, the *Abhidharma-kośa-śāstra*, and others. Between 1925 and 1930, Ui Hakuju published his six-volume masterpiece, *Indotetsugaku kenkyū*, for which he won the prize of the Tokyo Imperial Academy, tracing the development of Indian thought from pre-Buddhist religions up through Hinayana and Mahayana teachings. These men and their colleagues, in the space of two decades, raised the level of Japanese studies of Indian Buddhism above those of Europe, and at the same time contributed greatly to the systematization of Buddhist thought.

In the interwar period, the search for a fundamental truth expanded to include not merely a truth common to all Buddhist teachings but one that could unify even different religions, and perhaps the whole of human philosophy and culture. One sees evidence of this trend, for example, in the preface to Kimura Taiken's *Genshi bukkyō yori daijō bukkyō* (From original Buddhism to Mahayana Buddhism), where, in summing up the conviction informing his works, he states:

> Were I to describe my view of the human being, I would have to say mine is a philosophy of emancipation (*gedatsu shugi*), based on the eternal as the ideal. All things are in the process of moving toward emancipation in the eternal, and in directing everything toward liberation in the eternal, we find our value as human beings—that is my conviction. . . . Of course, given my position, a number of my essays [stemming from this conviction] deal with Buddhism, but among them are more than a few that I have developed from the standpoint of philosophy or religion in general.[17]

Attempting to reconcile divergent or even contradictory teachings on the basis of some greater truth forms an ancient part of the Buddhist tradition itself. In the interwar period, however, this trend was additionally fostered by specific intellectual currents of the time. During the Taishō period, an interest in democracy and its accompanying concerns for human rights and independence, the need for internal liberation from the past, confusion arising from rapid economic change, and the unease following World War I combined to awaken in intellectual circles a growing preoccupation with such questions as what is the human being, what is life, and how should it be lived. In pursuit of answers, intellectuals turned their eyes toward religion. But not the unscientific, divisive, confining religions of the past—rather, a cry was raised for "religious reformation." The religious focus that pervades thought and culture in the Taishō period was not the religion of a specific sect, or even necessarily religion in the sense of Buddhism versus Christianity, but a universal truth, in short,

---

[17] Kimura Taiken, preface, *Genshi bukkyō yori daijō bukkyō* (Tokyo: Sagi-no-miya shobō, 1968), p. 1.

religion stripped of its charismatic elements and virtually equated with humanism. Kurata Hyakuzō's 1917 drama *Shukke to sono deshi* (The priest and his disciples), mentioned in Thomas Rimer's essay, marked the beginning of a new wave of literature reflecting Buddhist themes or religious themes in general. Also for the first time, attempts were made to integrate Western philosophy and Buddhist thought, as represented by the works of Nishida Kitarō (1870–1945) and Watsuji Tetsurō (1889–1960).

The tendency in the Taishō period to modernize and "aestheticize" religion has since been criticized as a trend that robbed religion of the true power of faith and made it the toy of literary salons[18]—probably a valid criticism in some respects. It would seem however, to have aided the academic Buddhist movement considerably in its effort to transcend the bounds of sectarian *kyōgaku* or doctrinal studies, absorb the ideals and methods of modern Western scholarship, and integrate Buddhism into a single systematic framework.

For example, the demand for "religious reformation" and the humanizing of religion, aided by the influence of new studies in Europe and America, led to attempts to interpret Japanese religion or religion in general from historical and psychological perspectives. A pioneering work in this area was historian Hara Katsurō's *Tōsei no shūkyō kaikaku* (Religious reformations of East and West) published in 1911, among the first in a wave of publications comparing Eastern and Western religious thought. Drawing parallels between the Kamakura period of Japanese history and the European Renaissance, Hara interpreted the Kamakura Buddhist movement as a reformation and compared the accomplishments of Hōnen and Shinran to those of Luther and Calvin—interpretations that won instant favor and have only recently begun to be challenged.[19] New attention was focused on the Kamakura period of Japanese Buddhist history, and a tendency emerged to view the leaders of that move-

---

[18] See, for example, Tamura Yoshirō, *Nihon bukkyōshi nyūmon* (Tokyo: Kadokawa, 1969), p. 217.

[19] Kinoshita Naoe also compares Shinran to Luther in *Hōnen to Shinran* (1911), but not, as Hara did, from the standpoint of a historical specialist.

The notion of Kamakura Buddhism as a reformation also found its way into a number of English sources. For example, this idea is affirmed in Stanley Weinstein, "The Concept of Reformation in Japanese Buddhism," *International Conference on Japanese Studies Report* (Kyoto, 1972), 1:603–14; employed for comparative purposes in Robert N. Bellah, "Religious Evolution," in William A. Lessa and Evon Z. Vogt, eds., *Reader in Comparative Religions: An Anthropological Approach* (New York: Harper and Row, 1965), pp. 73–87; used in Whalen Lai, "After the Reformation: Post-Kamakura Buddhism," *Japanese Journal of Religious Studies* 5, 4 (December 1978):258–84; and finally challenged and dismissed in James H. Foard, "In Search of a Lost Reformation: A Reconsideration of Kamakura Buddhism," *Japanese Journal of Religious Studies* 7, 4 (December 1980):261–91.

ment—Hōnen, Shinran, Eisai, Dōgen, and Nichiren—not so much as the founders of sects but rather as the teachers of mankind.

These new trends in the interpretation of religion also appeared in the world of formal academic Buddhist studies. One sees evidence of a new sociohistorical orientation, for example, in the preface (and title, for that matter) of Anesaki's classic, *History of Japanese Religion, With Special Reference to the Social and Moral Life of the Nation.*[20]

> The author in no way cherishes the idea of being an apologist or a propagandist, but has ever been eager to be a scientific historian, whose function it is to weigh the balance of data and to obtain truthful insight into the movements of the human soul. Any degree of success he achieves, in carrying out this ambition, the author owes to his predecessors and teachers in this new branch of the science of religion and religious history. On the other hand, if there be any trace of undue estimation or reverence toward the religious leaders treated of in the book, he asks the reader's generosity to tolerate it, while critically weighing the circumstances, as it comes from the author's own religious heritage.[21]

Comparative religious studies also began to appear frequently in the realm of Buddhist scholarship, headed, among others by Takakusu Junjirō, who early on had begun to explore such themes as "God and Buddha" and "the Pure Land and Heaven," contrasting parallel concepts in Buddhism and Christianity. Takakusu eventually concluded that the West had tended to view the world in terms of matter and principles, and the East, in terms of the intuitive experience of living beings; the nation that could unite the two, he suggested, would support the future of the world. A quick glance at the titles of some of this influential scholar's works during the interwar period reveals some of the new directions emerging in Buddhist scholarship: *Bukkyō kokumin no risō* (The ideals of a Buddhist nation, 1916), *Uchū no koe toshite no bukkyō* (Buddhism as the voice of the universe, 1926), *Jinbun no kichō toshite no bukkyō* (Buddhism as the basis of civilization, 1929), *Ningengaku toshite no bukkyō* (Buddhism as the study of man, 1932), *Tōhō no hikari toshite no bukkyō* (Buddhism as the light of the East, 1934), and so on.

Such, briefly, were some of the major developments in Japanese Bud-

---

[20] Anesaki was a pioneer in this area. As early as 1905 he notes, in the preface to his *Nichiren, the Buddhist Prophet* (Cambridge: Harvard University Press, 1916) a debt to William James's *Varieties of Religious Experience* in enabling scholars to approach charismatic religious leaders from a psychological, rather than a doctrinal, viewpoint; to the psychological portraits of such figures done in the West, he now contributed a similar study of a major religious figure of Japan.

[21] Anesaki, preface, *History of Japanese Religion, With Special Reference to the Social and Moral Life of the Nation* (London: Kegan Paul, Trench, Trubner & Co., 1930; reprint ed. Tokyo: Charles E. Tuttle, 1963), p. vii.

dhist studies in the interval between the wars.[22] Vast amounts of research remain to be done in this area, but even this brief preliminary survey suggests that an examination of these trends may cast fully as much light on Japanese cultural assumptions during this period as on the history and teachings of Buddhism itself.

[22] In passing, a few other new developments in Buddhist studies of the interwar period should be noted. Archaeological studies marked a new endeavor for Japan: Outstanding in this area was the intrepid Tokiwa Daijō (1870–1945), a pupil of Murakami Senshō and scholar of Chinese Buddhist history at Tokyo Imperial University. Insisting that textual research alone formed an insufficient basis for proper study, he made five trips to the Chinese mainland between 1920 and 1929 to investigate Buddhist ruins. His field studies, along with his voluminous works on Chinese Buddhism, had a major impact on Japanese understanding of Chinese thought and of the history of Chinese culture and its influence upon Japan.

Also at this time Japanese Buddhist scholars, most notably Anesaki Masaharu, were beginning to write in English in an attempt to gain wider understanding of Japanese Buddhism in the world academic community. Academic exchange was also initiated. The noted French Buddhologist Sylvain Lévi visited Japan in 1923, and Anesaki and Takakusu went abroad: Anesaki lectured at Harvard, the University of Chicago, and Yale in 1913–15, occupying the chair of Japanese literature and life at Harvard during those years; at the University of California in 1918; and at the Collège de France in 1919; and Takakusu taught as visiting professor at the University of Hawaii from 1938 to 1939. His lectures during that period were compiled as *The Essentials of Buddhist Philosophy* (Honolulu: Office Appliance Co., 1956; reprint ed., Westport, Conn.: Greenwood Press, 1973), Takakusu's only major original work in English.

# 12

## A Turning in Taishō: Asia and Europe in the Early Writings of Watsuji Tetsurō

WILLIAM R. LaFLEUR

SQUEEZED between the Meiji and the Shōwa, two eras of considerable length and monumental changes, the Taishō era (1912–1926) often seems diminutive by comparison and an era whose best projects—democratization, for instance—all either withered away or were crushed by the overpowering historical developments of the subsequent Shōwa period. The Taishō, its ideas, and the men who conceived them have been good subjects for studies of monumental "failure."[1] Marxist analyses have tried to show that the intellectuals, in spite of their high ideals and lofty rhetoric, merely demonstrated and worked for the interest of their class.[2] But even other scholars, without a Marxist stress on class, have detected a profound naïveté about politics in the ideas and ideals of most liberal thinkers of the Taishō.[3] Many, especially the philosophers, seem to have unintentionally become patsies and ideological frontmen for others who were playing a harder, deadlier game.

Here I focus on Watsuji Tetsurō (1889–1960), a younger but very important intellectual of the Taishō period. As editor of the new journal *Shisō* and a key figure—perhaps the key figure—in what Maruyama

I express gratitude to the Social Science Research Council, The Japan Foundation, and the Academic Senate of UCLA, sources from which I received generous support for portions of this research.

[1] Especially Tatsuo Arima, *The Failure of Freedom: A Portrait of Modern Japanese Intellectuals* (Cambridge: Harvard University Press, 1969); William Miles Fletcher III, *The Search for a New Order: Intellectuals and Fascism in Prewar Japan* (Chapel Hill: University of North Carolina Press, 1982) focuses primarily on Shōwa developments.

[2] Tosaka Jun read Watsuji's thought as well as that of the "Kyoto School" as the ideology of the privileged class. See his severe criticisms in " 'Yamato-damashi' gakuha no Tetsugaku" and "Watsuji Hakushi. Fūdo Nihon" in *Tosaka Jun zenshū* (Tokyo: Keisō shobō, n.d.), 5:88–102.

[3] Peter Duus, "Liberal Intellectuals and Social Conflict in Taishō Japan," in Tetsuo Najita and J. Victor Koschmann, eds., *Conflict in Modern Japanese History: The Neglected Tradition* (Princeton: Princeton University Press, 1982), pp. 412–40.

Masao has called "Iwanami culture," Watsuji was influential and even a setter of certain intellectual trends. The most common judgment on him to date has been that, for all his brilliance, he provides virtually a classic instance of intellectual subornation. In a recent overview of the first half-century of the journal *Shisō* Nakamura Yūjirō sees the founding of that journal in 1921 and Watsuji's position therein as ideologically formed from the beginning.[4]

Even scholars less concerned with tracing the formation of ideology, however, have in the past tended to see Watsuji as an intellectual who at a very early date signaled a turn to the political right and became self-consciously nationalistic during the Taishō era. Robert N. Bellah, in an important essay published in 1965, focused on Watsuji to illustrate what he then called "national narcissism," a phenomenon that in the Japanese case turns out to be "comparatively speaking, extreme."[5] Bellah's essay, read widely in Japan, traced Watsuji's entire intellectual development and showed how certain Taishō writings of 1918 and 1919 indicate a basic change by Watsuji, who until then had expected much from Western philosophers but now "turn[ed] his back on individualism and return[ed] in his own way to the warm *gemeinschaft* community of Japanese life."[6] Bellah was concerned to show that in the Japanese case the power of particularized national identification has proven to be overwhelming and, especially in situations perceived to be crises, has effectively driven out universalized ethical concerns. To Bellah, Watsuji was a classic instance: "The humane and gracious figure of Watsuji Tetsurō would not be problematic for modern Japan were it not for the fact that partly behind the cloak of just such thinking as his, a profoundly pathological social movement brought Japan near to total disaster."[7]

If I offer here a somewhat different interpretation of Watsuji's thinking during the period around 1918, it is not to gainsay that Watsuji wrote things that meshed precisely with the needs of "ideological production" as Japanese imperialism deepened and expanded in the 1930s and 1940s. I merely wish to chart the finer nuances in Watsuji's earlier thinking, to show that his was not a simple switch from universalized concerns to chauvinistic particularism, and to delineate what seems to have been important to him, namely, a third option as alternative to what he deemed a suspect Euro-universalism, on one hand, and a narrow nationalism, on

---

[4] Nakamura Yūjirō, *Nihon no Shisōshi: jiko kakunin no tame ni* (Tokyo: Keisō shobō, 1967), pp. 8–14.

[5] Robert N. Bellah, "Japan's Cultural Identity: Some Reflections on the Work of Watsuji Tetsurō," *The Journal of Asian Studies* 24, 4 (August 1965): 573.

[6] Ibid., p. 587.

[7] Ibid., p. 573.

the other. To miss this is to overlook some of the specificity of the Taishō period.

It is important to recognize the degree of Watsuji's self-consciousness as a Taishō intellectual. In a perceptive essay Harry Harootunian has called attention to Taishō intellectuals' sense of the newness of their era—of living and writing in an epoch that they thought should be profoundly different from the Meiji.[8] It is important to explore that same point in Watsuji, whose writings during the late teens of our century are marked by a keen consciousness of Taishō as a period that ought to have intellectual bases and orientations very different from those of the preceding Meiji era. In this essay I focus on how Watsuji interpreted this change of ears, and how his symbolic representation of the Meiji-to-Taishō transition can be seen as a key element in understanding the contour of his own intellectual life.

Even before 1918, Watsuji had established himself as a young writer who had to be taken seriously. His initial publications, *Niichie kenkyū* (*Nietzsche studies*) and *Zēren Kierukegoru* (*Soren Kierkegaard*), came out in 1913 and 1915 respectively.[9] These had considerable success and have even been called "epoch-making."[10] Then, in May 1917, Watsuji did something the casual observer might dismiss as unimportant, but which I interpret as an event of profound symbolic importance. He and two or three of his friends went to Nara Prefecture, visited ancient Buddhist temples there, and took notes concerning the old icons of Nara and its vicinity. Two years later, in 1919, Watsuji was to publish these notes and reflections on that experience as an immensely popular work entitled *Koji junrei* (Pilgrimage to ancient temples).[11] In the intervening year, 1918, he published *Gūzō saikō* (Restoring idols),[12] a work many scholars see as marking a basic transition in Watsuji's intellectual life.

Unlike most evaluations of Watsuji during these years, I believe one must interpret *Restoring Idols* through its conceptual affinity with *Pil-*

[8] H. D. Harootunian, "Introduction: As Sense of an Ending and the Problem of Taishō," in Bernard S. Silberman and H. D. Harootunian, eds., *Japan in Crisis: Essays on Taishō Democracy* (Princeton: Princeton University Press, 1974), pp. 3–28.

[9] These works are republished in volume 1 of Abe Yoshinori et al., eds., *Watsuji Tetsurō zenshū* (Tokyo: Iwanami shoten), hereafter abbreviated as WTZ. *Niichie kenkyū* is in WTZ 1:1–391; *Zēren Kierukegoru* is in WTZ 1:393–679.

[10] Although scholarship on Nietzsche had existed in Japan since the mid-Meiji, Watsuji's study is generally regarded as a substantial breakthrough in terms of a real understanding. Shida Shōzō, in a study of Watsuji's *Niichie kenkyū*, holds that it constitutes "world-class scholarship" and for its day was unmatched, except for two or three studies, even in Europe. See Yuasa Yasuo, *Watsuji Tetsurō: Kindai Nihon tetsugaku no unmei* (Kyoto: Minerubua shobō, 1981), pp. 38–43.

[11] WTZ 2:1–192. This work is still readily available as an Iwanami paperback.

[12] WTZ 17:3–284.

*grimage*, although the latter is often regarded as merely a popular guide to Nara's temples and dismissed in attempts to chart the trajectory of Watsuji's intellectual life. I suspect that the wide and continuing popularity of *Pilgrimage* has masked its conceptual significance. It is not, however, just a layman's appreciative guide to old temples, but a work with ideas that, once unearthed, can indicate what was going on in Watsuji's mind and, more widely, that of his ear.

## I

In later life Watsuji himself professed distaste for the work entitled *Restoring Idols*, but most critics still see it as important, because in the initial essay of this 1918 collection Watsuji expressly referred to having undergone a "turn" in his way of thinking about things. He designated this by the word *tenkō*, a term that came to refer in the 1930s to the highly political act by which leftist or left-leaning intellectuals would disavow their previous inclinations and adopt a rightest political stance.[13] What is almost invariably overlooked, however, is that Watsuji's use of the term was very different from the ideological and even politically coerced use of it by others two decades later. Japan's social and political conditions at the time of Watsuji's professed *tenkō* differed widely from those that existed when thinkers in the late 1930s made their pressured about-faces. Whereas the *tenkō* events of the 1930s were prompted by strong external pressure to conform, Watsuji's was voluntary. It, moreover, was an act whose contents, while amenable to later employment for political or ideological purposes, were when it occurred quite free of such. In fact, as I hope to show here, this was a change of mind that ran counter to the ethos of nationalism rather than in lock-step with it.

Not all the complexly arranged components in Watsuji's self-conscious turning at this point in his life can be evaluated here. I hope merely to extricate what he wished to offer as a structured piece of cultural criticism tied to contrasts between the Meiji and Taishō eras. The initial point of inquiry must be the implications of things abumbrated by Watsuji in his use of the phrase "restoring idols."

Today one might be tempted to use a term such as "iconicity" or "symbolics" to categorize Watsuji's concern in this work. His initial uses of the term "idol," however, are largely in keeping with its pejorative sense as a

[13] There is a vast literature on the tenkō phenomenon. An overview of existing theories about the exact nature of Watsuji's tenkō is Izumiya Shuzaburō, "Watsuji Tetsurō no 'tenkō' ni tsuite—toku ni kojinshugi no mondai o megutte," in Ienaga Saburō and Komaki Osamu, eds., *Tetsugaku to Nihon shakai* (Tokyo: Kobundo, 1978), pp. 91–121. My interpretation differs considerably.

symbol whose meaning had ossified; as such it carries depleted meaning from the past and retards or scrambles effective communication in the present. Watsuji writes:

> There is no need to repeat the fact that the destruction of idols is necessary for human life to make progress; only through it can the flow of life be maintained. There are idols we have been unconsciously but continuously erecting, and it is these we must be continuously destroying—through efforts that are careful and yet also thorough. (p. 9)

Although man's capacity for symbolic activity is what prevents him from having a confused consciousness, Watsuji insists that, once they have become ossified and lifeless "idols," such symbols deserve to be destroyed—although, more precisely, it is the misunderstanding of them that needs to be cleared away.

Watsuji's conception of iconicity, however, is in no way detached from concrete expressions of it in history. He refers especially to religious icons and images concerning whose authenticity heated religious controversy arose in the past. While it is true that an "image" can be a mental phenomenon, Watsuji does not permit such abstract usage to obscure the fact that, especially in the history of religions in the West, the significance of wrought icons and intense struggle over their viability were what gave such bite to the notion of "idol." Use of the term invites recollection of moments of great conflict in history, and Watsuji gives his analysis of events in the history of Christianity in order to articulate the specificity of what he means by gūzō or "idol."

> Saint Paul was a man with a burning passion for demolishing idols. In his view idols were nothing more than the focus-points form the very superstitions that are obstacles to the true life. Once, when he was walking incognito through the city of Athens, what struck him most was his observation of how the superstitious, ignorant masses were completely intoxicated by the magnificence of their idols and were filled with a sense of their power. (p. 10)

A scene from the New Testament is depicted in some detail, especially self-mutilations carried on before the great icons of the Hellenistic world and temple prostitution there. Watsuji tells how Saint Paul went to the Acropolis, where an audience of Epicurean philosophers concurred with his judgment that superstitions are harmful but could not go along with his presentation of an immutable, Creator God. Their own philosophy was basically atomistic, and they maintained that all things are constellations of atoms that come together and then divide again.[14] Paul then

---

[14] In reference to "constellations of atoms that come together and then divide again," Watsuji was depicting not only Greek atomism but also probably a contemporaneous inter-

resorted to his "unknown God" argument, pointing out to his audience of philosophers that the city already contained an altar to such and that it was he, Paul, who could now reveal the real identity of the unknown deity who had been the object of local pieties. Such was, Paul insisted, the Creator of all things, not an idol fabricated by human hands.

Watsuji sees this as having imprinted subsequent European history, with the following long-range effect:

> [In Europe] Paul's fervor about these things held sway without interruption for a thousand years and some centuries beyond that. Even though cults developed dedicated to the worship of images of the Virgin and the saints, throughout the whole of the medieval period the statues of the beautiful Greek gods and goddesses of antiquity lay buried, hidden in darkness. In the eighth century a movement to get rid of idols did not even spare images of Christian saints. (pp. 11–12)

But finally, Watsuji notes, a "new era" opened. He vividly portrays the excavation of the sculpture of Venus by Praxiteles—something taken from the ground in all its radiant beauty, thereby ending a millennium of darkness. The people were afraid of what might happen if they were to deal with these pagan images. Zealous Christian priests were opposed to all this, but once these "restored idols" (*saikō sareta gūzō*) were rescued from darkness, they did not revert to being gods to be worshipped but were now appreciated as works of art.

> In this way the "restoration of idols" signified a resistance to a form of ecclesiastical suppression that had existed for more than a millennium. In the eyes of those involved in restoring these *"gūzō,"* it was really the ecclesiastical authority that itself was the "idol" that had to be destroyed. After all, the restoration of *old* idols is always hidden in the act of destroying *new* idols. [In the Renaissance] the restoration of the old images [of Greece and Rome] ushered in a very powerful materialist view of things and was also the stimulus for scientific activities. A splendid new way of looking at the world was concealed in all of this. . . . With the restoration of idols such as these, it was certain that Paul's God would in some sense have to die. (pp. 12–13)

Watsuji next briefly catalogues the items of medieval Christian belief that in his own judgment had become untenable in the context of the Renaissance. These include belief in the bodily resurrection of Christ, the creation of the world in seven days, parthenogenesis, the notion that the soul and body separate at death, and the imperishability of the soul. He

---

pretation of the nature of reality in early Buddhist philosophy. Greco-Buddhist links were important to Watsuji.

follows with an emphatic judgment, drawing from his studies of Nietzsche:

> It is only a personal cowardice in the face of the facts that keeps people today still believing in things like God or in a life-after-death. But to those for whom these things have for a long time already flown in the face of common sense, a declaration now such as the one that "God is dead!" says nothing really new at all. For them God had already been nonexistent all along.[15] (pp. 13–14)

It is important to note the subtle shift of focus in the last two sentences. Watsuji, with only a few words, makes half the global turn—and that turn is crucial to his whole argument. Since he writes in the language of adumbration, however, that point must be coaxed into visibility. What Watsuji is suggesting is that Asian civilizations in a very basic way had much earlier in history placed a good deal of intellectual distance between themselves and things that "fly in the face of common sense." Skepticism concerning theories of the soul, distaste for miracles, the penchant for empirical demonstration, and agnosticism about deities had all been demonstrated as comprising the earliest forms of Buddhism. Since by this point in his career Watsuji had begun to learn about European scholarship on Indian texts and knew from his readings in philosophy that both Schopenhauer and Nietzsche had been fascinated with the differences between Buddhism and Christianity, he was able to posit a contrast between Christianity's theism, belief in miracles, and postulation of bodily resurrection and classical Buddhism's decisive turn against such nondemonstrable tenets of faith. European scholarship and philosophers had also made such explicit contrasts.[16] By determining that this intellectual move in early Buddhism had fundamental and formative influence on subsequent cultural and intellectual life in all of East Asia, Watsuji was able to suggest a strong contrast between central religio-philosophical developments in Europe and those in Asia. For Watsuji's envisioned Asians, nourished for two and a half millennia on skepticism vis-à-vis deity, the boldness and bravery of the Nietzschean claim concerning the "death of God" comes, in fact, as old news and an anticlimax. "For these [Asians]," Watsuji writes, "God has already been nonexistent all along." Here there is the suggestion that Europeans, in this domain at least, lagged far behind Asians in grasping such things.

[15] It seems probable that the word *gūzō* and the title of this work were inspired in part by Nietzsche's *Götzen-Dämmerung* (Twilight of the idols); see *WTZ* 1:35 for reference to Nietzsche's work, translated into Japanese as *Gūzō no tasogare*.

[16] See Henri de Lubac, *La Rencontre du bouddhisme et de l'occident* (Paris: Abier, Editions montaigne, 1952), and Guy Richard Welbon, *The Buddhist Nirvana and Its Western Interpreters* (Chicago: University of Chicago Press, 1968), the latter for Nietzsche's interest in Buddhism.

Watsuji was undoubtedly commenting obliquely on nearly contemporaneous events in Europe and most especially in Russia. In *Restoring Idols* he refers pejoratively to miracle-mongering "Russian priests" (p. 57). The implication is that the October Revolution, which had taken place a year earlier, challenged religion, but religion that was very different from Japan's. Doctrinaire Marxism missed this fact. Watsuji's argument *in nuce* was that, because atheism was Buddhism's heritage from antiquity, the Asian cultures that had embraced that faith could be immune from the convulsions that were pulsing through Russia. *Restoring Idols* also held out a prospect whereby Asian societies—at least to the degree that they remained innoculated by Buddhism—had within themselves something that could protect them. "Materialism" for such societies, Watsuji implied, was neither new nor revolutionary and, consequently, should not greatly disturb or change them.

An analysis that focused primarily upon the ideological implications of this essay would find in them the only intentionality that really matters. Such an approach would likely agree with Tosaka Jun's indictment of all works of this type as nothing other than a reactionary articulation of "class interests." Such a reduction, however, would severely strain the evidence. The overwhelming concern and principal animus of Watsuji's writing in 1917 and 1918 was not directed against Marxism but against the intellectual and cultural style of the Meiji era. These essays were heralding something distinctively Taishō and as such had little use for the Meiji. That era's hostility toward Buddhism was taken as the index to its folly. Under the force of Meiji nation-building and the requisitioning of all intellectual life for such purposes, Buddhism had been classified among things of a past now to be either discarded or merely commandeered to serve nationalistic goals. Bent to the purpose of matching the West in attaining the latest technology and all the requisite indicators of being properly "civilized" (*bunmei*), those who called the tune during the Meiji saw no significant role for Buddhism. As the prototypical Meiji intellectual, Inoue Tetsujirō (1856–1944) showed in his pronouncements that Buddhism's role, when acknowledged at all, would be limited to that of supporting state ideology. Carol Gluck has rightly noted that this Meiji ideologue "criticized Buddhism for 'pessimistic tendencies' unsuitable to the march of progress and 'civilization.' "[17]

The Buddhists, of course, saw things differently. Their response to the harsh hand of Meiji authority was to secure training—especially philological—for the brightest young Buddhist scholars among their clergy. By study at major European centers with expertise in Indology and active

[17] Carol Gluck, *Japan's Modern Myths: Ideology in the Late Meiji Period* (Princeton: Princeton University Press, 1985), p. 134.

research on "primitive" or classical Buddhism, Japanese Buddhists laid the groundwork for what they hoped would be an intellectual recovery at home. Inoue Enryō (1858–1919) and Murakami Senshō (1851–1929) penned vigorous defenses of Buddhism; they stressed that at least its earliest form was empirical in its approach and comparatively free of superstition and unverifiable doctrines. To these Japanese Buddhists, feeling stifled and suppressed under the aegis of the Meiji Enlightenment and craze for things European, it was totally anomalous that Buddhism, disdained by the Meiji ideologues, was being hailed by some of Europe's most eminent researchers and thinkers as much more rational, empirical, and even up-to-date than Europe's own traditional religion, Christianity. There was, they felt, something absurd in all this.

What was important, then, about *Restoring Idols* was the degree to which, as a rhetorically skilled and clearly "literary" work by one of brighter young men of the Taishō period, it endorsed as fundamentally correct the Buddhists' long-standing complaint about an endemic blindness within Meiji ideology. Watsuji, it should be recalled, himself had a complicated but basically hostile personal relationship with none other than Inoue Tetsujirō, the prototypical Meiji intellectual. In 1912 Inoue had been in charge of Watsuji's program of study in philosophy at Tokyo Imperial University. At the very last moment he had opposed Watsuji's desire to write his degree paper on the philosophy of Nietzsche; Inoue declared that Nietzsche was not properly "philosophical" material for an essay. Unable to submit the work he had done on Nietzsche—much of it later published as a "epoch-making" book—Watsuji switched to Schopenhauer as a thesis topic. He rapidly wrote the thesis in English for the sake of Raphael von Koeber (1848–1923), one of the readers.[18] Watsuji's general dislike of Inoue extended not only to the latter's heavy-handedness and "heavy-mindedness," but also to what the younger man detected as a fairly feeble grasp of German on the part of a supposed authority on German thought. Watsuji regarded Koeber and Natsume Sōseki as his real mentors, especially after 1913 when he met the famous novelist and was privileged to join the study group that met periodically at his home. Inasmuch as Inoue and the ethos of Meiji were bound to coalesce in Watsuji's mind, it seems clear that he had a deep aversion to what he detected as the intellectual shallowness in both. A good deal of the Taishō sense of superiority vis-à-vis Meiji was rooted in precisely that sense of things.

*Restoring Idols* brings out this Taishō sense of superiority, and it is not without significance that Watsuji wrote of his tenkō as something for which a reappreciation of Buddhism acted as catalyst.[19] And that, in turn,

---

[18] "Kēberu Sensei" in *WTZ* 6:1–39.

[19] In the preface to its republication in 1937, Watsuji wrote that *Restoring Idols* is a work

was propelled, according to the text, by "the death of someone"—often assumed to be a veiled reference to the impact of not only Sōseki's demise on December 9, 1916, but also the interest the novelist had shown in Buddhism during his last years. In any case, *Restoring Idols* signals a profound change in Watsuji's interests and intellectual orientation; although he never jettisoned his studies of Western philosophy and history, from this point on he complemented them with ongoing studies of Asian Buddhism and the writing of innovative, often controversial, studies of Buddhist philosophy and ethics. Within a few years he would publish a study that would catapult the nearly unknown Kamakura Zen thinker Dōgen (1200–1253) from a position of near obscurity to recognition as one of early Japan's principal philosophical minds. Also *Genshi bukkyō no jissen tetsugaku* (The pragmatic philosophy of original Buddhism) (1927), Watsuji clearly demonstrates his interest in tracing the Buddhist component in East Asian culture back to its origins in India.

Whatever, then, may have been the exact nature of the "turning" referred to in *Restoring Idols*, that work was crucial in declaring what was to remain for Watsuji as a personal research program—namely, the attempt to document Buddhism as the principal cohesive factor in Asian civilization, and as a form of philosophy not only completely defensible in the twentieth century but one that, at least in its earliest forms, was already far in advance of European Christianity. In many ways this effort was to conceive of "Asia"—or at least eastern Asia—as a single cultural and intellectual milieu strongly patterned by the basic intellectual stance of earliest Buddhism. Watsuji imagined that part of the world not merely as a land mass but, at its roots, as a coherent cultural and intellectual entity.


## II


My aim here is to reconstruct what "Asia" meant as a central idea in Watsuji's writing during the years 1918 and 1919, and what these things can tell us about Watsuji's theory of the relationship between the Meiji and Taishō periods. In a subtle way, he wanted to reshape completely the popular understanding of the Meiji period in order to demonstrate to his contemporaries why the Taishō might prove to be very different and even vastly superior to it. Watsuji, I think, wanted to reverse many common views of the Meiji period; his readings in Nietzsche had instilled in him a

in which "one can find souvenirs left over from that period in my life when my interests were moving from Nietzsche and Kierkegaard to Buddhist arts and Japanese culture." *WTZ* 17:3.

certain delight in the transvaluation of received perspectives. Not only a "man of Taishō," Watsuji also desired a distinctively Taishō reading of the meaning of Meiji.

To this end, he employed an elaborate literary artifice. In *Restoring Idols*, for example, under a surface text concerning European history lies a subtext about Japanese history, which Watsuji wished his more perceptive readers to detect and approve. But to extract that subtext about Japan, one must look more closely at his point about "idols." Watsuji claimed that Paul's emphatic iconoclasm had shaped the consciousness of medieval Europe, led to Christian antagonism toward the sculptured gods and goddesses of classical Greece and Rome, and cast a pall over the age, which was lifted only when bold men of the Renaissance, contravening ecclesiastical authority, literally dug up and "restored the idols" of the classical period in all their ancient beauty. This same viewpoint was readily available in Western historical studies: the Medieval period was regarded as having been a Dark Age, and the Renaissance was seen as having reintroduced not only the antiquities but a corresponding light and sanity into society. Clearly, Watsuji identified with the spirit of rediscovery exhibited by the Renaissance.

Just as Asian Buddhists had known that "God is dead" long before Europeans moved to such a discovery, so too Asians had largely escaped a Dark Age like Europe's, one in which the treasures of the classical period were jettisoned and buried. But Watsuji's intent went deeper. He was not convinced that the Japanese, merely by virtue of being Asian, had solved all of their problems with the iconoclastic impulse. Although Buddhism historically had tempered the impulse to such destruction, when Buddhism was denigrated or neglected, that impulse reappeared and turned against Buddhism itself. In such times even Japan could not totally escape darkness and iconoclastic insanity.

Watsuji hid away in his text a structure of parallels with Europe. He imagined strict Japanese counterparts for three European forms of cultural life: a mode of artistic/iconic creativity; an iconoclastic mode in which idols were forgotten or destroyed; and a mode of recovery and restoration of what had been buried. In Europe's temporal sequence these corresponded to classical Greece (and Rome), the medieval period, and the Renaissance.

And what were their Japanese counterparts? The functional equivalent to Europe's classical antiquity appears to have been, at least in Watsuji's mind, the culture that developed in the capitals of the Nara plain between the sixth and the eighth centuries. Watsuji's *Pilgrimage* was on one level to connect with the iconic evidence of that epoch. He took the Buddhist sculpture located in temples on the Nara plain as parallel to that of ancient Greece; the entire epoch was, like Greece's, one of icon-creation.

To detect what filled the role of Europe's Medieval period, one must realize that for Watsuji a Dark Age by definition was one that exhibited no respect for the arts of antiquity. It was not, therefore, the "medieval" (chūsei) period of Japanese history, since the latter retained under the aegis of Buddhism, the ancient period's appreciation for artistic expression. Nor would the Edo period have been a Dark Age. Partly, perhaps, by default, but also because Watsuji seems to have detected in it real evidence for his theory, the Meiji period was the era that most clearly showed those traits that would warrant thinking of it as an equivalent of Europe's Dark Ages.

What data might support such an interpretative framework? The Meiji period was probably the first in Japanese history to witness literal iconoclasm—that is, large-scale physical destruction of religious icons. Part of this, no doubt, resulted from the reappearance during the Meiji of Christian missionaries, mostly Protestant this time, who clearly pinpointed existing religious sculpture, primarily Buddhist, as expressions of "idolatry" needing to be expunged from Japanese life in order to gain knowledge of Saint Paul's "true God." Christians in Meiji Japan identified Buddhist icons as "idols"; in their eyes, the Japanese landscape was littered with such idols, and their removal, along with the Buddhist and Shintō household altars was part of the program to Christianize Japan. To these Christians, the necessity for expunging idols from all of Japanese life was patent. Photographs from the period show crudely crafted placards hanging on outdoor Buddhist sculpture bearing the word "idol" in English. Watsuji clearly would have known of the Christian animus against Buddhist images.

This was not the major thrust of Meiji iconoclasm, however. Another variety, which came into being from a totally different source, was the result of long-standing nationalist and Nativist claims, advanced during the eighteenth century, to the effect that Buddhism was foreign in origin and unsuited to the Japanese mind. With the Meiji Restoration in 1868, these claims, long simmering in the minds of certain Nativists, took shape in overt attempts to remove Buddhism from Japanese cultural life. In 1871, attacks on Buddhism gathered such force that, in keeping with the slogan of haibutsu kishaku ("discard the Buddhas, cast out Śākyamuni"), there was widespread physical destruction of Buddhist icons.[20] This overtly anti-Buddhist iconoclastic movement was deeply etched into the consciousness of Japanese Buddhists as indicative of the extent to which

[20] See Tamamura Taijō, Nihon bukkyōshi 3:278–89; Itō Tomonobu, "Haibutsu kishaku ronsō," in Imai Jun and Ozawa Tomio, eds., Nihon shisō ronsōshi (Tokyo: Perikan sha, 1979), pp. 337–55; and Martin Collcutt, "Buddhism: The Threat of Eradication," in Marius B. Jansen and Gilbert Rozman, eds., Japan in Transition: From Tokugawa to Meiji (Princeton: Princeton University Press, 1986), pp. 143–67.

Meiji policies seemed bent on destroying the past in order to march pell-mell into the future.

Although it is not mentioned in *Restoring Idols*, one can be certain that Watsuji knew about the *haibutsu kishaku* movement, which had taken place eighteen years before his birth, and that it filled him with a sense of revulsion. In a revealing tribute to Okakura Kakuzō (1862–1913), Watsuji reminisced about having heard the famous art historian's lectures on Asian art at Tokyo Imperial University in 1911. Admitting that he had been deeply influenced by those lectures, Watsuji noted that the following stood out in his memory even many years later:

> Okakura told us students that during the Meiji period when the movement to "discard the Buddhas and cast out Śākyamuni" was in full swing, many masterpieces had either been burned or sold to Westerners for dirt-cheap prices. Being young, we were enraged in hearing this; it made us feel a degree of indignation hard to put into words. Okakura's words incensed us, but this was agitation of a positive type inasmuch as it awoke us to find something good in our own strong emotions.[21]

Clearly, learning about *haibutsu kishaku* was a deeply emotional event that catalyzed whole new ways of thinking among Watsuji and others of his generation. Inasmuch as *Restoring Idols* serves as a basic document of that generation's consciousness, the text represents one of the delayed results of Okakura's efforts to galvanize a new awareness of Asia and its art.

What remains is to fill in the third piece in the structure of cultural equivalences that shapes the subtext of Watsuji's work—that is, the functional equivalent to Europe's Renaissance. The thrust of Watsuji's argument was to say that the real Japanese renaissance began with his own and others' consciousness, especially when they saw through the Meiji rhetoric about itself as the period that had banished Edo's "darkness" and ushered in an "enlightenment."

Proof for such an equivalence between the Renaissance and the spirit of Taishō, if such was needed, was the very intensity with which Watsuji and his peers, inspired by Okakura, strove to unearth the artistic and intellectual wonders of the classical Nara period. Their writings were intended to lift the precious icons of Nara creativity back up into the consciousness of the Japanese people as a whole. Thus, the "restoration of idols" was really a code-phrase for the essence of every renaissance. As the title of Watsuji's book, it also suggested how that book might serve as a program for the work of an entire era. Not only was Buddhist art of the Nara period to be recovered, but, much more broadly Watsuji and his

---

[21] "Okakura Sensei no omoide," *WTZ* 17:354.

contemporaries were to discover the intellectual and religious implications of what it meant for the Japanese to be Buddhist. In addition, it meant a program for renewing the sense of a common Asian identity. All of these, in the minds of these young intellectuals, were concepts the Meiji period had tried to forget, ignore, and even destroy. The sense of indignation felt by those listening to Okakura in 1911 had in Watsuji's writings of 1918 and 1919 become a nuanced critique of what was seen as the Meiji's cultural blindness.

If visualized in graphic form, the whole of Watsuji's subtext about Japan lying below the surface of his writing about Europe, with implied equivalences, tied to distinguishable cultural modes, can be illustrated in the following manner.

| Europe | Japan | Cultural Mode |
| --- | --- | --- |
| Greece and Rome | Nara Plain cultures | icon creation |
| Medieval/Dark Ages | Meiji | icono-clasm |
| Renaissance | Taishō | icon restoration |

This, I maintain, was the model in Watsuji's mind. In addition, it seems clear that in this period he was conscious that his was a public voice with a growing audience within what was still perceived to be a new, bolder, and freer era in Japanese history. Consequently, when he wrote of "restoring images" in an essay that also declared that he himself had undergone a basic change in the direction of his thinking, he implied that his epoch as a whole either had undergone or ought to undergo its own version of tenkō.

This was no minor revision of the Meiji viewpoint. To use Watsuji's own words, it was about as iconoclastic an act of historiography as one might imagine at that time. He had turned what had been heralded as Japan's Enlightenment into the cultural equivalent of a Dark Age and had, by contrast, celebrated that early epoch during which continental Buddhism came to pervade Japanese cultural life as the most creative and important of Japan's history. It is not difficult to see that such an inversion of commonly accepted views had to be introduced with all the literary finesse and subtlety that Watsuji could muster—not so much from a fear concerning possible censorship or suppression, but simply because such a radical and novel transvalorization of Japanese history needed to win its way in the minds of readers through elusive suggestiveness rather than in the bold form of an outline such as the one offered here.[22]

[22] In other, similar contexts, Watsuji's rhetoric tended to be indirect. See my "Haikyō ni tatsu risei: sengo gōrisei ronsō ni okeru Watsuji Tetsurō no isō," in Tetsuo Najita, Maeda Ai, and Kamijima Jirō, eds., Sengo Nihon no seishinshi: Sono saikentō (Tokyo: Iwanami shoten, 1988), pp. 112–44.

## III

*Pilgrimage* was conceptually a companion work to *Restoring Idols*. In the former, Watsuji refashioned public thinking about the seventh and eighth centuries. But for him a rethinking was also a revisualization. Thus he went to Nara on an intellectual pilgrimage to see art as the physical embodiment of ideas.[23] Since the recovery of Buddhism was the essence of his own tenkō, he took it upon himself to make a literal and physical move into the remains of a culture thoroughly imbued with Buddhism, a turn back in time and space to an epoch and place that for him expressed all the best of the Asian traditions of the mind. Although Watsuji disclaimed any usual religious meaning in what he called his "pilgrimage," it was undoubtedly a symbolic journey for him at a time when his own sensitivity to the role of symbols was unusually sharp. Thus this was his own personal inversion of the *haibutsu kishaku* movement of 1871, a Taishō righting of all the wrongs of Meiji.

I accent the intellectual component in *Pilgrimage* and its importance in any account of the development of Watsuji's thinking in part because, as noted above, the book has had extraordinary popularity over the years, and also because today's art historians recognize it as more a literary work than a layman's guide to the art of Nara. Even Watsuji quickly recognized factual errors in it. When his friend and publisher Iwanami Shigeo (1881–1946) asked him to revise it so that a corrected, updated version might be published, Watsuji found that he could not rewrite the whole as he had wished. In 1947, when this new version appeared— twenty-eight years after the original—he penned this apology:

> I am, of course, grateful that this book has lots of readers and that they seem very fond of it. I think the reason for their affection is worth inquiring into. Since this book originally appeared, the development of historical research on Japanese art has proceeded apace, and there are many books on these topics on the market now. . . . Undoubtedly, my book is out of date in that sense. Still, however, many people like to read it, and I think I may have discovered the reason for this in the process of trying myself to revise and update it. In it are passions, enthusiasms, and youth—all qualities I now find missing in myself.[24]

The point was that a more dry, objective, and professional view of Nara's ancient Buddhas could be made, but only at the cost of depriving the book of the very youthful enthusiasm that endeared it to its readers. An old man's revisions of a younger man's vision are likely to be more accu-

[23] Tanikawa Tetsuzō, "Idē o miru gan" (1956), referred to Watsuji's ability to visualize ideas. Republished in Yuasa Yasuo, *Hito to shisō: Watsuji Tetsurō*, pp. 297–99.

[24] *WTZ* 2:4.

rate but also desiccated. Elsewhere he states that Okakura had told him and others to prize their first naive glimpses of the art of Nara.[25] Watsuji—for whatever reason—insists that he finally refused to sacrifice vividness for accuracy's sake.

There is, however, reason to suspect that there was more to the problem than simply a matter of youthful style. A transformation of *Pilgrimage* into a book acceptable to art historians would, Watsuji probably intuited, have involved not only the correction of multiple factual details but an evisceration of the book's whole purpose, which was not to describe works of art accurately but to represent in vivid prose the basic intellectual stance and style of the epoch that produced such art. Moreover, if we read this work not as a discrete work describing temples but rather as a key work in documenting the changes taking place in Watsuji's way of thinking about a variety of things, it becomes clear that *Pilgrimage* is much less innocent than its format—and Watsuji's profession of naïveté—would suggest. That is, although it reads as a series of spontaneous impressions recorded by a sensitive traveler in old Nara, it is replete with literary and rhetorical craft. The travel-record genre, an ancient one in Japan, is eminently useful for leaving the reader with the impression that certain key insights were forced upon one along the way—whereas in fact they may have been well known in advance and precisely what the author wanted to "find" along the journey.

The Nara portrayed in this book was thus intended to serve as the ancient exemplar for those things that Watsuji wanted his own era, the Taishō, to embody. What this author recovered he also promoted, and the point about Nara that interested Watsuji was that it was a thoroughly international culture. It thrived on cultural and intellectual exchange between Japan and the rest of Asia, and as such Nara served as the ideal of a Japan completely open and receptive to all cultures within its reach. Nara, to Watsuji, was a Japan transcending its own insularity; the Japan of that period was, above all, the Japan of the Shōsōin, the imperial storehouse holding treasures from the whole Silk Road. It was to Watsuji a city bound culturally and intellectually to all the known world.

This is the book's central point, and it is worked subtly into its structure and rhetoric. Watsuji begins his journey to Nara by spending a night in Kyoto. Although he himself was very fond of Kyoto, the book portrays it as a city of narrow streets, cramped lodgings, and necessarily limited vistas. Kyoto here is a city closed within itself—just as Japan during much of the time when Kyoto was the capital had less cultural exchange with the continent than it had had earlier when Nara was the capital. It is,

[25] WTZ 17:353.

significantly, *from* a city so described that Watsuji takes his leave to go into what to Watsuji was an even preferable past.

Watsuji notes that Nara, in obvious contrast to Kyoto, sits on a wide, open plain, and its temples majestically occupy places where all can see. Even before visiting his first temple, however, he "sees" his theme simply by looking at the ordinary citizens of Nara glimpsed in a public restaurant when stopping for a meal. He delights in the great variety he notices in the faces, hairlines, arms, and feet of the people—especially the women— he meets there, and this causes him to fall into a reverie about the pan-Asian racial stock that might be found in Nara. In the keynote of the book, Watsuji claims to have found in Nara something surprisingly "international" (p. 28).

His style, however, embraces an argument, even a polemic. One notion that Watsuji seems to have been especially eager to refute was the idea that the Tempyō period (729–48) was preeminently the period of the early poetic anthology, the *Man'yōshū*, something distinctively Japanese, a notion whose corollary was that the temples of Nara, precisely because they were so obviously of continental derivation, were not really Japanese in any genuine sense. To Watsuji this view, traceable to the Nativist movement, was precisely what needed overturning. Carefully, even tortuously, he counters it:

> The world of the *Man'yōshū* and that of the Buddhist arts [of the same epoch] are completely different, and this difference is not merely because the one art is that of lyric poetry whereas the other is that of the plastic arts. It is rather a difference of interests, requirements, and aspirations—in short, in very basic things having to do with the mind and heart. This sort of contemporaneity of two "worlds" within one time-frame, however, should not come as anything of a surprise to people like ourselves—people who right now in front of our own eyes can observe two different and separate "worlds." I think, therefore, it is jumping to too hasty a conclusion to judge that, because one can scarcely detect in the *Man'yōshū* any evidence of the absorption of foreign culture, the people of the Tempyō era had not yet come to grips with the culture from abroad. My point is that, even if it was still limited to a few specialists, the understanding of Buddhist philosophy had at that point begun in Japan. Then it is all the more true that the construction of monumental temples and pagodas constituted an event in society that certainly must have had a profound effect on the sensibility of ordinary people. One cannot imagine how this extraordinary development would not have deeply impressed the minds of people living then. Of course, they were imitating the Chinese in their reception and production of the arts of Buddhism; there was nothing characteristically Japanese in this. By contrast, in the *Man'yōshū* there is the expression of a typically Japanese mode of feeling. All of this notwithstanding, however, in our own time the artistic work created

by a Japanese who has studied painting in the Western style is nonetheless the artwork of a Japanese; it may, in fact, in some cases prove to be much better as art than work done in the characteristic style of traditional Japanese painting. In just the same way is it not possible that [in the Tempyō era] Buddhist sculpture and architecture executed by Japanese in imitation of the T'ang may have a value over and above the Japanese art that comes to expression in the lyrics of the *Man'yōshū*? It seems to me that there is no need to insist always on the distinctive "creativity" of the Japanese. If then the culture of the Tempyō era was the product of labor carried on cooperatively with foreigners, those foreigners became also our ancestors and, therefore, when it comes to the question of what constitutes the culture of our ancestors this is no different from any other. Certainly the poems of the *Man'yōshū* are a very valuable artistic expression, but they show only one part of the culture of the Tempyō era and do not in any way express the whole of it. Thus, also in the Buddhist art of that time we can read the minds of the people of Tempyō. (pp. 94–95)

There is cautious, measured stepping in an argument such as this.

It is important to note the degree to which Watsuji seems willing to include even foreigners—for instance, the Korean artisans who were then resident in Japan and undoubtedly contributed greatly to the art of Nara—among his and his contemporaries' "ancestors." Also important is the disavowal of any essentialist view of what constitutes Japaneseness; Watsuji makes a token acknowledgment of the poetry of the *Man'yōshū* as retaining ancient Japanese sentiments but immediately goes on to assert that such does not disallow as inherently "un-Japanese" those arts and art-forms that originated abroad. The intent would seem to have been to cast as wide a net as possible and to designate inclusivity rather than exclusivity as the cultural mode of the Japanese. This was bound to run counter to scholarship resulting from more than two centuries of Japanese studies in the Nativist mode—that is, scholarship insistent upon specifying what was "Japanese" by winnowing out all that was foreign.

Also apparent, however, is a subtly stated conjunction between Watsuji's own era and that of Nara. Concerning the coexistence of Buddhist sculpture and Man'yō sentiments he wrote: "This sort of contemporaneity of two "worlds" within one time-frame should not come as anything of a surprise to people like ourselves—people who right now in front of our own eyes observe two different, separate 'worlds.' " Here he used the prism of his own present to interpret the past, and vice versa. His "history" was also cultural criticism, and his point is that multiple "worlds" can coexist in one time-frame. Claiming that people of the Tempyō era were "like ourselves," Watsuji implies that the Taishō *ought* to be an era like the Tempyō. Such a coexistence of "worlds" within one culture can be maintained without friction. It was not, Watsuji suggests, the people of Nara Japan who perceived a conflict between continental Buddhism and their own indigenous culture; they managed to hold both, simultaneously and with ease. The conflict, he implies, lay in the minds of those in more recent periods who wanted to create a notion of Japan free of foreign influence and, by implication, a Japanese culture of isolation.

Certainly, many pages of the description of Nara in Watsuji's book will undoubtedly strike readers today as far from the Nara they know; the Nara of his 1919 account emerges as a relatively neglected and unvisited old city. Often he and his companions have great difficulty even locating what they wish to see, and there are instances of having literally to beat a path to ancient ruins. At one point the road is so bad that one of the companions, unable to continue, returns to the hotel. The Nara of Watsuji's book is a city that, if not in ruins, is at least terribly neglected—and the responsibility for that neglect is imputed to the ethos and policies of Meiji. Nara, like the Buddhism that nurtured it, is literally something that has now to be recovered.

Watsuji's journey becomes a personal act of "image recovery," and one full of histrionic possibilities. Within his book, moreover, there are depictions of even more dramatic recoveries. Always fond of archaeology and of portraying any discovery with vividness, Watsuji provides the following reconstruction of Ernest Fenollosa's uncovering of the Kannon image in the Yumedono Hall at the famous Hōryūji temple complex, south of Nara:

> Fenollosa's amazement when suddenly seeing this mysteriously beautiful Buddhist image is part of an event that is truly memorable—and should be unforgettable—in the history of art in Japan. Having received employment from the Japanese government, Fenollosa came here to Nara to study the arts of our antiquity. He was engaged in discussions with the monks at Hōryū-ji concerning the opening up of the miniature shrine of Yumedono, when suddenly he was told by the monk in charge that to attempt such an act of desecration would be to risk punishment from the Buddha—so that the entire temple might even collapse in a great earthquake. Such a thing was, therefore, completely out of the question. The monk then knew only that the icon enclosed therein was reputed to be an ancient Buddha image from Paekche, and that the shrine holding it had not been opened for at least two hundred years. This meant not only that the artistic value of an image had gone unappreciated during that time but also that it was something on which no single Japanese had laid eyes for at least two centuries. So Fenollosa, along with his companion, [Count] Kuki, must have been very excited as they anticipated even the possibility of getting a view of such an extraordinarily rare treasure. With single-minded tenacity they went about tearing down the resistance of the monk by their arguments and entreaties. At the conclusion of their long discussion the monk in charge finally took

out his key and proceeded to ascend the central platform. The two scholars must have been virtually quivering with excitement as they heard the sound of this key, one which had not been used for hundreds of years, turning in the terribly rusted lock. Inside the enclosure was standing a tall figure with its head wrapped in cotton cloth, on which was piled the dust of centuries. It was a monumental task to unravel all that cloth—while choking in the dust that filled the room. It is said that the binding cloth alone was about 450 meters in length. (p. 183)

Here was an example of "idol restoration" in its most literal sense, a quasi-archaeological recovery of an ancient icon. If one can designate figures that play heroic roles in the pages of *Pilgrimage*, the two that stand out most prominently would probably be Ernest Fenollosa (1853–1908) and Sir Aurel Stein (1862–1943), both depicted as having an intense desire to excavate and recover the glories of the Asian past, and both, of course, persons born in the West. Their value in Watsuji's eyes lay in their recognition and appreciation of the Asian heritage, in contrast to many of Watsuji's own countrymen, and especially those who still had minds in lock-step with Meiji ideology.

Watsuji did not miss making an explicit contrast with the Meiji, and especially with the folly of its anti-Buddhist, icon-destroying phase. *Pilgrimage* includes one episode in which, after having spent some pages describing the beauty of the Kannon image he had seen, Watsuji comments:

This magnificent piece of art, however, was only fifty years ago lying by the side of the road. This is what I have been told at least and I am not exactly certain of the truth in the account, but they say that this Buddhist image once had been the principal one in the temple associated with the Shintō shrine at Mount Miwa. Then, however, after the Meiji Restoration and under the baneful influence of the movement to keep Shintō and Buddhism apart from one another, this icon was pushed aside by the authorities pressing for a return to ancient Shintō. It suffered the misfortune of literally being thrown out into a place by the side of the road. It seemed for a while that there was no one in that area volunteering to take this discarded "idol" into his own keeping. So this marvelous Kannon lay there—covered with dirt and weeds for a very long time. Fortunately, and by mere chance, the priest of a very small Jōdo Shinshū temple called Shōrin-ji happened to pass along that road one day. Seeing the Kannon there he said: "What an incredible waste and impiety! If there is no one around here to pick it up, I myself will take care of it." With that he carried it off to his own temple. (pp. 46–47)

Whether his gathered information was accurate was—at least for the intention of this book—much less important than the occasion it gave Watsuji for a graphic depiction of the kind of cultural and artistic waste that the *haibutsu kishaku* mentality had produced. This instance was intended to demonstrate a trend in the Meiji—namely, a readiness to slice up Japanese culture in order to prize parts and dispense with others.

This concept of the Meiji served Watsuji as a negative counterpoint to what he was increasingly coming to define as a Japanese capacity to hold together and harmonize cultural elements that other people might find to be mutually antagonistic and fissionable. The Meiji ethos generally, and its *haibutsu kishaku* movement specifically, were to Watsuji perfect illustrations of everything he deemed incongruous with the real mode of Japanese cultural life. His theory was still in a formative stage. A few years later, in 1922, he was to assume his first university position and become an academic. Moving much more directly and deliberately into the world of academic debate, Watsuji would soon proffer "scientific" hypotheses and theories. One of the most important of these would be the concept of Japan's capacity for cultural assimilation and harmony, which would appear first in his *Zoku Nihon seishishi kenkyū* (Continued research on Japan's intellectual history) of 1926, wherein he coined the term *jūsōsei* (the quality of being stratified or laminated) to depict the layers of culture, much of it from abroad, that shaped Japan. Crucial to this theory is the assumption that, over the centuries, influences were accepted and made part of the multistrata structure of Japanese culture. That theory, later so commonly accepted by many Japanese that Watsuji's formulation of it is easily forgotten, has remained controversial among scholars.[26]

The earliest matrix of the theory appeared in the pages of *Restoring Idols* and *Pilgrimage*. There it was offered not to support nationalist ideology or as an embryonic form of "Japanism," but as a counter to the notion that "Japan" was a determinate entity that could be conceived of apart from other nations and cultures. That is, as originally proposed, the concept of Japan as a lamination of cultural levels was set forth in opposition to myopic chauvinism. As Watsuji said bluntly in a portion of *Restoring Idols* entitled "Of What Can Japan Be Proud?" those Japanese nationalists who forget that Japan was brought up by the cultures of India and China are simply being "blind to the facts."[27]

In his "turning," Watsuji did not so much dispense with his interest in the West and Western philosophy as begin research that complemented that interest with equal attention to Asian traditions. To add attention to Asia did not, he held, mean a subtraction of the West. Thus, later in the postwar context, Watsuji would attribute the disaster of the war to what

[26] WTZ 4:314ff. One could argue that this harmonistic theme operated to foreclose debate and forms of debate that should be legitimate. See, for instance, Najita and Koschmann, eds., *Conflict in Modern Japanese History*.

[27] WTZ 17:273.

had been a "closed" mentality of parochial nationalism and eclipse of Western values.[28] In 1918 and 1919, however, the crux of his critique of the Meiji was that it had "closed" in the other direction, namely, by eclipsing the Eastern past in the push to gain the West's technology.

There is a way to show this quite clearly. Watsuji, it must be remembered, was a thinker with a clear sense of symbolic action and its relationship to ideational choices. If his tenkō had involved for him a retrenchment back into the particularism of Japan, the site chose for his symbolic journey or pilgrimage would not have been Nara but certainly one associated with a specifically and uniquely Japanese identity. His pilgrimage, one can assume, would have been to Ise. But, of course, it was to Nara that he went, and once there, he set about describing the place and what he saw there as the node of ancient Japan's coexistence with all of Asia, and Japan's uniquely "international" city. This was, then, a tenkō that was far removed both in substance and in symbolism from those of Japanese leftists later coerced into professions of faith in the correctness of the positions of the political right.

*Pilgrimage* was one of the modern world's first books to visualize the extent and cultural significance of the Silk Route. Aurel Stein's discovery of the contents of the caves at Tun-Huang had taken place only a decade earlier, in 1906 and 1908; his *Ancient Khotan* was published in 1907, and his *Ruins of Desert Cathay* appeared in 1912. Watsuji knew these works early. Perhaps most interesting is that he took the existence of the Silk Route as proof that the world should not be simplistically divided into "East" and "West." That route, after all, led all the way back to the Mediterranean; the Shōsō-in treasures housed in Nara included art with demonstrable influences from that distant part of the world. This meant that the Buddhist art of even a distant place like Japan could be shown to have been influenced by that of Greco-Bactria.

All this seemed concrete and clear to Watsuji. During this phase of his career a cosmopolitanism grounded in historical materials was beginning to make much more sense to him than a conceptual universality derived from philosophy alone. He was becoming skeptical of theories or principles that, although having a genesis in the particularity of modern Europe, were touted as having universal validity and necessary application everywhere on the globe. Watsuji was just beginning to enter a period of doubt about the ability to universalize such theories, because they often seemed to be Euro-centrism masquerading as universally true. He was growing suspicious of such "universals"—especially when they seemed removed from the concrete cultural experience and history of Asian peo-

---

[28] Sakoku: Nihon no higeki (National closure: Japan's tragedy), in *WTZ* 15. In *Sakaku* he attributed this to an Edo rather than Meiji mentality. See my "Haikyō ni tatsu Risei."

ples. Thus he turned to the particulars of the history of Buddhism to try to demonstrate a form of cosmopolitanism already available in history to the Japanese. During the next few years the pages of *Shisō*, the Iwanami journal of ideas Watsuji edited, would be illustrated with reproductions of the art of classical Greece—even as its essays paid increasing attention to the discussion of themes in the history of Buddhism. Greco-Bactria gave him, he assumed, Europe's best combined with Asia's.

It is no exaggeration to say that Watsuji became obsessed with this form of Silk Route cosmopolitanism and his assumption that, through it, peoples as separated as the ancient Greeks and the Japanese had points of affinity. As he soon thereafter began a corresponding critique of modern European civilization—especially its Anglo-American expressions— he began to lay stress on a perceived intellectual and cultural gap between ancient Greece and the Roman Empire. In his *Genshi Kiristuto-kyō no bunkashiteki igi* (The import of the cultural history of primitive Christianity), a work first serialized in *Shisō* in 1921, he drew explicit parallels between Imperial Rome and both the imperialism and cultural style of Anglo-Saxon peoples, Americans in particular. Bellah and others have correctly noted that already at this point, Watsuji used his basic distaste for the Roman Empire as a way of targeting all that he disliked about American life and society—the basis of a criticism of America that would easily carry over into the war period, when he would write specifically on the American national character.[29]

Increasingly, Watsuji would begin to be coerced along by the rise of nationalist sentiments. In fact, he eventually found himself caught in the tangles of his own rhetoric. Ironically, what he had perceived and depicted as an ancient but still exemplary Asian ecumene, established culturally through Buddhism, was to become for Watsuji's politically ambitious contemporaries something to be unilaterally—even militarily— reconstituted as the Greater East Asia Co-Prosperity Sphere. Such a trajectory, one largely of the Shōwa era, would turn things out very differently than Watsuji had envisioned when he initially made his Taishō turning.

[29] Bellah, "Japan's Cultural Identity," p. 587; and Watsuji, "Amerika no Kokuminsei," in *WTZ* 17:451–81.

**Part V** —————————————————————————

ART AND THE CONCEPT OF CULTURE

IN MANY civilizations, and certainly in Japan, the arts have long represented a privileged domain in which the expression of various mentalities and attitudes seen as fundamental to human experience have been given pride of place. For the Japanese, the arts for many centuries have served not only as a means to enter into a dialogue with their cultural past, but as a way to achieve an authentic grasp of a significant level of truth that can arise from a contemplation of values that have often been regarded in Japanese thought as lying outside and beyond history as narrowly defined: the realms of space, time, and nature.

With the human aesthetic response playing such an important role in the Japanese definition of basic cultural values, any change in those values would naturally be reflected in both the development of new and contemporary arts and the way in which the meaning and significance of the art of the past might be redefined and newly evaluated in congruence with the consciousness of the present.

Virtually all of the shifts in the intellectual and philosophical orientations undertaken by modern Japanese writers, scholars, and intellectuals have been reflected, sometimes in the most poignant fashion, in the arts themselves. The increasing sense of the lonely autonomy of the interiorized individual produced by modern society was mirrored in the development of the modern Japanese novel. By the Taishō period, a significant portion of painting and sculpture now came to be created in consonance with Western ideals of taste, style, and proportion. A growing interest in the arts, both among the intelligentsia and for a more general public, as Shuji Takashina points out, changed considerably the nature of patronage as well as the relationships between high and popular culture in modern Japan.

The influx of Western ideas, ideals, and actual examples of art, whether in works of painting and sculpture or translated fiction and poetry, created in turn a new awareness, paralleling changes in other fields, of the differences between Western modalities and the principles that had governed the creation of the Japanese arts in the past. Imported Western methodologies of the study of art, quickly accepted in principle, provided a new means to examine in a fresh light the possibilities and difficulties involved in continuing to use older literary and artistic traditions; and indeed, many such traditions, from this new comparative standpoint, seemed to reveal a different level of significance, one seen by many as less central to the fundamental core of artistic values appreciated by a modern

Japanese intelligentsia, yet regarded by others as proof of Japanese uniqueness in terms of aesthetic insight. Whatever the shifts in importance assigned to traditional versus Westernized aesthetic experience, however, a common ground of belief in the primacy of the arts as a vehicle for understanding the nature and purposes of culture remained high, as Hajimu Nakano's essay on Kuki Shūzō makes evident. It was for that very reason that the artistic debates of the period were seen as so important and possessed such resonances for the development of modern Japanese culture. In the end, the often heroic efforts made to forge these new attempts at synthesis remain emblematic of the period, as in the case of the work of Ōnishi Yoshinori on *yūgen*, as described in Makoto Ueda's study, which suggests the struggles undertaken by many of the best minds of the interwar period to wrest some form of self-definition from the stubborn imported soil of Western ideas, ideologies, and methodologies.

# 13

## Kuki Shūzō and *The Structure of Iki*

HAJIMU NAKANO

## I

OF ALL the modern writers on Japanese aesthetics, judged in terms of their artistic and social significance, none has been as admired and studied as Kuki Shūzō (1888–1900), whose writings on *iki*, a Tokugawa category of aesthetic approbation that might be roughly translated as "chic," are among the most widely read and appreciated philosophic works in the cultural field.

Kuki Shūzō's life as an independent thinker spans the entire interwar period of Japan. In 1921, ten years after graduating from Tokyo University, where he studied European philosophy under the instruction of Raphael von Koeber,[1] he traveled to Europe at the age of thirty-three and remained there, mainly in France and Germany, for eight years. During this time he prepared himself for his own period of mature thought, both through his enthusiastic absorption of Western culture and through his involvement in the worldly life he found around him. The best view of Kuki's life during his European period can be gained from his *Parii shinkei* (Images of Paris), a collection of poems and traditional thirty-one-syllable *waka* he composed during his stay there. Many vividly depict his mental attitudes and the quality of his life at this time. It is true as well that, during this time, Kuki was already preparing himself for his study on iki, although his book *Iki no kōzō* (The structure of iki) would not

[1] Raphael von Koeber (1848–1923) was of German-Russian lineage. After studying music at the Moscow Conservatory, he traveled to Germany to take up his interests in philosophy, at both Jena and Heidelberg. In 1893 he was invited by the Japanese government at the recommendation of the noted philosopher Eduard von Hartmann to teach philosophy at Tokyo University and piano at the Tokyo Music Academy. His lectures in German philosophy attracted many brilliant students, a number of whom became important figures in the intellectual circles of interwar Japan. Kuki's own interest in philosophy doubtless stemmed from the interest shown in him during his studies at the First Higher School, where the brilliant but eccentric teacher Iwamoto Tei, himself a student of Koeber, was much attracted to the handsome and brilliant Kuki and became his intellectual mentor. For details on Iwamoto, see Donald Roden, *Schooldays in Imperial Japan* (Berkeley: University of California Press, 1980). The incident is described by Watsuji Tetsurō in his *Watsuji Tetsurō zenshū*, vol. 18 (Tokyo: Iwanami shoten).

appear until many years later. His first written work on the subject con-
sisted of an exploratory paper, prepared in 1926.

On returning home from his long stay abroad, Kuki began his academic
career in 1929 as a lecturer at Kyoto University. Rapidly promoted to
professor, he remained in Kyoto for thirteen years. His death in 1941
brought an end to his remarkable career just as war threw many of his
cherished values into question.

The effects of Kuki's European studies on his thinking were evident
from the work he did at Kyoto University. Particularly important were
the lectures he gave over the course of six years on the history of modern
Western philosophy. After his death, his friends and pupils arranged these
lectures for publication in two volumes as *Seiyō kinsei tetsugaku shi kō*
(A history of modern Western philosophy). Examining this material now,
it is clear that Kuki made strenuous efforts in preparing these lectures,
reading extensively in primary and secondary sources on his enormous
field of inquiry, which covered virtually all of Western philosophy. These
lectures represent in many ways the highest level that can be imagined for
a scholar not raised in the Western tradition; certainly there have been
few comprehensive works created in Japan since then that are comparable, either in breadth or depth, to Kuki's.

A second contribution involved Kuki's introduction into Japan of the
existential philosophy of Martin Heidegger through the publication in
1939 of his Kyoto University lectures, entitled *Ningen to jitsuzon* (Man
and existence), which dealt at least in part with what might be termed
philosophical anthropology. During Kuki's stay in Germany, he began to
study with Heinrich Rickert, a neo-Kantian philosopher active at the University of Heidelberg; he continued on at Freiburg with Edmund Husserl,
the founder of phenomenology. Kuki then met Heidegger, in 1927. He
attended the German master's lectures and seminars at Marburg for several semesters. At that time, the philosophical currents in Germany were
shifting from the older views of the neo-Kantians to the newer field of
phenomenology. Many young Japanese were to make the "Freiburg pilgrimage" to study with Husserl. Kuki, on the other hand, felt a great deal
of sympathy with what has been termed Heidegger's existentialism, and
he found these ideals consonant with his own developing ideas.[2] To intro-

---

[2] It is well known that Kuki served as a kind of reciprocal tutor to Jean-Paul Sartre in
Paris during the latter half of 1928. The young Sartre taught Kuki the various currents in
modern French philosophy, while Kuki taught him in exchange what he had learned of
Heidegger's ideas. It is said that when Sartre met Heidegger in Germany, he presented Ku-
ki's letter of introduction. Kuki thus played an unusual role as mediator between these two
great figures. Kuki himself is mentioned in Heidegger's writings, notably in the essay "A
Dialogue on Language," in Heidegger's *On the Way to Language* (New York: Harper &
Row, 1971). For the relationship between Sartre and Kuki, see Stephen Light, *Shūzō and*

duce Heidegger's philosophy into Japan, Kuki himself invented Japanese
equivalents for some of the key terms first coined in German. These concepts, so suggestively rendered in Japanese by Kuki, have since become
well-settled in academic and intellectual circles and are still very much in
use. The very term *jitsuzon* as the translation of "existence" is an obvious
example.

In his own writings, Kuki took up the problem of time and of contingency. Both concepts play a central role in existential philosophy. Indeed,
the concept of contingency had not undergone any appropriate examination in the history of ideas in the Western world before existential philosophers began to turn their full attention to the problem. Since the beginning of the Meiji period, Japanese academic philosophers had not
examined such issues, and Kuki was certainly the first modern Japanese
thinker to address the concept. Kuki's doctoral dissertation revealed his
lengthy concentration on the issue, which in turn formed the basis for his
book published in 1935, entitled *Gūzensei no mondai* (The probem of
contingency).[3] Kuki's study involved a series of elaborate and sophisticated schemata, some of which he later adapted for his use in *The Structure of Iki*. The concept of time also occupied him, as it did his mentor
Heidegger, for many years. As early as 1928, Kuki, stimulated by Heidegger, prepared and published in Paris a short study entitled *Propos sur le
temps*, in which he discussed the Oriental conception of time and eternity.
After returning to Kyoto, he wrote on the subject on numerous occasions,
with a particular emphasis on the ideas of Bergson and Heidegger. Kuki
had visited twice with Bergson during his years in Paris.


## II


Such intellectual performances certainly demonstrated Kuki's originality
and constituted a real contribution to scholarship in the field of philosophy in modern Japan. They do not, however, represent the best expression of his talents, nor his most significant importance for the history of
ideas. They show only one side of his learning and thought. They have
little to do with his keen emotional sensitivity, which constitutes the other
main factor in his personality, which, along with his intelligence, plays
such a crucial role in the constitution of his thought, particularly in the
area of aesthetics. Indeed, it is in this field that the combination of Kuki's
delicate personality and his extensive learning could flow together to such

---

*Jean-Paul Sartre* (Carbondale: Southern Illinois University Press, 1987), which also includes
a translation of *Propos sur le temps*.

[3] A French translation of the book, entitled *Le probleme de la contingence* was published
in 1966 by Tokyo University Press.

a remarkable degree. His major accomplishments in this field are represented by his *Structure of Iki*, published in 1930, and *Bungeiron* (On literature), published posthumously in 1941.[4] Kuki's originality came from two contrasting strains in his own personality, rational intelligence and emotional sensitivity. These strong contrasts were crucial not only for his work and thought but in his own behavior. His very existence showed a striking duality. Of course, many prominent thinkers have shown some kind of mental or emotional duality in their works and lives; it might be said that great thought in general cannot be formed without such duality of mind. In the case of Kuki, however, one finds a special peculiarity in that the contrast between these two elements is so clear-cut and reflects itself so vividly in his life and scholarly production.

This duality in Kuki presumably had certain genealogical roots. It would seem that, specifically, one element was derived from his father, and the other from his mother. Kuki Ryūichi, his father, came from a samurai family and, through shrewdness and ability, was able to become a noted bureaucrat in the Meiji government. He held several ranking posts and was successful in both political and administrative matters. As an officer in the Ministry of Education he took charge of various affairs relating to the preservation of the traditional arts in Japan. He was acquainted with the American philosopher Ernest Fenollosa, then teaching at Tokyo University, and with Fenollosa's disciple and colleague Okakura Tenshin. Their complicated relationships were to leave their mark on Ryūichi's fourth son, Shūzō.

Shūzō was born just after Ryūichi returned from a diplomatic mission to the United States. Shortly thereafter, the father was named a baron for his many services to the nation. Doubtless these inherent mental skills were transferred to his son, transformed from administrative to scholastic aptitude. Certainly it can be asserted that, in terms of intelligence, Kuki Shūzō was the son of his father. In some ways, however, the two must have felt some incompatibility. Ryūichi, although an able government officer, apparently lacked emotional sensitivity, the other and perhaps more important constituent of Shūzō's twofold nature. This second quality was evidently inherited from his mother, Hatsuko. Apparently coming from the demimonde of Kyoto (or, according to another source, from among the servants in the Kuki household), Hatsuko was both physically dainty and emotionally very sensitive. She was extremely accomplished in the polite arts, as practiced by geisha and other entertainers. Shūzō cherished a sincere love for his mother and felt a profound affinity for her responses to life.

[4] The latter is a collection of papers on related topics that connect the emotional life of the Japanese people to literary expression. Among the subjects treated are the metaphysics of literature, problems of rhyme in Japanese poetry, the meaning of the term *fūryū*, the fusion of art and life, and related topics.

Hatsuko's existence, however, was by no means a happy one. Because of her delicate personality, she began to feel herself in some discord with her husband, and symptoms of mental disorder appeared early in her married life. She lived for a time in Tokyo with her son, apart from her husband. During that period of separation, she fell deeply in love with Okakura Tenshin, who had brought her back to Japan from the United States.[5] Kuki's mother continued to press his father for a divorce, but he rejected the idea because of the harm it might bring to his prestige as a government administrator. All of these factors brought on an additional mental decline; eventually, having been granted a divorce, Hatsuko was placed in a mental asylum, where she died in 1931, at the age of seventy-one.[6]

Without such a maternal inheritance, Kuki might not have been able to write so intimately of his emotions, often tinged with eroticism, in his work *Images of Paris*. This collection of poetry may be seen as a crystallization of the delicacy and subtlety of his emotional life. In their way, Kuki's poems are reminiscent of the emotional states created by the poetry of Baudelaire or Verlaine. Some of the longer poems,—"Tango," "A Russian Song," "My Feelings"—are doubtless the best expression of Kuki's mentality at the time. A sample of his subtle feelings can be perhaps more quickly observed in the shorter *waka*, although translation blunts the complexity of the feelings he expresses so well in the original.

| | |
|---|---|
| Hitoyo nete | Touching the body of an actress |
| Onna-yakusha no | With whom I have slept a night |
| Hada ni fure | I smell the autumn roses in Paris. |
| Parii no aki no | |
| Bara no ka o kagu. | |
| | |
| Kushikezuru | What bliss—in the boudoir, |
| Brondo no kami | A girl combs her blonde hair, |
| Hi ni haete | Shining bright in the dim lamp. |
| Akashi sachi aru | |
| Neya no kuki yo. | |
| | |
| Kimi to nete | I sleep with you, |
| Bodoreru no | Humming softly a verse of Baudelaire, |
| Ku o utai | Late at night, in Paris, late in March. |
| Parii no yayoi | |
| Yo to tomo ni fuku | |

[5] Kuki described these situations in several unpublished essays now available in his *zenshū*, vol. 5. These essays chronicle Kuki's delicate and complicated feelings for Okakura.

[6] Much revealing information on the life of Kuki's mother can be found in Matsumoto Seichō, *Okakura Tenshin—sono uchinaru teki* (Tenshin—his inner enemies) (Tokyo: Shinchōsha, 1984).

| Hai-iro no | My worldly passions and desires |
| Chūshō no yo ni | Are too strong to live |
| Suman ni wa | In the grey world of abstract thought. |
| Koki ni sugitaru | |
| Bonnō no iro. | |

Kuki's paternal and maternal inheritance is thus well-reflected in his personality. He was both stoic and epicurean, serene and passionate, theoretical and emotional. The epicureanism is easily recognizable, of course, in the works contained in *Images of Paris*. The stoicism may seem more difficult to locate. Actually, Kuki wrote in a brief essay on the art of reading that his favorite author was Epictetus. In accordance with Kuki's personality, his way of living was twofold. On one hand, he led a studious life in Kyoto as a professor at the university, teaching and carrying out his administrative duties. By the same token, he took strong delight in the mundane pleasures he found all through his comparatively short life. He visited the gay quarters, and without shame, although many professors would certainly have refrained from such an act. As an extremely sensitive person, he was deeply conscious of the duality within him, and this in turn caused an internal agony evident from the *waka* poetry he wrote during his years in Kyoto. Those who knew nothing of his inner distress sometimes blamed him for his conduct, but he did not take notice of their censure. He knew that his own conduct made normal family life impossible. His way of living, on the other hand, sharpened and refined his sensitivities. With the agony, then, came a sense of relief, as he himself confessed in his essays and poems. On this point, Kuki might best be described as a worldly aesthete, rather than as an academic aesthetician or philosopher.

Kuki's duality finds expression as well in the contrast between the objects of his study and the methods employed in his research in his works on aesthetics, notably in his representative *The Structure of Iki*. In these areas of his concern, he took up as his object of research those phenomena related to the qualities he found inherent in Japanese emotional life. Kuki chose what he took to be those indigenous traits, particularly as revealed in the *ukiyo-e*, or woodblock prints. From an examination of such traits he made more general statements about the national character of the Japanese. His attempts to analyze such material with the kind of precise, rational methods he mastered in his study of Western philosophy reveal at once the contrast in the two elements, the pull between a traditional emotional object and an alien rational methodology. In this regard, Kuki is typical of most thinkers in modern Japan, since all had to learn from the Western world the rational methodologies required for their studies, mechanisms not part of the Japanese mental heritage. The foreigness of method was common to all. Yet in terms of objects of study, most Japanese thinkers, beginning with the preeminent modern philosopher, Nishida Kitarō (1870–1945), dealt with nonemotional issues. In this, Kuki was unique. *Iki*, the object of his study, is not only emotional, but also quite different from the traditional aesthetic values of the Japanese as evidenced in *yūgen*, the medieval term sometimes translated as "mystery and depth," studied in depth by Ōnishi Yoshinori. For iki, as an erotically tinged value, has something in common with *ukiyo-e*, while yūgen apparently has nothing to do with it. Kuki attempted to analyze this specific emotional value of iki with an exact theoretical method. This duality of method and object is thus most visible in *The Structure of Iki*, where the object of analysis lies in traditional taste as perceived by a modern aesthete, while the method of analysis functions through the mind of a Western-trained professional philosopher.

# III

*The Structure of Iki*, as a compound production of the two constituents of Kuki's nature, certainly deserves its reputation as a masterpiece. Kuki, with his keen aesthetic sense, discovered in iki a key concept that captures the essence of a kind of taste that can be defined as altogether Japanese. As iki reflects extremely delicate nuances of considerable intricacy indigenous to the life of the Japanese, it is difficult, if not impossible, to attempt to translate the word into any foreign language. There are certainly no appropriate equivalents in English. Such words as "refined," "chic," "dapper," and "smart" can express part but not the whole of the connotations that the term iki possesses. That which iki designates is not an inborn quality. A woman, for example, may be born pretty, but that does not mean that she shows the quality of iki. One must learn to possess it. And it cannot be learned easily. Iki is so subtle that it is difficult even for the Japanese to acquire the quality without a certain experience and training. Only adult, experienced men and women can possess it. Historically, iki was cultivated as a term to express the taste of the wealthy bourgeois during the Tokugawa period, who often haunted the pleasure quarters, always the main birthplace of those who knew iki. Iki thus functions as a symbol of ripened bourgeois culture, which is fostered exclusively in the society of the townsmen. Therefore, members of the other social classes (samurai, farmers, nobility) were usually not interested in developing this quality in themselves, although, as Kuki explained, the word itself may in its etymology show some relation to certain mental qualities associated with samurai. Iki thus designates, on one hand, an essential aspect of Japanese taste and, on the other hand, an aesthetic standard for an evaluation of taste, which can be applied to all kinds of style, both in cultural objects and in human behavior.[7]

*The Structure of Iki* is composed in six chapters. In chapter 1, which serves as the introduction to the whole work, Kuki points out that every nation has in its language special words that express its ethnic nature. For the Japanese, iki is such a word; and to understand what the Japanese mean by this word, an interpretation of their experience is indispensable. In chapter 2, "The Intensive Structure of Iki," Kuki maintains that three elements are suggested in this single term: coquetry, a proud spirit, and an attitude of resignation. For Kuki, coquetry suggests a sensual attitude that incorporates the kind of dynamic tension involved in erotic relationships between men and women. Iki, however, suggests the potentiality, not the actualization, of such relationships. In Kuki's explanation, the proud spirit suggested by iki represents above all the moral ideal of the citizens of Edo, the so-called Edokko, and bears some relationship to the morality of the samurai, *bushidō*. Iki, Kuki indicates, may trace its etymological roots to the term *ikiji*, a samurai quality suggesting a proud spirit. Iki thus gives rise to an unyielding quality; as a measure of taste, it possesses a strong moral connotation. Finally, resignation suggests an obedience to one's fate and a complete indifference to earthly success—money, love, and, in extreme cases, life itself. This *nil admirari* attitude in itself leads to a certain kind of refinement. Those who possess iki should therefore be able to abandon all things in order to maintain what they consider the highest spiritual values. Kuki then combines these three factors in order to define iki as "a refined and unyielding coquetry."

With this definition in mind, Kuki discusses in chapter 3, "The Extensive Structure of Iki," the relationship between iki and such related traditional expressions of taste as *shibumi, jimi,* and *hade*. He finds similarities between these words and iki but notes certain differences as well. He also examines opposing terms, such as *jōhin-gehin* (elegance-vulgarity), *hade-jimi* (gaudy-sober), and *iki-yabo* (chic-uncouth), explicating the implications of those relationships. In this chapter, Kuki employs particularly sophisticated schemata of the sort that he employed elsewhere in his philosophical writings. Such a scholarly analysis provides a useful contrast with the following chapter, "The Natural Expression of Iki." Here Kuki indicates the natural expression of iki, as opposed to a conscious

---

[7] Kuki indicated that the best illustration of *iki* in terms of the behavior of men and women could be seen in the amatory literature of the Tokugawa period referred to as *ninjōbon*, especially in the works of Tamenaga Shunsui, as well as in the light songs accompanied by *shamisen* referred to as *ha-uta, kiyomoto,* and *shinnai*. Such works were closely related to the life of the gay quarters, where *iki* was an important quality of life. *Sui* is another term with connotations like those of *iki*, but *sui* was more prevalent among the bourgeois in the Osaka area.

artistic statement, citing the spontaneous use of nuance in the human voice, and, visually, feminine posture and carriage, the wearing of clothing, bodily shapes, facial features, and so forth. In all of these natural expressions, Kuki indicates, there exists a dynamic tension suggesting a potential eroticism.

In chapter 5, "The Artistic Expression of Iki," Kuki points out that the true atmosphere of iki is more truly expressed indirectly in certain artistic elements that make up the life of the person involved, rather than being expressed directly and formally in works of art that are consciously created as such. Iki can thus be found in the colors and patterns of clothing, parts of architectural constructions, and musical melodies and rhythms; sculpture and painting cannot depict it directly. One can say that the cut and color of a kimono expresses iki, but not a particular picture. The art of the kimono is implicit; the painting is explicit. Iki, in its expression, is indirect, a quality more to be valued than any direct statement. From this point of view, Kuki goes on to compare various stripes, patterns, and colors of clothing, architectural styles and materials, and melodies and rhythms used in traditional Japanese music.

In chapter 6, Kuki concludes his study by indicating his conviction that iki is the product of sensual experience indigenous to the Japanese, both as individuals and as a race. Its study must therefore properly involve the hermeneutics of ethnic experience. For Kuki, iki has two components that make up its fundamental nature. One consists of a conscious attitude in the minds and emotions of the Japanese. The other is the manifestation of that attitude as expressed in various created objects. The basic attitude represents what is fundamental; what is created from that attitude thus remains a "symbol" of that attitude. Therefore, a study of iki must begin with an examination of that attitude. This fact, however, indicates what Kuki takes to be a serious problematic in the study of iki, for as it fundamentally represents a mental phenomenon, iki can only be grasped through experience. Iki is thus essentially beyond conceptual understanding. Does this mean, Kuki concludes, that his study is meaningless? Of course not, he replies. Certainly, he insists, "experience and conceptual cognition represent different realms. There is an impassable abyss between one and the other." Yet the true significance of any such theoretical study of emotional phenomena must lie in the attempt to theorize concerning objects of study about which it may seem impossible to theorize. Such is precisely the task of aesthetics. Thus, continues Kuki, a study of *iki* can and must be made. And indeed, from the reader's point of view, the very duality in Kuki's own nature as a man and as a scholar qualify him to make just such a study as this one.

Reading Kuki's study, one is always impressed by the fact that Kuki's approach is closely connected to the duality of his own nature. His own sharp sensitivities led him to discern exactly where in various phases of Japanese life iki really plays a part. On the other hand, Kuki's own lucid intelligence allowed him to discern and clarify the essential connotations of its conceptual forms. It might be observed as well that Kuki unifies in this study both the Oriental and Occidental ways of knowing. This unification of thought and method suggests in turn a connection of object and method of study that has significance in a broader context.

## IV

Kuki's position in the history of ideas during the interwar period in Japan indicates several significant points concerning the intellectual life of his times.

In the first place, it might be pointed out that this extraordinarily brilliant and original thinker was a solitary person. In Japanese academic life, as well as elsewhere, groups and schools can show strong influences. Kuki graduated from both the First Higher School and Tokyo University, highly influential academic bodies. Among his classmates were a number of prominent figures in Japanese philosophical circles. Yet Kuki seems to have been isolated from them, except for a few intimate friends such as Amano Teiyū, a professor of ethics at Kyoto University, and Iwashita Sōichi, a Catholic theologian. With these men he had important personal but no intellectual relations. He neither formed nor joined any academic groups. At Kyoto University, the so-called Kyoto School of philosophy[8] was already active, mainly in the faculty of letters, and it was in this environment that Kuki began to work when he returned from Europe. So far as philosophy was concerned, the leader of the Kyoto School remained Nishida Kitarō, followed by Tanabe Hajime (1885–1952), both of whom had studied under Koeber at Tokyo University. Nishida was quite friendly with Kuki, and indeed wrote an epitaph for his younger col-

---

[8] A precise description of the Kyoto School is difficult to give, and the term itself is rather ambiguous, as it is sometimes used in a laudatory way, sometimes partly pejoratively. There is by no means a firmly established opinion about who belonged to the group, or what its general characteristic may have been at this period. Generally speaking, when Kyoto University was founded, there were many professors of considerable learning, particularly in the faculty of letters, who were highly critical of the hegemony of the academic establishment represented by Tokyo University. These scholars therefore attempted to create a unique academic tradition completely independent of Tokyo University. These professors and their successors are thus collectively called the Kyoto School (Kyoto Gakuha). Yet within this "school," there are, of course, a variety of intellectual tendencies. For example, the specialists in history and literature can be characterized by their strict philological methods, while those teaching philosophy are noted for their strong emphasis on personal speculation.

league, adapting a translation of Goethe's well-known poem *Wanderers Nachtlied*, "A Traveler's Night Song." Yet Kuki remained altogether independent of the Kyoto School of thinkers. He seemed to have made efforts to keep himself apart from them.

In every aspect of his life, Kuki went his own way. He maintained his distance not only from his colleagues but from his students. He had few pupils in the field of the history of modern philosophy and none in the area of aesthetics, which did not represent his specialty insofar as the university was concerned. Indeed, in the latter field, he only once delivered a public lecture on literature.

In this regard, another remarkable peculiarity, Kuki's lack of social and political concern, might be pointed out. In his scholarly papers and articles, there are few serious comments on the actual issues of the day, although there were many important social and political incidents taking place not only in Japan but in the world at large. In this sense, he lived in isolation from the world. He certainly knew the world, yet he lived completely outside it. Such knowledge, and such indifference, provided the basis for his composition of *The Structure of Iki*. The book continues to find readers, and yet it too stands alone, and seems to have had little influence on later scholarship.

More important is the basic motivation in Kuki's thought and work, whether conscious or unconscious, to unite Occidental and Oriental ways of thought. This motivation operates in two directions. One attempts to appreciate and experience Occidental culture with an Oriental sensibility; the other attempts to explain Oriental sensibilities in terms of Occidental modes of reasoning. Kuki's life in Europe helped develop the first; his studies of aesthetics gave him the technique for the second. In this, Kuki was unique. After all, most thinkers in the Taishō period, especially those involved in the field of philosophy, were exclusively oriented to the West. Indeed, the whole ideal of *kyōyō shugi*, which might be translated as "culturalism" and was espoused by such writers as Abe Jirō, was altogether derived from European idealism, which Japanese scholars and writers made strenuous efforts to understand and to naturalize. Very few scholars in Kuki's generation paid attention to their own culture. For them, the word "philosophy" meant nothing but the study of European philosophy.

There were, on the other hand, two groups opposing that trend. A certain number of original thinkers preferred individual speculation to the study of foreign thought and became engrossed in their own vision of the world. Nishida and Tanabe might be considered the most successful representatives of this group. On the other hand, a small number of scholars, notably Watsuji Tetsurō and Yanagi Sōetsu, highly evaluated traditional Japanese culture. Watsuji, a classmate of Kuki, can serve as an interesting

point of comparison. He certainly had a profound grasp of European philosophy; indeed, he was one of several early specialists on Nietzsche in
Japan, and it was he who introduced the work of Kierkegaard to Japanese
intellectual circles. In his work as a professor of ethics, he founded his
own ethical system on a grand scale, drawing on his wide knowledge of
European philosophy. Yet since his youth, Watsuji paid constant attention to the traditional culture of Japan and to the Orient in general, and,
of course, he wrote many books on those subjects.

Watsuji's approaches to Japanese culture, however, were different from
those of Kuki. The objects of his study were not so closely linked to private emotions. Watsuji's attitude toward Europe is also different from
that of Kuki. Watsuji observed European culture. Kuki enjoyed European
life. It is unthinkable that Watsuji could have led the kind of life that Kuki
described in *Images of Paris*. These differences in turn are clearly visible
in the qualities of Watsuji's masterpiece, *Fūdo* (Climate), and *The Structure of Iki*. Kuki's intellectual concerns focused on the human beauty that
lies in the life of Japanese taste, not in concrete artistic productions. Watsuji, rather, was interested in the beauty of art and landscape. Kuki's sensitivity to beauty, it seems to me, is more delicate than that of Watsuji.
Yet, paradoxically, Kuki's methods of analysis are more rigorous, more
strictly conceptual than those of Watsuji. Kuki seems to have learned
more from the European intellectual tradition in his study of philosophy,
assimilating more than Watsuji did. In this sense, Kuki succeeded to a
higher degree than any of his contemporaries in attaining a unification of
Orient and Occident. This success indicates his unique position among
intellectuals in Japanese thought of the interwar period.

# 14

## Natsume Sōseki and the Development of Modern Japanese Art

SHUJI TAKASHINA

OF ALL the cultural figures in modern Japan, none has been more read, studied, and appreciated than the novelist and critic Natsume Sōseki (1867–1917); it is perhaps no surprise that his portrait has been chosen to grace the new thousand-yen note. Yet for all the sustenance that later writers, scholars, and intellectuals have drawn from his responses to a changing Japanese culture, surprisingly little attention has been paid to Sōseki's observations on the visual arts of his time. It is true that, while he made a number of casual references to art and artists in his stories, journals, and letters, Sōseki wrote only one sustained composition on the subject, "Bunten to geijitsu," first published in the *Asahi* in October 1912. The concerns he expressed in the article serve as a remarkable preview of the challenges that his younger contemporaries in all fields of creative endeavor would come to meet.

Despite the importance of the article, it has attracted relatively little attention. The text is easy enough to find in any set of Sōseki's complete works. I myself happened to write an article on it some years ago, and there is now available a small paperback reprint of the article, edited by Kagesato Tetsurō, director of the Mie Prefectural Museum, complete with an excellent set of illustrations and useful notes on the artists. But there remains much to be gained from a close reading of Sōseki on the subject of art.

To understand the scope of Sōseki's concerns, some general background on the sociology of modern Japanese art during the period is in order. The title of the article, "Bunten to geijitsu," can be translated as "Bunten and the Creative Arts." The term "Bunten" is an abbreviation for Monbushō Bijutsu Tenrankai, the Ministry of Education Art Exhibition. The Bunten exhibitions were begun in 1907 and represented the first official attempt by the Meiji government to organize government-controlled exhibitions of art in three categories, *Nihonga* (Japanese-style modern painting), *yōga*, (Western-style modern painting), and sculpture. The government undertook such an organization because of the proliferation of so many small groups of artists in every area of the creative arts. Nihonga painters, for example, were divided into several groups, some working in Tokyo, some in Kyoto, and the same pattern pertained to the other two categories as well. Both artists and government officials felt the need to create a centralized forum for the display of contemporary arts. In particular, the government hoped to establish an officially patronized annual exhibition that might resemble, in both design and influence, the French Salon. In the history of modern Japanese art, then, the creation of Bunten was truly an epoch-making event, and its importance is clear even today. For example, the national collections of modern Japanese art, now housed in the Tokyo National Museum of Modern Art in Chiyoda-ku, began with the first Bunten exhibit. Earlier paintings, even those created in the Western style, go automatically to the Tokyo National Museum in Ueno. The year 1907 thus has come to serve as a boundary for the development of modern Japanese art. Those official exhibitions were so successful that they continued to be organized, with some changes, every year until 1947. Beginning in 1948, the group changed its name to the Nihon Bijutsu Tenrankai (Japan Art Exhibition), customarily abbreviated as Nitten, and was placed under private control.

Sōseki chose to write on the sixth Bunten exhibit, held in 1912. In this particular year, one important change had come about in the organization of the exhibition. Up until that year, there were three categories in which artists could show their works: Nihonga, yōga, and sculpture. A number of conflicts, however, had grown up among the various practitioners of Nihonga, or Japanese-style modern painting, and their disagreements were such that the quarrel reached the floor of the Japanese parliament. The minister of education, asked to intervene, achieved an appropriately bureaucratic solution by making two sections for Nihonga, the First Section (Ikka) and the Second Section (Nika). Two years later, when new avant-garde artists painting in the Western style, many of them trained in Europe, found themselves frustrated by the conservative policies of the Ministry of Education, they left Bunten and created their own private society which they called Nika-kai, thus making ironic reference to the activities of their contemporaries in the field of Nihonga. The Nika-kai continues today as an important forum for independent artists.

The sixth Bunten exhibit was a particular success, attracting far more spectators than any previous exhibition. Some statistics may be of interest.

|               | Year | Attendance |
|---------------|------|------------|
| First Bunten  | 1907 | 43,741     |
| Second Bunten | 1908 | 48,535     |
| Third Bunten  | 1909 | 60,535     |

| Fourth Bunten | 1910 | 76,363  |
| Fifth Bunten  | 1911 | 92,765  |
| Sixth Bunten  | 1912 | 161,805 |

Even today, any exhibition in Tokyo that could attract more than 100,000 visitors would be considered a success. In 1912, however, the population of Tokyo was only around two million, so that the attendance can be judged to have been extraordinary. Every newspaper gave the exhibition an enormous amount of publicity, not only in the arts and literature sections, where one might expect a certain amount of attention given to the subject, but in the social pages as well.

The actual organization of the exhibit was along the lines of the French Salon. Any artist was free to submit his work. A jury was used to accept or reject the paintings submitted. Concerning this system, Sōseki himself mentioned the incident of a painter who, sure of his success, threw an elaborate party, only to find his work refused; his wife was so angry at the expense involved that she divorced him. Information of this sort appeared in the newspapers, creating an even greater interest in the exhibition.

The sixth Bunten ran from October 13 to November 17, 1912. In all, 1,811 works of art, in the various categories of painting and sculpture, were submitted to the juries. Only 186 were accepted. The competition was thus extremely severe. Along with other works especially added later, the show contained 239 works of art.

At this time in his career, Natsume Sōseki had already given up his teaching position and was working as a writer and editor for the *Asahi* newspaper. His article on the Bunten was written in serial form. The first part of the article was published on October 15; in all, his remarks required twelve installments, so that the whole text was fairly lengthy. Most of the first six installments were dedicated to an exposition of Sōseki's general views on the nature of art, the role of contemporary art, and other similar subjects. Only later in the series did Sōseki discuss the work of individual artists. Such an extended and personal structure was not unusual at the time; other writers often followed the same pattern. There was, for example, the famous case of Kojima Kikuo, a member of the editorial board of *Shirakaba* (White birch) magazine, the journal that did so much to promote a knowledge of Western art in Japan during this period. Kojima was also an art historian, and he later joined the faculty of Tokyo University in that capacity. He once wrote a twelve-point article on the sculpture seen in one of the Bunten exhibitions. For eleven of the twelve installments, Kojima wrote only concerning the true nature of sculpture, presenting an account of the general theory of the art based on examples from Greece, the Renaissance, Michelangelo, Rodin, and so forth. Only in the last section of the twelfth essay did he deign to speak about the actual exhibit. "Such," he wrote, "are the conditions required for true sculpture. Yet when we look at the current official exhibition, bearing in mind these requirements, we regret to say that there is not a single work worthy of the name of sculpture."

Sōseki was more reasonable. He did attempt to pick out certain works of painting and sculpture that he regarded as genuine works of art. Of the two parts of his article, however, the theoretical parts are of more compelling interest in terms of coming to an understanding of the state of culture at his time. His individual choices are of great interest, of course, in terms of art history, particularly when his opinions are juxtaposed with those expressed by other critics and scholars writing at the time. The exhibition contained, for example, a number of now famous paintings, among them works by Sakamoto Hanjirō and Aoki Shigeru, on which Sōseki commented.

Sōseki was not, as he made clear in his article, a professional art critic. An amateur in the area of art, he found himself free to record his own spontaneous impressions. The style of the article is free, easy, and full of humor. He discusses, for example, two portraits in the show painted by Wada Eisaku (1874–1959), an important Western-style painter who studied with Kuroda Seiki (1866–1924), an excellent artist who himself had worked in Paris and was responsible for much of the early development of Western-style painting in Japan. Wada himself was on the jury that made the selections for the exhibition.

> I would first like to mention the portrait of Baron Ishiguro, painted by Mr. Wada. I wish to state that, quite sincerely, I have no intention at all of speaking badly of the artist. I only wish to convey sincerely what I felt. The face of the Baron looks very much like a pumpkin, the color of which has begun to deteriorate. This may not be entirely the painter's fault. It may well be the truth that, in reality, the profile of the Baron may show some likeness to a pumpkin. Still, when it comes to the fact that the face of the Baron has dust all over its surface—and that fact may or may not emphasize its similarity to a pumpkin— that responsibility lies altogether with Mr. Wada. Or might we say that it is a defect of the light on his face? That seems unlikely to me.
>
> Mr. Wada has another painting in the exhibition, the portrait of Mrs. H. She has a color as disagreeable as that of the Baron. Perhaps it is because she appears to be seated in a dark, closed interior where there is not enough light; still, looking at the way in which the picture is painted, anyone would be convinced that it is not the space but Mrs. H's skin that is naturally dark. I felt very sorry for her.[1]

[1] Natsume Sōseki, "Bunten to geijutsu," in Sōseki zenshū (Tokyo: Iwanami shoten, 1966), 11:414.

In terms of cultural history, the most valuable sections of the article can be found in Sōseki's theoretical remarks. He begins with an aphorism, which he repeats, in one way and another, throughout the article. "Art," he writes, "begins with the expression of the self and ends with the expression of the self." Such is his viewpoint, and his attitude stands at opposite poles, for example, from that of the eminent lover of folk art, Yanagi Sōetsu (1889–1961) whose vision called for an art of the people, by the people, and for the people. For Sōseki, however, art is for the artist. He insisted that art as self-expression remains the fundamental rule of every form of creativity: painting, literature, music. An artist must try to express himself, and he must not create merely in terms of the effect that he thinks he will produce in terms of audience acceptance. Many artists, wrote Sōseki, are preoccupied with money, with the views of others, or, in the case of painting, with the views of the juries. All these factors, he insisted, must be seen as secondary. The artist must endeavor—and that effort is the essence of all art—to express himself.

The position taken by Sōseki is very much that of others active in creating the cultural and intellectual climate of his time. Those who wrote for *Shirakaba* show much the same cast of mind. Take, for example, the noted novelist Mushanōkoji Saneatsu (1885–1976), one of the most prominent spokesmen for that group. "For me," he wrote in the February 1912 issue of *Shirakaba*, "there is no greater authority than myself." The previous year, in the August 1911 issue, he had written, "I only understand myself; I only do my work; I only love myself. Everyone else, even my parents, my brother, my master, my friends, my beloved, are enemies to my growing self. Hated though I am, despised though I am, I go my own way." In this circle of intellectuals, such views were common. Sōseki, on this point, seems one with them.

Sōseki points out the potential conflict between society and the artist, or society and the sense the individual has of himself. The artist must be able to face resistance from society, and he must be willing to express his own intentions. Thus Sōseki always seeks to locate the expression of the individual personality of the artist in any particular work that he sees. Sōseki chooses a telling example from the Bunten exhibition to prove his point. In this case, he selected two paintings from the Second Section of the Nihonga group. Both artists had chosen the same subject matter, the traditional subject of "The Eight Views of Lake Tung T'ing," long a favorite of the literati painters who used imaginary views of China in their work. The two artists represented were Yokoyama Taikan (1868–1958), now considered as perhaps the last truly great artist in the literati tradition, and Terazaki Kōgyō (1866–1919), both disciples of the writer who brought new energies to the teaching of art in Meiji Japan, Okakura Ten-

shin (1862–1913). Sōseki, in comparing the two paintings, wrote as follows:

> Both Kōgyō and Taikan have illustrated the famous Eight Views, but their
> work looks quite different when the paintings are examined side by side. Kō-
> gyō's work is painted in a diligent fashion, with care, using fine brush strokes.
> In particular, in the rendering of the moon on the waves of the lake, the artist
> has covered the whole surface with small waves, like the surface of a fish's skin.
> This almost childlike, naive, and careful repetition gives to his work a certain
> gravity worthy of praise, but I also have the feeling that this kind of thing has
> already been done by the old Chinese painters, suggesting that Kōgyō's work
> shows less personality than Taikan's. On the whole, Taikan's painting con-
> vinced me that this artist was a man of Meiji, Yokoyama Taikan, and no other.[2]

Sōseki stressed that the subject matter chosen was traditional, and that,
while Kōgyō's painting was technically of high quality, he had merely
followed tradition, whereas Taikan, while working within the general
outlines of that tradition, had completely renovated its means of expression, thus making the painting a manifestation of the artist's own vision.
Even in traditional painting, Sōseki sought the same individualism that
constituted so much of the cultural climate of his time.

Such praise for personality and emphasis on creative individuality was
not altogether new. These attitudes were already visible at the beginning
of the century, at the end of the third decade of the Meiji period. Until
that time, there had been little expression of any sense of conflict between
society and the individual. By the time of the Russo-Japanese War (1904–
5), however, that conflict had become apparent. One trenchant example
of this shift of attitudes can be seen in the writings of Takayama Chogyū
(1871–1902). His famous article, "Biteki seikatsu o ronzu" (On the aesthetic life), written in 1901, served as a virtual manifesto on the creed of
individualism.

> What is happiness? We firmly believe that it can only be satisfied by the sat-
> isfaction of the instincts. What are the instincts? They are the natural demands
> of man. That which satisfies the natural demands of man is what we call the
> "aesthetic life."[3]

Chogyū placed what he called the natural demand of man in confrontation with social morality, and sharply criticized Confucian morality;
the natural demands of human personality, he was convinced, were in a
state of friction with such received ideas, and those who believed in his
doctrines must seek to perfect their own aesthetic lives. Such was Cho-

[2] Ibid., p. 408.
[3] Takayama Chogyū, *Chogyū zenshū* (Tokyo: Hakubunkan, 1914), 4:93.

gyū's position in 1901. Yet only six years before, in 1895, he expressed himself in a contrary fashion. In his article "Dotoku no risō o ronzu" (On the ideal of morals), he wrote:

> An individual does not have within himself any sufficiency great enough to constitute his own morality. Morals always emerge in the context of society. A society is not a simple conglomeration of individuals but constitutes a moral whole, which has its own personality; so is the state; so is mankind. The whole does not exist without the individual, of course, but the whole has its own life and personality, which cannot be found in each individual. To strengthen this personality of the whole and to develop its life is the ultimate object of the individual; and by participating in the ideal of the whole, each individual can also attain his ideal.[4]

Thus, in 1895, Chogyū saw that the whole has its own personality, and that there exists a harmonious relationship between society as a whole and the individual. He thus identified a kind of predestined harmony between society and the individual. At that point in his thinking, he found no conflict between the whole and the individual. Yet only six years later he saw clearly the friction between the two. His choice was for the individual, not for society.

Similar views appeared in other fields as well. Take, for example, the views of the poet and critic Masaoka Shiki (1867–1902). In an article entitled "Haiku taiyō" (The substance of haiku) in the October-December 1896 issue of the periodical *Nippon*, he wrote as follows:

> Haiku is a part of literature. Literature is a part of art. Therefore, the standards that apply to art apply to literature. The standards of literature are those of haiku. In other words, painting, sculpture, music, theatre, poetry, and fiction—all can be judged by the same standard.[5]

Shiki shows an optimistic belief in the wholeness of each genre, convinced that there is a standard applicable to every sphere of creation. Yet his optimistic belief was to collapse only five years later. In his famous essay "Bokujū-itteki" (A drop of ink), Shiki wrote that, "in my opinion, the tanka written by Yosano Tekkan and myself are based on completely different standards. If Shiki is right, then Tekkan is wrong."[6] Shiki could no longer posit a common standard for even one genre, that of tanka poetry. This shift to a pessimistic view now becomes central in Shiki's writing.

[4] Ibid., p. 857.
[5] Masaoka Shiki, *Shiki zenshū* (Tokyo: Kōdansha, 1975), 4:342.
[6] Ibid., 11:96–97. Yosano Tekkan (1873–1935), the husband of Yosano Akiko, was a poet who composed emotionally strong verse involving a kind of vivid imagery that Shiki found unsuitable for tanka.

There are other examples of such a change of view at the turn of the century. For instance, when the great poet and novelist Shimazaki Tōson (1872–1943) compiled his first volume of collected poems in 1904, he stated that his work represented a manifesto of a new poetry; "at last," he wrote (and his readers surely agreed with him), "the new age of poetry has come." The poet and sculptor Takamura Kōtarō (1883–1956), composed his own famous manifesto, "Midoriiro no taiyō" (The green sun) in 1910, in which he put forth the proposition that an artist had the right to paint his sun green, and the spectator to look at and judge that result in terms of the artist's intentions. The individualistic emphasis grew on and on. Natsume Sōseki himself wrote the novel *Sore kara* (And then) in 1910, the first of his important works in which he treated the conflicts between society and the individual.

There are other examples from popular culture that reveal similar trends, such as the development of popular military songs. At the end of the nineteenth century the Sino-Japanese War gave rise to a number of military songs that are popular even now, as any pachinko parlor addict can tell you. These songs, like "Yukan naru suihei" (The brave seamen) or "Yuki no shingun" (March in the snow), are all characterized by a spirit of great optimism. They are rapid, gay, and suggest bravery; they bring cheer to the listener. Yet, curiously enough, no song composed during the Russo-Japanese War has survived, with the notorious exception of "Senyū" (Comrade in arms). This melancholy song describes a soldier who dies in Manchuria and the sight of the red, setting sun from his grave. The song was so pessimistic in tone that it was prohibited by the Japanese Army during World War II, although it was still very popular. The suggestion is of a society moving from a spirit of harmony and optimism to a state of crisis. By the time of the Russo-Japanese War, the famous example of Yosano Akiko's antiwar poem, "Kimi shinitamau koto nakare" (You must not die), becomes possible as a protest against the military government.[7] The cultural atmosphere between these two wars, then, changed enormously, and the newer atmosphere carried on past 1912 into the Taishō period.

Such, I believe, is the background that must be kept in mind when the quality of Taishō moral concerns is examined. In addition, another social fact became important. I mentioned earlier the increasing number of visitors to the Bunten exhibits. By the Taishō period, it was apparent that a kind of mass-culture society had developed in Japan. More ordinary citizens became interested in the arts, and much larger crowds came to visit

[7] Yosano Akiko (1878–1941), one of the great women poets of modern Japan, wrote on a variety of provocative themes. A translation of the poem referred to here, "You Must Not Die," can be found in *The Japan Quarterly* 20, 2 (April–June 1974): 184.

the exhibitions. This very fact helped to emphasize in turn the position of the artist as a solitary genius. In the Taishō period there was a proliferation of art magazines and journals, beginning with *Shirakaba*, in 1910. The emergence of such artistic or literary journals, and the fact that increasing numbers of artists began to submit their works to exhibitions like the Bunten, may stand comparison with similar phenomena in the development of a mass culture in France eighty years before. Under the Louis Phillipe monarchy, the Salon grew enormously. Balzac described the situation vividly in his short novel *Pierre Grassou*, published in 1837, which dealt with the career of a successful *mondain* painter. At the beginning of his tale, Balzac writes, "The Salon has changed completely since 1830. Why? Because the Salon has been invaded by newcomers." By "newcomers," he was referring to a growing number of painters and a much larger number of visitors. For Balzac, the good works in the Salon could not be properly seen because there were so many bad works on display. By 1830, he insisted, the Salon was dead.

Such was the beginning of mass society in France, and so commenced what I would like to call the polarization of art: that is to say, on the one hand, there sprang up artists who were very successful with the large audiences drawn to the Salon, and on the other hand, there developed a new kind of creator, solitary, despised, misunderstood. The romantic myth of the artist-creator was born at this time in France, and something on a similar scale occurred in the Taishō period, with the emergence in Japan of a mass culture. Natsume Sōseki had real insight into that situation, for in his article he wrote a great deal about the life of the artist, particulary those who painted in the Western style, whose lives were still very difficult. In Sōseki's view, an authentically talented artist must strive for the comprehension of the public, even if he could not actually attain it. Sōseki thus anticipated the division between "mass art" and "pure art."

In the article, Sōseki attempted to show the state of art at his time; he was not, of course, a sociologist, and he did not make any formal analysis along rigorous lines. Still, his insights were profound. By 1912, Sōseki had divined precisely what the problems were that would come to change and deflect the culture of the coming generation. "Bunten and the Creative Arts," then, is a crucial document in our own cultural history.

# 15

## Yūgen and Erhabene: Ōnishi Yoshinori's Attempt to Synthesize Japanese and Western Aesthetics

MAKOTO UEDA

ŌNISHI YOSHINORI (1888–1959) began teaching aesthetics at Tokyo University in 1922 and continued doing so until his retirement in 1949. Shortly before his death, he recollected that the ultimate aim of his work throughout those years had been to digest Western aesthetics and reorganize it from a Japanese point of view.[1] Those who studied with him or read his books knew that all along. After publishing such works as *Gendai bigaku no mondai* (Problems in modern aesthetics, 1927), *Kanto no handanryoku hihan no kenkyū* (Kant's *Critique of Judgment*: A study, 1931), and *Genshōgakuha no bigaku* (Phenomenologist aesthetics, 1937) to introduce Western aesthetics to Japan, he went on to write books like *Yūgen to awaré* (Yūgen and awaré, 1939), *Fūga ron* (On Fūga, 1940),[2] and *Man'yōshū no shizen kanjō* (Feelings toward nature in the *Man'yōshū*, 1943) in an attempt to analyze traditional Japanese concepts of beauty. Eventually he established his own system of aesthetics, which was based on Western models but was broad enough to include traditional Japanese ideas as well. By all indications it appears that he had formulated the system in the 1930s, but the public had no chance to see it in its totality until a massive book, simply entitled *Bigaku* (Aesthetics), was published posthumously in 1959–60.

Ōnishi's aesthetic system cannot be presented in its entirety in an essay as brief as this. What I wish to do in the following pages is focus on his study of *yūgen* and show how he integrated it into his elaborate scheme. Before doing so, however, I will briefly trace the evolution of aesthetics in

[1] Cited by Takeuchi Toshio in his preface to Ōnishi Yoshinori, *Bigaku* (Tokyo: Kōbundō, 1959–60), 1:3.

[2] *Yūgen, awaré*, and *fūga* are three of the major aesthetic ideals pursued by premodern Japanese poets. The meaning of *yūgen* is discussed in the present essay. Awaré (sometimes called *mono no awaré*) implies a deep, emphatic appreciation of the ephemeral beauty manifest in nature and human life. *Fūga*, a concept developed by *haikai* poets, refers to the refined taste of a recluse living in the heart of nature and enjoying the pleasures of poetry and the arts.

modern Japan prior to his time, so that there will be some sense of the historical background against which he did his ambitious work.

## I

Western aesthetics was first introduced to Japan in 1870, when Nishi Amane (1829–97) touched on it in a series of lectures he gave at two educational institutions in Tokyo. Apparently he had a considerable interest in the subject, for two years later he authored *Bimyōgaku setsu* (Lectures in aesthetics), the first scholarly work on aesthetics ever written in Japan, in preparation for the lectures he delivered in the Meiji emperor's presence. The work was based on a variety of Western sources, especially on psychological studies analyzing the sense of beauty. In 1878–79 Nishi published one such source, Joseph Haven's *Mental Philosophy*, in Japanese translation.[3]

The 1880s saw a number of Western aesthetic theories flowing into Japan. Beginning in 1881, Ernest Fenollosa (1853–1908) gave several public lectures on Japanese art, deriving his aesthetic principles from Hegelian idealism, Spencerian evolutionism, and the eclecticism of Victor Cousin and Théodore Jouffroy.[4] In 1883–84 Nakae Chōmin (1847–1901) published a translation of Eugène Véron's *L'Eesthétique*,[5] thereby establishing, among other things, *bigaku* as the standard Japanese word for "aesthetics." A little later Futabatei Shimei (1864–1909) began introducing aesthetic concepts of Russian philosophers like V. G. Belinski and M. G. Pavlov,[6] while Ōnishi Hajime (1864–1900) published several essays on art that showed the influence of neo-Kantian scholars. In 1890 Toyama Masakazu (1848–1900) gave a famous lecture on the future of

[3] Joseph Haven (1816–74) was professor of intellectual and moral philosophy at Amherst College. His *Mental Philosophy* was published in 1858.

[4] Victor Cousin (1792–1867) and his student Théodore Jouffroy (1796–1842) both taught philosophy at the Sorbonne. They tried to integrate German idealist aesthetics into contemporary French thought, which was more moralistic and practical.

[5] Eugène Véron (1825–89) was a French journalist who edited the magazine *L'Art*. His book *L'Esthétique*, published in 1878 as the fourth volume of the *Bibliothèque des sciences contemporaines*, is built around an expressive theory of art, with an emphasis on the artist's individuality.

[6] V. G. Belinski (1810–48), a Russian critic and journalist, was at first under the influence of German idealism and romanticism, but later he came to stress realistic and social elements in art. M. G. Pavlov (1793–1840), professor of agriculture and physics at Moscow University, published articles on a wide variety of subjects, including "On the Distinction between the Fine Arts and the Sciences," which especially interested Futabatei.

Japanese painting, which reflected some of the ideas of Hippolyte Taine and John Ruskin.

None of those Western aestheticians, however, became as influential—and controversial—in early modern Japan as Eduard von Hartmann,[7] whose works began to be translated by Mori Ōgai (1862–1922) in the early 1890s. Especially famous was his *Philosophie des Schönen*, which was adapted into Japanese in 1889 by Ōgai and Ōmura Seigai (1868–1927) under the title *Shinbi kōryō* (The outline of aesthetics). Ōgai and Seigai had been attracted to Hartmann because they believed his aesthetic theory successfully combined both idealistic and psychological approaches to the subject, but what looked like a good synthesis to them seemed nothing more than an ineffectual compromise to Takayama Chogyū (1871–1902), who criticized the book harshly. Chogyū had a higher regard for other theories, such as "realistic" aesthetics of J. H. von Kirchmann and hedonistic aesthetics of Henry Rutgers Marshall.[8] Ōnishi Hajime, citing physiological aesthetics of Grant Allen and sociological aesthetics of Jean Marie Guyau,[9] also wondered how many contemporary scholars in Europe accepted Hartmann's theory. In later years Ōgai himself published books and articles introducing other aestheticians, such as Johannes Volkelt and Otto Liebmann.[10]

In response to the increasing interest in aesthetic studies, Japanese universities began offering courses in the field, too. At Tokyo University, aesthetics was first taught by Fenollosa and Toyama as part of a course in Western philosophy, starting in 1881. It became an independent course in 1885 and was given by George William Knox (1853–1912) and Ludwig Busse (1862–1907). Other universities soon followed suit: In 1892 Ōgai initiated a course in aesthetics at Keiō University, and Ōtsuka Yasuji

[7] Eduard von Hartmann (1842–1906) a German philosopher and author of the popular *Philosophie des Unbewussten* (1868), published his *Ästhetik* in 1887, proposing therein the notion of aesthetic *Schein* (semblance) as the source of all beauty. *Philosophie des Schönen* is volume 2 of *Ästhetik*.

[8] J. H. von Kirchmann (1802–84), a German empiricist philosopher, was the author of *Ästhetik auf realistischer Grundlage* (1868), a book that caught Chogyū's attention. Henry Rutgers Marshall (1852–1927), an American architect and philosopher, examined the sense of beauty from a psychological viewpoint in such books as *Pain, Pleasure, and Aesthetics* (1894), *Aesthetic Principles* (1895), and *The Beautiful* (1924).

[9] British novelist and scientific writer Grant Allen (1848–99), in his *Physiological Aesthetics* (1877), tried to trace the sense of beauty to its physical source and determine its relation to the nerve system. French philosopher Jean Marie Guyau (1854–88), in his *L'Art au point de vue sociologique* (1889), stressed the importance of communal feelings in art.

[10] In 1898–99 Ōgai serialized in a magazine an outline of *Ästhetische Zeitfragen* (1895) by Johannes Volkelt (1848–1930), a German philosopher who developed an aesthetic theory based on psychological studies of empathy. Two years later Ōgai published in the same magazine a partial translation of *Zur Analysis der Wirklichkeit* (1900) by Otto Liebmann (1840–1912), a neo-Kantian philosopher who taught at Strassburg and Jena universities.

(1863–1931) did the same at Waseda University. Busse, Ōgai, and Ōtsuka all gave lectures that relied heavily on Hartmann's concepts. In 1893 Tokyo University founded a degree-granting program in aesthetics and invited Raphael von Koeber (1848–1923) to head it. Although he himself was not a specialist in aesthetics, Koeber became an inspirational mentor for a number of young Japanese scholars who were later to become leaders in the field.

Western aesthetic theories continued to flow into Japan after the turn of the century. The work of Alexander Bain,[11] for example, was introduced by Tsunashima Ryōsen (1873–1907) in 1901; Liebmann's *Zur Analysis de Wirklichkeit* was partially translated by Ōgai in 1902; George Santayana's *The Sense of Beauty*, Marshall's *Pain, Pleasure, and Aesthetics*, and Theodor Lipps's *Ästhetik*[12] were all discussed by Shimamura Hōgetsu (1871–1918) in his lectures published in 1911. Leading scholars of the new generation were no longer content, however, to play the role of someone who merely introduced Western theories. They were becoming painfully aware of the dichotomy between theories imported from the West and actual works of art produced in Japan. They had to be apprehensive of the value of their scholarship when they saw that contemporary Japanese artists—even those working in Western-style arts—paid little or no attention to the aesthetic theories they were lecturing on. The main task for the younger scholars, then, was to become completely versed in Western theories and then create their own system that fitted Japanese reality. It was a daunting task, however. How daunting it was can be inferred from the fact that three of the most talented scholars of the generation did not write a single book on the subject of aesthetics. Ōtsuka, who succeeded Koeber at Tokyo University and served as professor of aesthetics there from 1900 to 1929, made extensive studies of European—especially German—aesthetic theories, first focusing on Hartmann's, then on Wilhelm Max Wundt's, and finally on Wilhelm Dilthey's,[13] but he was reluctant to systematize his vast knowledge of the field. Fukada Yasukazu (1878–1927), Koeber's disciple and professor of aesthetics at Kyoto University from 1910 until his death, was also an er-

[11] Alexander Bain (1818–1903) was a British philosopher who, in such books as *Emotions and the Will* (1859) and *Mental and Moral Science* (1868), attempted to distinguish "aesthetic emotions" from other feelings.

[12] Theodor Lipps (1851–1914), a German philosopher, is famous for having formulated an elaborate theory of empathy, which he applied to various branches of philosophy, including aesthetics. He published a massive book entitled *Ästhetik* in 1903–6.

[13] Wilhelm Max Wundt (1832–1920), a German physiologist, wrote extensively on philosophical and aesthetic issues from a physiological viewpoint. Wilhelm Dilthey (1833–1911), a German philosopher, did the same from a more historical and cultural angle. Ōtsuka in his later years became increasingly attracted to the kind of cultural typology Dilthey had proposed.

udite scholar familiar with all the major aesthetic thoughts in Europe, but
he seemed to regard himself as someone who ought to do groundwork
for later scholars. Abe Jirō (1883–1959), who lectured on aesthetics at
three major universities from 1913 to 1945, did publish a book called
*Bigaku* (Aesthetics) in 1917, yet the book was, by his own admission,
little more than a restatement of Lipps's aesthetic theory. Abe intimated
that he would like to write "a book of aesthetics purely my own," but the
idea never materialized. The difficulty faced by those eminent scholars in
early twentieth-century Japan shows how challenging a task it was to try
to formulate one's own theory, especially a theory that incorporates traditional Japanese concepts.

In the meantime, less ambitious scholars had attempted to examine
specific aspects of Japanese art in the light of Western aesthetic thought.
In 1885–86 Tsubouchi Shōyō (1859–1934) published his famous *Shōsetsu shinzui* (The essence of the novel), in which he utilized some of Fenollosa's ideas to criticize didacticism in contemporary Japanese fiction.
Ōnishi Hajime, in two essays written in 1888–89, resorted to Hegel's *Ästhetik* to chide his fellow Japanese for their failure to produce first-rate
poetry and music. Hōgetsu, in an article published in 1895, tried to define
the famous but enigmatic concept in Oriental art, *kiin seidō* (the spirit's
circulation—life's motion), by referring to the ideas of Friedrich von
Schiller and George Trumbull Ladd.[14] Watsuji Tetsurō (1889–1960), in
his essay on *mono no aware* written in 1922, analyzed the well-known
Japanese literary ideal by using a philological method learned from European scholars like Gilbert Murray. Then, as discussed in Dr. Nakano's
essay elsewhere in this book, Kuki Shūzō (1888–1941) in 1930 published
his brilliant study on the structure of iki, in which he utilized his rich
knowledge of modern Western philosophy to expound the Edo aesthetic
concept. Those and many other, similar studies contributed immensely to
the understanding of traditional Japanese aesthetic ideals, which had
never been exposed to close scholarly scrutiny until then. What remained
to be done was a comprehensive study that would integrate those ideas
into a systematic whole.

Ōnishi Yoshinori, who succeeded Ōtsuka as professor of aesthetics at
Tokyo University, squarely met that challenge. He undertook a close examination of three concepts central to traditional Japanese aesthetics—
*yūgen*, *aware*, and *sabi*—and not only did he analyze them from the
standpoint of a specialist in European aesthetics, but he made them part
of a comprehensive aesthetic structure that was uniquely his own. No

---

[14] George Trumbull Ladd (1842–1921), professor of metaphysics and moral philosophy
at Yale University, helped to introduce experimental psychology to the United States. In
1892 and 1899 he lectured in Japan.

scholar before him had carried out a study of traditional Japanese aesthetic thought so methodically and on so large a scale. He would have been better known to the general public if he had written some popular books in the manner of Abe Jirō or Watsuji Tetsurō, but he directed all his writings toward specialists in the field and did not seek a wide circulation of his ideas. It is reported that he even did not want to publish his lifework, *Aesthetics*, until his students persuaded him to change his mind.

## II

Ōnishi's study of yūgen, entitled "Yūgen ron" (On yūgen), was first published in the May and June 1938 issues of the journal *Shisō*. With some minor revisions, it was incorporated into his book *Yūgen and Awaré* the following year. It is divided into eight chapters. In the first chapter the author gives a general view of waka poetry and poetics from the standpoint of a specialist in Western aesthetics. In the next three chapters he traces the evolution of the concept yūgen from its rise in the Heian period to its decline in the Muromachi period. Chapters 5 and 6 comprise his reflections on problems that have bothered modern scholars who tried to define the term. In the final two chapters the author himself analyzes the concept and then suggests a way to integrate it into Western aesthetics.

The most important part of chapter 1 is where the author compares the creative processes in Eastern and Western art. According to Ōnishi, the way in which a work of art is created in the West can be expressed in one of two formulas. The simpler formula is:

$$\text{art-aesthetic moment} + \text{material} = \text{work of art}$$

"Art-aesthetic moment"—Ōnishi uses the German term *kunstästhetische Momente* as well as its Japanese equivalent, *geijutsukan-teki keisei*—refers to the artist's expressive impulse, a psychic force waiting for a chance to express itself. When that impulse is applied to the material, a work of art emerges. Ōnishi has derived this formula from the aesthetic theory of Rudolf Odebrecht,[15] but he feels it overemphasizes the artist's role. He would rather apply the second formula to Western art:

$$\text{art-aesthetic moment} + (\text{nature-aesthetic moment} + \text{material})$$
$$= \text{work of art}$$

[15] Rudolf Odebrecht (1883–1945), a German philosopher, wrote a number of books and articles on aesthetics, including *Grundlegung einer ästhetischen Werttheorie* (1927) and *Schleiermachers System der Ästhetik* (1932). He advocated "value aesthetics" in opposition to psychological approaches.

"Nature-aesthetic moment"—*naturästhetische Momente* or *shizenkan-teki keisei*—alludes to man's response to beauty in nature. According to this formula, the Western artist recognizes natural beauty in the material, and that recognition stimulates his artistic impulse. When the impulse and the response are united, a work of art is born. The second formula allows nature to play a part in the creative process.

Ōnishi contends that different formulas are at work with the Eastern (by which he means East Asian) artist. One of them is:

$$(\text{art-aesthetic moment} + \text{nature-aesthetic moment}) + \text{material} = \text{work of art}$$

This formula indicates that the Eastern artist, on facing his material, feels no artistic impulse clearly distinct from his response to natural beauty. Because of the long tradition of Oriental art which always emphasized the importance of nature, the artist's aesthetic sense has become inseparable from his appreciation of beauty in nature. The role of nature in the creative process is even more significant than in the second formula.

In the fourth formula, also reserved for the Oriental artist, Ōnishi brings in a new element:

$$\text{artistic moment} + [(\text{art-aesthetic moment} + \text{nature aesthetic moment}) + \text{material}] = \text{work of art}$$

By "artistic moment"—*artistische Momente* or *geijutsu-teki keisei*—Ōnishi means awareness of a comprehensive set of values which the Japanese traditionally called *geidō*, the Way of Art. In his opinion, art in the Orient has often become a superart, a large conceptual framework that embraces not only art but aspects of ethics, philosophy, and religion. When the Eastern artist sets out to work, he is motivated not only by his aesthetic impulse (which has been nurtured in close relation to his response to beauty in nature), but also by his awareness of the Way of Art that permeates his entire personality.

In presenting these formulas, Onishi repeatedly stresses that he is talking in generalities and would be willing to allow exceptions. Indeed, he concedes that the last formula may be in operation with certain Western artists subscribing to romanticism. However, his conviction in the centrality of nature in Oriental art is a firm one and extends to other aspects of his discussion of Japanese poetry. He points out, for instance, that a prominent feature of waka is a close union of lyric and descriptive impulses within the poet, which results in an expression of emotion through nature imagery. Another feature lies in the language of waka poetics, which often uses an image from nature to suggest the essence of a poem. Only from such a tradition could there emerge a teaching such as "You must write waka in the manner of pouring water over an iris five feet tall."[16] The main purpose of Ōnishi's introductory chapter is to make the reader aware of this unique waka tradition before he begins discussing yūgen.

The next three chapters constitute an outline history of yūgen. In roughly chronological order, Ōnishi presents different implications of the term as used in the works of such authors as Ki no Yoshimochi (d. 919), Mibu no Tadamine (d. 920?), Fujiwara no Mototoshi (b. 1142), Fijiwara no Shunzei (1114–1204), Kamo no Chōmei (1155–1216), Fujiwara no Teika (1162–1241), Shōtetsu (1381–1459), Shinkei (1406–75), Zeami (1364?–1443), and Zenchiku (1405–1468). As can be expected, the implications differ considerably from one author to another. All the authors recognize one or more of such semantic ingredients as mystery, depth, elegance, and sadness in the term yūgen, but they differ in emphasizing one or another of those ingredients. As for Ōnishi's position, he believes that the concept reached its greatest sophistication in meaning with the writings of Shunzei and, helped by Shunzei's high reputation as poet, became the highest ideal of Japanese poetry in the twelfth century. After his death it temporarily went on a decline because his son Teika, the most prestigious poet in the next generation, came to hold ushin[17] as the ideal ambiance of waka. But yūgen was again restored to its supreme place in later years, especially in the writings of poets like Shōtetsu and Shinkei and of nō actors like Zeami and Zenchiku. When both the waka and the nō began to decline after the fifteenth century, yūgen became less and less viable as an aesthetic ideal.

Ōnishi's outline of the historical evolution of yūgen adds little that is new to the existing scholarship. Ōnishi himself has stated that he is not an expert in classical Japanese literature, and that he has largely depended on the findings of past scholars in the field. He feels, however, that from a nonspecialist's point of view, he might be able to make some contributions toward the resolution of controversies that have long plagued specialists in classical Japanese literature.

Ōnishi's main contributions are two, and they are presented in chapters 5 and 6. The first concerns the relationship between the concept of yūgen advocated by Shunzei and the idea of ushin put forward by Teika. Earlier scholars' controversies have centered on how to relate these two concepts developed by the father and the son, both supposedly belonging to the same school of waka. In an attempt to solve the problem, Ōnishi intro-

---

[16] Yūgen to aware (Tokyo: Iwanami shoten, 1939), p. 17. The teaching, attributed to the poet Shun'e (b. 1113), is cited in various medieval treatises on poetry, such as Gotobain gokuden and Sasamegoto.

[17] Ushin, a term with a wide range of meanings, initially denoted a style laden with intense emotion, but Teika gave more emphasis to the serenity and profundity of mind that enables the poet to perceive the most ethereal type of beauty.

duces a Western-type analytical method. He believes that yūgen, as used in Shunzei's writings, alludes to a total aesthetic experience of writing or reading a certain kind of poem. On the other hand, the term ushin as used by Teika emphasizes the poet's frame of mind in composing a poem. Teika demanded that the poet have the utmost serenity of mind before taking up the writing brush. In Ōnishi's opinion, a poem written in such a frame of mind would come to emanate the beauty of yūgen. Ōnishi concludes that Shunzei's yūgen and Teika's ushin are like two sides of a triangle that eventually meet at the top.

The other main contribution by Ōnishi has to do with the idea of style. Referring to Goethe, Volkelt, Kainz,[18] and other Western authors, he points out that there have been many different concepts of style that have to be carefully defined and discriminated. In his opinion, the term yūgen as used in Heian and medieval Japan involves at least four different concepts of style. What the Japanese poets had in mind were: (1) a specific style distinguished by certain verbal features; (2) a style representing the highest achievement in waka; (3) a style representing the highest achievement within a specific style such as (1); and (4) the highest of various styles, of which (1) is an example. Ōnishi believes that confusion among modern scholars regarding the meaning of yūgen is largely due to their failure to distinguish between different concepts of style applied to yūgen.

How, then, should yūgen be defined? Ōnishi responds to this question in his concluding chapters. As he sees it, the concept of yūgen is made of seven components. The first is "concealment" (inpei), the presence of a veil that hides an object from direct viewing. The second is "crepuscularity" (hakumei), a type of dim darkness that causes not fear but a sense of softness or gentleness in the onlooker's mind. The third is "calm" (seijaku), a serene state of mind that is the ultimate of softness and gentleness mentioned above. Then there is "depth" (shin'en), signifying not depth in space but spiritual profundity or religious esotericism. Another ingredient is "fullness" (jūjitsusō), the finite in appearance containing the infinite in substance. Next comes the sense of "mystery" (shinpisei), a cosmic sense that emerges when the human soul is united with the soul of nature. The seventh and last component is "indescribability" (fukasetsu), an ambiance so delicate and subtle that no word or phrase could do it justice.

Of these seven components, Ōnishi regards depth as central to the meaning of yūgen. The concept of depth, he contents, combines the implications of yūgen and ushin and relates them to the poet's state of mind. To support his contention, Ōnishi also points out how important the idea

---

[18] Friedrich Kainz (1897–1977), an Austrian philosopher, formulated "personalistic aesthetics" under William Stern's influence. He is the author of *Personalistische Ästhetik* (1932)

of *kokoro* (mind, heart) was in traditional Japanese poetics, and how central the concept of depth is in the aesthetic theory formulated by Lipps. Unlike Lipps, however, Ōnishi believes that this aesthetic depth is derived less from the poet's ethical or moral attainment than from his calm contemplation of nature. As has been seen, Ōnishi holds that "nature-aesthetic moment" plays a major role in the creative process of a Japanese artist. The depth essential to yūgen comes from the poet's pure contemplation of nature, and from the resultant glimpse by the poet into the Idea of Being. Here Ōnishi relates yūgen to the Western concept of "the sublime" (*Erhabene*) and "darkness" (*Dunkelheit*) as defined by Vischer.[19] Explaining this darkness, Ōnishi says:

> In my opinion, this "darkness" is a kind of "shadow" cast on the totality of aesthetic experience by the symbol of the Idea of Being itself as sensed through the nature-aesthetic impulse. My phrase "the symbol of the Idea of Being itself" may need further explanation. What I refer to is an occasion when the artist suppresses the creative function of his mind as much as he can and submerges it in the provisions of nature until he enters a state of pure contemplation. On such an occasion, nature and the human mind, or the object and the subject, merge into one and allow him a momentary glimpse of the Being in its totality; at that moment "the individual" is absorbed into "the whole," and the microcosm expands into the macrocosm. A specific aspect of aesthetic experience arising from such a moment is what I mean by the phrase.[20]

In Ōnishi's idea, depth in yūgen signifies such an aspect of aesthetic experience. Beauty of a work of art created by man is "clear" and "superficial"; by contrast, beauty of nature is "dark" and "deep."

In an attempt to clarify himself further, Ōnishi quotes a medieval waka which he thinks had this type of depth:

| Nagamureba | I gaze into the mist |
| kiri tachikomete | enshrouding the wide expanse |
| nio no umi ya | of Grebe Lake |
| nami no izuko ni | and I wonder: Where beyond |
| ariake no tsuki.[21] | those waves is the moon of dawn? |

According to Ōnishi's reading, this poem embodies the kind of aesthetic experience he described earlier. The poet brushed with the Being in its

---

[19] Friedrich Theodor Vischer (1807–87) elaborated on the idealist aesthetics of his mentor, Hegel, in his voluminous work entitled *Ästhetik oder Wissenschaft des Schönen* (1847–57).

[20] *Yūgen to awaré*, pp. 99–100.

[21] Ibid., p. 101. The waka appears in *Sanjū-ban uta-awase*, a poetry contest referred by Ton'a. See *Gunsho ruijū* (Tokyo: Naigai shoseki, 1928–37), 10:88. Grebe Lake is another name for Lake Biwa.

totality, and his experience of the moment crystallized into the poem. Its ambiance is dark and deep, and that is precisely what yūgen is.

At the end of his essay "On yūgen," Ōnishi suggests a way by which to integrate yūgen into a general aesthetic system that includes both Eastern and Western ideas. He believes that yūgen can be considered a type of beauty derived from "the sublime," which has long been recognized as one of the basic types of beauty in Western aesthetics. He says he is pre-pared to explain this point in detail but does not have the space to do so. One recalls that the essay was first published in a journal: that fact had imposed restrictions on the author. The essay, therefore, ends in a tanta-lizing tone.

## III

Fortunately, we now have Ōnishi's *Aesthetics*, a study that responds to the unanswered question. In this posthumous publication one can find out in more detail what he had in mind. Although he probably wrote the book after his retirement from teaching in 1949, there is no doubt that he had conceived the scheme many years earlier. Indeed, much of his earlier essay, "On yūgen," is incorporated into the book verbatim.

*Aesthetics* is a thick two-volume book, nearly a thousand pages in all. The author begins with an introductory chapter discussing various meth-odologies of aesthetics conceived in the West. He then goes on to the next section, entitled "Structure of Aesthetic Experience," where he takes up major problems in the philosophy of beauty, such as perception vs. feel-ing, natural beauty vs. artistic beauty, and criteria for aesthetic judgment. By and large his frame of reference is to Western—especially German—aesthetics, although he touches on the Japanese point of view in his dis-cussion of natural and artistic beauty. He continues to look toward the West, too, in the third section called "Nature of Art," a section dealing with problems in the philosophy of art, such as form vs. content, genres and types of art, forms of art, and so forth. Volume 1 ends here.

Volume 2 is almost exclusively devoted to discussions of "aesthetic cat-egories" (*biteki hanchū*), by which Ōnishi means types of beauty. After introducing various Western ideas on the subject, and eventually agreeing with Hermann Cohen,[22] he proposes to set up three basic types of beauty, "the beautiful" (*Schöne* or *bi*), "the sublime" (*Erhabene* or *sūkō*), and "humor" (*Humor* or *fumōru*). He then conceives of six derivative types of beauty: "the tragic" (*hisō*), yūgen, "the graceful" (*yūen*), awaré, "the

[22] Hermann Cohen (1842–1918), founder of the Marburg School of neo-Kantianism, published *Kants Bergründung der Ästhetik* in 1889 and *Ästhetik des reinen Gefühls* in 1912. Ōnishi's reference seems to be to the latter book.

comic" (*kokkei*), and sabi.[23] According to him, tragic beauty emerges when factors that generally produce sublimity are, for some natural or human reason, made to focus more on man's life or mind; when the same factors focus more on nature, there appears yūgen. The basic type of beauty termed as the beautiful gives birth to a variation called the graceful when it is modified by certain conditions unique to human activities; it is transformed into awaré when modified by an experience in nature. The same kind of nature-man dichotomy is the basis of distinction between the remaining two types, the comic and sabi, both of which are derived from humor.

What, then, is the sublime as conceived by Ōnishi, and how is yūgen derived from it? According to him, a work of art embodying sublimity emerges when the nature-aesthetic moment is a more dominant factor than the art-aesthetic moment in the artist's creative process. All objects in nature, as against artifacts, contain varying degrees of darkness or translucency to the human eye, and as long as the artist recognizes that quality and makes it participate in the creative process, there is a basis for the sublime. By contrast, a work of art emanating humor includes little or no such darkness, because the art-aesthetic moment dominates the process. The beautiful, which stands on a harmony between humor and sublimity, may contain some amount of darkness.

Under what circumstances would the nature-aesthetic moment dominate the creative process? Ōnishi, like many Western theorists of the past, here brings in the concept of great size or bulk: an object in nature that is exceedingly large in one sense or another tends to awe the onlooker and brings out a sublime feeling. Following Kant, Ōnishi talks of "mathematical sublimity" and "dynamic sublimity": a boundless ocean and the spacious night sky are among the examples of the former, while a ranging storm and a turbulent sea are among the instances of the latter. Ōnishi differs from Kant, however: whereas the German philosopher stressed the resistance of human reason against nature's overwhelming force, the Japanese scholar wants to emphasize man's love for and harmony with nature. He believes that sublime beauty arises when the artist faces nature not as an enemy to conquer but as an object of aesthetic contemplation, an object with which he ultimately entrusts his soul.

Ōnishi allows that a certain type of man-made object may effect a sublime impact, too. Generally, following Vischer, he argues that such objects usually create an impression of "the whole," although an exception should be made when divisiveness is of such a kind as to increase the sense

---

[23] *Sabi*, as used in medieval literary criticism, referred to a lonely, cold type of beauty. Haikai poets in the Edo period, however, mitigated that loneliness by adding elements of resignation, acceptance, and even humor, thereby elevating sabi to a higher and more complex concept.

of large size. A cathedral is one such exception: it gains in grandeur by giving an impression of many parts being piled up. Tallness also enhances the impression of sublime beauty. When a tower points straight up toward the sky, the onlooker's imagination is drawn heavenward and expands to infinity. Vischer believed that an extremely tall object intensifies the sublime feeling because of its association with freedom and independence, but Ōnishi thinks this is so because it suggests transcendence of the human mind and entry into the consciousness of nature.

Man-made objects that emanate sublime beauty need not have a physically large size. Ōnishi believes that something small can create an impression of grandeur when there is a certain tension between its form and content. In his opinion, the Italian Renaissance sculptor Verrocchio's equestrian statue of Colleoni imparts a sublime impression because of the tension between the visible shape of the mounted soldier and his invisible willpower suggested in that shape. Other similar examples Ōnishi cites from Western art are Michelangelo's "Captives," music of Beethoven, and paintings of Rubens, Goya, and Delacroix. He speculates that literature is a better medium to express the sublime because it can leave more room for the appreciator's imagination. His examples are Aeschylus' *Prometheus Bound*, Dante's *Divine Comedy*, Byron's *Cain*, certain scenes in Goethe's *Faust*, and an early poem by Schiller entitled "Die Grösse der Welt."

Ōnishi thinks that sublime beauty is manifest in certain works of Oriental literature, too, but with a slight difference in its mode. According to him, Western authors tend to create sublimity in a clear language spoken by the characters, whereas European poets and writers prefer letting the reader experience the sublime feeling himself or herself. While the former would make a character say that something is sublime, the latter merely suggest it through some subtle literary technique. For such an example of the sublime, Ōnishi quotes a famous *hokku* by Matsuo Bashō (1644–1694):

| Araumi ya | The wild sea: |
|---|---|
| Sado ni yokotau | extending over Sado Isle |
| amanogawa.[24] | the River of Heaven. |

Another example he uses is from the *Man'yōshū*:

| Ōumi ni | On the vast ocean |
|---|---|
| shima mo aranaku ni | not a single island in sight |
| unabara no | and yet, far beyond |
| tayutō nami ni | the rolling surface of the sea, |
| tateru shirakumo.[25] | white clouds rising high. |

[24] *Bigaku* 2:76. The *hokku* is included in Bashō's *Oku no hosomichi*.
[25] Ibid. The waka is no. 1089 in the *Man'yōshū*.

Ōnishi speculates that Heian literature was generally lacking in this type of sublime beauty because court life did not allow contemporary authors to see nature in its broad manifestations. *The Tale of Genji* does include a storm scene in the chapter "Suma," but the scene is presented through the awestricken minds of Prince Genji and other courtiers present; the method is closer to that of Western authors.

The two poems cited above illustrate that sublime beauty can be manifest in a dimunitive art form, but their subjects are things in nature that are spacious. As has been seen, however, there are also works of art that do not allude to a great ocean or the boundless sky and yet create a sublime impression. Presumably, they contain some quality which is metaphorically "large." What is that quality?

In answering the question, Ōnishi rejects Kant and excludes intellect from the quality that leads to sublime beauty. In his opinion, a great power of reason may incite admiration and respect, but not an aesthetic feeling; also, it is lacking in the type of darkness characteristic of the sublime. Ōnishi's own answer has to do with that part of human nature that man shares with external nature. It includes vigor, instinct, willpower, and all the feelings that are categorized as passions. When they become "large," or "exalted," they come to have a quality essential to sublime beauty. Here Ōnishi divides those exalted passions into three types by the direction in which the elevation takes place: "moral," "religious," and "social." The first type occurs in cases where a work of art expresses the artist's impassioned effort for artistic or moral perfection; examples are Michelangelo's Prophets on the ceiling of the Sistine Chapel and a climactic scene of Schiller's *Wallenstein*. The second type emerges when a work of art embodies the artist's lofty aspirations for transcendence from the mundane and absorption into the divine; all great works of religious art exude this type of beauty. Ōnishi's examples include Giorgione's *Concept Champêtre*, Botticelli's *Primavera*, and Buddhist images from the Suiko and Tempyō periods. The third type of sublimity is seen when the work of art gives out an impression of majestic power reigning over human society; among the examples cited are *Apollo Belvedere*, David's depiction of Napoleon, European baroque architecture, Kanō Eitoku's paintings, and Nikkō Shrine.

This third type is an extreme variety of the sublime, insofar as the kind of darkness inherent in nature is here minimized by the dominance of humanity. It is more the majesty of man than the magnitude of nature that is exalted. When the artist goes farther in this direction and makes a great power of man crash against a great power of nature, his work will come to embody a derivative type of beauty, which Ōnishi called the tragic. When the artist goes in the opposite direction and lets his humanity completely dissolved in the majestic force of nature, there will emerge the beauty of yūgen. Because the artist has here abandoned his effort to penetrate into nature with his intellect, his work will contain an abundance of darkness, more so than a work of sublime beauty would. As a result, the onlooker or reader will be struck by a greater sense of mystery and depth. Yūgen is sublime beauty with a larger ingredient of unknown nature and its accompanying ambiance, crepuscular beauty.

To illustrate the beauty of yūgen, Ōnishi quoted a waka on Grebe Lake in his essay "On Yūgen." In *Aesthetics* he adds several more waka to his examples, although he gives no specific explanation for any one of them. One of the examples is a celebrated poem by Shunzei:

| Yū sareba | As the nightfall nears |
| nobe no akikaze | autumn winds from the field |
| mi ni shimite | have grown chillier |
| uzura nakunari | and a quail has begun to cry |
| Fukakusa no sato.[26] | here at Fukakusa. |

Fukakusa, literally meaning "deep grass," was located in the southern outskirts of Kyoto. To courtiers living in the capital, it signified a remote village where many imperial gravemounds were located. That image and the images of nearing nightfall, approaching winter, and the lonely cry of a quail all combine to suggest a type of mystery and depth that defies intellectual analysis. Another poem cited by Ōnishi is a waka by Priest Saigyō (1118–90), which Shunzei said has a yūgen form:

| Tsu no kuni no | Spring at Naniwa |
| Naniwa no haru wa | in the province of Tsu . . . |
| yume nare ya | Was all that a dream? |
| ashi no kareha ni | Over the dead bulrush leaves |
| kaze wataru nari.[27] | a wind blows, and blows again. |

The poem alludes to another waka, written by Priest Nōin (b. 988) more than a century earlier:

| Kokoro aramu | How I wish to show |
| hito ni misebaya | to those who have the heart |
| Tsu no kuni no | this spring scene |
| Naniwa watari no | around the town of Naniwa |
| haru no keshiki wo.[28] | in the province of Tsu! |

Naniwa, the modern Osaka, used to be a rustic town whose vicinity was noted for a beautiful view of bulrushes. Priest Nōin, traveling through the area one spring in the early eleventh century, enjoyed the view and wrote the poem. The nation, however, became war-torn in the decades that fol-

---

[26] Ibid., p. 235. The waka is no. 258 in the *Senzaishū*.

[27] Ibid., The waka is no. 625 in the *Shinkokinshū*.

[28] *Goshūishū*, no. 43.

lowed. Saigyō, visiting the same area in the twelfth century, thought of the glorious past and of some great unknown force that had since brought winter to nature and human society alike. Again the poem suggests something dark and mysterious working in a sphere impenetrable by intellect.

Ōnishi does not cite any example of yūgen in Western literature or art, although he says that theoretically yūgen is not confined to Japanese or Oriental aesthetics. In his view, yūgen has manifested itself in Japanese culture in such abundance because of certain historical and social factors, especially because of the way in which the concept of beauty evolved in the history of Japanese culture. Yūgen, then, is a universal ambiance that claims a place in international aesthetics, but that has showed an especially high degree of development in Japan.

# IV

Ōnishi's study of yūgen and other traditional aesthetic ideals was not widely read in contemporary Japan. Although *Yūgen and Aware* and *On Fūga* were published in wartime when readers craved new books, it seems that his scholarly prose style intimidated readers. Specialists in the field did read the books, but their reactions were mixed. In general, they expressed an admiration for Ōnishi's incisive intellect, methodical approach, and broad knowledge of Western aesthetics. On the other hand, they did not like his abstract language, lack of proof for his arguments, and what seemed to be a rather arrogant attitude toward scholars specializing in Japanese literature. The reviewers were polite toward this erudite professor of aesthetics at Tokyo University, but they were not ready to embrace his findings with enthusiasm.

A good example is a brief review of *Yūgen and Aware* published in the newspaper *Asahi*, written by the renowned poet Saitō Mokichi shortly after the publication of the book. Saitō is impressed by Ōnishi's effort to discuss Oriental ideas of beauty in the international context, as well as by the meticulously logical way in which he formulated his arguments. But the reviewer does not forget to remind the readers that "for us people of Japan it is of prime importance to train ourselves in such a way that we can appreciate yūgen and aware directly, leaving them intact."[29] By "leaving them intact," Saitō means "without dissecting them" as Ōnishi has done. The reviewer also points out that Japanese poetry began to decline when poets became too theoretical in discussing yūgen. Obviously Ōnishi's analytical method, derived from Western philosophy, did not find much sympathy with Saitō, a practicing poet.

[29] *Saitō Mokichi zenshū* (Tokyo: Iwanami shoten: 1952–57), 41:57.

Another example that illustrates the book's contemporary reputation is a review written by Oda Takuji, a specialist on *renga*, which appeared in the journal *Kokugo kokubun*. In the review Oda commends the book for its intellectual depth and chides his fellow scholars in Japanese literature for their overemphasis on bibliographical and historical studies. He also praises *Yūgen and Aware* for the incisive, methodical way in which its conclusions are induced. He wonders, however, whether the conclusions are not what scholars or premodern Japanese literature had known all along. Of course, these scholars were lacking in a philosophical framework with which to systematize their knowledge, but Oda is not sure if Ōnishi's aesthetic approach is the best answer. "Does aware," he asks, "demand to be treated as an aesthetic category as Dr. Ōnishi thinks it does? And will it endure such a treatment?"[30] He also questions about the precise meaning of some of Ōnishi's terms, such as "nature-aesthetic moment" and even the word "nature" itself.

An even more negative opinion on Ōnishi's study is voiced by another scholar in Japanese literature, Imoto Nōichi, who published a review of *On Fūga* in the journal *Kokugo to kokubungaku*. A scholar known for his studies in *haikai*, Imoto apparently waited to vent his feelings until this book on *sabi* appeared, although he had previously seen Ōnishi's essay on yūgen. He criticizes the book for several reasons. Ōnishi, he says, has built his argument often on a fragile foundation, relying upon dubious sources. Ōnishi's heavy reliance on the writings of Kagami Shikō (1665–1731) draws especially sharp criticism from Imoto, who is convinced that Shikō's idea of *haikai* deviated far from the orthodox tradition. But Imoto's most basic reservation about the book, and about Ōnishi's study in general, lies elsewhere. It is summed up in the following passage:

> Generally speaking, the author is so eager to comply with the demand of his aesthetic system that in a considerable number of instances he seems to make a far-fetched interpretation of the text or formulate a theory for the sake of theory. At first sight his arguments look impeccably logical, but in that very logicality I cannot help feeling something hollow, something distant from the historical reality of literature.[31]

Imoto is here voicing his basic misgivings about Ōnishi's deductive method. To him, Ōnishi's study seems too neat and too often negligent of the complex, sometimes even chaotic, aspect of beauty arising from the actual literary text.

Today, Ōnishi's books are all but forgotten. Of course, he is still a re-

[30] *Kokugo kokubun* (November 1939): 96.
[31] *Kokugo to kokubungaku* (September 1940): 86.

vered figure among his countrymen specializing in the field: a leading scholar among them called Ōnishi's *Aesthetics* "practically the only high-standard work in aesthetic theory ever written by a Japanese."[32] But aestheticians nowadays, Japanese or Western, do not seem to be as concerned with types of beauty as Ōnishi was. Outside the field of aesthetics, Ōnishi's books have even fewer readers. Those who want to know about yūgen today are likely to go to Nose Asaji's *Yūgen ron* (On yūgen), a more historical and comprehensive study of the subject done by an esteemed scholar in Japanese literature. For aware, students would consult many writings on the topic by such scholars as Hisamatsu Sen'ichi and Okazaki Yoshie. As for *sabi*, studies by Imoto Nōichi are well known. The only book by Ōnishi that still has some appeal to students of Japanese literature is *Feelings Toward Nature in the Man'yōshū*, which is the least theoretical among his works.

It might be argued, however, that Ōnishi's writings did make a lasting impact on the Japanese scholarly scene, albeit an indirect one. Ōnishi was one of those intellectuals of the interwar period who firmly believed that world culture did exist, and he wanted to demonstrate, in the field of his specialization, what position Japan occupied in that culture. Today's Japanese aestheticians do not have to be so internationally conscious in their studies, because they are aware of what Ōnishi did. They know that Japanese aesthetic ideals can be discussed in the same terms as Western ones. Scholars in classical Japanese literature have been slower in being convinced. Yet, the borderline between Japanese and comparative literature, which was once so clearly delineated, is gradually becoming ambiguous. Even Imoto, in theorizing his idea of sabi, has resorted to the Western concept of irony, and he has used the German word *Ironie* to express it in his writings. Ōnishi's lofty aesthetic structure may be becoming a monument of the past, but the parts making up the whole, as well as the ideas lying behind it, continue to inspire those who wish to study aesthetic aspects of Japanese culture from an international point of view.

[32] Imamichi Tomonobu, *Bi ni tsuite* (Tokyo: Kōdansha, 1973), p. 239.

# Contributors _____

*Thomas W. Burkman,* Associate Professor of History and Director of the Institute of Asian Studies at Old Dominion University, has a special interest in Japan's international relations during the interwar years as well as in the Allied Occupation. His writing focuses on Japan's relationship to the League of Nations.

*Brett de Bary,* Associate Professor of Asian Studies at Cornell University, has done extensive research on postwar and postmodern Japanese literature and criticism. Her *Three Works by Nakano Shigeharu* contains translations of fiction by Nakano Shigeharu.

*H. D. Harootunian,* who teaches history at the University of Chicago, has long been recognized as an important authority on Japanese intellectual history. His most recent book, *Things Seen and Unseen,* is a treatment of the place of *kokugaku* ("Nativism" in his rendering) in Japan's Tokugawa period.

*Germaine A. Hoston,* Associate Professor of Political Science at Johns Hopkins University, is a specialist on Chinese and Japanese politics, as well as in comparative politics and comparative intellectual and cultural history. Her recent book, *Marxism and the Crisis of Development in Prewar Japan,* treats the history of Marxist debates over the development of capitalism in Japan.

*Nozomu Kawamura,* who teaches in the Department of Sociology and Social Anthropology at Tokyo Metropolitan University, has remained for many years one of the foremost scholars writing in the field of Japanese economic and social history.

*Stephen W. Kohl,* Associate Professor of Japanese at the University of Oregon, has written on Japanese interwar literature and has published translations of such twentieth-century authors as Tachihara Masaaki, Inoue Yasushi, and Ōba Minako.

*William R. LaFleur* is Professor of Japanese at the University of Pennsylvania. Widely respected as a scholar of traditional Japanese religion and Buddhism, his book *The Karma of Words: Buddhism and the Literary*

*Arts in Medieval Japan* is an important treatment of religious ideas in their historical contexts.

*Hajimu Nakano*, who writes on modern Japanese intellectual history, is Professor of Philosophy at the University of the Air in Japan.

*J. Thomas Rimer*, Professor of Japanese Literature at the University of Maryland, College Park, has published studies of modern Japanese fiction, theater, and cultural history. His most recent book, *Pilgrimages: Aspects of Japanese Literature and Culture*, treats a variety of cultural themes in the modern and traditional arts.

*Donald Roden*, Associate Professor of History at Rutgers University, has wide interests in various aspects of modern Japanese history and culture. His book *Schooldays in Imperial Japan: A Study in the Culture of a Student Elite* represents an important analysis of a Japanese institution examined in terms of its social and psychological context.

*Miriam Silverberg*, Assistant Professor of History at the University of California, Los Angeles, has a special interest in modern Japanese intellectual and cultural history. Her recent book, *Changing Song: The Marxist Manifestos of Nakano Shigeharu*, deals with the work of the writer and poet Nakano Shigeharu in relation to the Western Marxist tradition.

*Eugene Soviak*, Associate Professor of History at Washington University in St. Louis, has a strong interest in modern Japanese social and intellectual history. He has recently completed, in collaboration with Tamie Kamiyama, a translation of *Ankoku nikki*, the confidential war diary of Kiyosawa Kiyoshi.

*Jackie Stone* is completing her Ph.D. degree in Buddhist studies at the University of California, Los Angeles. Her thesis addresses problems involved in understanding the Japanese Buddhist thinker Nichiren (1222–1282) in his intellectual and historical context.

*Shuji Takashina* is Professor of the History of Art at the University of Tokyo. An expert on European art, he has translated a number of important Western works of art history into Japanese and has published distinguished essays on modern Japanese art.

*Makoto Ueda*, Professor of Japanese and Comparative Literature at Stanford University, has written several highly regarded studies on the aesthetic theories of art, fiction, and poetry in traditional and modern Japan, among them *Modern Japanese Poets and the Nature of Literature* and *Modern Japanese Writers and the Nature of Literature*.

# Index

Abe Isoo, 64, 66
Abe Jirō, viii, ix, 5, 7–21, 32, 49, 55, 59, 271, 286, 287; *The Diary of Santarō* (Santarō no nikki), 8–21
Abe Yoshishige, 32
Adams, Henry, viii
Adorno, Theodor W., 131, 146n
Aeschylus, 294
Akamatsu Katsumaro, 170
Akutagawa Ryūnosuke, 18, 135, 142, 152
Allen, Grant, 284
Anesaki Masaharu, 221, 228, 232, 233n
Anglo-Japanese Alliance of 1902, 193, 205, 207
Anti-Security Treaty struggle, 166
Aoki Shigeru, 236
Ara Masato, 157
Araki Shigeru, 50
Arendt, Hannah, 152n
Ariga Nagao, 62
Arishima Takeo, 9
Aristophanes, 17, 18, 49
Aristotle, 160
Aruga Kizaemon, 75, 78–81, 100, 123, 125, 126
Ashida Hitoshi, 208, 209
Ashio Copper Mine incident, 7
Ashiwara Kuniko, 48
Awano Kenjirō, 51

Bain, Alexander, 285
Balzac, Honoré de, 281
Baudelaire, Charles-Pierre, 265
Beethoven, Ludwig von, 294
Belinski, V. G., 283
Benjamin, Walter, 131, 132, 145–48, 149, 151, 152, 153
Bergson, Henri, viii, 36, 198, 263
Bible: New Testament, 12, 30, 62, 238
Blake, William, 30
Bloch, Ernest, 100
Bluchner, Heinrich, 152n
Bogdanov, Alexander, 97n
Botticelli, Sandro, 293

Bougle, Célestin C. A., 75n
Brecht, Bertolt, 133, 146n, 152, 153
Buddhism, 30, 157, 169, 171, 177, 178, 180, 199, 217–33, 239n, 240, 242, 243, 245, 248, 250
Buddhist sculpture, 295
Bunten, 273–78
Buñuel, Luis, 37
Burke, Kenneth, 158
Bushidō, 268
Busse, Ludwig, 284, 285
Bryon, George Gordon, 294

Calvin, John, 231
Carnegie Endowment, 198
Castoriadis, Cornelius, 105n
Chikamatsu Chūkō, 33
Christianity, 22, 30, 35, 36, 192, 199, 230, 240, 242, 256
Claudel, Paul, 147n
Cohen, Hermann, 292
Comintern, 168, 169, 181, 185
communism, 76
Compte, Auguste, 67
Confucian classics, 177
Confucianism, 171, 178, 180
Cooley, Charles Horton, 74n
Corfu Incident (1923), 202
Cousin, Victor, 283

Dai Ajia Kyōkai, 210, 211, 213
Dai Ajia Rengō, 211
Dali, Salvador, 37
Dante Alighieri, 15, 20, 294
David, Jacques Louis, 295
Delacroix, F. V. Eugène, 294
de Man, Paul, 158
Derrida, Jacques, 109n
Dewey, John, 41
Dilthey, Wilhelm, viii, 285
Dōbunkai, 210
Dōgen, 232, 243
Dostoevski, Feodor Mikhailovich, 30
*Dream of the Red Chamber*, 177
Dreyer, Carl Theodor, 37

Drummond, Sir Eric, 200, 201
Durkheim, Émile, viii, ix, 59, 74

Eckhardt, Wolf von, 40
Eisai, 232
Ellis, Havelock, 45
Emerson, Ralph Waldo, viii
emperor system, 62–63, 67, 68, 70, 74, 76,
    80, 103, 163, 182, 183
Engels, Friedrich, 75n, 181
Epictitus, 266

Far Eastern League, 212
Fenollosa, Ernest, 252, 253, 264, 283, 284,
    286
Foucault, Michel, 109n
Four-Power Consortium, 194, 196
Four-Power Pact, 207, 210
Freud, Sigmund, 40, 45, 55
fūga, 282
Fujiwara no Mototoshi, 289
Fujiwara no Shunzei, 289, 290, 296
Fujiwara no Teika, 289, 290
Fukada Yasukazu, 285
Fukuda Tokuzō, 84
Fukuzawa Yukichi, 8, 65
Futabatei Shimei, 8, 9, 283

Gandi, Dino, 208
Genyōsha, 210
Giddings, Franklin Henry, 65, 70, 74n,
    75n
Giorgione, 295
Gluck, Carol, 241
Goethe, Johann Wolfgang von, 3, 16, 20,
    224, 271, 290, 294
Gorky, Maxim, 97n
Goya, Francisco José de, 294
Gramsci, Antonio, 99
Greater East Asian Co-Prosperity Sphere,
    184, 256
Greek Sophists, 157
Guyau, Jean Marie, 284
Guanzi (Kuan Tzu), 177

Habuto Eiji, 45, 46
Hagiwara Sakutarō, 158
haibutsu kishaku movement, 218, 245,
    246, 254
haiku, 279
Han Feizi (Han Fei Tzu), 177, 178

Hani Gorō, 105n
Haniya Yutaka, 132, 155–67; Credo Quia
    Absurdum, 156–67
Hara Katsurō, 231
Hara Kei, 191, 194, 196, 197
Harootunian, Harry, 236
Hartmann, Eduard von, 4, 261n, 284, 285
Hasegawa Kazuo, 49, 53
Hasegawa Nyozekan, 54
Hatano Kanae, 84
Haven, Joseph, 283
Hayashi Fusao, 156
Heidegger, Martin, viii, 132, 262, 263
Hegel, Georg Wilhelm Friedrich, viii, ix, 4,
    12, 20, 63, 175, 176, 178, 283, 286. See
    also Young Hegelians
Heine, Heinrich, 143, 224
Hesse, Hermann, 38, 41
Hibiya Riots, 87
Hiller, Kurt, 40
Hirano Ken, 157
Hirata Atsutane, 110, 113, 114
Hirato Renkichi, 154
Hiratsuka Raichō, 44
Hirohito (as Prince Regent), 200
Hirotsu Kazuo, 42
Hirschfeld, Magnus, 37, 45, 55
Hisamatsu Sen'ichi, 299
Hobbes, Thomas, 175
Hōnen, 231, 232
Hori Tatsuo, 50
Hughes, H. Stuart, ix
Hughes, Langston, 133, 152, 153
Husserl, Edmund, 262

Ide Tadashi, 84
Imanaka Tsugimaro, 84
Imoto Nōichi, 298, 299
Inage Sōfu, 47
Inoue Enryō, 218, 224, 242
Inoue Tetsujirō, 44, 55, 241, 242
Institute of Pacific Relations, 192, 203,
    209, 215
International Committee for Intellectual
    Cooperation, 198
International Labor Organization, 198
Irokawa Daikichi, 111
Ishii Kikujirō, 202, 207
Ishikawa Takuboku, 132
Itō Noe, 43
Iwamoto Tei, 26n, 51

Iwamoto Zenji, 41
Iwanami Shigeo, 5, 32, 235, 248, 256
Iwashita Shōichi, 270

James, William, viii, 24, 232n
Jameson, Frederic, 158
Japan Communist Party (JCP), 184, 185
Jouffroy, Théodore, 283
Joyce, James, 154, 158

*kabuki*, 17, 42
Kadota Ashiko, 48
Kagami Shikō, 298
Kainz, Friedrich, 290
Kajii, Motojirō, 158
Kamikawa Hikomatsu, 212, 213, 215
Kamo no Chōmei, 14, 289
Kaneko Daiei, 84
Kanō Eitoku, 295
Kanō Kōkichi, 51
Kant, Immanuel, viii, 4, 32, 34, 157, 159,
    160, 161, 162, 165, 283, 293, 295. *See
    also* neo-Kantianism
Katayama Sen, 63, 64
Katō Hiroyuki, 64–65, 66–67
Katō Kōmei, 193
Katō Tadashi, 122
Kawabata Yasunari, 50, 154
Kawakami Hajime, 83, 84, 175
Kawakami Kiyoshi, 197
Kellogg-Briand Pact of 1928, 204, 206,
    210
Ki no Yoshimochi, 289
Kierkegaard, Søren, 160, 243, 272
Kimura Taiken, 229, 230
Kinoshita Naoe, 64, 66, 231n
Kinugasa Teinosuke, 49
Kirchmann, J. H. von, 284
Kitamura Tōkoku, 3, 31, 43
Knox, George William, 284
Kobayashi Ichizō, 47, 53
Koeber, Raphael von, 4, 23, 32, 242, 261,
    270, 285
*Kojiki*, 177
Kojima Kikuo, 275
Kokuryūkai, 210
Kokusai Bunka Shinkōkai (KBS), 211
*kokutai*, 169, 171, 178, 182, 183
Komura Jutarō, 195
Komura Kin'ichi, 195, 196
Konoe Astumaro, 210, 211

Konoe Fumimaro, 212, 214, 215
Kōtoku Shūsui, 4, 7, 64, 66, 69, 71, 132
Kraft-Ebing, Richard, 45
Kraus, Karl, 148
Kuki Hatsuko, 264, 265
Kuki Ryūichi, 252, 264
Kuki Shūzō, 260, 261–72, 282; *Images of
    Paris* (Parii shinkei), 261, 265–66, 272;
    *The Structure of Iki* (Iki no kōzō), 261–
    72
Kumagusa Minakata, 103
Kunikida Doppo, 24, 31, 75
Kurata Hyakuzō, 5, 6, 16, 22–36, 49, 59,
    231; *The Origins of Love and Under-
    standing* (Ai to ninshiki to no suppatsu),
    5, 22–36
Kuroda Seiki, 276
Kuwaki Gen'yoku, 32, 54, 55
Kyokutō Renmei, 213
*kyōyō shugi*, 271

Ladd, George Trumbull, 286
Lang, Fritz, 38
Lao Tze, 152
Lautréamont, Compte de, 154
Laurent, Henri, 39
League of Nations, 192, 194, 195, 197,
    204, 207, 209, 210, 212, 215, 216
League of Nations Association, 201
League of Nations Covenant, 214
Lefebvre, Henri, 141, 142
LeFort, Claude, 105n
Lenin, Vladimir Ilyich, 166, 178, 182
Lévi, Sylvain, 225, 233n
Li Dazhao (Li ta-chao), 180
Liebmann, Otto, 284, 285
Lipps, Theodor, 285
Locarno Conference, 202
Locarno Pact, 207, 208, 209, 210
Locke, John, 175
Lukács, Georg, 131, 132
Lunacharsky, Anatoly Vasilyevich, 97n
Luther, Martin, 231

McDougall, William, 74n
Machiavelli Niccolò, 178
MacIver, Robert Morrison, 74n
Maeda Tamon, 203
Makino Nobuaki, Baron, 196, 197
Mallarmé, Stéphane, 154
Manchukuo, 207, 208, 213

Manchuria, 198, 206, 208, 209, 215, 280
Manchurian crisis, 192, 193, 199, 200
Manchurian Incident, 170, 183, 205
Mann, Thomas, viii
Man'yōshū, 116, 177, 250, 282, 294, 299
Mao Zedong (Mao Tse-tung), 180
Marcuse, Herbert, 125, 126
Marin, Louis, 107n
Marshall, Henry Rutgers, 284, 285
Maruyama Masao, 234
Marx, Karl, viii, 75n, 135, 137, 138, 140,
    141, 143, 166, 176, 178
Marxism, 75, 83, 87, 96, 121, 122, 125,
    131, 154, 168–86, 234, 241
Masaoka Shiki, 279
Matsumoto Bunzaburō, 221n
Matsuo Bashō, 32, 294
Matsuoka Yosuke, 207, 212, 215
Matsuzawa Kenjin, 84
May Fourth Movement, 193
Meiji Emperor, 7, 17, 283
Meinecke, Friedrich, 40
Meirokusha, 65
Mibu no Tadamine, 289
Michelangelo, 275, 294, 295
Mikhailovsky, N. K., 181
Miki Kyoshi, ix, 84, 122, 131, 132, 212
Minobe Tatsukichi, 171
missionaries, Christian, 245
Miwata Masako, 41
Miyamoto Yuriko, 50, 131, 155n, 156
Mizuno Shigeo, 170
Mizutani Chōzaburō, 84
mono no aware, 27, 115, 282
Morgan, Lewis Henry, 74n
Mori Ōgai, 3, 5, 7, 22, 23, 284, 285
Motoori Norinaga, 60, 115
Motoyoshi Yujirō, 64, 65
Mozi (Mo Tzu), 177
Müller, F. Max, 219, 220, 225
Murai, Tomoshi, 64
Murakami Senshō, 220, 221, 229, 233n
Murō Saisei, 135
Murray, Gilbert, 286
Mushanokōji Saneatsu, 9, 33, 277
Mutai Risaku, 84

Nabeyama Sadachika, 155, 168
Nagai Kafū, 8
Nāgārjuna, 219
Nakae Chōmin, 283

Nakano Shigeharu, 132, 133–53
Nanjō Bun'yū, 219, 225
Nara Miyako, 48
Natsume Sōseki, 3, 7, 8, 9, 15, 19, 32, 33,
    242, 243, 273–81
neo-Kantianism, 23, 32, 51, 54, 84, 283.
    See also Kant, Immanuel
New Perception School, 154
Nichiren, 232
Nietzsche, Friedrich, viii, 4, 11, 12, 16, 20,
    30, 236, 240, 242, 243, 272
Nihon Seiji Keizai Kinkyūjo, 169
Nihon Shakaigakuin, 69
Nihon Shakaito, 68
Nihonga, 273, 274
Nihon-shoki, 177
Nine-Power Pact, 204
Nishi Amane, 61, 283
Nishida Kitarō, viii, xii, 24, 29, 32, 36, 84,
    92n, 199, 231, 267, 270, 271
Nitobe Inazō, 42, 104, 192–216
Nogami Toshio, 44
Nogi Maresuke, 17, 29
Nōin, 296
norito (Shinto ritual prayers), 177
Nose Asaji, 299

October Revolution (Russia), 241
Oda Takuji, 298
Odagiri Hideo, 157
Odake Kazue, 44
Odebrecht, Rudolf, 287
Oka Arajirō, 84
Okakura Tenshin (Kakuzō), 246, 264, 265,
    277
Okazaki Yoshie, 299
Ōmura Seigai, 284
Onchi Kōshirō, xii
Ōnishi Hajime, 283, 284, 286
Ōnishi Yoshinori, 199, 260, 267, 282–99
onnagata (in kabuki), 17, 18
Origuchi Shinobu, 60, 100, 101, 102,
    105n, 106, 110, 113–21, 122, 123, 126,
    127
Ōtsuka Yasuji, 284, 285, 286
Ōya Sōichi, 53, 54, 55

Pacific War, 184
Paris Peace Conference, 195, 197
Paul, Saint, 238, 244, 245
Paul, M. Eden, and Cedar, 97

Pavlov, M. G., 283
Plato, 17, 18
positivism, 73
Praxiteles, 239
Profintern (Red International of Trade Unions), 168
Proudhon, Pierre-Joseph, 166
Public Peace Law, 66

Rhys Davids, T. W., 220
Rice Riots of 1918, 7
Rickert, Heinrich, 132, 262
Rilke, Rainer Maria, 38, 41, 50
Rimbaud, Arthur, 158
Rodin, Auguste, 275
Rōyama Masamichi, 204, 212, 214
Rubens, Peter Paul, 294
Ruskin, John, 284
Russo-Japanese Alliance of 1916, 193
Russo-Japanese War, 4, 66, 67, 68, 69, 211, 280

Saigyō, 296, 297
Saionji Kinmochi, 194, 197
Saitō Mokichi, 297
Sakamoto Hanjirō, 276
Santayana, George, 285
Sano Manabu, 132, 155, 168–86
Sartre, Jean-Paul, viii, ix, 262n
Sasaki Kiichi, 157
Sawada Junjirō, 45, 46, 55
Scheler, Max, 120
Schiller, Friedrich von, 286, 294, 295
Schoenberg, Arnold, 38
Scholars, The, 177
Schopenhauer, Arthur, 4, 15, 20, 224, 240, 242
senmyō (ancient imperial proclamations), 177
Senuma Shigeki, 154
Shakai Gakkai, 63
Shakaigaku Kenkyūkai, 64
Shakaishugi Kenkyūkai, 64
Shakaishugi Kyōkai, 66
Shangzi (Shang Tzu), 177
Shaw, Glen W., 31
Shidehara Kijūrō, 191, 207
Shiga Naoya, 13, 15, 16, 18
Shiga Shigetaka, 200
Shigemitsu, Mamoru, 211
Shimaki Kensaku, 156

Shimamura Hōgetsu, 34, 285, 286
Shimazaki Tōson, 3, 75, 280
Shimonaka Yasaburō, 84
Shinkei, 289
Shinran, 30, 231, 232
Shintō, 171, 177
Shirakaba (White birch) magazine, 9, 275, 277, 281
Shōtetsu, 289
Shotwell, James T., 198
Shōwa Kenkyūkai, 212, 214
Shrine Merger Act, 99, 103, 104
Siberian Intervention, 193
Simmel, Georg, ix, 59, 70, 71, 72
Sino-Japanese War of 1894–95, 280
Sino-Japanese War of 1937, 214
Small, Albion Woodbury, 70
social Darwinism, 65, 66, 191
Social Democratic Party, 66
socialism, 96, 173, 180
socialism, Christian, 64
Socrates, 17
Spanish-American War, 191
Spencer, Herbert, 65, 283
Spengler, Oswald, 41
Stein, Sir Aurel, 253, 255
Stimpson, Henry, 198
Stimpson Doctrine, 206, 210
Strindberg, August, 30
Sun Yat-sen, 211
Sweig, Stefan, 37

Taine, Hippolyte, 284
Takabatake Motoyuki, 169, 175, 182
Takagi Masayoshi, 64, 65, 67
Takagi Yasaka, 203, 209, 210, 215
Takahashi Kamekichi, 169, 184
Takakura Teru, 84
Takakusu Junjirō, 199, 221, 225, 226, 229, 232, 233n
Takamine Taeko, 47
Takamura Kōtarō, 280
Takarazuka Theatre, 47–48
Takata Yasuma, 71, 72, 74, 100, 122–27
Takayama Chogyū, xii, 278, 279, 284
Takayanagi Kenzō, 203, 205
Tale of Genji (Genji monogatari), 14, 16, 295
Tamenaga Shunsui, 268n
Tanabe Hajime, 32, 270, 271
Tanaka Kinuyo, 49

Tanaka Ōdō, 84
Tanikawa Tetsuzō, 84
Tanizaki Jun'ichirō, 50
Tarde, J. Gabriel de, 74n, 75n
Tatebe Tongo, 66, 67, 68, 69, 70
Tayama Katai, 9, 75
Tazoe Tetsuji, 69
tenkō, 155, 162–64, 165, 167, 168, 169–
    86, 237
Terazaki Kōgyō, 277, 278
Toa Renmei Kyōkai, 211
Toa Shinchitsujo (New Order in East Asia),
    191, 212, 214, 215, 216
Toda Teizō, 73, 74
Tokiwa Daijō, 322n
Tokunaga Sunao, 156
Tokutomi Sohō, 45
Tolstoi, Lev N., 17, 30, 36
Tönnies, Ferdinand, 122
Tosaka Jun, 84, 122, 234n, 241
Toyama Shōichi (Masakazu), 65, 283, 284
Tripartite Pact of 1940, 213
Tsubouchi Shōyō, 286
Tsuchida Kyōson, 59, 83–98
Tsunashima Ryōsen, 285
Tsurumi Shunsuke, 157, 158, 159, 160,
    161, 162, 163, 164, 165, 166
Tsurumi Yūsuke, 203
Twenty-one Demands, 193, 194

Uchida Yasuya, 215
Ugaki, Kazushige, 52
Ui Hakuju, 177, 217, 229, 230
ukiyo-e (woodblock prints), 266
United States Immigration Act of 1924,
    202
Urabe Kumeko, 48

Vasubandhu, 219
Verlaine, Paul, 265
Véron, Eugène, 283
Verrocchio, Andrea del, 294
Vischer, Friedrich Theodor, 291, 293
Volkelt, Johannes, 284, 290

Wada Eisaku, 276
Wagner, Richard, 224
Ward, Lester Frank, 70
Washington Disarmament Conference, 194
watakushi-shōsetsu (I-novel), 155
Watanabe Kaigyoku, 212n, 221, 222, 223,
    224, 225, 226
Watsuji Tetsurō, ix, 5, 100, 199, 231, 234–
    56, 261n, 271, 272, 286, 287; Pilgrim-
    age to Ancient Temples (Koji junrei),
    236, 248–56; Restoring Idols (Gūzō
    saikō), 236–43, 244, 246
Weber, Max, 75n, 177
Weimar Republic, 37–41
Wells, Herbert George, 110
Williams, Raymond, x, 156
Wilson, Woodrow, 193
Windelband, Wilhelm, 24
Woolf, Virginia, 38
Wundt, Wilhelm Max, 285

Yanagi Sōetsu, xii, 271, 277
Yanagisawa Sanji, 52
Yanagita Kunio, ix, 60, 75–80, 99–113,
    115, 118, 119, 120, 121, 122, 123, 125,
    126
Yano Jin'ichi, 211
Yasuda Tokutarō, 54, 55
yōga, 273, 274
Yokomitsu Riichi, 154
Yokota Kisaburō, 209, 210, 215
Yokoyama Taikan, 277
Yoneda Shōtarō, 70, 71
Yosano Akiko, 43, 279n, 280
Yosano Tekkan, 279
Yoshimoto Takaaki, 111
Yoshino Sakuzō, 194
Young Hegelians, 171. See also Hegel,
    G.W.F.
yūgen, 267, 282, 287–92

Zeami, 289
Zenchiku, 289